D0148572

Nabokov's Fifth Arc

Vladimir Nabokov in the Montreux Palace Hotel, at the time of the work on his last novel, *Look at the Harlequins!*
Photo: J. E. Rivers

Nabokov's Fifth Arc

NABOKOV AND OTHERS ON HIS LIFE'S WORK

Edited by J. E. Rivers and Charles Nicol

UNIVERSITY OF TEXAS PRESS, AUSTIN

THE DAN DANCIGER PUBLICATION SERIES

Copyright © 1982 by the University of Texas Press
"Notes to *Ada* by Vivian Darkbloom" and "Postscript to the Russian
Edition of *Lolita*" copyright © 1982 by Véra Nabokov
"A Few Things That Must Be Said on Behalf of Vladimir Nabokov"
copyright © 1982 by Dmitri Nabokov
All rights reserved
Printed in the United States of America
First Edition, 1982

Requests for permission to reproduce material from this work
should be sent to Permissions, University of Texas Press,
Box 7819, Austin, Texas 78712.

Library of Congress Cataloging in Publication Data
Main entry under title:
Nabokov's fifth arc.
   (The Dan Danciger publication series)
   Bibliography: p.
   1. Nabokov, Vladimir Vladimirovich, 1899–1977—Criticism and
interpretation—Addresses, essays, lectures.   I. Nabokov, Vladimir
Vladimirovich, 1899–1977.   II. Rivers, J. E. (Julius Edwin), 1944–
III. Nicol, Charles, 1940–   .   IV. Series.
PG3476.N3Z793   813'.54   81-14764
ISBN 0-292-75522-8   AACR2

OLSON LIBRARY
NORTHERN MICHIGAN UNIVERSITY
MARQUETTE. MICHIGAN 49855

To David and John and to
Ed and Martha Lee,
Jonathan and Judy,
Tommy and Kim

Contents

Acknowledgments

The editors would like to thank Véra and Dmitri Nabokov, Philip Anderson, Stephen Jan Parker, Jim Rivers, Earl Sampson, and William Walker for their help and advice in the preparation of this book. Special thanks are due to Véra Nabokov for her permission to publish Nabokov's "Notes to *Ada* by Vivian Darkbloom" and "Postscript" to the Russian *Lolita* and for her help in proofreading these texts. We would also like to thank our contributors for their willingness to revise, polish, and repolish their essays in our shared attempt to create a fit memorial to Nabokov. And we would like to acknowledge our debt to the editors with whom we worked at the University of Texas Press: Suzanne Comer and Kathleen Lewis.

Alfred Appel, Jr.'s "Nabokov: A Portrait" first appeared in the *Atlantic* in September 1971. A version of Paul S. Bruss's essay "The Problem of Text: Nabokov's Last Two Novels" appeared in his book *Victims* (Bucknell University Press, 1981). Portions of "Notes to Vivian Darkbloom's Notes to *Ada*" by J. E. Rivers and William Walker were originally published in the third issue of the *Vladimir Nabokov Research Newsletter*.

A grant from the Indiana State University Faculty Research Fund assisted in the preparation of this study.

Introduction

CHARLES NICOL AND J. E. RIVERS

The fourteenth chapter of Nabokov's autobiography begins with one of his discoveries, part pun and part revelation: "The spiral is a spiritualized circle." Noting further that the Hegelian dialectic describes "the essential spirality of all things in their relation to time," Nabokov goes on to apply his discovery to himself:

> Twirl follows twirl, and every synthesis is the thesis of the next series. If we consider the simplest spiral, three stages may be distinguished in it, corresponding to those of the triad: We can call "thetic" the small curve or arc that initiates the convolution centrally, "antithetic" the larger arc that faces the first in the process of continuing it; and "synthetic" the still ampler arc that continues the second while following the first along the outer side.
>
> A colored spiral in a small ball of glass, this is how I see my own life. The twenty years I spent in my native Russia (1899–1911) take care of the thetic arc. Twenty-one years of voluntary exile in England, Germany and France (1919–1940) supply the obvious antithesis. The decade I have already spent in my adopted country (1940–50) looks like the beginning of a synthetic envelopment.

Like Nabokov, the autobiography described a spiral. Originally titled *Conclusive Evidence*, it soon acquired the new title *Speak, Memory*. Then Nabokov wrote a Russian version (*Drugie berega*) with significant changes. Finally, *Speak, Memory* went through a third, synthetic arc, returning to English with the subtitle *An Autobiography Revisited*. By this time Nabokov had completed his own third arc, and the last sentence of the above passage from *Conclusive Evidence* became, "The period spent in my adopted country (1940–1960) forms a synthesis—and a new thesis." Furthermore, in revising the autobiography Nabokov added the words "And so on" to the end of the first paragraph quoted above, apparently to emphasize that "twirl follows twirl" not in a simple series of three but in an infinitely expanding pattern.

From the above quotation and its later additions we must draw the uncanny conclusion that Nabokov's move back to Europe in 1960 was already implicit in his original description of the spiraling patterns of his life in 1950. And the prophecy contained in the phrase "And so on" was also fulfilled, for Nabokov's residence in Europe from 1960 until his death in the summer of 1977 fell just short of describing another full arc of twenty years. Nabokov's life thus comes very close to achieving the formal perfection he sought in both life and art.

But Nabokovian forms are open forms, and there is always the implicit "And so on." To the four arcs of Nabokov's life—the Russian, the European, the American, and the neo-European—a fifth arc is now being added: the arc of Nabokov's continuing life as an artist who speaks and will speak in many different voices to many different generations. The fifth arc is the arc of literary history. "Dead is the mandible," says John Shade in *Pale Fire*, "alive the song."

This book is intended as a metaphor for Nabokov's fifth arc and as a first stage in its continuing climb through the crystal land into the reflected sky. The essays that follow study both individual works and their relation to the life's work. At the same time, they engage in a constant dialogue with previous criticism of Nabokov. In all these respects, they stand as tributes to Nabokov, celebrations as well as investigations of his unique literary achievement.

Our book begins with this fifth arc—with the end that is also a new beginning. "Part I: The Fifth Arc" opens with Alfred Appel, Jr.'s portrait of Nabokov during the last period of his life—the lionized, world-famous sage of Montreux. Appel's memoir is followed by three aggressive and perhaps controversial essays concerned less with interpreting individual works than with abandoning, refining, or extending traditional viewpoints and techniques. James M. Rambeau describes the traps Nabokov's writings hold for their critics; Dmitri Nabokov objects on behalf of his father to some recent commentators; and Phyllis A. Roth ventures into a psychological approach that Nabokov himself might have discouraged. The first section thus serves as a microcosm of the whole by highlighting the transition from Nabokov's life as a practicing writer to his continuing life as a stimulating and controversial figure in literary history.

We then return to the two earliest arcs of the spiral, to Nabokov's Russian and first European periods. Beverly Lyon Clark analyzes his little-known translation of *Alice's Adventures in Wonderland*; Walter Evans delineates the neglected major story "The Potato

Elf"; William C. Carroll traces the philosophical and literary tradition behind *Despair*, generally regarded as Nabokov's first major novel; and Margaret Byrd Boegeman closes our second arc with an analysis that shows *Invitation to a Beheading* to be, among other things, Nabokov's farewell to the Russian language.

Our third arc begins with Beverly Gray Bienstock's analysis of the film imagery in *Bend Sinister*, the first novel Nabokov wrote in America, followed by Larry R. Andrews' close scrutiny of the brief but brilliant story "Signs and Symbols." This section continues with major contributions to the growing literature on *Lolita*: Gladys M. Clifton shows that we must take Lolita's point of view into account in order to understand Humbert and his narrative, and Thomas R. Frosch reveals heretofore unsuspected shades of irony and paradox in the novel's treatment of the literary traditions of which it is a part. Then Nabokov himself speaks out on his masterpiece: his critically neglected but highly revealing postscript to the Russian version of *Lolita* is presented here in its first English translation. The third arc concludes with Julian W. Connolly's analysis of the spiraling patterns of "recurrence and transformation" in *Pnin*.

In our consideration of Nabokov's fourth, Swiss period, Marilyn Edelstein analyzes the complex consciousness that informs *Pale Fire*, and Carol Shloss discusses the interplay of aristocratic and aesthetic motifs in *Speak, Memory*, a work that underwent its final revision and metamorphosis during this period of Nabokov's life. We then present our second major grouping of materials, on *Ada*: an essay by Charles Nicol on the unreliability of Van Veen as narrator, Nabokov's own "Notes to *Ada* by Vivian Darkbloom," and a commentary on those notes by J. E. Rivers and William Walker. This section concludes with Paul S. Bruss's demonstration that Nabokov's last two novels explore the metaphor of life as a difficult, perhaps corrupt, perhaps ultimately impenetrable text. Our final section thus presents searching new interpretations of the novels published during the final period of Nabokov's life, shows how they relate to more familiar works, and suggests several ways in which the masterpieces of the fourth period recapitulate the spiral of Nabokov's career as a whole.

Our broad chronological scope and close interpretation of individual works allow this book to supplement and complement another recently published memorial to Nabokov: *Vladimir Nabokov: A Tribute*, edited by Peter Quennell (1980). The Quennell collection is concerned more with the spirit than with the development of Nabokov's fiction and contains only one essay on an individual text (Robert Alter's reading of *Ada*). Our book combines an overview of

Nabokov's entire career with detailed readings of works from every period of his creative life. We believe it is important at this point in the ongoing assessment of Nabokov's achievement to review his career as a whole and to appreciate its sweep, its variety, and its inclusiveness.

The book has, then, a structure and a progression. What it does not have, and purposely so, is a consistently held critical outlook. In the following pages we present twenty-one individual minds exercising themselves from an assortment of critical perspectives on the problems and pleasures of Nabokov's fiction. The book approaches Nabokov as he often encourages us to approach "reality": not from a single, inflexible point of view but from many points of view which, taken together, may reveal something of the true complexity of the subject at hand. Some of the essays emphasize Nabokov the Russian, some Nabokov the American. Others scrutinize more elusive identities: the American within the Russian and the Russian within the American, the man behind the artist and the artist behind the man. Some are traditional in their approach and in their conclusions. Others are experimental in their conception and tentative in their findings. We have tried, in short, to create a book that will be both a commentary on and an example of the current state of Nabokov studies. Furthermore, the book is aimed at a wide audience. The general reader, we hope, will be able to use the book as an introduction to Nabokov, but it is an introduction that constantly challenges the general reader to explore in the company of experts hitherto uncharted territory in Nabokov scholarship. The specialist will find ideas that are new to the field and suggestions for further innovative research together with constant reminders that worthwhile discoveries can still be made through traditional methods and approaches. There is an essay attacking annotation as a way of understanding Nabokov. But there are also two sets of annotations to one of Nabokov's most complex novels, with one set acting as a commentary on the other. Not all the contributions are so antithetical. But the book does strive for—and we hope it achieves—a wide spectrum of argument and opinion.

The lively and occasionally sharp tone of the essays is due in part to the fact that some were first presented at the special seminars devoted to Nabokov at recent conventions of the Modern Language Association, seminars that have now metamorphosed into meetings of the newly formed Vladimir Nabokov Society. The editors served as discussion leaders for the first and second of these seminars, and the idea for the book grew out of their association with each other and with other Nabokov scholars at these annual gatherings. The book was conceived, then, in a spirit of debate and intellectual exchange, and we have tried to preserve this spirit in the form the book has now attained. Nabokov loved a good intellectual joust, and any tribute to him that did not recall and honor this aspect of the man would be incomplete.

If we were asked to summarize what the essays have in common aside from their esteem for Nabokov, their occasionally pugnacious tone, and their ultimately synthetic purpose, we would answer as follows. First, they attempt to focus attention on the human qualities of Nabokov's art and on the humanity that underlies and vivifies what is often interpreted as artifice for its own sake. Second, they attempt to illustrate the various genres and traditions that intermingle in Nabokov's work and to use these as a basis for defining his artistic originality. Third, they attempt to view Nabokov within the context of his era and to begin the task of assessing his contributions to modern literature. Each of the essays addresses at least one of these topics, and many of them address all three.

Having thus begun to define the fifth arc of Nabokov's literary life, let us return for a moment to the third arc, to the beginning of his career as an American writer. In what is now a rare and little-known book—*New Directions in Prose and Poetry, 1941*, edited by James Laughlin—there is a section devoted to "Soviet Russian Poetry." One of the contributions to this section is "Hodassevich: A Note and Translation, by Vladimir Nabokov." The "Notes on Contributors" describe this newcomer to America as follows:

> Vladimir Nabokov, who translates Hodassevich in our Russian section, is now lecturing at Wellesley College. A Russian, member of a great aristocratic family, cousin of the composer Nicholas Nabokov, he was educated at Cambridge and lived in France and Germany after the Revolution. He wrote some twenty books—novels and stories—which were widely translated in Europe, winning him an important reputation. New Directions has just issued his novel *The Real Life of Sebastian Knight* and a number of his stories have appeared recently in *The Atlantic*. Several years ago Bobbs-Merrill published his novel *Laughter in the Dark*. His other books have not yet been done in English translations, but they will be. Nabokov is a chess fiend and a lepidopterologist. He is married and has a young son.

Nabokov's fantastically productive third arc began at this point of transition from his European to his American incarnation. Edmund Wilson was introducing him to New Directions, the *New Repub-*

lic, and the *Atlantic*, as later he would introduce him to the *New Yorker*. And already, in his second extant letter to Wilson (15 December 1940), Nabokov was explaining that "you are quite wrong about Hegel's triad being based upon the triangle"; instead, he continued, it "is really the idea of a circle." Now, at another point of transition, this time from the fourth to the fifth arc, the circle once again becomes spiritualized, bodies forth harmonies and congruences, and turns, at the same time, toward new directions.

Part 1

The Fifth Arc

2 July 1977: Vladimir Nabokov dies in Switzerland.

Nabokov: A Portrait

ALFRED APPEL, JR.

They know that Hamlet and Lear are gay
Gaiety transfiguring all that dread.
                    —W. B. Yeats, "Lapis Lazuli"

"I'm as American as apple pie," said Vladimir Nabokov as we walked through the main lobby of the Palace Hotel in Montreux, Switzerland. "You have a funny accent, Captain," I drawled, imitating Peter Sellers' impersonation of drunken and deranged Quilty being confronted by gun-toting Humbert Humbert in the film version of *Lolita*. Nabokov laughed, a full-bodied, very Russian laugh; his accent, however, is quite English, the language of his nursery and his university. He and his wife Véra have lived in the Montreux Palace since 1960. "Gogol began *Dead Souls* nearby, you know," said Nabokov, "and Tolstoy stayed here, and risked his health by chasing chambermaids down these endless halls."

Montreux, says Nabokov, is "a rosy place for our riparian exile." Situated in the eastern corner of Lake Geneva, the little town is quiet save for the tourist season, when its main attraction is Byron's Castle of Chillon. "Our Alp," as Nabokov calls it, is visible from their window. The rococo Palace Hotel, erected in 1835, resembles the grand hotels at which Nabokov's family vacationed during his privileged childhood. There are personal and practical reasons, he says, for their staying there now: his sister, Elena, lives nearby in Geneva; their son, Dmitri, an opera singer, resides in Milan; and one of Nabokov's current works-in-progress, an illustrated history of the butterfly in art, "from Egyptian antiquity to the Renaissance," calls for research trips to various European museums. Montreux is not lonely, however, or without its social life. "There are the crested grebes of Lake Geneva," he says, "and we are always happy to see American intellectuals."

Nabokov's long absence from America is reflected in his work. *Lolita* (1955) and *Pnin* (1957) have American settings, but *Pale Fire*

(1962), conceived in the States but completed in Europe, is only partly American in locale, and *Ada* (1969) is a fantasia that only in its final few pages touches ground, in Switzerland. "I can't use a contemporary American setting now," says Nabokov, "because I've lost touch with the slang." It is fitting that the last work he should have completed in America, after twenty years there (1940–1960), was his monumental translation of Pushkin's *Eugene Onegin*. If, as Nabokov says, "the writer's art is his real passport," then *Ada*, the first and only classic of Amerussian literature, makes it more difficult than ever for academic pigeonholers and census-takers to "place" him.

Vladimir Vladimirovich Nabokov was born in St. Petersburg on 23 April 1899, a birthday he shares with William Shakespeare and Shirley Temple, as he likes to point out, thereby defining the polar extremes of the vast areas of knowledge at his disposal as scholar and novelist. Widely read in three languages by the age of seventeen, when he inherited from his uncle a country estate and the equivalent of a few million dollars, Nabokov took with him into exile no legacy, but a mind filled with literature and memories of a loving and "harmonious world of perfect childhood," re-created with eloquence and elegance in his memoir, *Speak, Memory* (1951, revised edition, 1966). His was a truly distinguished as well as aristocratic family, with a long tradition of culture and public service. His father, Vladimir Dmitrievich, was an eminent jurist, the author of several books and thousands of articles, including "The Blood Bath of Kishinev," a famous protest against the 1903 pogrom in which hundreds of Jews were massacred. A leader of the prerevolutionary opposition party and a member of the first imperial parliament (Duma), he moved his family to the Crimea in 1917 (as Minister of Justice in the anti-Soviet government), and two years later, into exile in Berlin. His son noted that occasion with several poems, including one called "Hotel Room" (translated by Nabokov and included in his book *Poems and Problems*, copyright © Vladimir Nabokov, 1971):

> Not quite a bed, not quite a bench.
> Wallpaper: a grim yellow.
> A pair of chairs. A squinty looking-glass.
> We enter—my shadow and I.
>
> We open with a vibrant sound the window:
> the light's reflection slides down to the ground.
> The night is breathless. Distant dogs
> with varied barks fracture the stillness.

> Stirless, I stand there at the window,
> and in the black bowl of the sky
> glows like a golden drop of honey
> the mellow moon.

Written shortly before his twentieth birthday, in Sebastopol, "Hotel Metropole, room 7, April 8, 1919, a few days before leaving Russia," the poem provides the foreground frame of an infinite regress of rented rooms.

Nabokov's exile defines a state of mind and spirit and is not simply a matter of his being a so-called "White Russian." The figure of the exile embodies the human condition in our time, and it has become a commonplace to point out how many writers have either chosen this role or been cast literally in it: Joyce, Mann, Toller, Brecht, Beckett, Ionesco, and Russians too numerous to name, for they seem to have had all of modern history with which to contend. Nabokov's cousin and childhood playmate was killed by the Soviets in 1919; his brother died in a German concentration camp in 1945; and his father, age fifty-two, was shot at a political meeting in Berlin in 1922, as he was shielding a speaker from two Russian monarchist assassins. Under Hitler, Vladimir Dmitrievich's killer became chief of the Gestapo's émigré section.

The sorrows of exile were infinite: isolation, poverty, despair, disease, early death, suicide, or—if the émigré writer survived, languageless in some distant land—silence, obscurity, and the nightmare of nostalgia. "I haf nofing, I haf nofing," wails Pnin, and,

> Beyond the seas where I have lost a sceptre,
> I hear the neighing of my dappled nouns,
> soft participles coming down the steps,
> treading on leaves, trailing their rustling gowns

writes Nabokov in "An Evening of Russian Poetry" (1945), the year he became an American citizen. Only the vulgar persist in believing that Nabokov scorns the Russian Revolution simply because it wiped out his wealth.

Nabokov graduated in 1922 from Trinity College, Cambridge, with a "first-class" (Honors) degree in foreign languages (French and Russian). From 1922 until 1937, except for many summers, he lived in Berlin, where he wrote prolifically in Russian—numerous translations, fifty reviews and essays, hundreds of poems, nine plays, forty short stories, and nine novels—almost all under the pseudonym of "V. Sirin," which he adopted in 1920 so as to avoid confusion with his father, in whose newspaper, the liberal émigré publication *Rul' (The Rudder)*, he often published.

One evening on her way back to their apartment, Véra Nabokov witnessed one of the first of the Berlin book-burnings, and the passage of time has not dulled her or her husband's memories. They have not revisited Germany since their return to Europe ten years ago; they cannot forget the crimes, or forgive a criminal, however hapless he may now seem. "It is always the year one," as one of his narrators says. Thus the vehemence with which Nabokov noted the news coverage describing the return to Hamilton College in 1969 of a famous American poet whose activities as an Axis broadcaster are barely remembered: "That bit about Mr. E. Pound, a venerable mediocrity, making a 'sentimental visit' to his alma mater in Clinton, New York, and being given a standing ovation by the commencement audience—consisting, apparently, of morons and madmen."

Too many readers have taken Nabokov too literally when, in the prefaces issued from his present tower, he says he is not a political writer. He is no ideologue, to be sure, but *Invitation to a Beheading* (1935–1936) and *Bend Sinister* (1947) are in the best sense "political," and Nabokov's detractors should submit themselves to Adam Krug's anguish in *Bend Sinister* when he discovers that the State has murdered his young son by mistake, or the vision in *Pale Fire* of obscene Gradus, the political assassin, fighting the effects of less-than-fresh *pommes frites* as he rushes to discharge his gun rather than his bowels.

Unable to obtain an academic job in England, which he visited during the winter of 1939, Nabokov, his wife, and their son, Dmitri, emigrated to America in May 1940. On the Continent, Nabokov had supported his family by reading his works to Russian émigré audiences and by giving lessons in tennis and English. There was less demand for such services in America. During his first year he wrote reviews on Russian subjects and received modest grants. The summer of 1940 was spent at the Vermont summer home of an old friend, Mihel Karpovich, a professor at Harvard. One day at Karpovich's the mail produced an invitation to contribute to the *New Republic*. The letter was signed by someone named Edmund Wilson, who also enclosed a copy of a book he had just published, *To the Finland Station*, thereby inaugurating a friendship that would last some twenty-five years. At about the same time a telegram arrived from the Tolstoy Committee (an organization that, among other things, helped émigrés to resettle), advising Nabokov to return immediately to New York City; a job had been found for him in publishing. Nabokov hurried back to the city. The Tolstoy Committee's secretary told him to present himself at the main desk of Scribner's Bookshop, which is located below their editorial offices on Fifth Avenue. "And stand up straight," she added, "you'll make a better impression." At Scribner's he was received by a man named Wraden, whom he had known in Europe, and who was somewhat nonplussed to see who had been sent over, since the job opening was for a delivery boy on a bicycle. When young Dmitri registered at school, he wrote "tennis coach" in the blank space above "father's occupation."

Nabokov's vocational identity was firmer by 1941. That summer he taught Russian literature and a creative-writing course at Stanford University, and in the fall began teaching Russian grammar and literature at Wellesley College. The salary was in the neighborhood of $2000. "Not bad for a beginning boy of forty-one," he says today, smiling slyly. There were other upward turns. *The Real Life of Sebastian Knight*, which he had written in English in Paris, was "bought for $150 in 1941 by New Directions." Lucie Léon had gone over the manuscript in Paris; and now, still concerned with what he calls "the fragility of my English at the time of my abandoning Russian in 1939," Nabokov "begged the late Agnes Perkins, the admirable head of the English department at Wellesley, to assist me in reading the galleys of the book." It was published just a few days after Pearl Harbor and did not eclipse *The Song of Bernadette*, *The Robe*, or any of the other timely best sellers of the moment.

The Real Life of Sebastian Knight was not his first publication in English. Gleb Struve, the émigré critic and scholar, had placed translations of Nabokov stories in *This Quarter*, an English-language little magazine based in Montparnasse (1932), and in *Lovat Dickson's Magazine* in England (1934—the misspelled byline read "V. Nobokov-Sirin"). An offer of further Nabokov stories was rebuffed by a famous "liberal" magazine in London because it was against their policy, during the worst years of Stalin's reign of terror, to publish those reactionary "White Russians." Encouraged by the English publication in 1936 of Winifred Roy's translation of *Laughter in the Dark* (1932), Nabokov himself translated *Despair* (1934) at the end of 1936, and it appeared in London the next year. "This was my first serious attempt," he says, "to use English for what may be loosely termed an artistic purpose." It sold badly, however, and the entire publisher's stock was destroyed by German bombs in 1940.

Publication in America continued to elude Nabokov. After Ivan Bunin won the Nobel Prize for Literature in 1933, H. L. Mencken asked Albert Parry (now chairman of the Russian Department at Case–Western Reserve University) if there were any other émigré writers who deserved an American audience, and if he would write a piece on them for Mencken's *American Mercury.* Parry said there were, and his article, which also focused on Mark Aldanov and Nina Berberova, represents the first mention of Nabokov in America. It prompted the following letter to Parry from Slovo, the émigré publishing house in Berlin (dated 1 September 1933):

> Dear Sir,
>   We have had the pleasure of reading your fine article—"Belles-lettres among the Russian Emigrés"—in the July issue of the "American Mercury."
>   We are the publishers of Mr. Sirin's works and in this capacity highly appreciate your recognizing that author's great merits. You are right in supposing that Mr. Sirin's brilliant novels and short stories (with the only exception of one short story published in "The Quarter") have not yet been translated either in America or in England. We should be very much obliged to you for any suggestion or advice you should care to give in regard to the chance of Mr. Sirin's works finding a publisher in America.
>   We hope that you will kindly give your attention to this matter, and remain, dear Sir,
>
> Yours faithfully
> (signed)

Alfred A. Knopf, Bunin's publisher, saw Parry's article and invited him to his office to discuss Sirin, but nothing came of it; the economic realities of the Depression did not encourage Knopf to introduce another foreign author. But in 1938, Bobbs-Merrill published Roy's rather flat translation of *Laughter in the Dark,* revised anew by the novelist, who at the time transliterated his name as "Nabokoff." While he was still living in Paris he also made his debut in an American magazine, the December 1939 *Esquire,* wherein appeared Sirin's "The Potato Elf," a dark and haunting tale about a dwarf, quite out of place in a gala Christmas issue.

Sebastian Knight and *Laughter in the Dark* each had its American admirers, but only after "Hurricane Lolita" (to quote *Pale Fire*) did Nabokov's eight other Russian novels begin to appear in the United States in English translations. In the mid-1940s, one of Dmitri's teachers asked him who his favorite Russian writers were. "Pushkin and my father," he answered, a piquant enough response, given the sudden disappearance of Sirin, and the scant evidence in America that he had existed.

In addition to *The Real Life of Sebastian Knight,* 1941 saw the publication also of "Cloud, Castle, Lake" and "The Aurelian" in the

Atlantic Monthly. Translations of short stories from the thirties, they were only the first of seven stories, both old and new, which Nabokov would contribute to that magazine in the forties; they made him visible. A novel, of course, is on its own, for better or worse, and *The Real Life of Sebastian Knight* and his next novel, *Bend Sinister* (1947), turned out to be lonely creatures indeed. The *Atlantic*, however, provided Nabokov with a body of readers large enough to call an audience, and these stories in turn formed the main content of *Nine Stories* (1947).

That first American audience included Professor Morris Bishop of Cornell University, who in 1947 found himself chairman of a committee searching for a new professor of Russian literature. Bishop sought out Nabokov, even though the latter had neither advanced degrees nor, worse yet, a record of academic publications. Nabokov liked Wellesley, especially since its proximity to Cambridge allowed him to work on lepidoptera many hours every day (including Sundays) at the Harvard Museum of Comparative Zoology, but after seven years he still did not have tenure. He was invited to Cornell to present a paper and endure the customary "looking over," and shortly afterwards, in 1948, was offered an associate professorship, which he accepted—"though at heart," says Nabokov, "I have always remained a lean visiting lecturer."

The Bishops remember how Nabokov, seated in their living room before giving the paper, suddenly clasped his coat against his chest to see if his folded lecture was there, a heart-arresting gesture sufficiently reminiscent of Nabokov's own creation, the myopic and addlepated Professor Pnin. Lecturer Nabokov had his share of Pninian experiences. One letter of invitation from a department chairman was signed "Vladimir Nabokov." Only four people showed up for the resulting lecture: "I forgot to advertise," said the chairman, a genius of absentmindedness. As Nabokov began to speak, half of the audience, a mother and son, got up and left. They were in the wrong room. "Vladimir Vladimirovich, we are all Pnins," said an émigré colleague in the History Department as they were walking across the snowbound Cornell campus shortly after one of the *Pnin* chapters had appeared in the *New Yorker*. "You know, he'd forgotten I'd written it," says Nabokov, fifteen years later, his disbelief firmly intact. But Nabokov is not Pnin. He did not take the wrong train to Cornell, or arrive at the Bishops' a week too early, and the folded pages were in their place, as Morris Bishop fondly recalls.

Nabokov is one with Pnin, however, in his abhorrence of Soviet totalitarianism and "the Philistine essence of Leninism." The decision to leave Wellesley had been hastened by the person in high authority there who had suggested to Nabokov that he tone down his classroom criticism of Soviet writers: "They are our allies, you know." Of the writers he met in this country only Robert Frost seemed to share his opinion of Communism, but their fleeting political kinship was neutralized for Nabokov when Frost was gratuitously and excessively rude to their kind host. "My main regret," says Nabokov, is "that I didn't emigrate earlier to America." If he had lived in New York City in the thirties he might have offered "free lessons to pro-Soviet boosters." After receiving Edmund Wilson's presentation copy of *To the Finland Station*, Nabokov sent him an errata and a critique, which insisted, among other things, that the oft-repeated story about Lenin sparing a fox's life was both apocryphal and symbolically meaningless, considering certain facts and statistics.

Nabokov and Wilson met often thereafter, particularly in the forties, and exchanged "frank letters" for years. Wilson was kind in many ways, some of them professional—a long blurb for *Sebastian Knight*, a publisher for *Bend Sinister*—while Nabokov quietly aided and abetted Wilson backstage in his long struggle with the Russian language.

It would not be cheap or easy psychologizing to suggest that Wilson's famous 1965 assault on his old friend's *Eugene Onegin* translation was a monumental self-assertion dating back to their preceptorials in Russian. Wilson nevertheless sent the Nabokovs his customary Christmas card that year, enclosing a little wind-up paper butterfly. "It didn't work," complains Nabokov. "Made in Japan."

Politics and pedagogy converge in Nabokov's view of the "student revolution." Lamenting the conformity of "group beards and group protests," he says that "rowdies are never true revolutionaries." Nabokov would be unhappy on today's campuses for more than one reason. "After all," he notes, "my method of teaching precluded genuine contact with my students," and it is, of course, that kind of contact which many students now demand.

Although Nabokov gave some seminars at Cornell—in Pushkin, for example—the subject matter and the catalogue description ("Prerequisite, proficiency in Russian") led no one to expect a rap session. Nabokov's other courses were conducted as lectures, even if the enrollment was modest, as in his survey of Russian literature. Few of his pre-*Lolita* students knew he was a writer. He was an immensely popular teacher, however, particularly in his Literature 311–312 course, "Masterpieces of European Fiction." The course was unique in the smallest of ways (witness the "bonus system" employed in examinations, allowing students two extra points per effort whenever they could garnish an answer with a substantial and accurate quotation—"a gem"—drawn from the text in question).

Carefully handwritten and then typed out, an artist-scientist's anatomical examination of the books he admired and adored, Nabokov's lectures ranged widely and wildly in mood, from the most moving to the most farcical of moments. "You cannot understand a writer if you cannot pronounce his name," he would say, introducing Gogol ("Gaw-gol, not Gogal!"). He would then rehearse Gogol's death agonies, his head thrown back in pain and terror, nostrils distended, eyes shut, his beseechments filling the hushed lecture hall. Urging his students to become "creative readers," he would ask them to develop "the passion of the scientist and the precision of the artist"—double takes on the part of notetakers; didn't he mean the opposite?—and, digressing for the minute, Nabokov would toss brickbats at "Old Dusty" or "the Viennese quack," eliciting from the gallery as many gasps as laughs. He would conclude a lecture with a rhapsodic apostrophe to our writer's style: "Feel it in your spine; let us worship the spine—the upper spine, the vertebrae tipped at the head with a divine flame!" And then, as the hour ended, he would ask to see the students who had occupied seats 102 and 103 during the recent midterm examination. "I suspect mental telepathy!"

"My assistant," he always called her, with a decorous, business-like impersonality, but everyone knew she was Véra Nabokov. Depending on the lecture room, she would sit either in the first row or at the end of the platform, her cool, steady gaze taking in the audience, one by one, it seemed. "My assistant has forgotten one label on the diagram . . . oh, it is a very important label," he said one day, rushing to the blackboard and picking up a piece of chalk. It was the only time anyone had seen her smile in class, even at one of his jokes, or, rather, *especially* at one of those jokes, since most of his funniest "asides" were in script, and, an experienced trouper, she had heard it all before, many times, and had no doubt typed it up. A woman of great dignity and natural elegance, Véra Nabokov has been a totally devoted collaborator, handling her husband's correspondence and business transactions, driving the car, grading thousands of examination papers, and running the household, such as it was. Fiercely intelligent, she is at once his ideal reader and only real editor. Since their marriage in Berlin in 1925, he has read to her all of his works at least twice, and she has reread them while typing them; *Ada* was the first manuscript to have been prepared by a professional secretary.

"Véra's Russian is stupendous," he says, and she learned Italian in order to be able to check the translations of his novels into that tongue. She reads widely in several languages, and is very much "up" on contemporary American letters. "He has digested his Nabokov," she says of a well-known young novelist, genus Black Humor. "Trash," she says of another. Her memory may be better than her husband's. He does not remember Thomas Pynchon, a student in Literature 311–312, circa 1957, nor has he read *V.* ("Lovely title, lovely," says Nabokov), but she quickly responds, "Yes, I remember him, he had an unusual handwriting: half printing, half script." Nor is Véra Nabokov too shy to disagree with her husband, and their games of Scrabble (in English, and *Skrebl* in Russian) have the aura of an infinite series of good-natured rematches between Dempsey and Tunney. Inseparable, self-sufficient, they form a multitude of two.

Although he taught at major institutions, published in *Partisan Review* as well as the *New Yorker*, and had friends such as Edmund Wilson and Harvard's Harry Levin, Nabokov remained through his years at Cornell aloof from "literary circles" and naively unaware of their existence. One summer in the forties he taught at a Writers' Conference at the University of Salt Lake City. He remembers that the faculty included Wallace Stegner, Oscar Williams, and another man. "I don't remember his name," he says. "White-haired, eyeglasses, he wore a conservative suit and looked like a banker, yet wrote some extraordinary verse: 'Bells . . . Bells'—not Poe!—'Bells for John Whiteside's Daughter,' I liked particularly." The mystery faculty member was John Crowe Ransom, at that time one of the two or three most influential poet-critics in America and editor of the *Kenyon Review.* A well-known younger poet of that period, who died in middle age, sat next to Nabokov on a bus trip after they had both given readings. "He didn't want to talk about poetry," says Nabokov, "only about the reputations of other poets." Nabokov also remembers how a distinguished professor of English at Cornell cut short a budding literary discussion at a cocktail party: "It's after five; no shop talk!" Nabokov laughs. "A strange man," he adds. But it is with no bemusement that he recalls the expert in linguistics who could not speak the language of the department he chaired, a phenomenon preserved in the pages of *Pnin.* Many of the most fantastic and grotesque perversions of learning in *Pnin* happen to be drawn from "real life" in the academy; it is the only novel he has ever written that bears the disclaimer, "All of the characters in this book are fictitious, and any resemblance to actual persons, living or dead, is purely coincidental."

Never once during his almost twenty years on campus did Nabokov write an academic article or attend a meeting of the Modern

Language Association, but he did contribute continually to *Psyche* and other lepidopterological journals, and occasionally participated in scientific meetings. Once, at the American Museum of Natural History in New York, where several of Nabokov's specimens are deposited, he met a rather stuffy old gentleman, a banker or businessman, who told Nabokov that he had recently caught a unique butterfly. As Nabokov re-creates the scene in the museum, the man, eyes aglow, reached into his vest pocket and produced a little tin specimen box. He opened the box, and playing it close to the vest in the most literal sense of that cliché, he held it in his cupped palm, against his ample stomach, like a vendor of pornographic postcards in front of a church or school yard. Nabokov mimes his manner, and impersonating himself, leans over to see the proffered butterfly. Stolid and staid, the old gentleman had also experienced the quiet rapture of discovering an undescribed species, and like a long line of Nabokov's fictional creations, from Luzhin in *The Defense* to Humbert in *Lolita*, he too had pursued a secret life, an ardent desire, an obsessive quest.

Nabokov went butterfly-hunting every summer, and these adventures as a "lepist" carried him through two hundred motel rooms in forty-six states, along the same roads traveled by Humbert and Lolita. Though he had tenure at Cornell, the Nabokovs continued to rent, moving every year, sometimes every term—a mobility he bestowed on refugee Humbert. Morris Bishop, Nabokov's only close friend at Cornell, remembers visiting them after they had moved into the tastelessly furnished home of an absent professor. "I couldn't have lived in a place like that," says Bishop, "but it delighted him. He seemed to relish every awful detail." In a few years Bishop realized that these moves were a form of field research enabling Nabokov to study the natural habitat of Humbert's prey. *Lolita* was under way.

Nabokov usually has at least two works-in-progress at roughly the same time, and these literary companions often turn out to complement each other in extraordinary ways; this is most true of *Lolita* and *Speak, Memory* (or *Conclusive Evidence*, as its first, shorter edition was titled in 1951).

In *Speak, Memory*, his fifth book in English, Nabokov became the master of a variegated and virtuoso prose; henceforth he would seek no further advice on English. *Speak, Memory* released him to write *Lolita*, and Lolita in her turn released him from the circumscribing spell of *Speak, Memory*, the cul-de-sac of nostalgia. It is no coincidence that after losing Lolita to Quilty, it takes Humbert three years to find her again, the same number of years Nabokov spent writing *Speak, Memory*. "The past is the past," she tells him, after he has finally located but not recaptured his ineffable girl, now wan, veiny-armed, pregnant, a nymphet no more and badly in need of a few bucks.

The novel developed slowly as Nabokov faced technical problems and absorbed the necessary *couleur locale*—as Humbert might say—by renting Charlotte Haze's house, sampling teen-talk on school buses, reading case studies and movie magazines, observing, observing, wherever he went. Robert M. Adams, then in the English Department at Cornell ("Ah, a duel!" Nabokov had exclaimed, when Adams appeared at the departmental office one morning with his newly broken arm in a sling), remembers a Monday morning in June circa 1951, during the calm between commencement and summer session. A convocation of a youth group was to begin that day—the Young Lutherans or Future Farmers of America—and as Adams approached the wide bridge that separates the campus from the main dormitory area, he saw heading toward him, on the left side of the bridge, radiating the healthiness of a breakfast-food ad, a seemingly endless swarm of blond and apple-cheeked junior- and senior-high-schoolers, and on the other side, walking alone in the opposite direction, his gaze taking them in, a man wearing hiking shoes, knee socks, baggy Bermuda shorts, a sporty cap, and carrying a butterfly net. As it crossed the bridge, the Norman Rockwell *tableau vivant* turned as one to stare in astonishment at *him*, since Nabokov was no doubt the first typical American college professor they had ever seen.

Written before class in Ithaca, or in a parked car on cloudy Colorado afternoons while butterflies slept, or at night in a motel after a long day of "lepping," *Lolita* was finally completed in the spring of 1954, surely no placid period for the Nabokovs. Back in 1950, when he had been discouraged, Véra Nabokov had prevented her husband from throwing the initial chapters into the garden incinerator, but now that the book was a reality, she must have experienced some misgivings and anxieties about its publication and possible reception; even tenured professors are vulnerable. "But she had no doubts about *Lolita*," says Mrs. Bishop; "she knew it would be a classic." Véra Nabokov was absent from lecture the last two weeks of the term (typing the manuscript, no doubt), and one day Nabokov startled the class by appearing without tie or jacket, in old tennis shoes, clearly a distracted man. One friend urged Nabokov to issue the novel anonymously; another refused to publish it for fear that they'd both be imprisoned. With no fanfare whatsoever the Paris-based Olympia Press brought out *Lolita* in 1955. Three years later it was published in America.

"A painful birth, a difficult baby, but a kind daughter," *Lolita* enabled Nabokov, at sixty, to resign his professorship. Part of the fortune lost in 1919 had been restored exactly forty years later, the rubles miraculously converted to dollars, and the Nabokovs soon moved again, first to Hollywood to script *Lolita*, and then to Switzerland in 1960.

Fifty years of renting furnished quarters has made Nabokov, along with Samuel Beckett, a laureate of the lonely room. He has learned to travel light, and his ambience at the Montreux Palace sustains this sense of him. The Palace is a grand hotel in the old tradition, with wide, spacious salons and lovely gardens, but there is nothing opulent about the Nabokovs' apartment on the sixth floor, overlooking Lake Geneva. The living room, where they receive guests, is small, as are the other rooms. There is no TV; they rent a set for important events such as the moon landing and the World Cup soccer championship (Nabokov, who played goalie at Cambridge, notes that Brazil's spectacular player, Pele, "is powerful but has no style"). A card table next to the couch is stacked with books of recent vintage—mostly sent by publishers—which they are sampling and, in a few instances, reading. Nabokov recommends *The Godbotherers*, a novel by Philip Oakes, an Englishman, and is even more enthusiastic about *The Butterflies of Japan*. Paul McCartney, whom he has never met, has sent them his latest record album, the presentation note signed, "With love, Paul and Linda." A still life recently painted by Dmitri, his son's first try at oils, adds a genuine personal touch to the wall above the couch. Nabokov's study, in the next room, contains a lectern, a desk and chair, and a bed. Although he prefers to write standing up, he may use any of the three, depending on the hour and the pull of gravity. The walls are bare, but arranged along the top of the desk are a little family photograph, a framed butterfly, and postcard reproductions of a Picasso still life, *Pitcher, Candle, and Casserole*, and Fra Angelico's *Annunciation*, the radiant rainbow wings of the angel Gabriel easily outshining those of the framed specimen. A conspicuous presence in the room is a multivolume Russian dictionary and a well-worn *Webster's Unabridged*, second edition. Except for the back bedroom, which their part-time secretary has converted into an office, the Nabokovs' apartment gives the impression that they could be packed and ready to leave on the shortest notice.

Nabokov rises at six A.M. and, armed with the discoveries of creative insomnia, begins to write immediately; *Transparent Things* is the title of the novel now in its early stages. By ten thirty, when he draws a hot bath, Nabokov has put in what many writers would call a full day's work. The fair-weather schedule he was following during my most recent visit (August 1970) would next find him, at around eleven o'clock, walking down to the Montreux station to buy his three daily newspapers, the *Times* of London, *Le Monde*, and the *Paris Herald-Tribune*, where he follows, with determined loyalty and attention, the open-ended comic strip adventures of *Buzz Sawyer* and *Rex Morgan, M.D.* Returning along the lakeside, Nabokov comments on its flora, fauna, and filth; Lake Geneva has not been immune to the waste that has so befouled America. "I saw it coming in the States twenty years ago, and would tell people that," says Nabokov, shaking his head, then deploring "the faddist aspects of the antipollution movement." He points out a ginkgo tree he is very fond of, and pauses to examine the venation of one of its butterfly-like leaves (a small wonder also marked in *Pale Fire*, note to line 49). Further on, he stops to watch some swans. "An overrated bird," he says, "the postures of its neck are grotesque, aesthetically absurd, and," he adds, "how can you respect or trust a creature that goes about with such a dirty neck?"

After lunch, there is coffee and conversation in the Nabokovs' apartment: the butterfly in art, the prosody of prose (Bely and Melville), the art of Keaton, Chaplin, the Marx Brothers, and his favorites, Laurel and Hardy. That subject leads logically to Nabokov's experiences in Hollywood while scripting *Lolita*: excellent "lepping" in the Hollywood hills, and stimulating discussions with the film's producer, who wanted Humbert to marry Lolita, a small compromise Nabokov was unwilling to make.

The conversation turns to cannibalism. "It is not as uncommon as you'd think," Nabokov says, recalling a Belgian poet he had known in the 1930s. The poet's father had been a stationmaster. One day a terrible accident had severed a man's leg, and the poet, then a very young man, had helped himself to the limb, "prepared and waiting on the track."

"I never believed that story," says Véra Nabokov, with a tolerant smile.

"It happened, it happened!" insists her husband. "I couldn't make up such a story."

"I like people who have the gift of gab," says Nabokov, generalizing. "I mean 'good conversationalists,'" he adds, correcting himself, not wishing to hurt the feelings of anyone present. Nabokov clearly relishes good gab; gossip, anecdotes, and jokes pour forth from him, and he is one of those people whose laughter threatens to unseat them. To emphasize a point or underscore a punch line, he will often lower his head, wrinkle his brow, and peer over the top of his eyeglasses, a parody of a professor. His face, even at less animated moments, is very expressive, mobile; photographs reveal its protean qualities. "I've frequently been told I don't look like me," he says, pausing for a moment to enjoy the paradox. "Recently, a stranger, a tourist, approached me in the [hotel] garden, and said, 'I know you! You're . . . you're . . . *you're General MacArthur's brother!*" Nabokov shakes with mirth, and dabs his eyes with a handkerchief, and catches his empty coffee cup and saucer as they are about to topple from his lap.

By three in the afternoon Nabokov retires for a rest and more work: the polishing of Dmitri's rendering into English of *Podvig* (1931)—*The Exploit*, now retitled *Glory*—the last of his untranslated Russian novels (Nabokov was delighted to find a forgotten passage in which the reverie of his fantasizing hero seems to anticipate Thurber's "The Secret Life of Walter Mitty," a story much admired by Nabokov). Then drinks and more conversation. Close students of the artist's metabolic patterns should note that Nabokov usually goes to bed by nine o'clock.

When Nabokov doesn't have visitors, he may spend the early afternoon reading in the hotel's poolside garden (always keeping notepaper by his side in case the Muse speaks unexpectedly), or else take long walks, sometimes for three or four hours, doing a lot of work in his head. In the spring, when the butterfly-hunting is best, Nabokov may walk (and run) as many as fifteen or twenty miles a day. It is not surprising that he is deeply tanned, firmly muscled, and looks considerably younger than his seventy-two years. Watching him kick around a soccer ball with Raffaello, one of the hotel's cabana boys, underscores the connection between his penchant for exercise and the enormous enthusiasm and creative energy which have resulted in, among many other things, three major works since his sixty-third birthday (*Pale Fire*, the four-volume *Onegin* translation, and *Ada*).

Wordplay is very much a part of Nabokov's personal manner. He has a habit of repeating a phrase that he has just spoken, of spearing a word in midair and toying with the pieces. "No, tape recorders are out," he says. "No speaking off the Nabocuff. When I see one of those machines I start hemming and hawing . . . hemming and hawing. Hemingwaying all over the place."

When reviewers use the tag "Nabokovian," they are acknowledging that he is that rarest of artists—a man and a writer who discovers, defines, and expresses himself and his world in a voice that is consistently and uniquely his. Nabokov's voice is most vibrant and identifiable when he is describing either his "passion for lepidopterological research" or his abhorrence of certain writers. "Had there been no Russian Revolution, I probably would have devoted myself solely to lepidopterology," says Nabokov, whose aesthetic of objectivity and precision is clearly that of a naturalist: "The use of symbols [is] hateful because it substitutes a dead general idea for a live specific impression. . . . In high art and pure science detail is everything." His statements go far in helping to place in a quite reasonable context his remarks on other writers, remarks which are variously thought to be arrogant, eccentric, outrageous, indefensible, funny but frivolous. The zest with which he exorcises "bogeys and shams from the hall of false fame" and the verbs he favors ("detest," "loathe") are bound to set sensitive teeth on edge, while his inscrutable dismissals of famous works (*Death in Venice* is "asinine") rarely clarify his objections to them, or suggest the seriousness and consistency of his position or its source in the literary wars of Russia a hundred years ago. In the 1860s and '70s Nikolai Chernyshevsky and other influential radical polemicists insisted that literary artists be topical reporters and social commentators, and the proselytizing, ideological, and sociological nature of much nineteenth-century Russian literature testifies to their success. Pushkin and Chekhov were attacked for their failure to be "relevant" and *engagé* (to use today's trite terms), as Sirin would be in the 1930s, and today's Socialist Realism is the police state's transmutation of those earlier criteria and supposedly progressive principles. Beleaguered or not, Solzhenitsyn is in the main tradition of Russian literature, and the ironies are, of course, tragic.

When the first chapters of *The Defense* came out in 1929 in the leading émigré journal, the Paris-based *Sovremennye Zapiski* (*Contemporary Annals*), Nina Berberova knew that "a great Russian writer, like a phoenix [had been] born from the fire and ashes of revolution and exile. Our existence from now on acquired a meaning. All my generation were justified. We were saved," she writes in her recent memoir (*The Italics Are Mine*). She was not alone in her estimation of Nabokov, but a number of other émigré critics vilified him for being "un-Russian" in his concerns. So taken for granted were these assumptions about the writer's social responsibilities that the liberal editors of *Sovremennye Zapiski*, not wishing to offend their readers, refused in 1937 to publish Nabokov's satirical biography of Chernyshevsky, now intact as chapter 4 of *The Gift*, which they were then in the process of serializing.

Living in Switzerland, writing in English, Nabokov is never more Russian than when offering to journalists and interviewers those seemingly fripperous remarks about writers he deems short on style and/or long on argument and advice. Those remarks, hardly random, enable him to sustain his miraculous open-ended debate with Chernyshevsky, thereby fulfilling his own polemical respon- sibilities as the embodiment of the other great Russian tradition: Pushkin, Chekhov, and the Tolstoy who wrote *Anna Karenina*, or at least most of it. "Skip the hymn to the wheat," Nabokov would in- struct his students, referring to Tolstoy's Populist attitudes and Levin's day in the field.

Contrary to rumor, Nabokov is not totally ungenerous, and has praised in print many writers, from Shakespeare to Sirin. Of the fa- mous moderns, he most admires Joyce, Proust, Kafka, and H. G. Wells, his favorite boyhood author. When Nabokov mentions his continued esteem for Wells, especially his "romances"—*The Time Machine, The Invisible Man, The War of the Worlds*—I ask him about chapter 3 of *Ada*, where he describes Aqua Veen's private "War of the Worlds," and, in a haunting passage, her howling disin- tegration. Did he have in mind, I wondered, the final pages of Wells's fantasia, when the silence of devastated and darkened London is dis- turbed by the terrible last lamentations of those mammoth invaders from Mars, toppled by lowly bacteria?

"Yes," says Nabokov, "I can still hear those creatures," and the expression on his face and the tone of his voice remind me of two moments during other visits to Montreux. Late one afternoon in Jan- uary 1968, our conversation had turned to the dark days of the mid-1930s, when the Nabokovs were planning their permanent de- parture from Germany. Because Véra Nabokov is Jewish, a future there seemed even more uncertain. Nabokov recalled Ivan Bunin's visit to Berlin in 1934. The most famous of the émigré writers, Bunin had recently received the Nobel Prize, and was making a kind of triumphal tour. Nabokov attended the public ceremony in Bu- nin's honor, and a few days later lunched with him at a Berlin restau- rant. They were seated, Nabokov remembers, at the rear of a crowd- ed room, beneath a huge Nazi flag. When they met again shortly afterwards, in Paris, Bunin told Nabokov and several others how on his departure from Berlin he had been stopped by the Gestapo, ever on the alert for that most stable of émigré commodities, a smuggled jewel or two. The handsome and erect old gentleman was interro- gated, searched, stripped, and searched again. An empty bucket was placed behind the Nobel laureate, who was then given a strong and immensely successful dose of castor oil. The search of the naked man was completed by the Gestapo agent who wiped him. As

Nabokov finished the story, his forehead twisted into a tangle of lines, and he stared, unblinking, at a point considerably distant from this small, nondescript room in a Swiss hotel.

Late in the last evening of my September 1966 visit we were talking about Soviet writers. Nabokov spoke contemptuously of "the literary double agents," "the party hacks," "the purveyors of works-to-order." Were there any writers of the Soviet period whom he admired? Yes, there were, and Nabokov spoke of several, concluding with Sinyavsky and Daniel, pacing back and forth across the living room as he talked, clasping and unclasping his hands behind his back as he summarized their stratagems for survival. "All these people were enormously gifted," he said, softly, "but the regime finally caught up with them and they disappeared, one by one, in nameless camps." His voice trailed off, and for the first time he looked his age. It was eleven o'clock, late indeed for an early riser and insomniac who usually retires by nine. He stood by the open doorway of his small balcony; it was warm and muggy, the darkness over Lake Geneva was softened by a heavy mist, and he was the last free Russian writer.

"By the way, do you know how a dung beetle lays its eggs?" he asked, moments later, picking up an unresolved thread of conversation from earlier in the evening, when he had entomologically identified Kafka's metamorphosed Gregor Samsa. Since I had to confess that I did not know how a dung beetle laid its eggs, Nabokov imitated the process as best he could, bending his head toward his waist as he slowly walked away from the darkened doorway, making a dung-rolling motion with his hands until his head was buried in them and the eggs were laid.

Laughter in the Dark is clearly a resonant title. That it embodies the ample spirit of the man as well as his work is best illustrated for me by an incident at Cornell in 1953, when I was one of thirty or so students enrolled in Nabokov's Russian literature course. The class was held at the end of a long, dimly lit corridor in the basement of Goldwin Smith Hall. I was rushing to class one wintry morning, three or four minutes late, but slackened my stride when I noticed that Professor Nabokov was also late, and walking ahead of me halfway down the hall. He hurried into a classroom, and my heart sank as I realized it was one door too soon. I entered the class to find Nabokov several sentences into his lecture; not wanting to waste another minute, he was stooped over his notes, intently reading them to thirty stunned students, a shell-shocked platoon belonging to an even tardier don. Trying to be as transparent as possible, I approached the lectern and touched Nabokov on the sleeve. He turned, and peered down at me over his eyeglasses, amazed. "Mr. Nabokov," I said very quietly, "you are in the wrong classroom." He readjusted his glasses on his nose, focused his gaze on the motionless figures seated before him, and calmly announced, "You have just seen the 'Coming Attraction' for Literature 325. If you are interested, you may register next fall." Pnin no more, he closed his folder of notes and moved one door down the hall. "A most extraordinary thing just happened, most extraordinary," he told the students of Literature 325, chuckling to himself as he opened his folder once more and, not bothering to explain what had happened, began to lecture.

Nabokov's Critical Strategy

JAMES M. RAMBEAU

The first American edition of Vladimir Nabokov's *Lolita* was published in 1958, after several years of negotiation and timidity on the part of various publishers. Within four years Stanley Kubrick had directed a movie version, and in 1971 a musical version called *Lolita, My Love*, with book and lyrics by Alan Jay Lerner, opened (and quickly closed). In short, *Lolita* is a success in almost every way open to the American novel, and from it Nabokov earned enough money to give up his post at Cornell and retire to Switzerland, "kept," as he put it, "by a little girl named Lolita."[1]

In 1970, the success of *Lolita* was celebrated in another and perhaps equally ambiguous way, by the publication of Alfred Appel, Jr.'s edition of *Lolita*. Apparently completed with the full blessing of Nabokov, the text is ornamented by Appel with a 4-page preface, a 57-page introduction, 5 pages of bibliography, and, after the text is inserted, 121 pages of notes, which incorporate corrections of the 1958 text. We can witness another example of the contemporary acceleration in time: *Lolita* has progressed from bestseller to movie to critical success to enshrined masterpiece in about the same time span that it took Lolita herself to ripen just enough for Humbert Humbert's delectation—twelve years.

Reading *The Annotated Lolita* is an unsettling experience. Appel tells us in the preface, "This annotated edition is designed for the general reader and particularly for use in college literature courses."[2] A flush general reader might still hesitate at the cost of the hardback edition but be willing to buy the paperback edition of this elaborate enterprise. I suspect that most college literature courses will continue to content themselves with the unannotated paperback edition.

Appel adds that college students and other readers "are more troubled by Humbert Humbert's use of language and lore than by his abuse of Lolita and law" (p. ix). Of course they are, but it should be true that the pleasure of reading Nabokov is the often wonderfully funny "interplay between recognition and bafflement, puzzle and surprise."[3] This edition, wrapped as it is around the text of *Lolita*, does a disservice by creating the illusion that the mysteries and difficulties of the text are herein solved. To undergraduates being introduced to the original and always odd world of Nabokov's fiction, such an edition would be intimidating as well.

But the book has more limited purposes, according to Appel: "As with Joyce and Melville, the reader of *Lolita* attempts to arrive at some sense of its overall 'meaning,' while at the same time having to struggle, often page by page, with the difficulties posed by the recondite materials and rich, elaborate verbal textures. The main purpose of this edition is to solve such local problems and to show how they contribute to the total design of the novel. Neither the Introduction nor the Notes attempts a total interpretation of *Lolita*" (p. ix). Surely the recondite materials, and their unfamiliarity, are part of the amusement of reading *Lolita*: we are overhearing Humbert Humbert's feverish, odd, overstocked mind at work, most often at work in contemplation of a banal if perverse passion. The fact—which Appel mentions as if it were a liability—that *Lolita* has "rich, elaborate verbal textures" is the delight of reading the novel; to suggest that such textures are "local problems," to be solved and then fitted into "the total design of the novel," is to imply that we must reconstruct the novel, casebook style, and find out in paraphrase what it really means. If there is any sense to the widespread notion that style and expression *are* what the novelist or poet is "saying," then we have once more been deluded into comfort and assured a security that is simply never possible when we are truly reading in the best sense of that word.

Appel is intensely aware of the difficulties raised for any commentator and annotator of Nabokov's work; it is, in fact, his awareness of these difficulties which makes this edition really interesting. For in spite of what I think are self-defeating purposes in preparing an annotated *Lolita*—which lead us to a question I will later examine about Nabokov's endorsement of the project—the kind of admiration which Appel feels for *Lolita*, and which he wants to express in some concrete way, is understandable. He is inevitably self-conscious about the enterprise: "Of course, the annotator and editor of a novel written by the creator of Kinbote and John Ray, Jr., runs the real risk of being mistaken for another fiction, when at most he resembles those gentlemen only figuratively. But the annotator exists; he is a veteran and a father, a teacher and taxpayer, and has not been invented by Vladimir Nabokov" (p. xii). "In Place of a Note on the Text," Appel quotes from the conclusion of Charles Kinbote's foreword to *Pale Fire*: "To this statement my dear poet would probably not have subscribed, but, for better or worse, it is the commentator who has the last word" (p. lxxvii). In the course of the introduction, Appel urges us to pause, turn to Nabokov's afterword to *Lolita*, and then return to *his* introduction, having marked the place, possibly with "a brightly colored piece of clothing" (p. xxxvii). Printed after this suggestion is a hand with index finger directing the reader to the back of the book.

Appel's self-consciousness about his own role and intense awareness of his proximity to parody have led him to these measures. And yet, inevitably, such self-consciousness only makes him sound more like Kinbote than ever.

Responding to this self-conscious quality, A. Alvarez, reviewing *The Annotated Lolita*, has suggested that Alfred Appel, Jr., does not exist but is another invention of Vladimir Nabokov.[4] He goes on to suggest that he himself might be too. Alvarez' joke was anticipated by Appel in his assertion of his own existence; but the joke was presumably irresistible to Alvarez. What is equally clear is that Alvarez' jokes are formed out of the same self-consciousness which informed Appel's work, and that both of them are, in a sense, the victims of Nabokov's strategies.

They are victims for the following reasons. Readers of Nabokov, delighted with his playfulness, are not obligated in any way to define that playfulness. But critics are; in some way, they must try to show that they are aware of *how* Nabokov operates. The conventional way to display this awareness is through a scholarly or critical voice of interpretation. But Nabokov, in the voices of the biographer of *The Gift*, in John Ray's introduction to *Lolita*, in Charles Kinbote's commentary on the poem in *Pale Fire*, and in the notes on prosody, the commentary, and biography of Abram Gannibal in his 1964 edition of *Eugene Onegin*, has made that voice suspect. In order to dissociate *their* voices from Nabokov's parodies and uses, critics are obliged to display awareness of their own tenuous position. In the fantastic worlds of recondite learning, obscure puns, and shifting references which Nabokov has himself created, the self-consciousness, intensified at every turn, can only strengthen the possibility that the critic *is* another version of Nabokov at play.

Nor is this victimization of the critic and annotator rare for Nabokov. The foreword of Carl Proffer's *Keys to "Lolita"* (1968) concludes: "Some may say my commentary is a parody of Nabokov. This, of course, is probably untrue."[5] Andrew Field, whose first full-length study of Nabokov appeared in 1967, and who records there the cooperation, again, of Nabokov, states in his foreword, entitled "In Place of a Foreword" (as is the Russian custom for informal works):

> The second unusual aspect of *Nabokov: His Life in Art* is its innovatory nature as a work of criticism: it is *formed*, that is, it is structured in a way roughly corresponding to that of the narrative in fiction. . . . In short, I have treated Nabokov's novels, poems, stories, plays, and essays as characters in a novel, and each has its role and place carefully prefigured and integrated into the whole. . . . Only in an effort to satisfy all these conditions of contents, form, and style, respectively, can literary criticism aspire to be considered an art in any rigorous sense of the term. And I see no reason why it should not.[6]

There are many reasons why literary criticism should not aspire to being considered an art, the most important of which is that it is *not* an art. And if we are to consider it one, for whatever reason, we then read literary criticism not for illumination of a novelist and his or her work but to enjoy a critic's *performance* as a critic. This phenomenon happens often enough, as we know—consider Empson's *Milton's God*, for example, or Nabokov's *Nikolai Gogol*—but surely the argument is untenable, for it insists on the importance of the critics' skills at the expense of their object, which is to teach us things we did not know about someone else's art. That critical skills are indispensable we have no doubt; but criticism is not an art and should not be displayed in artful terms, which are by definition elliptical, indirect, and even, in MacLeish's famous definition, "mute." These matters have been fully explored in the "Polemical Introduction" of Frye's *Anatomy of Criticism*, in which Frye reminds us of John Stuart Mill's phrase "art is not heard, but overheard."[7] The qualities of muteness, of being overheard, are what literary critics must deal with, must articulate, must explain; they will not do these difficult chores well if they are, in some sense, in competition with their subjects in creating works of art.

It is, in fact, as competitors with their subject's work that Alfred Appel, Jr., and Andrew Field strike us, at least when they are making their claims. Here is the conclusion of Andrew Field's "In Place of a Foreword" (p. 8):

> Nabokov, I have mastered your themes. (*Nabokov, have I mastered your themes?*) See how your books lie carefully ar-

OLSON LIBRARY
NORTHERN MICHIGAN UNIVERSITY
MARQUETTE, MICHIGAN 49855

ranged in the window of my critical eye. (*I return your books, neatly packed and unsoiled, but I have kept and cut the pages and taken up the images.*) Each is an essential cubist plane of a bookish portrait that, in the necessary cultural perspective and light, is your truest and most palpable biography. (*Together they form your future monument, the shadow of which even now extends from Moscow to New York.*)

The name of our writer is (say it quickly) Vla*deem*ear Nah*boak*off.

If the text of Field's first book on Nabokov continued in this vein, reminding us of *The Gift* and the problems that novel raises, we can only imagine what it would be like. Fortunately, it does not: it is a solid and thorough book, the first study of all of Nabokov's work by someone who knows Russian as well as English and who therefore has *read* most of Nabokov's fiction. In his "Concluding Remarks," Field cites with obvious approval the opening remark of an anonymous article: "To approach Nabokov's novels with anything less than complete humility is not only an act of arrogance but of foolishness" (p. 383). It is between these excesses—on the one hand in competition with the subject, on the other hand rendered helpless before it—that criticism of Nabokov can exist, and can say something. And it is between them that Field actually does operate, and Appel too, in several articles on *Lolita* and *Speak, Memory*.[8]

Field's *Nabokov: His Life in Part* (1977) reveals some of the same problems. The epigraph's allusion to Dr. Johnson and Field's device of presenting himself as being in a running conversation with the Nabokovs (indicated by boldface intrusions) cause our attention to the often fascinating details of Nabokov's family and early life to be seen within the context of Nabokov's disagreements with the attempted modifications of his biographer. The conclusion becomes a celebration of the biography's being done; our last glimpse of Nabokov—a wonderful one, as he smartly claps for a porter in Ithaca, New York, sometime in the 1960s—is thus followed by what is, after all, given the subject in whom we are interested, an irrelevance (p. 284):

> —And has it all been true and kind and necessary?
> —Ah, let us avoid jokes now. Envy the sculptor who does with a single gesture.
> —Done and done then. A portrait of Vladimir Nabokov. Russian-American writer of our time and of his own reality.
> The End. Oh. The End.

The problems of self-consciousness in criticism are intensified in writing about Nabokov, as they have been intensified in writing about the Swift of *A Tale of a Tub* or the Joyce of *Finnegans Wake*, because of the existence in Nabokov's fiction of a mad annotator, an obsessive misreader of a poem by John Shade—Charles Kinbote of *Pale Fire*. Appel is certainly aware of the problems and refers to his annotated edition as "*A Tale of a Tub* for our time" (p. xi). As we have seen, he also feels obliged to insist on his own existence, to assert boldly that he has not been invented. And yet, if we examine some of Kinbote's annotations of "Pale Fire," Nabokov's annotations and commentaries for *Eugene Onegin*, and Appel's annotations for *Lolita*, it is easy to see why Alvarez' mock doubts about Appel's existence are justified. First, let us consider examples from *Pale Fire*, a novel which derives its form from various annotated editions, and which parodies a scholarly voice.

Let us focus on Kinbote's peculiar thickheadedness concerning the title of the poem, "Pale Fire." In the first note in which he mentions the actual source of the title, Shakespeare's *Timon of Athens*, Kinbote mentions it for other reasons and cites the passage from which it comes in his own re-Englishing of a Zemblan translation of *Timon* (pp. 79–80). The phrase "pale fire" does not appear. The note also refers us to line 962 of the poem—"Help me, Will! *Pale Fire*"— and *its* note, in which Kinbote explains that he is unable to remember the source, because he is annotating in a cabin with only a Zemblan version of *Timon of Athens* for company (p. 285). The note then goes on to recall the translating prowess of his uncle Conmal, duke of Aros in Zembla, who lived to be 100; after translating all of Shakespeare, "he went on to Milton and other poets, steadily drilling through the ages, and had just completed Kipling's 'The Rhyme of the Three Sealers' . . . when he fell ill and soon expired" (p. 285). A further annotation, locating an allusion to Browning, peevishly attacks the principle of extracting titles from works of the past (p. 240). Under "Kinbote" in the index, we find a reference to this note and an allusion to *The Tempest*, which is not mentioned in the note. Kinbote alludes to the title, to Shakespeare, and to *Timon of Athens* elsewhere as well, but we see the point: as an annotator, Kinbote is helpless. Further, the ways in which Kinbote "reads into" the text of Shade's poem the history of his exposed lost family and kingdom is a parody of scholarly overkill, as well as a frightening portrait of a madman of a very particular kind.

We know that *Pale Fire* was written while Nabokov was also preparing the four-volume edition and translation with commentary of Pushkin's *Eugene Onegin*, published two years after *Pale Fire*, in 1964. While I will not try to judge the merits of his translation and commentary (about which Nabokov carried on a famous controversy, with Edmund Wilson among others, during 1965), it is worth looking at his commentary and trying to judge it as a voice, related in some ways to Kinbote's. For example, the essay on Abram Gannibal, Pushkin's supposed African ancestor, contains a fantastic display of research and information of all kinds and is dazzling in its wit; it concludes in pyrotechnical speculation:

> One's marginal imagination conjures up here many a pleasing possibility. We recall Coleridge's Abyssinian maid (*Kubla Khan*, 1797) singing of "Mount Abora," which (unless it merely echoes the name of the musical instrument) is, I suggest, either Mt. Tabor, an amba (natural citadel), some 3000 feet high in the Siré district of the Tigré, or still more exactly the unlocated amba Abora, which I find mentioned by the chronicler Za-Ouald (in Basset's translation) as being the burial place of a certain high official named Gyorgis (one of Poncet's two governors?) in 1707. We may further imagine that Coleridge's and Poncet's doleful singer was none other than Pushkin's great-great-grandmother; that her lord, either of Poncet's two hosts, was Pushkin's great-great-grandfather; and that the latter was a son of Cella Christos, Dr. Johnson's Rasselas. There is nothing in the annals of Russian Pushkinology to restrain one from the elaboration of such fancies.[9]

Now this is a case of the annotator's "marginal imagination" taking over with a vengeance, with speculation of a dubious sort giving way, in the final sentence, to a joke. But Nabokov is still in control, for part of his point is to comment on the "annals of Russian Pushkinology," to show that the absence of known facts inevitably leads one to such speculation, which—as he shows us—is fun and, in this case at least (where it is shown to be playful), harmless.

If there is any similarity at all between Kinbote and his creator, as annotators, it is only that they are both inventive; in the edition of *Eugene Onegin*, the editor displays considerable learning and lore, but does not claim significance which only he can see, and Nabokov's oft-stated theories of literal translation have been followed in the way in which he presents Pushkin's text.

I want now to return briefly to the annotations we find in *The Annotated Lolita*. We are not faced with a fictional editor and commentator, nor with an editor on holiday in an appendix; rather, we are reading a series of notes about the novel of a contemporary author who aided the project. The only useful function of such notes is—or should be—to illuminate *Lolita.*

The notes are often concerned with rounding up Nabokov's literary allusions—Poe ranks first with over twenty allusions, "followed by Mérimée, Shakespeare, and Joyce, in that order" (p. 331)—translating French phrases, both long and short, glossing unfamiliar words like "natatoriums" (p. 386), and so on. But there are, as I have said, 121 pages of notes, in a typeface much smaller than that of the text. Not even the many obscurities of Humbert Humbert's style could fill that much, nor could the considerable cross-referencing of other novels.

I can only indicate how Appel extends the annotations to such length by quoting one, by no means unusual in its length or range of reference. We will remember that "John Ray, Jr., Ph.D.," who wrote the foreword, mentions the fate of various characters. One character is described in this way: "'*Vivian Darkbloom' has written a biography, 'My Cue,' to be published shortly, and critics who have perused the manuscript call it her best book*" (p. 6). Here is Appel's annotation of this sentence in full (p. 344):

> 6/9 "*Vivian Darkbloom*" . . . "*My Cue*": "Vivian Darkbloom"
> is Clare Quilty's mistress and an anagram of "Vladimir
> Nabokov" (see my 1967 *Wisconsin Studies* article, p. 216, and
> my 1968 *Denver Quarterly* article, p. 32 [see bibliography]).
> Among her alphabetical cousins are "Vivian Bloodmark, a phil-
> osophical friend of mine," who appears in *Speak, Memory* (p.
> 218), and "Mr. Vivian Badlook," a photographer and teacher of
> English in the 1968 translation of the 1928 novel *King, Queen,
> Knave* (p. 153)—and they all descend from "Vivian Calm-
> brood" (see Field, *op. cit.*, p. 73), the alleged author of *The
> Wanderers*, an uncompleted play written by Nabokov in Rus-
> sian (the anagram is helped along by the fact that in Cyrillic,
> the *c* is a *k*). One act of it was published in the émigré almanac
> *Facets* (1923), as an English play written by Vivian Calmbrood
> in 1768 and translated by V. Sirin (the pen name under which
> all of Nabokov's Russian work appeared). In a discussion in
> *Ada* (1969) of Van Veen's first novel, *Letters from Terra*, men-
> tion is made of the influence "of an obscene ancient Arab, ex-
> pounder of anagrammatic dreams, Ben Sirine" (p. 344).

As for H. H. and John Ray, unless characters in a novel can be said to have miraculously fashioned their creators, someone else must be responsible for an anagram of the author's name, and such phenomena undermine the narrative's realistic base by pointing beyond the book to Nabokov, the stage manager, ventriloquist, and puppeteer, who might simply state, "My cue." Because Nabokov considered publishing *Lolita* anonymously (see p. 315), there was also a purely utilitarian reason for anagrammatizing his name, as proof of authorship. "Cue" is also the cognomen of Clare Quilty, who pursues H. H. throughout the novel. But who *is* Quilty?—a question the reader will surely ask (see the Introduction, pp. xiii–lxviii, and 33/9). As with H. H. and Lolita (*née* Dolores Haze), Quilty's name lends itself to wordplay by turns jocose (see 225/1) and significant, since H. H. suggests that Clare Quilty is clearly guilty. Clare is also a town in Michigan (see 161/1), and, although Nabokov did not know it until this note came into being, Quilty is a town in County Clare, Ireland, appropriate to a verbally playful novel in which there are several apt references to James Joyce. See 6/11.

The internal evidence of this note leads us to conclude that its author, while neither Kinbotean in his invention nor Nabokovian in his playfulness, is an annotator who has completely lost his sense of proportion, and who has therefore become a parody of an annotator. In spite of this annotator's genuine existence, Nabokov has invented him better, and to more purpose, elsewhere. It is because of this apparently helpless drift into parody which occurs in the notes to *The Annotated Lolita* that Appel is right in feeling obliged to assert his existence—and Alvarez is right to question it.

But we should remember that Alvarez, in *his* self-consciousness, suggests that we should doubt his existence too, and also remember the kinds of self-consciousness displayed by Andrew Field and Carl Proffer. These facts lead us back to a matter I have questioned before: why would Nabokov lend his implicit approval to books of this kind?[10] The answer is that Nabokov has managed to create a body of work which is, in one way, close to critic-proof.

The kinds of duplicity, of mirror-images and self-contained stories within stories, of parodies and games which Nabokov plays with his readers, place his critics in a defensive position: they must first prove they understand what Nabokov is *doing* before they can judge the final effects of his fiction. And, while Nabokov has never been simple or straightforward, it is in his English-language fiction and as his career has extended that he is most cryptic, allusive, and difficult. *Lolita* presents many difficulties, and *Pale Fire* and *Ada* many more; but when we track down every possible reference and suggestion and pun, and expose them all by careful explanation, even then Nabokov has his fun—for then, most of all, his critic becomes part of the apparatus of the novel. Kinbote, quoted by Appel, says that "it is the commentator who has the last word." But if the last word is the annotations to *Lolita*, then the critic has become part of the labyrinth, and a victim of Nabokov's methods, instead of the ideal reader who can lead us out of the obscure.

But of course *The Annotated Lolita* is not the last word, and common sense can prevail here as elsewhere in the discussion of difficult literature and difficult uses of literature. Richard Poirier, discussing "the politics of self-parody" in *The Performing Self*, distinguishes Joyce and Nabokov from Borges, Barth, and Murdoch in terms of the "vitality" of their "competitive response" to the "assumption that the public world they live in is also compulsively fictional."[11] He adds: "Borges, Barth, and Miss Murdoch, however different from one another in many respects, share a debilitating assumption: that it is interesting, in and of itself, to make the formal properties of fiction into the subject matter of fiction. While it isn't wholly uninteresting to do so, those readers most capable of appreciating the idea are also apt to be the most impatient with any lengthy demonstrations, with the repetitive effort, page after page, to show that literature is, to take a phrase from *Finnegans Wake*, 'the hoax that joke bilked'" (p. 31).

The effect of *The Annotated Lolita* is to suggest strongly in its arrangements and sheer bulk that "the formal properties of fiction," most particularly parody, are "the subject matter of fiction." That this proposition is simply not true of *Lolita*, nor generally of Nabokov, can be demonstrated by looking at the sort of criticism which best explains the final appeal of the book.

An example of this criticism is the Minnesota pamphlet *Vladimir Nabokov*, by Julian Moynahan, not only because of its common sense, but also because of its necessarily synoptic quality. When Moynahan discusses Humbert Humbert briefly, it is in terms of our interest in the changes which occur in Humbert toward the end of the novel (pp. 32–33, ellipsis in original):

> Lolita has written him after years of silence and absence to say she is married, pregnant, and in need of money. He finds her in a shack in "Coalmont," eight hundred miles from New York City, big-bellied, worn out at seventeen, and he wants to steal her away again or kill her if she will not come. But then he realizes that he loves her *as she is*, not merely as the echo or memory "of the nymphet I had rolled myself upon with such cries in the past . . . Thank God it was not that echo alone that

I worshipped." The "echo" of course points to the "eidolon" he had pursued lifelong, spying into "jewel-bright" windows and depraving little girls because the print of sexual characteristics was still so faintly impressed upon their childish bodies that he could pretend when savaging them that he was cleaving to a pure form and recapturing the lost Edenic time he had spent in childhood with "Annabel Lee."

This brief passage tells us considerably more about Humbert's conversion to love from lust toward the end of the novel than anything in Appel's notes. Compare, too, Appel's remarks on the same matter in *The Annotated Lolita* (p. lxviii):

The reader sees Humbert move beyond his obsessional passion to a not altogether straightforward declaration of genuine love (pp. 279–280) and, finally, to a realization of the loss suffered not by him but by Lolita (pp. 309–310). It is expressed on the next to the last page in a long and eloquent passage that, for the first time in the novel, is in no way undercut by parody or qualified by irony. Midway through this "last mirage of wonder and hopelessness," the reader is invoked again, because Humbert's moral apotheosis, so uniquely straightforward, constitutes the end game and Nabokov's final *trompe-l'oeil*. If the reader has long since decided that there is no "moral reality" in the novel, and in his sophisticated way has accepted that, he may well miss this unexpected move in the farthest corner of the board and lose the game after all. It is the last time the reader will be addressed directly, for the game is about over, as is the novel.

Appel's extremity of self-consciousness is again apparent; even the crucial matter of Humbert's conversion must be seen as part of the chess game metaphor; "moral reality" must be assigned quotation marks.

"The formal properties of fiction," no matter how cleverly used, are not "the subject matter of fiction." It is no doubt part of the duty of Nabokov's critics and editors and annotators to detect what they can in his elaborate ruses, but their final duty is to avoid the entrapment within his strategies which Appel's edition illustrates.

I might conclude with another example of the best sort of suggestiveness of which Nabokov's critics are capable. I quote again from Julian Moynahan, writing in another place:

The great theme in Nabokov is not that of the past recaptured, and for me he is simply floundering in a moral and metaphysical quagmire when he insists, as he has been wont to do in recent years, pronouncements and works, upon the omnipotence of his or anyone else's creative thought. Nabokov's great theme, which he shares with the Beethoven of *Fidelio* and the Gluck of *Orfeo* and *Alceste*, is that of married love. In *Fidelio*, when Leonora penetrates to the dark dungeon where Florestan languishes in fetters and brings him up to light and freedom, she is acting out, in all the tenderness and courage of uxorious passion, a great moral positive that I find, either fulfilled or blighted, in all of Nabokov's major work. The connection is between loving and making free in a bond of two against the loneliness of exile, the imprisoning world, the irredeemable nature of time, the voidness of eternity. I am thinking of *The Gift*, that great wedding song, of widower Krug's agony of loss in *Bend Sinister*, of the sinister parodies of wedded states in *Kamera Obskura*, *Lolita*, and *King, Queen, Knave*, of Tatyana's blighted marriage hopes in the Pushkin translation, of the poor prisoner in *Invitation*—that mock-*Fidelio*—cursed with a foolish unfaithful wife, of old John and Sybil Shade in *Pale Fire*, whose life together is such an irritating unfathomable mystery to the mad solitary neighbor spying on them from the shrubbery.[12]

What Moynahan talks about here is what, finally, makes Nabokov worth reading. Beyond all the games, the ultimately sterile parodies, the splendid verbal jokes and puns, Nabokov creates for us characters who touch us. Timofey Pnin, in all his confusion, interests us most when he recalls a dead girl or weeps at a bad movie. Humbert Humbert matters to us when he begins to understand what he has done toward the end of his story; Lolita herself gains our affection at the same time, and we are reminded of her bleak death in Gray Star.

We need to be reminded of these human concerns, and Nabokov's critics can only discuss them when they lose the self-consciousness induced by Nabokov's complex and sophisticated literary games. And it is only possible to lose that self-consciousness by recognizing how small a part those games finally play in Nabokov's genuine appeal to his readers.

Nabokov has suggested this central interest to us, too, in some of the remarks he has made about his work. In his remarks about *Bend Sinister*, he observes that the "main theme" of the novel "is the beating of Krug's loving heart"; "it is for the sake of the pages about David and his father that the book was written and should be read."[13] Among the "nerves of the novel" he points out for *Lolita* are "the Kasbeam barber (who cost me a month of work)" and "pale, pregnant, beloved, irretrievable Dolly Schiller dying in Gray Star."[14] The Kasbeam barber speaks of his son, dead for thirty years, as if he were alive; and Dolly Schiller is of course Lolita herself, beloved of Humbert Humbert at last, and dead in childbirth.

NOTES

1. Quoted and translated in Andrew Field, *Nabokov: His Life in Art*, p. 11.
2. Vladimir Nabokov, *The Annotated Lolita*, ed. Alfred Appel, Jr., p. ix. Hereafter cited in text.
3. A. Alvarez, "'A Tale of a Tub' for Our Time," *Saturday Review of Literature* 53, no. 24 (13 June 1970), 45.
4. Ibid., pp. 27–28, 45.
5. Carl R. Proffer, *Keys to "Lolita,"* p. vii.
6. Field, *Life in Art*, pp. 6–7. Hereafter cited in text.
7. Northrop Frye, *Anatomy of Criticism* (Princeton: Princeton University Press, 1957), p. 5. The relevant discussion is on pp. 4–5.
8. Appel's earlier work on *Lolita* is partly incorporated into the introduction to *The Annotated Lolita*, pp. xv–lxxi (for his other publications, see Appel's bibliography in the same volume, p. lxxiv). An excellent article on Nabokov's techniques, "Nabokov's Puppet Show," appeared in the *New Republic* issues of 14 and 21 January 1967 and has been reprinted with minor changes in *The Single Voice*, ed. Jerome Charyn, pp. 76–95. The second part of the article is also reprinted in the introduction to *The Annotated Lolita*.
9. Vladimir Nabokov, *Notes on Prosody and Abram Gannibal*, p. 161.
10. Nabokov made his approval of *The Annotated Lolita* even more ambiguous in an interview: "Nabokov described Appel as 'my pedant. A pedant straight out of *Pale Fire*. Every writer should have a pedant.'" Quoted by Alan Levy, "Understanding Vladimir Nabokov—A Red Autumn Leaf Is a Red Autumn Leaf, Not a Deflowered Nymphet," *New York Times Magazine* (31 October 1971), 30.
11. Richard Poirier, *The Performing Self*, p. 31. Hereafter cited in text.
12. Julian Moynahan, "*Lolita* and Related Memories," in *Nabokov*, ed. Appel and Newman, p. 251.
13. Vladimir Nabokov, *Bend Sinister* (1973), introduction, p. viii.
14. Vladimir Nabokov, "On a Book Entitled *Lolita*," *The Annotated Lolita*, p. 318.

A Few Things That Must Be Said on Behalf of Vladimir Nabokov

DMITRI NABOKOV

I think my favorite fact about myself is that I have never been dismayed by a critic's bilge or bile, and have never once in my life asked or thanked a reviewer for a review. My second favorite fact—or shall I stop at one?
—Vladimir Nabokov, *Strong Opinions*

Vladimir Nabokov very seldom bothered to react to criticism or chance comments that might have been offensive. He felt his time was better spent writing. However, in certain instances of questioned honor or of gross factual error concerning some important aspect of his life or of one of his fields of expertise, he felt it his duty to set the record straight. It is in that spirit that I take the opportunity to comment on a few posthumous slurs that have appeared here and there quite apart from the many perceptive and brilliant comments.

In *Le Monde des Livres* published on 15 July 1977—only a few days after Father's death—Maurice Girodias writes about Vladimir Nabokov in an article titled "Lolita, héroïne de toutes les censures" ("Lolita, Heroine of All Censorships"): "Je m'efforçai de lui faire honte, et il finit par se résigner au courage et à signer le livre de son nom" ("I did my utmost to shame him, and in the end he resigned himself to courageous action and signed his name to the book").

Girodias is very optimistic if he thinks his opinions had any influence on Nabokov's decision not to use a pseudonym for *Lolita*. On the advice of a kind and wise friend, Father had indeed consid-
Girodias is very optimistic if he thinks his opinions had any influence on Nabokov's decision not to use a pseudonym for *Lolita*. On the advice of a kind and wise friend, Father had indeed considered doing so. His principal motive would have been concern that the "bilge and bile" surrounding Girodias' activities might in some way reflect on his loyalty to an institution with which he had had a long and happy relationship. What Father writes regarding his insis-

tence that Girodias abstain from mentioning Cornell in his "publicity splashes" is equally applicable to his considering and rejecting the idea of a pseudonym:

> Only a very helical mind could twist my request into a semblance of frailty. By signing *Lolita* I had shown my complete acceptance of whatever responsibility an author has to take; but as long as an unhealthy flurry of scandal surrounded my innocent *Lolita*, I certainly was justified in acting as I did [i.e., asking that Cornell not be referred to], lest a shadow of my responsibility fall on the university that had given me unbelievable freedom in conducting my courses (they were never meddled with by the department or departments under which they were nominally listed); nor did I care to embarrass the close friend who had brought me there to enjoy that true academic freedom.[1]

For further sidelights on Girodias' behavior, see Nabokov's article "*Lolita* and Mr. Girodias"[2] and letter on the same subject.[3] In any case it should be clear to those with any notion of Nabokov's ways and work that he was quite able to make his own decisions and that, if he ever sought advice (particularly when declining that of an old and trusted friend), he would never have turned to someone of Girodias' ilk.

"A few years later in Paris," writes a 1954 graduate in a letter to the *Cornell Alumni News* for April 1977, "I purchased the Olympia Press edition of *Lolita*. Needless to say I was struck by the book and surprised that the professor I knew had written it. On reflection I decided it was pure *tour de force* on his part—a simple effort to make enough money to live the rest of his days in comfort—which he has done. . . ." If Father ever seriously considered using a *nom de plume* for *Lolita*, it was because of his aversion to just such philistine idiocy as this (even though, unlike the writings of certain fellow sages, this correspondent's basically benevolent bilge suggests that to him such a ploy might be a perfectly honorable way of making a fast buck). If a son's firsthand testimony is of any value, I can recall how lovingly Father would speak of his "innocent *Lolita*," what a unique inflection he would give to the very title (*moya Lola*, with the thick Russian *l*), and how often he said privately as well as publicly that he considered it his "best thing in English." As for a presumed lust for money, it has been amply documented in Nabokov's writings that he never lamented the loss of a sizable fortune in the Revolution and found joy in a sometimes meager existence on condition that it permitted him to write, take an occasional butterfly ramble, play a game of chess or tennis now and then, and—far from least—be with his small beloved and loving family. Moreover, not only was *Lolita* anything but a money-making scheme: Father was so skeptical of the book's ever being published that he even considered destroying the typescript. Read *Strong Opinions*, my friend.

If this nonsense may be explained by naivete or ignorance, those excuses can hardly be applied to some of the absurdities written by a friend of long standing, the late Edmund Wilson. It is not my intention to add to or subtract from *The Nabokov–Wilson Letters*. I have simply selected a few points that certain critics have seen fit to belabor. One of them writes in a magazine review: "In his attack on [Nabokov's] *Onegin* tetralogy,[4] [Wilson] noted 'the perversity of Nabokov's tricks to startle or stick pins in the reader,' and went on to 'his sadomasochistic Dostoevskian tendencies so acutely noted by Sartre.' This led up to the remark in Wilson's memoir *Upstate*: 'The element in [Nabokov's] work that I find repellent is his addiction to *Schadenfreude*. Everybody is always being humiliated.'" If anyone is sticking pins in this quoted passage, it is Wilson, who refers to a diatribe by Sartre—whom Nabokov despised—and to Dostoevsky—for whom he had little esteem—in the hope that the kick might reach a sensitive region (it did not). Should not genius startle? As for *Schadenfreude*—gloating over another's misfortunes—what could be farther from the compassion felt by author and reader for poor Pnin, who brings young Victor the unwanted soccer ball, for Cincinnatus, who is tormented for an unspoken crime, for Krug, in anguish over his tortured child? If pins are stuck here, they are of the empathic, tingling kind, the pins that, through art, make the reader feel the pathos of a book. It is Nabokov who is on the side of the persecuted. And if we are to speak of sadomasochism and of *Schadenfreude*, may we not suspect that he who sticks "this particularly thick and rusty pin into [Nabokov's] effigy"[5] has a guilty conscience? (Wilson, who once saw the milk spurt from a just-fed kitten pierced by a lady's heel, confided to Father that the sight gave him a tingle of sexual excitement.)

Another old friend—and professor of literature—who definitely knows better, makes several disparaging and unfair comments in a recent publication. In reference to Nabokov's translation of *Eugene Onegin* and a certain versificator's prior attempt, he writes, "Nabokov—instead of drawing upon his stylistic skills to eclipse his predecessor [i.e., to do a better *versified* version]—sought to crush him with a high-handed review." It is odd that this specialist in literature, and attentive reader of books, disregarded the fact that, in translating *Eugene Onegin*, Nabokov had set himself—and brilliantly accomplished—a specific task. This critic should also have realized that VN's purpose was not to "crush" the poor man "with a high-handed review" but to put on record something that was of the utmost importance to him: the protection of Pushkin's poem from cheap verse translations, and a presentation to the English-language reader of the true meaning and true worth of the poem. What a ridiculous notion that Nabokov ought to have "[drawn] upon his stylistic skills to eclipse" someone in an enterprise that, from the outset of his work on *Onegin* (and after most thorough consideration), he judged to be worthless. In "Reply to My Critics" Father defines his review as "an indignant examination of the insults dealt out to Pushkin's masterpiece in yet another arty translation."[6] What were his objections? After a substantial list, and explanation, of the more gross mistranslations, Nabokov concludes: "[the translator's] most bizarre observation, however, comes on page vi, towards the end of his preface: 'The present new translation . . . is not aimed primarily at the academic and literary expert, but at a public of English-speaking students and others interested in a central work of world literature in a compact and readable form,'—which is tantamount to proclaiming: 'I know this is an inferior product but it is gaily colored and nicely packed, and is, anyway, just for students and such people.'"[7] Nabokov is speaking here not only in Pushkin's defense, but the reader's as well. The publishers of the versified version tried to patch things up a bit with "A 'Second Printing, revised' of [the] 'translation' . . . . but despite the note saying that 'several emendations were suggested by Vladimir Nabokov's criticism at various times' this 'revised' version still remains as abominable as before."[8]

Nabokov has spoken for himself on matters pertaining to prosody, to his *Eugene Onegin* translation, and to sundry attacks thereon, but a few other echoes of the *Nabokov–Wilson Letters* require comment. A critic for a major American book review refers, in the spring of 1979, to the "confusing technical wrangle about English and Russian prosody." In another review, published shortly thereafter, a well-known writer says, "Nabokov refused to understand Wilson when he spoke of secondary stress in English polysyllables." The first reviewer seems to have read a "wrangle" into the exchange that ensued, instead of realizing that Nabokov was painstakingly explaining his theory of prosody to a non-Russian non-poet—perhaps on too high a plane, given Wilson's total lack of grounding in Russian versification. While the discourse conceivably is difficult for the reader who lacks a specialization in the technical aspects of poetry, it should be evident to both reviewers that there was no argument on Father's part about English prosody—he merely used examples in English for clarity: "Now will you please study the following six examples of R^0, R^1, R^2, R^3, R^{1+3}, and R^{2+3}, all of them taken from "Count Nulin," with translation attempting to render the rhythm in English. Let me repeat that this is not an attempt to force alien rhythms upon English versification but an effort to show that similar rhythmical variations may be—artificially perhaps—illustrated by English lines, bad as they are, or, in other words, that there is no need whatever to resort to phonetics in order to understand Russian versification."[9] Not only did Nabokov use the English examples for illustration only, but he went further: he even claimed (generously and much too modestly) that he had only a *shapochnoe znakomstvo*—a nodding acquaintance—with English versification.[10]

A critic for a mid-American journal singles out the following from Wilson's letter 139: "Your last line[11] . . . is a conspicuous example of your failure to master the English subjunctive." If the gentleman had read on to the next letter, he would have found a pellucid reply: "The 'was' in the last line of the 'Sail' was intentional as 'there were' seemed cacophonic to me, and sagging."

Since Father's death certain other critics have written as they would hardly have ventured to do in his lifetime. A case in point is a review in the *TLS* of Nabokov's *Lectures on Literature* by one John Simon. I have selected for comment only a few pearls from his diatribe to give an idea of his hostility to the poetic and the ingenious. One also suspects that the inside of his cheek has never felt the tip of his tongue. And one finds that he plays fast and loose with the chronology of certain events.

Mr. Simon quotes VN as saying that *A la recherche du temps perdu* is "the greatest novel of the first half of the twentieth century." Father's presumed presumptuousness is then illustrated in the following aside: ". . . which, we shall recall, is the half that did not produce *Lolita, Pnin, Pale Fire* and *Ada*." The critic overlooks the fact that the comment about Proust occurs in a lecture composed and delivered many times before any of these novels by Nabokov appeared. The ice Mr. Simon treads is creaking.

Father was full of humor, and so are his *Lectures*. But humor is anathema to this kind of person. When Nabokov, in an interview, extols a "comfortable campus" as "a fine milieu for a writer," and adds (tongue in cheek), "There is, of course, the problem of educating the young," or when he jokingly suggests that his meticulously prepared lectures might be delivered by tape recorder, Mr. Simon can be felt reddening with rage at such lèse majesté. Judging from this reviewer's remarks, we should presume it a sin for the teacher to mention the year in which a novel was written, or to require that his students take note of concrete detail—the topography of Joyce's Dublin, the arrangement of Tolstoy's sleeping car, the fact that Gregor Samsa was a beetle and not a cockroach.

What to Mr. Simon is perhaps Nabokov's supreme sin is based on pure hypothesis. At a place where two pages of the manuscript are missing, Father's sentence breaks off after "a creative writer . . . cannot help feeling that in his rejecting the world of the matter-of-fact, in his taking sides with the irrational, the illogical, the inexplicable and fundamentally good, he is performing something similar in a rudimentary way to what—." The sentence was to end, Mr. Simon theorizes, with a comparison to an act of God. Here a Freudian might glimpse the hidden key to the reviewer's captiousness, for Mr. Simon finds, further on, a resemblance between a rather tame bon mot of his own and how "[Nabokov] himself might have put it" (Simon-Nabokov-God?).

I shall not bother with the reviewer's pedantry in picking at misprints, or with his chagrin that Father omitted or failed to esteem this or that writer, other than to note that VN was not a literary historian dealing in overviews (he was not interested in the valleys of literature but rather in its snowy summits).

Mr. Simon's concluding quip is no more felicitous than the rest of his snidely hostile article: "Dirty Lit." to which a "dirty little girl" [Lolita] supposedly put an end was a student sobriquet not for Father's course but for that of his predecessor, a certain Prof. Weir. Here the ice finally cracks, and Mr. Simon plunges into Lake Cayuga's chilly waters.

Some particularly astonishing nonsense recently appeared in a Missouri reviewer's piece: "What torments Nabokov must have felt when he, an unknown foreigner cast upon our shores by his third exile, . . . had to ingratiate himself with Wilson. . . ." and on in the same vein. "Ingratiate" used reflexively means to insinuate oneself, to curry favor. Father's whole life proves that he never sought anyone's patronage through compromise of any kind. If help was proffered spontaneously by someone he respected—and he did respect Wilson—he felt free to accept it. When a friendship developed—as it did in this case—Father might ask as well as extend a favor. But he remained, at all times, utterly true to his principles, and when there was disagreement—say, on an artistic or a political matter—he spoke as no self-ingratiator would: one has only to read, very early on in the correspondence with Wilson (letter 4, December 1940), his remarks on Lenin's axmanship, or the brilliant piece on Malraux, or the prosody lesson itself, or, finally, in letter 176 (28 May 1950), "Once [and] for all you should tell yourself that in these questions of prosody . . . you are wrong and I am right, always." If Nabokov had been capable of ingratiating himself, he had ample opportunity to court influential people other than Wilson. Perhaps the reason he never did can best be made clear, to those who did not know him well, through an illustration of his attitude in declining numerous memberships, honorary degrees, and other flattering offers he received. They came from prestigious literary associations, including the American Academy of Arts and Letters, the American Academy of Arts and Sciences, the Royal Literature Society, the Zurich Academy, and from some of the most illustrious universities in America and England. Father's reply would generally be along these lines: "I am deeply honored by the invitation. . . . but to my extreme regret I must decline. . . . I wish to explain that throughout my writing life I have accepted medals and awards (Guggenheim, American Academy, Brandeis University, etc.) but have invariably refused membership in any literary academy, organization or society, no matter how glorious."[12] Or "Nature has not equipped me with the virtues which make a person a useful member of an active organization. In the absence of such virtues I would find it embarrassing to accept a title without being able to contribute anything in exchange."[13]

Finally, a truth about Vladimir Nabokov that some have failed to grasp (and this goes not only for critics of the *Onegin* translation), a truth that should stand as an introduction to every one of his works. When Wilson ascribed to Father an "addiction to rare and unfamiliar words," he received a nutshell reply: "It does not occur to him that I may have rare and unfamiliar things to convey."[14]

NOTES

1. Vladimir Nabokov, "*Lolita* and Mr. Girodias," in *Strong Opinions*, pp. 274–75.
2. Nabokov, *Strong Opinions*, pp. 268–79.
3. Ibid., pp. 211–12.
4. Vladimir Nabokov, trans., *Eugene Onegin*, by Aleksandr Pushkin.
5. Nabokov, *Strong Opinions*, p. 250.
6. Ibid.
7. Nabokov, *Strong Opinions*, p. 240.
8. Ibid.

9. Vladimir Nabokov and Edmund Wilson, *The Nabokov–Wilson Letters*, ed. Simon Karlinsky, p. 73.
10. Ibid.
11. In Father's translation of Lermontov's poem "The Solitary White Sail," later published in *Three Russian Poets*.
12. Nabokov, unpublished letter, 1969.
13. Nabokov, unpublished letter, 1964.
14. Nabokov, *Strong Opinions*, p. 250.

Toward the Man
behind the Mystification

PHYLLIS A. ROTH

The relationship between the life and the art of Vladimir Nabokov has always been intriguing. Nabokov would have his critics believe it totally determined by deliberate choice and absolute artistic control. In response, many critics have elected to treat the relationship as if it were tenuous or insignificant, as if the fiction sprang full blown from the top of Nabokov's head without any engagement of the viscera of the artist's experience. Of course, critics have recognized some biographical parallels and Nabokov himself has provided others; furthermore, we are generally aware that Nabokov's exile from Russia and the subsequent years he spent in America had some significance for the concerns and development of the fiction. Beyond this, however, Nabokov's critics have feared to tread: some perhaps because to do so is not their concern; others because Nabokov has so energetically blocked the way, prefacing his novels with denials and peppering them with mocking assaults on Freud and Freudianism. Nevertheless, as Andrew Field has reluctantly corroborated in his recent biography, Nabokov read psychological case studies and took an active if hostile interest in psychoanalysis and other psychologies.[1] Moreover, Nabokov employed psychoanalytic insights extensively in the fiction, typically parodically, though not exclusively so.[2]

As a result, a psychoanalytic approach to Nabokov's work which subsumes the relationship between the work and the life is, as one would expect, extremely complicated and difficult. It is not, however, to be dismissed easily in the flick-of-the-wrist manner Nabokov would like his critics to emulate. This is especially true since Nabokov himself has not been able so to dismiss it. No single article, however, can do more than indicate the outlines of the territory and some of the obvious questions to be considered—in brief, open the field for further investigation. What follows is not an exhaustive analysis, certainly not yet thoroughly psychoanalytic, but an indication of a set of possibilities which I believe are worth further psychoanalytic investigation.

The place to begin is precisely with the concept of absolute artistic control, for certainly artistic control and that which Nabokov believes it can offer, as many of his critics have argued, is not only the technique of the fictions but their subject matter as well—the hallmark of his "metafiction." But artistic control is not an answer to a question; it is itself a problem. What type of control—and of what? Other, even broader questions come as immediately to mind, but for my purposes, these are the pertinent ones. I will conclude that despite his asseverations to the contrary, Nabokov, like others, employed his art to master fears, anxieties, and unacceptable desires, transforming them into a transcendent fiction which is acceptably "aesthetic." I hope to suggest a way of understanding Nabokov's statement that his characters are "like the mournful monsters of a cathedral façade—demons placed there merely to show that they have been booted out"[3]—to show, in other words, that his fictions are means of enabling him to smile at his experience and, as he put it, "to fight the utter degradation, ridicule and horror of having developed an infinity of sensation and thought within a finite existence."[4]

I am not arguing that his fiction is shallow, merely self-serving, or ultimately reducible to childhood traumas. On the contrary, I am affirming the genius of Nabokov's imagination, an imagination which employs experiences of this life to body forth visions of other worlds; to confirm for us that this transformation of memories can indeed enable us to progress beyond the sources of those memories, although we are finally, as Nabokov was well aware, "consumed by that which we were nourished by."

To begin, then, with Nabokov's awareness of death as that which finally cannot be transcended is to begin with what Nabokov's critics have already established. As Nabokov himself tells us, the deceit of art is a way of achieving control over merely mortal considerations. *Speak, Memory* shows that Nabokov relished that deceit, finding room for its exercise even in the composition of chess problems (pp. 291–92):

> I remember one particular problem I had been trying to compose for months. There came a night when I managed at last to express that particular theme. It was meant for the delectation of the very expert solver. The unsophisticated might miss the point of the problem entirely, and discover its fairly simple, "thetic" solution without having passed through the pleasurable torments prepared for the sophisticated one. The latter would start by falling for an illusory pattern of play based on a fashionable avant-garde theme . . . , which the composer had

taken the greatest pains to "plant". . . . Having passed through this "antithetic" inferno the by now ultrasophisticated solver would reach the simple key move . . . as somebody on a wild goose chase might go from Albany to New York by way of Vancouver, Eurasia and the Azores. The pleasant experience of the roundabout route (strange landscapes, gongs, tigers, exotic customs, the thrice-repeated circuit of a newly married couple around the sacred fire of an earthen brazier) would amply reward him for the misery of the deceit, and after that, his arrival at the simple key move would provide him with a synthesis of poignant artistic delight.

We can, then, equate deceit with artistic control and deal with it in the terms I have suggested: the mastery through transformation of lifelong preoccupations (fears, anxieties, and desires). Nabokov's constant need for control—over not only chess but also lepidoptera, literature, and soccer—is demonstrated throughout his work. Nabokov, like the insects he so admired, required protective markings and coloration to divert the attention of those whom he considered predators while he revealed and revelled in his own control.

For the purposes of this introductory study, I will focus almost exclusively on *Speak, Memory*. I will view the autobiography as Nabokov's *Interpretation of Dreams*, a rendering of his experiences which, while it is controlled so as to rival (or forestall) its psychoanalytic prototype, is nonetheless more psychologically revealing than has been argued to date. I am interested in the preoccupation with artistic control and in discovering what required the control provided by art.

Nabokov refers throughout his autobiography to dreams and nightmares; he says he has "ransacked [his] oldest dreams for keys and clues—[but rejects] completely the vulgar, shabby, fundamentally medieval world of Freud, with its crankish quest for sexual symbols . . . and its bitter little embryos spying, from their natural nooks, upon the love life of their parents" (p. 20). Nabokov's skill at *reductio ad absurdum* arguments against symbol-mongering[5] is not to be slighted, but he is as aware as any psychoanalyst of the significance of childhood for establishing patterns of desire and response; he mentions elsewhere "the odd fact that whenever possible the scenery of our infancy is used by an economically minded producer as a ready-made setting for our adult dreams" (p. 130). But again, while *Speak, Memory* is Nabokov's personal handbook of dreams fulfilled and dreams shattered, nightmares realized and those transcended, it is as carefully and artfully controlled and structured as any of the fictions. I need not repeat Dabney Stuart's evidence for this conclusion; it is better to recommend Stuart's excellent piece, "The Novelist's Composure: *Speak, Memory* as Fiction."[6] But it is worthwhile to provide at least one other example which demonstrates this control in some of its subtlety. Careful readers of chapter 12, separately entitled "Tamara," will pay special attention to this: "During the beginning of that summer and all through the previous one, Tamara's name had kept cropping up . . ." (p. 229). Also, on the next page: "She slapped dead the horsefly that she had been waiting for to light and proceeded to catch up with two other, less pretty girls who were calling to her." Returning to the preceding chapter, one finds that, indeed, Tamara's name had a way of cropping up: "On a floorboard at my feet a dead horsefly lay on its back. . . . And the patches of disintegrating whitewash on the inside of the door had been used by various trespassers for such jottings as: 'Dasha, Tamara and Lena have been here' or 'Down with Austria!'" (p. 216). This type of control indicates primarily that the artist knows what he is doing, knows it backwards and forwards. Other more extended sections of *Speak, Memory* demonstrate Nabokov's *need* to control what he is doing.

Nabokov shares with many of his characters an insomnia and fear of loss of consciousness entailed by sleep. During a lengthy description of the fascination of trains, Nabokov gives us a view of the mastery of sleep's terrors provided by art (p. 145):

> I would put myself to sleep by the simple act of identifying myself with the engine driver. A sense of drowsy well-being invaded my veins as soon as I had everything nicely arranged— the carefree passengers in their rooms enjoying the ride I was giving them, smoking, exchanging knowing smiles, nodding, dozing; the waiters and cooks and train guards (whom I had to place somewhere) carousing in the diner; and myself, goggled and begrimed, peering out of the engine cab at the tapering track, at the ruby or emerald point in the black distance. And then, in my sleep, I would see something totally different—a glass marble rolling under a grand piano or a toy engine lying on its side with its wheels still working gamely.

Among the most noteworthy elements of this passage are those of the "sense of . . . well-being" which results from the artist's mastery of his materials and his imagination. Notice that Nabokov is in control of the scene because he both creates it and is the engine driver: he is thus the engineer in two senses.[7] But then, "in my sleep, I would see something totally different." The train is now a toy, derailed, "with its wheels still working gamely."

Nabokov's preoccupation with control, his desire to be the engineer, is evident in the various activities he pursued in addition to literature and chess. His pleasure in soccer, for example, reveals his desire to stand above or away from the crowd in order to maintain his autonomy. In *Speak, Memory*, Nabokov describes his position as goalkeeper this way: "Aloof, solitary, impassive, the crack goalie is followed in the streets by entranced small boys. . . . His sweater, his peaked cap, his kneeguards, the gloves protruding from the hip pocket of his shorts, set him apart from the rest of the team. He is the lone eagle, the man of mystery, the last defender. . . . the stadium roars in approval as he remains for a moment or two lying full length where he fell, his goal still intact" (p. 267). Andrew Field adds a delightful, and I would argue emblematic, anecdote: "His last soccer game was played in 1935. . . . Nabokov was knocked unconscious with the ball in his grip and had to be carried from the field. . . . Nabokov remembers that when he came to, the first thing he was aware of was a teammate impatiently trying to pry the ball, frozen in his grip, out of his arms."[8]

One thinks, too, and perhaps more immediately, of lepidoptera. Nabokov's comparison between nature's "mysteries of mimicry" and those of art is worth pursuing: "Both were a form of magic, both were a game of intricate enchantment and deception." We find in his descriptions of mimesis among insects the transformation of the grotesque into the brilliantly artful which characterizes both his fiction and his perceptions: "Consider the imitation of oozing poison by bubblelike macules on a wing . . . or by glossy yellow knobs on a chrysalis ('Don't eat me—I have already been squashed, sampled and rejected'). Consider the tricks of an acrobatic caterpillar . . . which in infancy looks like bird's dung, but after molting develops scrabbly hymenopteroid appendages and baroque characteristics, allowing the extraordinary fellow to play two parts at once . . . : that of a writhing larva and that of a big ant seemingly harrowing it" (pp. 124–25). Of course, it is no easy matter to distinguish the ant from the larva here, to distinguish play from what is necessary for survival. It seems to me most helpful to consider play and survival as two descriptions of the same phenomenon. Viewing them this way, we can reconsider Nabokov's statement that "deceit to the point of diabolism, and originality, verging upon the grotesque, were my notions of strategy" (p. 289). We can take as our point of departure Nabokov's reference here to "the grotesque," and attempt to understand its relation to his survival through artistic control.

While the term is problematic, and especially so in relation to Nabokov, Wolfgang Kayser's study of the grotesque is helpful.[9] Kayser argues that the grotesque "contradicts the very laws which rule our familiar world. . . . The basic feeling . . . is one of surprise and horror, an agonizing fear in the presence of a world which breaks apart and remains inaccessible." "The grotesque is the estranged world . . . it is our world which ceases to be reliable." Perhaps paradoxically, but certainly usefully for us, Kayser concludes his analysis with a "final interpretation" of the grotesque, which would better be called the anti-grotesque, as "an attempt to invoke and subdue the demonic aspects of the world."

These observations illuminate the sources of the recurrent themes and repetitively elaborated structures of Nabokov's art. Nabokov's experience and his perception of that experience were such that he had to come to terms with the grotesque as Kayser defines it. Outcast from the idealized world of his Russian childhood, married to a Jew and in exile in Nazi Germany, bereft of a beloved father assassinated by mistake, Nabokov could not avoid "the estranged world." Moreover, *Speak, Memory* indicates earlier experiences of the grotesque in the nightmares which so plagued Nabokov and which suggest correlations both with the characters in the fiction and with those anxieties, those demons, he needed to subdue. Early in the autobiography, Nabokov describes the visions he sees under his eyelids as he attempts to sleep: "They come and go, without the drowsy observer's participation. They are often grotesque. I am pestered by roguish profiles, by some coarse-featured and florid dwarf with a swelling nostril or ear" (p. 34). Nabokov's experience of the grotesque typically occurs in his encounters with what he can control only in his art; most often, the uncontrollable is death and the visions of "death's second self," sleep. At the end of chapter 2 of *Speak, Memory*—a chapter devoted to Nabokov's recollections of his mother, to his awareness that it was she who taught him how to defy mortality by deliberate acts of memory—the themes of death, the grotesque, and their transcendence by art are revealed to us (p. 50):

> Whenever in my dreams I see the dead, they always appear silent, bothered, strangely depressed, quite unlike their dear, bright selves. I am aware of them, without any astonishment, in surroundings they never visited during their earthly existence, in the house of some friend of mine they never knew. They sit apart, frowning at the floor, as if death were a dark taint, a shameful family secret. It is certainly not then—not in dreams—but when one is wide awake, at moments of robust

joy and achievement, on the highest terrace of consciousness, that mortality has a chance to peer beyond its own limits, from the mast, from the past and its castle tower.

Several brief portraits in *Speak, Memory* remind us of the way the grotesque is transformed into fiction. For example, a portrayal of "Somnus" himself, "that black-masked headsman binding me to the block . . . the familiar ax . . . coming out of its great velvet-lined double-base case" (p. 109), reminds us of the cellmate of Cincinnatus C. There is, too, the scathing portrait of the most monstrous character in the autobiography, "a young German university student, well-bred, quiet, bespectacled, whose hobby was capital punishment" and who described his interest to Nabokov in vivid detail with photographic illustrations of executions. The conclusion of this portrait is instructive both for its bitter tone and for the way in which it enables us to recognize Nabokov's mastery of horror (p. 279):

> At our third and last encounter (there still remained bits of him I wanted to file for possible use) he related to me, more in sorrow than in anger, that he had once spent a whole night patiently watching a good friend of his who had decided to shoot himself and had agreed to do so, in the roof of the mouth, facing the hobbyist in a good light, but having no ambition or sense of honor, had got hopelessly tight instead. Although I have lost track of Dietrich long ago, I can well imagine the look of calm satisfaction in his fish-blue eyes as he shows, nowadays (perhaps at the very minute I am writing this), a never-expected profusion of treasures to his thigh-clapping, guffawing co-veterans—the absolutely *wunderbar* pictures he took during Hitler's reign.

The parenthetical references to "possible use" and to his writing about Dietrich reveal Nabokov's desire to fashion the student into a fiction. Nevertheless, we are reminded by this portrait of the Nabokovs' all-too-real experience of living in Hitler's Germany until 1937. Field argues that Nabokov failed to take Nazism seriously for quite a time; he describes Nabokov's feelings in the early 1930s as "heedless disgust." Ultimately, however, Nabokov not only repudiated Germany utterly but felt the need to do something. In understanding the sense of mastery his literary and lepidopteral pursuits afforded him, we can better understand his characteristic and only seemingly callous desire to "enlist [in the U.S. Army] and go to fight in Morocco (. . . there was a particular kind of butterfly in North Africa which he longed to capture)."[10] In other words, we cannot understand Nabokov's vision of the estranged world unless we remember Bolshevik Russia and Nazi Germany.

In the chapter in *Speak, Memory* originally entitled "Mademoiselle O," Nabokov makes explicit the process whereby he transforms a set of memories, frequently unattractive and painful, by imaginatively synthesizing them with later experience and associations. He describes the chapter as "my desperate attempt to save what is left of poor Mademoiselle" from the artist in him which frequently gives away his past to the characters of his novels (p. 95). But, and this is most important, it is the artist in him who attempts, in both the autobiography and the fiction, to save his childhood in Russia by subduing the demons of an estranged world. He does this throughout *Speak, Memory* by, to use his terms, creating a dialectic of his experience. Here, the dialectic maintains the balance between thesis (Mademoiselle in Russia) and antithesis (Mademoiselle in Switzerland) and synthesizes the two to provide a new spiral of meaning, one which never would have been revealed otherwise. The elements in the thematic spiral are Nabokov's memory of Mademoiselle summarized as "the shallowness of her culture, the bitterness of her temper, the banality of her mind" (p. 113); his visit during which she lies about the past and attempts to deceive him about the efficacy of a hearing aid he has brought her; the image of "an aged swan, a large, uncouth, dodo-like creature, making ridiculous efforts to hoist himself into a moored boat" (p. 116), which somehow is associated with Mademoiselle; and his hearing that Mademoiselle has died. The associations of all these events, taken in the context of his life, result in a new perception (p. 117):

> Just before the rhythm I hear falters and fades, I catch myself
> wondering whether, during the years I knew her, I had not
> kept utterly missing something in her that was far more she
> than her chins or her ways or even her French—something per-
> haps akin to that last glimpse of her, to the radiant deceit she
> had used in order to have me depart pleased with my own
> kindness, or to that swan whose agony was so much closer to
> artistic truth than a drooping dancer's pale arms; something,
> in short, that I could appreciate only after the things and
> beings that I had most loved in the security of my childhood
> had been turned to ashes or shot through the heart.

What I have been moving toward in this discussion of the grotesque is an attempt to explain why, for Nabokov—who has succeeded over all these years in presenting himself as predominantly

cerebral, aristocratic, elitist, perhaps a bit effete, dwelling in a rare-
fied atmosphere of the true and the beautiful—the uncouth swan's
agony is much closer to artistic truth than a drooping dancer's pale
arms. His extraordinarily happy Russian childhood, his heterosex-
ually active youth, his long and devoted relationship with Véra, and
his eminently successful exile are facts, but his fictions are located
in an asylum of tortured grotesques, frequently homosexual and
mad to one degree or another. The reason is that this too was his
experience, the underside of the idyllic life. This part of his experience was dominated by death and loss and pain and guilt occasioned
by the end of childhood, the end of homeland, the loss of those well
loved, who made of that Russian childhood the nurturing environment for the child and the future artist. This may explain why, in
seeming to compare the uncouth swan to Mademoiselle, Nabokov
conceives the swan as male; perhaps Nabokov saw behind his own
"radiant deceit" a similar agony.

The fiction, then, is a way of controlling the uncontrollable, of
creating not only a world generated by memory in which, as a result,
nothing is ever lost, no one ever dies, but also a world of which Nabokov is the engineer, able to assert and perpetuate his distance
from the grotesque. As he put it so plainly, "the writing of a novel
relieved me of . . . fertile emotion" (pp. 244–45).

I have tried to indicate the special need and nature of control in
Nabokov's art; I would like now to consider more fully the specific
sources of the satisfaction gained by the artistic transformation of
personal experiences. The direction followed here derives from Nabokov's relationships with the significant men of his childhood; surprisingly, given the number of homosexuals in the fiction, Nabokov's critics have not pursued the leads the autobiography provides.

The transformative and cathartic functions of Nabokov's writing about homosexuals clearly find their imperatives in Nabokov's
memories of his brother Sergey and Uncle Ruka. While Nabokov
never uses the term "homosexual" when describing them, Field cor-
roborates its accuracy. Field also adds the following, presumably on
the basis of discussion with Nabokov:

Nabokov shares his father's view of homosexuality as an illness . . . transmitted exclusively by heredity . . . though in my
own mind I myself cannot disregard entirely the hothouse atmosphere in which the Nabokovs lived at the turn of the century and which seems to have allowed so many propensities of
all manner and kind to grow and flourish exceptionally well. I
hasten now (too slowly, thinks Nabokov) to leave this subject.

The discomfiture which it caused decades ago in the Nabokov
family has, at least in part, inspired an artistic interest in the
subject which has provided a remarkable gallery of homosexual characters in Nabokov's writing.[11]

There is, then, evidence to support the view, as the fiction certainly
does, that Nabokov saw homosexuality as an illness which was of
particular personal concern and "discomfort." Further, a special set
of associations with both Uncle Ruka and Sergey undoubtedly was
cause for additional anxiety, indeed even guilt, in his feelings about
them. Both stuttered and had difficulty expressing themselves, difficulty it is impossible to imagine for Nabokov. Both were part of the
immediate family group, yet clearly not among those to whom Nabokov paid especial attention; nor did his parents pay as much attention to them as to him. Yet Uncle Ruka left Nabokov an estate
worth two or three million dollars and, while we may believe Nabokov when he says the material loss went unnoticed in his exile, we
must understand the feeling underlying the following description of
his uncle: "He insisted that he had an incurable heart ailment and
that, when the seizures came, he could obtain relief only by lying
supine on the floor. Nobody took him seriously, and after he did die
of angina pectoris, all alone, in Paris, at the end of 1916, aged forty-
five, it was with a quite special pang that one recalled those after-
dinner incidents in the drawing room" (p. 71), when Uncle Ruka
sprawled on the floor.

   Even clearer is Nabokov's difficulty in discussing Sergey, a difficulty which does not stem—and here I am arguing with Nabokov's
description—from unfamiliarity. Nabokov claims that "except for
the two or three poor little adventures I have sketched in earlier
chapters, his boyhood and mine seldom mingled" (p. 257). In fact,
the earlier chapters of *Speak, Memory* indicate that Sergey was present wherever Vladimir went, on all trips and vacations with parents,
sharing rooms and tutors, up through college in England. What Nabokov refers to here as "poor little adventures" are episodes he painfully recalls of his torturing Sergey; for instance, he admits, "I kept
self-sufficiently overtaking poor gamely stumbling Sergey, one of
those galling little pictures that revolve on and on in one's mind" (p.
205). Perhaps most crucially here, when the brothers were attending
different schools, Nabokov read "a page from his diary . . . , and in
stupid wonder showed [it] to my tutor, who promptly showed it to
my father, [a page which] abruptly provided a retroactive clarifica-
tion of certain oddities of behavior on his part" (pp. 257–58). Nabokov himself again provides us with an assessment of his feelings;

concluding the section on Sergey in a tone reminiscent of that evident in the description of Uncle Ruka's death, Nabokov says: "A frank and fearless man, [Sergey] criticized the regime in front of colleagues, who denounced him. He was arrested, accused of being a 'British spy' and sent to a Hamburg concentration camp where he died of inanition, on January 10, 1945. It is one of those lives that hopelessly claim a belated something—compassion, understanding, no matter what—which the mere recognition of such a want can neither replace nor redeem" (p. 258).

Some redemption exists, however—the redemption provided of course by art, the art of *Speak, Memory* and of the fiction, in which the grotesque and mortal underside of experience is divested of its bitterness by the artist who smiles in spite of mortality, even in spite of guilt and remorse. Nabokov puts it most eloquently at the end of his discussion of Uncle Ruka, significantly when he recalls Uncle Ruka's delight at rereading the books beloved in childhood, and his own similar delight (pp. 76–77):

> In my own case . . . I not only go through the same agony and delight that my uncle did, but have to cope with an additional burden—the recollection I have of him, reliving his childhood with the help of those very books. I see again my schoolroom in Vyra, the blue roses of the wallpaper, the open window. Its reflection fills the oval mirror above the leathern couch where my uncle sits, gloating over a tattered book. A sense of security, of well-being, of summer warmth pervades my memory. That robust reality makes a ghost of the present. The mirror brims with brightness; a bumblebee has entered the room and bumps against the ceiling. Everything is as it should be, nothing will ever change, nobody will ever die.

Art, then, redeems from time what would otherwise be lost. Everything is as it *should* be. For Nabokov this means, among other things, that his complicity in the temporal—indeed, I would argue, his complicity with death—is, on one level, absolved. The goal, the "synthesis of poignant artistic delight," is achieved by means of what Van Veen calls "sudden juxtapositions that revived the part while vivifying the whole."[12] The use of "revived" and "vivifying" emphasizes the life-sustaining function of temporal associations. These juxtapositions and their function are especially significant in relation to two additional portraits from *Speak, Memory*, those of Nabokov's father and of his cousin Yuri, which call for a unified analysis.

Throughout *Speak, Memory*, Nabokov foreshadows his father's tragic death, indicating the ubiquitousness of this experience in his memory. For example, Nabokov notes that his grandfather, Dmitri Nabokov, died "on March 28, 1904, exactly eighteen years, day for day, before my father" (p. 59). Chapter 1 concludes with the following proleptic reminiscence, in which the homage of the local peasants who tossed Vladimir Dmitrievich in the air turns abruptly into the image of a funeral (pp. 31–32):

> Thrice, to the mighty heave-ho of his invisible tossers, he would fly up in this fashion, and the second time he would go higher than the first and then there he would be, on his last and loftiest flight, reclining, as if for good, against the cobalt blue of the summer noon, like one of those paradisiac personages who comfortably soar, with such a wealth of folds in their garments, on the vaulted ceiling of a church while below, one by one, the wax tapers in mortal hands light up to make a swarm of minute flames in the mist of incense, and the priest chants of eternal repose, and funeral lilies conceal the face of whoever lies there, among the swimming lights, in the open coffin.

Moreover, these temporal juxtapositions enable Nabokov to work backward through his experiences to affirm that he fully appreciates the far past in light of subsequent events. This transformation of time and emotion is strikingly evident in the description of his response to the duel his father was to have fought (pp. 191–93):

> And behind it all there was yet a very special emotional abyss that I was desperately trying to skirt, lest I burst into a tempest of tears, and this was the tender friendship underlying my respect for my father; the charm of our perfect accord; the Wimbledon matches we followed in the London papers; the chess problems we solved; the Pushkin iambics that rolled off his tongue so triumphantly whenever I mentioned some minor poet of the day. Our relationship was marked by that habitual exchange of homespun nonsense, comically garbled words, proposed imitations of supposed intonations, and all those private jokes which is the secret code of happy families. . . .
> At last I was home, and immediately upon entering the vestibule I became aware of loud, cheerful voices. . . . I knew at once that there would be no duel, that the challenge had been met by an apology, that all was right. . . . I saw my mother's serene everyday face, but I could not look at my fa-

ther. And then it happened: my heart welled in me . . . and I had no handkerchief, and ten years were to pass before a certain night in 1922, at a public lecture in Berlin, when my father shielded the lecturer (his old friend Milyukov) from the bullets of two Russian Fascists and, while vigorously knocking down one of the assassins, was fatally shot by the other. But no shadow was cast by that future event upon the bright stairs of our St. Petersburg house; the large, cool hand resting on my head did not quaver, and several lines of play in a difficult chess composition were not blended yet on the board.

We are, of course, reminded of the death of Mademoiselle, which concludes with the statement, "I could appreciate [the memory] only after the things and beings that I had most loved in the security of my childhood had been turned to ashes or shot through the heart."

In the depiction of Yuri we can see the very special way Nabokov felt death as his personal enemy. Additionally, Nabokov's attempt to come to terms with the emotional experience by transforming it artistically and setting it into a literary context—much as he sets his father's death into the context of a chess game—reveals the depth of the pain and anxiety. Nabokov describes his relationship with his cousin in chapter 10 of the autobiography, immediately following the summary of his father's assassination. Chapter 10 begins with a plot summary of *The Headless Horseman* by Mayne Reid: "two friends swap clothes, hats, mounts, and the wrong man gets murdered" (p. 195). In his introduction of Yuri, Nabokov remarks, "I suddenly see myself in the uniform of an officers' training school: we are strolling again villageward, in 1916, and . . . have exchanged clothes—Yuri is wearing my white flannels and striped tie." Then the wrong-man-murdered theme continues its evolution (pp. 199–200):

> During the short week he stayed that year we devised a singular entertainment which I have not seen described anywhere. There was a swing in the center of a small circular playground surrounded by jasmins [sic], at the bottom of our garden. We adjusted the ropes in such a way as to have the green swingboard pass just a couple of inches above one's forehead and nose if one lay supine on the sand beneath. One of us would start the fun by standing on the board and swinging with increasing momentum; the other would lie down with the back of his head on a marked spot, and from what seemed an enormous height the swinger's board would swish swiftly above the supine one's face. And three years later, as a cavalry officer

in Denikin's army, he was killed fighting the Reds in northern Crimea. I saw him dead in Yalta, the whole front of his skull pushed back by the impact of several bullets, which had hit him like the iron board of a monstrous swing, when having outstripped his detachment he was in the act of recklessly attacking alone a Red machinegun nest. Thus was quenched his lifelong thirst for intrepid conduct in battle, for that ultimate gallant gallop with drawn pistol or unsheathed sword. Had I been competent to write his epitaph, I might have summed up matters by saying—in richer words than I can muster here— that all emotions, all thoughts, were governed in Yuri by one gift: a sense of honor equivalent, morally, to absolute pitch.

Not only is this passage dominated by a sense of the monstrous, it is startling for the sense of inadequacy Nabokov conveys. Nevertheless, the experience of inadequacy is only apparently atypical. Further, the line of association in this chapter is obvious. Yuri is associated with Nabokov's father since both were murdered by cosmic error and injustice, both had their deaths foreshadowed by earlier events, and both were similarly beloved and admired. Indeed, Nabokov's description of Yuri's greater sophistication indicates that Yuri was a paternal model for Vladimir. Undoubtedly, and consciously, Nabokov would have done anything to prevent their deaths. However, the emotional complexity of Nabokov's attitude is indicated by the correlation of Yuri's death with the swing game, with the fact that the cousins often played with guns and staged duels together, and with the wrong-man-murdered theme.

It is clear, then, that death and loss were among the most moving experiences of Nabokov's life, that associated with these experiences were guilt and the need both to recall the emotions of the past and to make up for its losses. The way Nabokov found to deal with the hideous experience of mortality was to work on the memories so as to make them permanent compensations for loss and inadequacy, and through the fictions to distance himself from painful experiences, denying the implications of death and of his complicity in it. In this way, I think, we can understand the recurrence of character types and experiences in the fiction. We might think for a moment of the wrong-man-murdered theme, and its association with the grotesque and the guilty, in *Despair*, *Pale Fire*, and *Lolita*. The fiction reiteratively revitalizes and vivifies, as well as transforms and distances, the past and its inhabitants. Moreover, in subduing the grotesque by the artful, life is redeemed from the "shameful family secret" and "dark taint" of death.

Finally, however, Nabokov's art acknowledges the unfortunate truth that the transcendence of mortality is contingent on mortality; it is this truth which the fictions consciously and continuously affirm by demonstrating that to deny it, as almost all the characters do, is to opt for madness and suicide. In other words, Nabokov, unlike his characters, knows that the past must never be confused with the present, the imaginatively recreated memory with the event itself. Describing his childhood return to Russia from Germany in 1905, for instance, Nabokov says: "I was not quite six, but that year abroad, a year of difficult decisions and liberal hopes, had exposed a small Russian boy to grown-up conversations. He could not help being affected in some way of his own by a mother's nostalgia and a father's patriotism. In result, that particular return to Russia, my first *conscious* return, seems to me now, sixty years later, a rehearsal—not of the grand homecoming that will never take place, but of its constant dream in my long years of exile" (pp. 96–97). The distinction between his dreams of return to the past and the actual return which can never occur is a distinction which certain of Nabokov's characters (Martin Edelweiss, Humbert Humbert, Van Veen) fail to make. However reluctantly, Nabokov affirms the existence of the present, its inescapable presence. For example, in a description of Mademoiselle's journey from the railroad station to the Vyra estate, Nabokov concludes with a scene he can only imagine since he "was not there to greet her" (pp. 98, 99–100):

> Very lovely, very lonesome. But what am I doing in this stereoscopic dreamland? How did I get here? Somehow, the two sleighs have slipped away, leaving behind a passportless spy standing on the blue-white road in his New England snowboots and stormcoat. The vibration in my ears is no longer their receding bells, but only my old blood singing. All is still, spellbound, enthralled by the moon, fancy's rear-vision mirror. The snow is real, though, and as I bend to it and scoop up a handful, sixty years crumble to glittering frost-dust between my fingers.

The point and the poignancy of this scene are located in the dialectical tension between temporal opposites and between artifice and reality. Nabokov's characters often become trapped in pasts or in other identities because they are unable to bear this tension; their mental confusion and the fusion of opposites it generates define their grotesqueness. Perhaps only V. in *The Real Life of Sebastian Knight* clearly recognizes the deceit, the artifice, of artistic truth: "And then the masquerade draws to a close. The bald little prompter shuts his book, as the light fades gently. The end, the end. They all go back to their everyday life . . . —but the hero remains, for, try as I may, I cannot get out of my part: Sebastian's mask clings to my face, the likeness will not be washed off. I am Sebastian, or Sebastian is I, or perhaps we both are someone whom neither of us knows."[13]

Speak, Memory, then, provides a model for the creation of artistic truths out of memories and experience, by means of enchanting and diabolical deceit. Nabokov's pained yet delighted awareness of the deceit is a bar against which the imaginations of his characters can be measured. Further, in concluding with the issue of deceit I am returning to my initial discussion of Nabokov's need for the control provided by art.

It is my hope that I have been able to some degree to trace the antithetic inferno of the "real life" of Vladimir Nabokov, to suggest ways in which prior notions of "sufficient explanations" must be overturned.[14] The necessity for doing so is evident when we recall that reluctance to deal with Nabokov as a human has led to frequent questioning of the value of his fictions. Most recently, the question was rephrased in a tribute to Nabokov occasioned by his death: "Was it all a game, an elaborate, brilliant, obsessive, but finally sterile mental exercise, like a game of chess . . . which leads to nowhere and tells us nothing of value about the human predicament? Or after you've worked your way through the maze, is there someone there, a real man with real values, who, for his own reasons, had to make you play the game before he would reward you with the vision?"[15] The author responds affirmatively, of course, to the latter question. Yet the evidence to prove the assertion is not brought forth. In fact, we make it impossible to answer questions raised about Nabokov the artist until we constitute Nabokov the man behind the mystification.

NOTES

1. Describing Nabokov's father's library and therefore the books Nabokov grew up with, Field reveals a strongly defensive posture about approaches such as mine: "There one may find titles such as *The Sexual Instinct and Its Morbid Manifestations* and a good collection of Havelock Ellis. . . . the young Nabokov certainly did acquire a taste for this sort of reading, for when he was confined to bed for a time years later in Berlin, he sent a friend to the library to take out psychological case studies for him. It is a very simple and unexciting but sufficient explanation of the origins of Nabokovian neurotics and psychotics such as Smurov in *The Eye*, Herman Karlovich in *Despair*, and Humbert Humbert" (*Nabokov: His Life in Part*, p. 96). I am, of course, disagreeing with Field's notion of a "sufficient explanation."

2. As I have tried to demonstrate at length in "The Psychology of the Double in Nabokov's *Pale Fire," Essays in Literature* 2 (1975), 209–29.
3. Nabokov, *Strong Opinions*, p. 19.
4. Nabokov, *Speak, Memory*, p. 297. Hereafter cited in text.
5. He seems uncomfortable, for example, about what the symbol-monger might do with the very special pencil his mother bought him when he was ill as a child. Both the beginning and conclusion of the narrative of that event are defensive. He begins, "the future specialist in such dull literary lore as autoplagiarism will like to collate a protagonist's experience . . . with the original event" (p. 37); and ends, "the shopman had been obliged to ring up an agent, a 'Doctor' Libner (as if the transaction possessed indeed some pathological import)" (pp. 38–39).
6. Dabney Stuart, "The Novelist's Composure: *Speak, Memory* as Fiction," *Modern Language Quarterly* 36 (1975), 179.
7. The multiple control and the pleasure it affords are also evident in the task of *Speak, Memory* itself: "This re-Englishing of a Russian reversion of what had been an English re-telling of Russian memories in the first place, proved to be a diabolical task, but some consolation was given me by the thought that such multiple metamorphosis, familiar to butterflies, had not been tried by any human before" (pp. 12–13).
8. Field, *Life in Part*, p. 154.
9. Wolfgang Kayser, *The Grotesque in Art and Literature*, trans. Ulrich Weisstein (Bloomington: Indiana University Press, 1963), pp. 31, 184–85, 188.
10. Field, *Life in Part*, p. 250.
11. Ibid., pp. 62–63.
12. Nabokov, *Ada*, p. 31.
13. Nabokov, *The Real Life of Sebastian Knight*, p. 205.
14. See note 1 above.
15. Carll Tucker, "The Back Door," *Saturday Review* (20 August 1977), 80.

Part 2

The First and Second Arcs

22 April 1899: Vladimir Nabokov is born in St. Petersburg.

1919: The Nabokovs emigrate from Russia to Germany.

1919–1923: Studies at Cambridge University.

1922: Father assassinated in Berlin.

1923–1937: Lives in Berlin.

1923: Publishes Russian translation of *Alice's Adventures in Wonderland*.

1925: Marries Véra Evseevna Slonim.

1926: *Mashenka* (*Mary*)

1928: *Korol', dama, valet* (*King, Queen, Knave*)

1929: "Kartofel'nyy el'f" ("The Potato Elf") published in the émigré daily *Rul'* (Berlin).

1930: *Zashchita Luzhina* (*The Defense*)

Vozvrashchenie Chorba (*The Return of Chorb*), containing "The Potato Elf"

1932: *Podvig* (*Glory*)

Kamera obskura (*Laughter in the Dark*)

1934: Nabokov's son Dmitri is born.

1936: *Otchayanie* (*Despair*)

Kamera obskura published in English as *Camera Obscura*.

1937–1940: Lives in Paris.

1937–1938: *Dar* (*The Gift*) published in part.

1938: *Priglashenie na kazn'* (*Invitation to a Beheading*)

Laughter in the Dark (revised translation of *Kamera obskura*)

Nabokov's Assault on Wonderland

BEVERLY LYON CLARK

In 1966 Vladimir Nabokov could proselytize for literal translations (especially when translating the work of someone else and especially when that someone else was Pushkin), by lamenting that "the canned music of rhymed versions is enthusiastically advertised, and accepted, and the sacrifice of textual precision applauded as something rather heroic, whereas only suspicion and bloodhounds await the gaunt, graceless literalist groping around in despair for the obscure word that would satisfy impassioned fidelity and accumulating in the process a wealth of information which only makes the advocates of pretty camouflage tremble or sneer."[1] In 1923, however, he might not have so argued. In that year he published *Anya v stranye chudes*, his translation of *Alice's Adventures in Wonderland*, a translation that is far from literal. In *Anya* Nabokov launches his experimentation with the fantastic in fiction, an experimentation that would mature in Humbert Humbert's fantasy-filled view of Lolita and in Charles Kinbote's fantastic Zembla. *Anya* may adhere more or less closely to Lewis Carroll's original, but it is not a literal translation, and the changes Nabokov makes suggest, even this early in his career, his fondness for wordplay and, in general, for a merging of fantasy and "reality."[2]

One kind of change that Nabokov makes is to give *Alice* a Russian setting. Simon Karlinsky points out, in his excellent brief article, that Nabokov does not simply translate Carroll's parodies of English poems but rather parodies Russian poems.[3] But beyond this, Karlinsky notes how Nabokov has naturalized other aspects of *Alice* as well, unlike an earlier Russian translator, Polykhena Solovyeva, whose Alice supposedly lives in England yet encounters parodies of Russian rather than English poems. In particular, Nabokov changes the foreign-sounding Alice into the more familiar Anya, and Ada and Mabel into Ada and Asya, while the French-speaking Mouse has come over with Napoleon rather than with William the Conqueror.[4] Other changes include the changing of a hundred pounds[5] to a thousand roubles,[6] of the British institution of orange marmalade (*Alice*, p. 8) to the less specifically British strawberry jam (*Anya*, p. 6), and of the Cheshire Cat to the Carnival Cat.[7] Nabokov also omits explicit references to England—Alice attempts to reach conclusions about the English coast (*Alice*, p. 18), while Anya tries to make deductions about the seaside in general (*Anya*, p. 17)—as well as references to Shakespeare (*Alice*, p. 23; *Anya*, p. 24).

Another kind of change results from Nabokov's attempts to render Carroll's wordplay in Russian. One of Nabokov's most successful renditions is his translation of "Reeling and Writhing" (*Alice*, p. 76), two of the Mock Turtle's regular subjects when he went to school in the sea. Both Karlinsky and the publishers of the 1976 *Anya* have singled out the translation of this passage for special comment.[8] Nabokov manages to come up with "chesat' i pitat'" (*Anya*, p. 85), or "grooming and feeding," a clever substitute for "chitat' i pisat'," or "reading and writing." In fact, Nabokov's version is even more clever and elegant than Carroll's, for Nabokov simply exchanges the middle consonants in the verbs.[9] It is as if Carroll had been able to come up with "Reating and Wriding." Not all of Nabokov's renditions are quite as successful, but many of them are strikingly apt.

In addition to translating Carroll's wordplay cleverly, Nabokov adds some wordplay of his own. The publishers of the 1976 *Anya*, for instance, discuss the title of Nabokov's first chapter, "Nyrok v krolich'yu norku," which means "A Dive into the Rabbit-Hole" and is close to Carroll's "Down the Rabbit-Hole." But in addition Nabokov has juxtaposed the similar-sounding *Nyrok* and *norku*, which are also the Russian words for other animals, a duck and a mink ("Publisher's Note," in *Anya*, p. 2). Likewise, we might look at Nabokov's rendition of the seventh verse of "Father William." What basically corresponds to *"Yet you balanced an eel on the end of your nose—"* (*Alice*, p. 40) is "Sazhaesh' ty ugrya zhivogo / Na ugrevatyy nos" (*Anya*, p. 43), or roughly, "You put a live eel / On your pimpled nose." Nabokov has here added "pimpled" or "blackheaded" or even "eel-like" (*ugrevatyy*) in order to play with its similarity in sound to "eel" (*ugrya*). Another embellishment occurs in Nabokov's translation of "'We quarreled last March—just before *he* went mad, you know—' (pointing his teaspoon at the March Hare,)" (*Alice*, p. 57). Throughout his translation Nabokov translates "March Hare" straightforwardly as *Martovskiy Zayats*, but here he translates "March" in "We quarreled last March" as *Martobre* (*Anya*, p. 62), or, in English, "Marchober." *Martobr'* is, appropriately enough, an allusion to Gogol's "Diary of a Madman," where one of the entries in the madman's diary is headed *"Martobrya 86 chisla,"*[10] or "the 86th of Marchober."

Certainly Nabokov's added wordplay is largely in the spirit of Carroll's own. Yet Nabokov's use of more and also slightly different types of wordplay can be seen as an early adumbration of his mature style and technique. In particular, Nabokov's overall concern for the sounds of words reflects his general interest in words for their own sakes. Although Carroll has more interest in words as entities than realistic novelists do, he still limits his interest in many ways—we do not see him, for instance, juxtaposing words like *nyrok* and *norku* or *ugrya* and *ugrevatyy* for the sheer joy of playing with their sounds. Carroll's wordplay is characterized by puns which produce comic confusion, as when Alice means "tails" and "knots" and the Mouse means "tales" and "nots," and by near-puns which hint at the fantastic differences between Wonderland and Alice's "real" world, as is the case with "Reeling and Writhing." And when Carroll uses similar-sounding words he is usually using them to rhyme or alliterate in his verse—within the constraints, in other words, of a traditional form where rhyme and alliteration are expected.

We can gain a better understanding of how Nabokov and Carroll use somewhat different types of wordplay by examining their uses of alliteration and related forms of repetition. Carroll uses much less alliteration, and what alliteration he does allow tends to be confined to the dialogue, including the spoken verse (as with his other forms of wordplay), though alliteration may slip into a chapter title like "Pig and Pepper" (or "Wool and Water" in *Through the Looking-Glass*). When Carroll uses alliteration he is also likely to use it self-consciously, carefully pointing out that he is making a game of finding words that begin with a particular letter, as the Dormouse does with the letter *M* when he lists "mouse-traps, and the moon, and memory, and muchness" (*Alice*, p. 60) or as Alice does when she plays "I love my love with an H" in *Through the Looking-Glass* (*Alice*, p. 170).

One part of the dialogue that is especially prone to alliteration in *Alice* is the verse that various characters recite. The first verse of "*'Tis the voice of the Lobster,*" for instance, is especially rich in alliteration, with its *"baked me too brown," "his belt and his buttons," "turns out his toes,"* and *"timid and tremulous"* (*Alice*, p. 82). Similarly, the Duchess' apothegms alliterate freely: "Take care of the sense, and the sounds will take care of themselves"; "Birds of a feather flock together"; "The more there is of mine, the less there is of yours" (*Alice*, pp. 71–72). In addition, particular characters, such as the Mock Turtle, with his "school in the sea" (*Alice*, pp. 74, 75) and "somersault in the sea" (*Alice*, p. 78), tend to speak more alliteratively than others. Similar examples include Alice's "Latitude or Longitude" (*Alice*, p. 8), the Hatter's "Why is a raven like a writing-desk?" (*Alice*, p. 55), and the Hare's "*best* butter" (*Alice*, p. 56). Only rarely does alliteration creep from dialogue into the narrative itself, as it does in "simple sorrows" (*Alice*, p. 99) and "there was a Duck and a Dodo, a Lory and an Eaglet, and several other curious creatures" (*Alice*, p. 20); and even these instances can be explained in part as the insidious tendency of lists to become alliterative.

Nabokov, on the other hand, includes more alliteration, and the resemblances among his words are more likely to continue beyond the initial sounds to produce assonance and consonance.[11] In his rendition of "*Speak roughly to your little boy*," for instance, Nabokov concludes each verse with the words "*Bayushki bayu*" (roughly equivalent to "Hushaby, lullaby"), which are linked through both alliteration and assonance, and whose alliteration and assonance recall the "*pob'yu*" ("I will beat") and "*b'yu*" ("I beat") elsewhere in the verse (*Anya*, p. 53).[12] And in "The Lobster-Quadrille" Nabokov translates "*There's a porpoise close behind us*" (*Alice*, p. 79) as, roughly, "A cuttlefish rolls up from behind" in order to get "*Karakatitsa katitsya szadi*" (*Anya*, p. 90).

Furthermore, Nabokov's alliteration is not limited to his verse and dialogue. They do contain alliteration (the examples in the preceding paragraph are drawn from his verse), but so does the discursive text that surrounds them. In Nabokov's dialogue, "I never could abide figures!" (*Alice*, p. 48) becomes "Ya nik*ogd*a ne m*ogl*a vynosit' vychis*len'*ia!" (*Anya*, p. 53). And in Nabokov's narrative "she felt that she was losing her temper" (*Alice*, p. 41) becomes "ona *ch*uvstvovala, *ch*to *t*eryaet *t*erpen'e" (*Anya*, p. 44);[13] "a graceful zigzag" (*Alice*, p. 42) becomes "*iz*yashchnuyu *iz*vilinu" (*Anya*, p. 46); and "the roof was thatched with fur" (*Alice*, p. 53) becomes "*krysh*a byla *kry*ta *sh*erst'yu" (*Anya*, p. 58). More extended examples include Nabokov's translation of "in a deep, hollow tone" (*Alice*, p. 74) as "*glubo*kim, *gul*kim *golo*som" (*Anya*, p. 84); his translation of "in her haste, she had put the Lizard in head downwards" (*Alice*, p. 93) as "ona *v*popykhakh *v*tisnula *Yash*u-*Yash*cheritsu *v*niz golo*v*oy" (*Anya*, p. 106);[14] and his translation of "At this moment the door of the house opened, and a large plate came skimming out, straight at the Footman's head: it just grazed his nose, and broke to pieces against one of the trees behind him" (*Alice*, p. 46) as "Tut *dver'* *d*oma na mig raspakhnulas', i bol'shaya tarelka, vyletev ottuda, proneslas' dugoy nad samoy golovoy *la*keya, *leg*ko *ko*snuvshis' *kon*chi*ka* ego nosa, i razbilas' o *so*sedniy *st*vol" (*Anya*, p. 50).

Nabokov's alliteration is thus more extensive than Carroll's in two ways: it is more likely to include assonance and consonance, and it is less confined to verse and dialogue.[15] As a result, we are more conscious of the mediation of the narrator and of the ways in which he plays with words.

Another instance in which Nabokov focuses attention on words as words and on the narrator is his change of the Duchess' apothegm from "Take care of the sense, and the sounds will take care of themselves" (*Alice*, p. 71) to "slova est'—znachen'e temno il' nichtozhno" (*Anya*, p. 79), or, in Simon Karlinsky's translation, "There are words whose meaning is obscure or insignificant."[16] In other words, Nabokov reduces Carroll's emphasis on the "sense" or referential meaning and emphasizes the sounds, the words themselves.

Such tendencies are reinforced by other aspects of Nabokov's translation. We might look particularly at other ways in which Nabokov subtly makes the narrator more prominent. In Carroll's *Alice* we learn about Wonderland through the mediation of Alice's consciousness, as Walter de la Mare points out.[17] Carroll may not limit himself to Alice's consciousness as consistently as James does with some of his protagonists, but only rarely are we told something that Alice does not know: we are often told her thoughts, for instance, but rarely those of other characters. Carroll's narrator rarely expresses a point of view different from that of Alice, though he does intrude with his own perspective a few times near the beginning, when he is orienting us to her. Yet even then he sets off such comments as "Which was very likely true" (*Alice*, p. 8) and "she tried to curtsey as she spoke—fancy, *curtseying* as you're falling through the air! Do you think you could manage it?" (*Alice*, pp. 8–9) from the rest of the narrative by placing them in parentheses. At the very end, also, the narrator leaves Alice's consciousness and enters that of her sister, as he enlarges the spatial and temporal contexts of his story and returns to "reality."

The tendency of Nabokov's translation, on the other hand, is to blur Carroll's initial and final distinction between the narrator and the protagonist but at the same time to create new distinctions in the main body of the narrative. Nabokov does not radically alter the point of view: his *Anya* is still told largely from the perspective of the central character. And yet there is a tendency in Nabokov's version to de-emphasize the primacy of Alice's perspective by qualifying it with other points of view.

Nabokov's blurring of Carroll's demarcation between narrator and protagonist at the beginning and end of *Alice* can be illustrated by his handling of the phrases cited above. Carroll's "Which was very likely true" (*Alice*, p. 8) becomes "Eto uzhe, konechno" (*Anya*, p. 7), or roughly, "That is so, of course." The translation is not significantly different, but Nabokov encloses it within the quotation marks surrounding Anya's preceding thoughts and hence attributes it to Anya rather than to the narrator. In a similar vein, Nabokov reduces Carroll's "she tried to curtsey as she spoke—fancy, *curtseying* as you're falling through the air! Do you think you could manage it?" (*Alice*, pp. 8–9) to "Tut ona poprobovala prisest'—na vozdukhe-to!" (*Anya*, p. 7), or literally, "Then she tried to curtsey—in the air!" Nabokov does not completely omit the narrator's interjection, but he does omit some of the narrator's distinct personality. Similar examples occur near the end, when Carroll's narrator again becomes obtrusive. Carroll's text reads, for example, "So Alice got up and ran off, thinking while she ran, as well she might, what a wonderful dream it had been" (*Alice*, p. 98). Nabokov's translation omits the judgmental "as well she might" (*Anya*, p. 113).

After Carroll has distinguished between Alice and the narrator at the beginning of *Alice*, so that in effect the narrator introduces us to Alice, the two perspectives become very similar: the narrator's consciousness is virtually identical to Alice's. In *Anya*, on the other hand, the narrator is not given as distinct a voice at the beginning, so that his introductory role is minimized; and later in the book he tends to maintain more distance from his protagonist than Carroll's narrator does. When the Queen of Hearts orders her around, "Alice join[s] the procession, wondering very much what w[ill] happen next" (*Alice*, p. 65). In Nabokov's text, however, "wondering very much what w[ill] happen next" is entirely omitted (*Anya*, p. 72). Later, when the Mock Turtle tells Alice about the lessening of lessons, we are told, "This was quite a new idea to Alice, and she thought it over a little before she made her next remark" (*Alice*, p. 77). Nabokov's version, however, is simply "Anya podumala nad etim" (*Anya*, p. 87), or "Anya thought about this for a little while"— we do not explicitly learn that this is a new idea to her. Nabokov thus minimizes the extent to which his narrator enters Anya's mind.

On the other hand, Nabokov's narrator frequently enters the minds of other characters. For instance, Carroll's narrator describes the appearance of the Cheshire Cat from Alice's point of view: "The Cat seemed to think that there was enough of it now in sight" (*Alice*, p. 67). In Nabokov's version, however, we are told not what the Cat seems to think but what is actually going on in its mind: "Kot reshil, chto on teper' dostatochno na vidu" (*Anya*, p. 74), or roughly, "The Cat decided that it was now sufficiently visible." A similar example occurs earlier, when "the cook was busily stirring the soup, and seemed not to be listening" (*Alice*, p. 48). In Nabokov's rendering, "seemed not to be listening" becomes "was not listening" (*Anya*, p. 53). A final example occurs in Nabokov's version of the passage describing the jurors in the chapter entitled "Who Stole the Tarts?" Carroll tells us that "she could even make out that one of them didn't know how to spell 'stupid,' and that he had to ask his neighbour to tell him" (*Alice*, p. 87). Nabokov's version is "Kraynyy ne znal, kak pishetsya 'glupye,' i obratilsya k sosedu, ispuganno khlopaya glazami" (*Anya*, p. 99), or roughly, "The last one did not know how to write 'stupid,' and with a startled, blank look turned to his neighbor." Nabokov describes the juror as being startled and also omits the reference to Alice's perspective in "she could even make out," thereby doubly minimizing the alliance between the narrator's consciousness and Anya's.

Thus Nabokov does not, like Carroll, first establish credibility for Alice's perspective and then work almost entirely within it. Instead, Nabokov's translation tends to blur Carroll's initial and final distinctions between Alice and the narrator, only to undermine our reliance on Alice's point of view in other sections of the narrative. Through this slight alteration in point of view, Nabokov eliminates some of Alice's function as the realistic norm in a fantastic world. What happens in *Anya* is that Nabokov harries the boundaries between the fantastic and the realistic, allowing fantasy to assault "reality," and the de-emphasis on Alice's "realistic" normative perspective is one part of this. As Nabokov himself has pointed out, "If read very carefully, [Carroll's *Alice*] will be seen to imply, by humorous juxtaposition, the presence of a quite solid, and rather sentimental, world, behind the semi-detached dream."[18] In his translation, however, that too solid and sentimental world has begun to melt.

Another instance in which Carroll maintains the boundaries and underscores the difference between Alice's "real" world and Wonderland occurs when she responds to the Caterpillar's question, "Who are *you*?" with "I—I hardly know, Sir, just at present—at least I know who I *was* when I got up this morning, but I think I must have been changed several times since then" (*Alice*, p. 35). In the "real" world, in other words, Carroll's Alice has a stable identity, and it is only in Wonderland that she begins to question it. Nabokov's translation of Alice's response, however, is "Ya . . . ya ne sovsem tochno znayu, kem ya byla, kogda vstala utrom, a krome togo c tekh por ya neskol'ko raz 'menialas'" (*Anya*, p. 39, ellipsis in original), or roughly, "I . . . I am not entirely sure who I was when I got up this morning, and furthermore since that time I have 'changed' several times." Nabokov's Anya, in short, does not even have a stable identity in the "real" world, for she is unsure as to her identity when she got up that morning.[19] Thus, much as Anya's reduced normative function allows for greater merging of the "real" world and the fantasy world, so too does Anya's uncertain memory of her identity.

Another realistic norm which Nabokov minimizes is Carroll's precise specifications of Alice's height at various times in Wonderland. These specifications serve to orient us and give us a clear idea of how the world of Wonderland compares to the "real" world. Nabokov simply omits many of these specifications.[20] Nabokov may tell us, as Carroll does, that her head struck the ceiling (*Anya*, p. 14), but he entirely omits "in fact she was now rather more than nine feet high" (*Alice*, p. 15); Nabokov may tell us that she measured herself against the table and found herself lower than it (*Anya*, p. 16), but he omits that she "found that, as nearly as she could guess, she was now about two feet high" (*Alice*, p. 18). Nabokov also omits heights when Alice raises herself to about two feet high in order to visit the March Hare (*Alice*, p. 53; *Anya*, p. 58); when she makes herself about a foot high in order to enter the Queen's garden (*Alice*, p. 61; *Anya*, p. 67); and when the Queen claims that Alice is nearly two miles high (*Alice*, p. 93; *Anya*, p. 108).

Heights are not the only numbers with which Nabokov plays in his translation. When he changes other numbers, he tends to make ordered numbers more random and unrelated numbers related. The verse that Carroll's King attributes to the Knave contains the lines "*I gave her one, they gave him two, / You gave us three or more*" (*Alice*, p. 95), which corresponds to Nabokov's "Ya dal ey sem', emuzhe desyat', / On ey—chetyre ili pyat'" (*Anya*, p. 110), or "I gave her seven, [I gave] him ten, / He [gave] her four or five." Nabokov thus introduces greater randomness into phrases that Carroll has ordered by numerical progression. Nabokov also subtracts a referential ordering principle when he completely omits "There was no 'One, two, three, and away!'" at the start of the Caucus-race (*Alice*, p. 23; *Anya*, p. 24). Carroll's reminder of the lack of this ordering principle in the race serves as a realistic standard, like Alice's specified heights, against which the events of Wonderland should be measured. Nabokov, as usual, does not care to remind us of any presumably more ordered and "normal" phase of existence, as if to suggest that "real" life is never really that ordered.

Besides making ordered numbers more random (when they are not omitted altogether), Nabokov also tends to relate numbers that are otherwise unrelated.[21] When Carroll's jury writes down three dates—the fourteenth, fifteenth, and sixteenth of March—then adds them up, they "reduced the answer to shillings and pence" (*Alice*, p.

88). Nabokov, for once, actually adds a number to the text at this point, for his jury specifically comes up with the wrong answer—forty-four kopeks (*Anya*, p. 101). Later, Carroll's King invokes Rule Forty-two (*Alice*, p. 93), while Nabokov's invokes Rule Forty-four (*Anya*, p. 108). The kopeks and the rule number should, in "realistic" terms, be quite unrelated, but Nabokov gives each the same arbitrary number, as if to suggest that the true ordering principles in the world are not the agreed-upon ones, that the only possible order in the natural world is "topsy-turvical coincidence," or paradoxically, artistry:

> Some kind of link-and-bobolink, some kind
> Of correlated pattern in the game,
> Plexed artistry . . .[22]

Nabokov thus rearranges numbers to undermine traditional conceptions of order and to suggest that perhaps the only possible orderings are seemingly accidental coincidences or artistic re-orderings. In other respects, too, he impugns the existence of traditional order and absolutes and asserts relativity instead. Carroll's Mock Turtle tells Alice, "Ah! Then yours wasn't a really good school" (*Alice*, p. 76), while Nabokov's Mock Turtle is more relative: he tells Anya that her school is not as good as his (*Anya*, p. 85). Likewise, after hearing the verse about the Owl and the Panther, Carroll's Mock Turtle exclaims, "It's by far the most confusing thing that *I* ever heard!" (*Alice*, p. 84). Nabokov's Mock Turtle, on the other hand, omits the superlative and simply exclaims, "It is such a puzzle!" (*Anya*, p. 95). Finally, we might note that both Carroll and Nabokov refer their readers to an illustration to see how the King of Hearts manages to wear his crown over his wig; Carroll then goes on to suggest that "it was certainly not becoming" (*Alice*, p. 86), while Nabokov invites his readers to decide for themselves how well it became the judge (*Anya*, p. 99).

Perhaps Nabokov's change of the chapter title "The Queen's Croquet-Ground" to "Koroleva igraet v kroket," or "The Queen Plays Croquet," has a similar basis. Nabokov places less emphasis on the "absolute" of location in space and more on the activity undertaken, because in a world of relativity an activity may be more knowable than a location indicated by external coordinates. Analogously, when Alice interrupts the Dormouse's story by objecting that treacle-wells do not exist, Carroll's Alice finally tries to mollify the Dormouse by admitting, "I dare say there may be *one*" (*Alice*, p. 59). Nabokov's Anya, on the other hand, says, "Pozhaluysta, khot' kakoy-nibud' razskaz!" (*Anya*, p. 65) or roughly, "Let's please have at least some kind of story!" Nabokov shifts the emphasis from the possibility of the "real" existence of something to the possibility of an admitted artifice, the story.

Nabokov thus tends throughout his translation to de-emphasize absolutes, to admit greater relativity, and to emphasize words as words and narrative as narrative. Without radically altering Carroll's book, Nabokov nonetheless uses his translation as a vehicle for his own style and vision. In Nabokov's Wonderland, fantasy is kept less firmly in its place as something to be carefully differentiated from and excluded from "reality," something which creatures from "reality" can invade and then leave with impunity. Instead, the assault on Wonderland triggers a reciprocal assault on "reality," making it relative, making it fantastic. In many ways, then, *Anya* is a proleptic reflection of Nabokov's later work, an intimation of the fantasy worlds of Humberland, Zembla, and Antiterra.

NOTES

1. Nabokov, *Strong Opinions*, p. 242.
2. Andrew Field quotes Nabokov as saying of his *Alice* translation, "It is not a very good translation, I'm afraid, except those bits of poetry. The prose is a little stilted" (*Nabokov: His Life in Part*, p. 240). Nabokov has also said, "How much better I could have done it fifteen years later! The only good bits are the poems and the word-play" (*Strong Opinions*, p. 286).
3. Simon Karlinsky, "Anya in Wonderland: Nabokov's Russified Lewis Carroll," in *Nabokov*, ed. Appel and Newman, pp. 310–15. See also Warren Weaver, *Alice in Many Tongues: The Translations of "Alice in Wonderland"* (Madison: University of Wisconsin Press, 1964), pp. 90–91, and Jane Grayson, *Nabokov Translated*, pp. 19–21.
4. Karlinsky, "Anya in Wonderland," p. 312.
5. Charles Dodgson [Lewis Carroll], *Alice in Wonderland: Authoritative Texts of "Alice's Adventures in Wonderland," "Through the Looking-Glass," "The Hunting of the Snark," Backgrounds, Essays in Criticism*, ed. Donald J. Gray (New York: Norton, 1971), p. 20. Hereafter cited in text. All parenthetical references to *Alice* are to this edition, including citations of *Through the Looking-Glass and What Alice Found There*. All italics are Carroll's unless otherwise indicated.
6. Vladimir Nabokov [V. Sirin], trans., *Anya v stranye chudes*, by Charles Dodgson [Lewis Carroll], p. 19. Hereafter cited in text.
7. The Russian is *Maslyanichnyy Kot* (*Anya*, p. 51 et passim). It derives from the Russian proverb, "Ne vse kotu maslyanitsa, budet i velikiy post," which translates roughly as "It is not always carnival time for a cat, [for] Lent too will come," or more generally, "Good things don't last forever."

8. Karlinsky, "Anya in Wonderland," p. 315, n. 6; "Publisher's Note," in *Anya*, p. 2.

9. The unstressed vowels *e* and *i* sound very similar, and for our purposes the difference can be ignored.

10. N. V. Gogol, "Zapiski sumasshedshego," in *Povesti*, introduction by Vladimir Nabokov [V. Sirin] (New York: Chekhov, 1952), p. 59. Italics Gogol's. I am indebted to Patricia Arant for pointing out the allusion to me.

11. This playing with sounds is a tendency that continues in Nabokov's more recent fiction, as Carl R. Proffer demonstrates in *Keys to "Lolita,"* pp. 81–119, and as Jane Grayson demonstrates in her discussion of Nabokov's translations of his earlier Russian work into English (*Nabokov Translated*, pp. 52, 63 et passim).

12. To highlight the sound instrumentation I have italicized individual letters in these and subsequent quotations from the Russian.

13. Although the *ch* sounds in *chuvstvovala* and *chto* are not identical, there is at least visual alliteration here, if not aural alliteration.

14. Nabokov's inclusion of the Lizard's name *Yasha*—while Carroll omits the corresponding name Bill—reminds us that Nabokov tends to let names be determined by their sounds. He replaces Bill with *Yasha* because of the similarity of *Yasha* to *Yashcheritsa*, or Lizard. Likewise, Alice, Ada, and Mabel become Anya, Ada, and Asya, while Elsie, Lacie, and Tillie (*Alice*, p. 58) become Masya, Pasya, and Dasya (*Anya*, p. 64). Carroll's closest approach to letting sound influence naming in *Alice* is his use of the alliterative "Fish-Footman" and "Frog-Footman"; even the Tweedles and Humpty Dumpty in *Through the Looking-Glass* have the names they have because of their nursery-rhyme derivations, not because of Carroll's playful naming.

15. In examining Nabokov's changes I have tried to avoid instances of added wordplay which could be attributed to differences between Russian and English. Because of the inflected nature of Russian, for instance, many word endings are similar simply because the words are in the same case. In the previously cited "glubokim gulkim golosom," the similarity of the final *im*'s and *om* is due simply to the use of the instrumental case. The ubiquity of prefixes in Russian may also make it easier for Nabokov to repeat the initial sounds of words, but he still needs to make the choice to alliterate when he decides to juxtapose words like *vynosit'* and *vychislen'ya* or *sosedniy* and *stvol* (choosing *stvol* over *derevo*, the more common translation of "tree"). For general discussions of the influence of Russian on Nabokov's style, and of differences between Russian and English, see William Woodin Rowe, *Nabokov's Deceptive World*, pp. 21–48, and Jane Grayson, *Nabokov Translated*, pp. 182–212. See also Nabokov's postscript to his Russian translation of *Lolita*, pp. 296–97 (translated in its entirety later in this book).

16. This line is, as Karlinsky points out ("Anya in Wonderland," p. 313), reminiscent of a poem by Lermontov (see M. Yu. Lermontov, *Stikhot-*

voreniya 1832–1841, vol. 2 of *Sochineniya v shesti tomakh* [Moscow: Akademiya Nauk, 1954], p. 144].

17. Walter de la Mare, *Lewis Carroll* (London: Faber, 1932), p. 55.
18. Nabokov, *Strong Opinions*, p. 184.
19. Earlier Carroll hints that Alice doubts that she was quite the same that morning, for Alice wonders, "Dear, dear! How queer everything is to-day! And yesterday things went on just as usual. I wonder if I've changed in the night? Let me think: was I the same when I got up this morning? I almost think I can remember feeling a little different" [*Alice*, p. 15]. Yet Alice is simply speculating here, and later when talking to the Caterpil-lar she asserts that she knew who she was that morning—and presum-ably was the same as she had been the day before—instead of believing, like Anya, that she has indeed changed before entering Wonderland.
20. This is despite Nabokov's own strong interest in specificity. His fantas-tic worlds are usually rich in precisely specified details. Even elsewhere in his *Alice* translation Nabokov adds many details to Carroll's descrip-tions. (Although Nabokov also omits some details, the balance of change is in favor of additions.) The White Rabbit's house in Nabokov's translation, for example, has acquired blue wallpaper [*Anya*, p. 30; see *Alice*, p. 27]; the elbow Anya props against the door is specified as her left elbow [*Anya*, p. 31; see *Alice*, p. 28]; the puppy's tongue is specified as being crimson [*Anya*, p. 38; see *Alice*, p. 33]; the King's crown on its crimson cushion is described as ruby [*Anya*, p. 70; see *Alice*, p. 63]; and the Mock Turtle draws his breath, in Nabokov's version, with a whistle [*Anya*, p. 93; see *Alice*, p. 82]. All this suggests that Nabokov's omission of height specifications, because it is in opposition to his usual ten-dency, is significant.
21. This is a tendency in Nabokov's other fiction as well. As L. L. Lee notes in "Vladimir Nabokov's Great Spiral of Being," *Western Humanities Re-view* 18 (1964), 231, Nabokov's numbers "are not magic numbers, sym-bolic numbers, but connectives, linking this to that."
22. Nabokov, *Pale Fire*, p. 63.

The Conjuror in "The Potato Elf"

WALTER EVANS

The first of Nabokov's stories published in an American magazine (*Esquire*, December 1939), "The Potato Elf" or "Kartofel'nyy el'f" was originally written in Russian in 1929.[1] Andrew Field considers the story not merely a "masterpiece" but Nabokov's "greatest short story"; yet his description of the conjuror Shock as a "sorrowful and even tragic figure" suggests that Field misinterprets that character's role in the story, picturing him much more as a victim of fate or of the potato elf than Nabokov ever does.[2] Marina Turkevich Naumann clearly errs in depicting Shock as a godlike presence exercising "supernatural" powers over life and death (even Shock's wife Nora never draws such a conclusion) and in treating the piece primarily as "a love story."[3] William Woodin Rowe's treatment combines plot summary with sex-symbol-mongering[4] and has been specifically discredited by Nabokov himself.[5]

These critics respond with a proper enthusiasm for the story's bizarre power but finally give Nabokov and the story too little credit: a masterpiece by Nabokov, one featuring a magician or conjuror at that, could hardly be as superficial, as barren of interesting games and compelling manipulations as these critics imply. They not only seriously misunderstand the plot: they miss Nabokov's point. Fortunately, Nabokov reveals his intentions rather clearly in certain passages of the story and also in some details that distinguish the story's first translation (by Serge Bertenson and Irene Kosinska), which Nabokov felt "betrayed" him, from his own later Englished version: "retranslating it properly is a precious personal victory that seldom falls to a betrayed author's lot."[6] For example, a native speaker of English would be tempted to use more or less synonymously the words "magician" (employed throughout the first translation) and "conjuror" (Nabokov's own consistent choice). But those careful of their diction—and non-native speakers who consult a dictionary—will be aware of a slight but crucial distinction. In addition to the general connotations of magic and legerdemain and sleight-of-hand, the word "conjure" means "to summon a demon, spirit, etc. by a magic spell" (Second College Edition of *Webster's New World Dictionary*). In substituting "conjuror" for "magician" in his own translation of the story, Nabokov deliberately emphasizes this mysterious character's creative power to "conjure up" rather than merely manipulate.

All this is essentially irrelevant to the interpretations of critics like Rowe and Field and Naumann; one infers that so far as they are concerned the conjuror might as well have been a milliner or bee-keeper or librarian. They see him as a wronged husband, innocently betrayed by his wife and his friend, faking suicide (or in Naumann's remarkably naive reading, returning from death's threshold) for some sort of bizarre revenge on his wife, arranging—apparently out of sheer coincidence—to leave England for America immediately after the adultery. Nonsense. Nabokov develops his characters much more carefully than that.

Nabokov constantly represents the conjuror in this story as a figure of power and control. For example, he repeatedly compares Shock to a poet and his conjuring to poetry: "He resembled a poet more than a stage magician" (p. 223); he is rumored to compose "lyrical poems" (Shock denies the rumor); and his wife understands that "conjuror Shock was, in his own way, a poet" (p. 227). For Nabokov, the artist is preeminently the one who orders or controls, who employs illusions intelligently to manipulate an audience for some purposeful effect. In the story Shock unambiguously earns his title of artist generally and of conjuror specifically.

Let us consider the story carefully before continuing to generalize about it. The brief first paragraph introduces the dwarf Fred Dobson, whose stage name is the Potato Elf, and his friend and partner, the conjuror Shock. The second paragraph foreshadows the story's central episode—in fact, it would seem, Dobson's monologue here provides the inspiration which Shock's fertile mind seizes on as the basis for his most successful bit of conjuring: " 'a few months before I was born, my gin-soaked dad rigged up one of those wax-work cherubs, you know—sailor suit, with a lad's first long trousers—and put it in my mother's bed. It's a wonder the poor thing did not have a miscarriage. . . . this is, apparently, the secret reason I am—' " (p. 221). Fred thus ascribes his dwarfishness to the trauma caused his pregnant mother by his father's trick with a dummy. The much more artful Shock conspires a similar trick, only the boy-sized creature he maneuvers into his wife's bed is alive and the result quite different.

Fred, "the virginal dwarf," is bedeviled by lust. In the second paragraph of the story's second section Shock tells him: "What you need is a female dwarf" (p. 224). Apparently none is immediately available, but in the following paragraph, as Fred passes by the door to the female acrobats' room, the two women "both half-undressed" teasingly invite him in. Moments later Fred, "empurpled with lust, rolled like a ball in the embrace of the bare-armed teases" (p. 225). The acrobats' male partner unexpectedly appears and "silently, without any resentment," throws Fred out. Whom does Fred encounter but "Shock, who happened to be wandering past"? Perhaps all this is coincidence, but the next step can hardly be. "'Bad luck, old boy,'" Shock sighs. "'I told you not to butt in. Now you got it. A dwarf woman is what you need.'" Wheels turn in Shock's head, and he immediately announces: "'You'll sleep at my place to-night'" (p. 225) —a curious choice of words when we realize Fred does "sleep" in the conjuror's "place," that is, with Nora.

Shock's wife, Nora, is, if not physically dwarfish, certainly spiritually so. The daughter of a "respectable" hack artist of conventionally realistic paintings, Nora is "of uncertain age," skinny, untidy, lifeless, altogether the sort of woman who "could hardly attract many men" (p. 226). Shock presents Fred to Nora as if he were a child and tersely announces: "Must be adopted" (p. 228). Careless readers may assume this is Shock's practical joke, as Nora seems to: "'I'm not so easy to fool,' she sneered." But the masterful conjuror Nabokov has created could hardly stoop to a trick so obvious, petty, unimaginative, and easily foiled. That evening Nora mothers Fred, picturing in him the son whom Shock, or God, or Nature, or Nabokov has denied her. The next morning: "With an abstract smile Mr. Shock left for an unknown destination" (p. 229). The conjuror, so alive to both Fred's needs and his wife's, abandons them to human nature, which follows its course.

That afternoon Fred visits a cafe "where all kinds of performers gathered" (p. 233) and there encounters Shock, "who never frequented taverns" (pp. 233–34). Pure coincidence? That depends on one's frame of reference. Fred decides to confess everything, but before he can begin Shock announces to his partner, friend, "adoptee": "By the way, tonight I appear together with you for the last time. That chap is taking me to America. Things look pretty good" (p. 235).

Why should Shock, who has in the last few hours shown such a solicitous concern for his partner, at this point (he hasn't seen Nora since leaving that morning) abruptly announce his departure for America? Because Shock already knows what Dobson now incoherently tries to explain to him: "Be brave, Shock. I love your wife. This morning, after you left, she and I, we two, I mean, she—." Shock seems to pay absolutely no attention, wanders into anecdote, then back to the topic: "You were about to tell me something, my little friend?" (p. 235). Did Shock miss the point? That's hard to believe of one who elsewhere exercises such masterful control, one who even when "immersed in astral fancies" is always "keenly observing everything around him" (p. 226). It's much easier to believe that here as throughout the story Shock has anticipated the other's action, remains perfectly in control, and is carefully creating precisely the effect he desires.

The following scene opens with Nora alone. We learn first that she feels contempt for "the dwarf," next that she imagines the secret of her adultery will for the first time give her power over the superior husband she has begun to resent almost to the point of hatred. Shock arrives and she considers him, gloating: "With grim pleasure she thought, 'Ah, if you only knew. You'll never find out. That's my power!'" (p. 238). Here, incidentally, we clearly glimpse one of the story's and Nabokov's major themes—the awesome power residing in manipulation of illusion.

Shock's oneupmanship continues, however. He convinces the initially quite skeptical Nora that he's in the last throes of a suicide by poison, and this "shock" coincides with her "shock" of recognition that, after all, she profoundly loves her husband. After screaming into the telephone for a doctor, she discovers the immaculate Shock before a mirror, methodically arranging "the black ends of his silk bow" (p. 240). She's been tricked again.

Next we discover Fred, eight years later, having retired to rural England. The pain of unrequited love has finally numbed; he suffers a few heart attacks; he lives anonymously, unseen by the villagers except when disguised as a child in his occasional nighttime rambles. Suddenly Nora appears alone at the door, in a black gown, veiled. His affection completely dissipated over the years, Fred regretfully believes she must have come to renew their affair, but she has appeared for a different purpose (p. 248, ellipsis in original):

> It was then that she told him in a very soft voice:
> "The fact is I had a son from you."
> The dwarf froze, his gaze fixing a minuscule casement burning on the side of a dark blue cup. A timid smile of amazement flashed at the corners of his lips, then it spread and lit up his cheeks with a purplish flush.
> "My . . . son . . ."
> And all at once he understood everything, all the meaning

of life, of his long anguish, of the little bright window upon the cup.

She tells him the child is normal. When he asks to see the boy, she agrees but abruptly insists she must catch a train, and leaves. Heart swelling, Fred tries to imagine his son, and solely by this act of imagining (his own conjuring), "by the act of transferring his own aspect onto his boy, he ceased to feel that he was a dwarf" (p. 249).

Abruptly realizing he's without Nora's new address, Fred quickly dresses to go out—for the first time in many years as a man, not as a mock boy—and, vainly "trying to forget the heart breaking his chest with a burning ram" (p. 250), runs after Nora, pursued by a swelling mob of mocking boys and townspeople (p. 251):

> She looked back, she stopped. The dwarf reached her and clutched at the folds of her skirt.
> With a smile of happiness he glanced up at her, attempted to speak, but instead raised his eyebrows in surprise and collapsed in slow motion on the sidewalk.

Nora, however, regards his corpse almost indifferently: "'Leave me alone,' said Nora in a toneless voice. 'I don't know anything. My son died a few days ago.'"

A masterful story—throughout it Nabokov impresses us with the fact that he himself as artist functions as the master conjuror, the final source of power (which Nora explicitly identifies with deception) and of "shock." The character Nabokov most closely associates with artfully controlled illusion and with the creative use of "fiction" is the conjuror, who at first appears intentionally cruel. He seems to show contempt for both the adult dwarf and the childless Nora in introducing Fred as a candidate for adoption, later pretends not to comprehend Fred's attempted confession of the adultery Shock himself manipulates, and with the fake suicide drives Nora to hysteria.

Yet, viewed from another perspective, the conjuror's imaginative, creative use of illusion results in enormous boons for those he manipulates. Apparently potent only in the world of imagination and appearances, Shock has not physically produced a child for his frustrated wife, but his tricks finally result in one. What is to be valued more than life? Love? The false suicide "shocks" Nora into comprehending "that she loved him more than anything in the world" (p. 240).

Fred, quite as frustrated as Nora, benefits from Shock's manipulations in achieving the bliss life has so far denied him—not only sexual intercourse but also a love for Nora which "shocks" him out of a narrow, if understandable, egotism. What could be more important than such love? Perhaps a sense of human dignity. The conjuror's manipulations "shock" Fred out of his dehumanizing life as a sideshow freak. As he writes to Nora: "Now you understand why I cannot continue to live as before. What feelings would you experience knowing that every evening the common herd rocks with laughter at the sight of your chosen one?" (p. 236).

A longed-for child, love, human dignity—close analysis reveals the almost divine benevolence of Shock's manipulations of imagination, conjuring up for these characters what a comparatively sterile reality has denied them.

"The Potato Elf" celebrates the creative manipulation of the imagination, but Nabokov clearly denies that trickery is a panacea, deception a utopia. "Practice no hurtful deception," counseled Ben Franklin. Nabokov represents as ugly, and as properly frustrated, Nora's intention secretly to triumph over the conjuror through the power she gains in deceiving him with the potato elf ("You'll never find out. That's my power!"). We should condemn her here, but Nabokov leads us to judge otherwise of Nora's impulsive attempt (she arrives dressed in mourning) to deceive Fred into believing his son still lives. Nora's final conversion to creative and benevolent employment of illusion seems a great moral triumph.

What of Frederick Dobson, the potato elf himself? Fred too practices deception, hiding himself away in the daytime pretending to be a normally proportioned invalid, then occasionally donning a wig and child's clothes to circulate in the village in darkness. The conjuror has allowed Fred to leave a painful life in "reality," to dream, to retire to Drowse (the unsubtly chosen name of the village in which Fred locates), there to play games of chess with Dr. Knight. The conjuror's manipulations have lent Fred a courage and a sense of human dignity which enable him to avoid ridicule and to lead a life he has freely chosen. Admittedly, the illusion's success prevents him from penetrating his pervasive loneliness and forming meaningful human attachments, but Nabokov keeps reminding the reader of Fred's imperfect heart (angina pectoris, p. 243). The inevitable stimulation of attachments in the "real" world must carry an enormous threat to his life.

Nabokov dramatically ascribes the potato elf's climactic death not to illusion but to a surfeit of reality—perhaps more precisely a final refusal to remain in the benevolent realm of imagination. Fred expires because of a fatal compulsion wholeheartedly to embrace reality. Illusion showers Fred with benefits life otherwise denies him.

But Fred literally destroys himself in refusing to be satisfied, in attempting to "realize" (make real) his now purely illusory child. Heart and life both fail when he madly pursues the dark chimaera of reality—Nora suitably garbed in mourning—into alien daylit streets mobbed with ridicule and contempt.

So we have finally, in "The Potato Elf," not a conventional fiction in which "the major theme is a love story" but a Nabokovian masterpiece in which the major themes are conjuring, illusion, imagination, and the distinction between sterile reality and fertile illusion. Nabokov is the ultimate conjuror, and the story brilliantly celebrates the creative virtue inherent in such conjuring.

NOTES

1. To quote from Nabokov's introduction to the story in *A Russian Beauty and Other Stories*: "This is the first faithful translation of 'Kartofel'nyy el'f,' written in 1929 in Berlin, published there in the émigré daily *Rul* (December 15, 17, 18, and 19, 1929) and included in *Vozvrashchenie Chorba*, Slovo, Berlin, 1930, a collection of my stories. A very different English version (by Serge Bertenson and Irene Kosinska), full of mistakes and omissions, appeared in *Esquire*, December, 1939, and has been reprinted in an anthology (*The Single Voice*, Collier, London, 1969)" (p. 220). The last-mentioned book, edited by Jerome Charyn, was published in America in the same year by Collier Books in New York.
2. Andrew Field, *Nabokov: His Life in Art*, pp. 147, 104, 252.
3. Marina Turkevich Naumann, *Blue Evenings in Berlin*, pp. 139, 137.
4. William Woodin Rowe, *Nabokov's Deceptive World*, pp. 76–78.
5. Nabokov, *Strong Opinions*, pp. 304–7.
6. Nabokov, *A Russian Beauty*, p. 220. Hereafter cited in text.

The Cartesian Nightmare of *Despair*

WILLIAM C. CARROLL

For all its baroque modernity, its arch allusiveness, its fashionably shifting relationships among author, narrator, reader, and character, *Despair* succeeds largely because of its old-fashioned virtue: the creation of a concretely realized world of intriguing interest.

What is peculiar and unique about *Despair* is the nature of this world, and the methods by which the reader, as opposed to the main character, apprehends it: "The dogs are barking. I am cold. That mortal inextricable pain . . . Pointed with his stick. Stick. What words can be twisted out of 'stick'? Sick, tick, kit, it, is, ski, skit, sit. Abominably cold. Dogs barking: one of them begins and then all the others join in. It is raining. The electric lights here are wan, yellow. What on earth have I done?"[1] These are the rhythms of madness —non-sequiturs, compulsive repetitions, disintegrating linguistic identities, words as fluid and formless as the self, an alienation so profound as to provoke wonder. These rhythms operate from the first paragraph, and eventually dominate the book. After all, this novel is narrated by a madman, one of the first of the series of such narrators Nabokov has bequeathed to posterity.

In 1937, the émigré poet and critic Vladislav Khodasevich described *Despair* as "one of Sirin's [Nabokov's pen name] best novels."[2] He was referring to the first version of the novel, *Otchayanie*, written in Russian in 1932 and serialized in 1934; it was later transmuted into English by Nabokov in 1936 and published in London in 1937. The second and final English version, published in 1966 with considerable revisions,[3] is my text here; it has garnered the praise of Andrew Field: "measured against the outstanding fiction of this century, it is a major novel."[4] But *Despair* as we now have it has not enjoyed the popularity of Nabokov's best work. Too often regarded as an anticipation of *Lolita*, it suffers by comparison.

Despair seems to me not only one of Nabokov's best novels but, after *Pale Fire*, his most bizarre. This weirdness does not reside merely in the overt plot, or in the "real" plot behind the "obvious" one,[5] but in the secondary details, the nuances of Hermann's world —the melting shapes, ominous conspiracies, unlocalized itchings— which constitute the originality and genius of this novel. Nabokov reifies insanity as no one else ever has. *Despair* represents an important stage in his long exploration of paranoia and the more extreme forms of lunacy.

Hermann is a spectacularly unreliable narrator. We are duped on the second page of the novel when Hermann describes his parents' noble background. A paragraph later he confesses that the "bit about my mother was a deliberate lie. In reality, she was a woman of the people, simple and coarse, sordidly dressed in a kind of blouse hanging loose at the waist. I could, of course, have crossed it out, but I purposely leave it there as a sample of one of my essential traits: my light-hearted, inspired lying" (p. 14). Given this early admission, we must be unusually cautious readers, but we need not go so far as Stephen Suagee, who feels that the "more drastic instances of delusion . . . totally discredit Hermann as a reporter," and concludes, "in the end, we cannot decide what is real and what unreal."[6] What "really" happens is less important than what Hermann believes has happened, and if we are cast adrift with few external bearings, it isn't the only time in Nabokov.

We might best proceed by considering two related aspects of the novel which help create its particular symbolic world: the ironic allusions and the "philosophical" issues openly raised by Hermann. Literary allusions lace through all of Nabokov's novels, helping form the unusual geography of their symbolic worlds. But simply to identify such an allusion in Nabokov, especially in *Despair*, is only half of a difficult battle; an understanding of the allusion's full context proves equally necessary. Several complex allusions serve *Despair*, creating a pervasive if inconsistent irony that envelops and eventually strangles its narrator. Pushkin, Gogol, Turgenev, Dostoevsky, Wilde, and Conan Doyle—forces as "real" as the weather—haunt the text and continually betray Hermann.

First, as always, there is Pushkin. Clarence Brown has brilliantly demonstrated how "Pushkin is Nabokov's Fate,"[7] and we can argue in turn that Hermann's fate is Pushkin's. Nabokov obligingly invokes Pushkin in the foreword, where he tells us that "the lines and fragments of lines Hermann mutters in Chapter Four come from Pushkin's short poem addressed to his wife in the eighteen-thirties" (p. 9). He then translates it for us (p. 10, ellipsis in original):

'Tis time, my dear, 'tis time. The heart demands repose.
Day after day flits by, and with each hour there goes

A little bit of life; but meanwhile you and I
Together plan to dwell . . . yet lo! 'tis then we die.
There is no bliss on earth: there's peace and freedom, though.
An enviable lot I long have yearned to know:
Long have I, weary slave, been contemplating flight
To a remote abode of work and pure delight.

A knowledge of Pushkin's fate, just a few years after writing this poem, and of the degree of his wife's responsibility (not to mention her general attitude toward his art), immediately reveals a parallel with Hermann's fate—his wife is deceiving him, disaster overtakes him, his art goes unappreciated by her because she prefers Ardalion's portraits. The shared "remote abode" eludes Hermann as it did Pushkin.

Hermann first quotes the lines a few days before 1 October, when he will meet Felix in Tarnitz. Lydia remarks that it is autumn, that it must be lovely in Russia now. Hermann then begins to recite from the poem in a disconnected manner while Lydia continues to talk about Ardalion (pp. 72–73). Thus Nabokov sharpens the analogy between these two "artists" with unfaithful wives. But the analogy takes on a different irony with Hermann's next admission: "Now, I want to be quite frank: I did not experience any special craving for a rest; but latterly such had become the standing topic between me and my wife. Barely did we find ourselves alone than with blunt obstinacy I turned the conversation towards 'the abode of pure delight'—as that Pushkin poem has it" (p. 73). This admission may be part of some game Hermann conducts with his wife. Throughout the novel, he reveals an obtuseness to her infidelity that borders on the subhuman, yet there are frequent hints that he knows but cannot admit the truth. He recalls that in school, "when rendering 'in my own words' the plot of *Othello* (which was, mind you, perfectly familiar to me) I made the Moor skeptical and Desdemona unfaithful" (p. 56). (Carl Proffer has pointed out that *Otchayanie* has a comparably twisted allusion to Pushkin's story "The Shot" in place of the *Othello* reference.)[8] Felix asks Hermann, "could you name a single [woman] who did not deceive her husband?" (p. 86), and, upon assuming Felix's identity, Hermann parrots the idea: "show me one wife who is true" (p. 185). Quoting the Pushkin poem seems to be a covert admission by Hermann that something is wrong.

As usual, Nabokov has not quite told the whole story in his foreword, for the poem continues to echo in the novel beyond chapter 4. In chapter 7, Hermann and Ardalion have a nervous conversation in which Ardalion senses Hermann's knowledge of his affair with Hermann's wife, even though Hermann still seems to remain obtuse. Hermann's offer to finance a trip to Italy, one remote abode at least, is taken by Ardalion as an attempt to buy him off: "'Oh, drop it, Hermann Karlovich,' said he, using for the first time, I think, my name and patronymic. 'You quite understand what I'm driving at. Lend me two hundred fifty marks, or make it dollars, and I'll pray for your soul in all the Florentine churches'" (p. 138). When Hermann apparently doesn't understand, Ardalion risks suggesting that Lydia go along with him. With the subject of his wife's relation to Ardalion brought forth again, Hermann quotes once more from the Pushkin poem: "Maybe she'll come later on. Maybe we'll both come. Long have I, weary slave, been planning my escape to the far land of art and the translucent grape" (p. 139). Finally, when explaining to Lydia about his long-lost "brother," Hermann again lapses into echoing and now undermining Pushkin: "also I'm sick of everything and yearn for a remote land, where I'll devote myself to contemplation and poultry breeding" (p. 151). The invocation has become virtually automatic, but not as irrelevant as Hermann claims it is.

Allusions to other works by Pushkin operate in the same way. Earlier in the lengthy conversation with Ardalion, Hermann says, "An artist cannot live without mistresses and cypresses, as Pushkin says somewhere or should have said" (p. 136). The idea of the artist's mistress is appropriate enough here, but Hermann has also recognized a pun that Pushkin once employed in *Onegin's Journey*—"cypress" is also "cypris," a euphemism for venereal disease.[9] Later, filled with pride over his artistic murder, boasting of his powers, Hermann says, "Things that pass are treasured later, as the poet sang. One fine day at last Lydia joined me abroad" (p. 188). Lydia, of course, never joins him, and Hermann soon admits that his epilogue is another fantasy of impossible wish-fulfillment. Moreover, the line he quotes, from an untitled poem by Pushkin, is slightly misleading out of context. I quote from Arndt's "linear" version:

If life deceives you,
Do not sorrow, do not rage!
On the day of grief submit:
The day of joy, believe, will come.

In the future lives the heart;
[If] the present is dismal,
All is momentary, all will pass;
What has passed, will be dear.[10]

It is a conventional sentiment, but Hermann's transformation of the final line, linked again with Lydia, distorts the meaning of the poem, casting a revealing and ironic light on the line "if life deceives you."

Finally, two of the alternative titles Hermann considers for his work are "An Answer to Critics" and "The Poet and the Rabble" (p. 211). The first may be an allusion to Pushkin's unfinished article "The Refutation of Criticism," in which he explains and defends some of his earlier works; his contempt for his stupidest reviewers anticipates Hermann's hysterical reaction to the "critics" of his crime, those who point out the inaccurate details he has let slip by: "such small and quite immaterial blemishes as would, given a deeper and finer attitude towards my masterpiece, pass unnoticed, the way a beautiful book is not in the least impaired by a misprint or a slip of the pen" (p. 202). The second title, "The Poet and the Rabble," unquestionably refers to Pushkin's poem of the same name. At the moment he realizes how Felix's stick has betrayed him, Hermann laments the shattered remains of his marvelous construction, "and an accursed voice shrieked into my ear that the rabble which refused me recognition was perchance right" (p. 213). Pushkin depicts The Poet responding to the carping of the "babbling throng," defending his craft and power in exalted terms against the materialistic, corrupt notions of "the unhallowed of the land." With similar intensity but considerably less justification, Hermann remains confident that, "as happens with wonderful works of art which the mob refuses, for a long time, to understand, to acknowledge, and the spell of which it resists" (pp. 132–33), his moment of recognition will someday come.

Yet Hermann's greatest debt to Pushkin, unknown to him, is his very name, taken from the protagonist of "The Queen of Spades." Pushkin's story ends with the German-born Hermann insane: "Hermann went mad. He is now installed in Room 17 at the Obukhov Hospital," a fate which Nabokov's Hermann equally deserves. Moreover, the dualism and schizophrenia of Nabokov's Hermann are anticipated in Pushkin's figure, whose "German" and "Russian" halves are in conflict. Pushkin's final chapter begins with a comment that might serve nicely as an epigraph to *Despair*, suggesting the impossibility of any doppelgänger: "Two fixed ideas can no more exist in one mind than, in the physical sense, two bodies can occupy one and the same place."[11]

Turgenev provides a parallel series of ironic allusions. Reflecting on one of Ardalion's many visits, Hermann offers it "as a sample of an evening gaily and profitably spent," and then quotes one of his own "literary exercises," which in turn "reminds me of Turgenev's prose poems. . . . 'How fair, how fresh were the roses' to the accompaniment of the piano. So may I trouble you for a little music" (pp. 116–17; ellipsis in original). In *Dream Tales*, Turgenev's prose poem reveals a first-person narrator huddled up in a corner, freezing in winter, who reflects back on summer and love: "in my head the line ['how fair,' etc.] keeps echoing and echoing." For Hermann, "the coy trifles composed that winter have been destroyed, but one of them still lingers in my memory" (p. 116). Turgenev's narrator recalls a beautiful, innocent girl, thoughts of loving children (presumably his own), and warmth. But the flickering candle and the memories go out, and his canine companion dies shuddering at his feet. The melodramatic tale ends: "I'm cold . . . I'm frozen . . . and all of them are dead . . . dead . . . *'How fair, how fresh were the roses . . .'*"[12] Hermann has recalled the sentimental refrain accurately enough, but has repressed the knowledge that it heralds the loss of love and the loneliness of death. The ironic context of Hermann's recollection—another visit from his wife's lover—also goes unremarked.

Once beyond Pushkin and Turgenev, we are still confronted with a bewildering array of allusions, direct and oblique, all of which function similarly to suggest a constriction of detail and coincidence which Hermann denies but which the reader recognizes. Many of the allusions relate to the theme of the doppelgänger. Hermann considers as a prospective title for his manuscript "'The Double' . . . But Russian literature possessed one already" (p. 211). Dostoevsky usually comes in for a hard time in Nabokov, and *Despair* is no exception. Golyadkin's descent into madness, precipitated and symbolized by the mysterious appearance of his "double," parallels Hermann's madness, with the added irony that Felix is actually a "false double," as Nabokov said in an interview.[13] Moreover, Nabokov has described *The Double* as Dostoevsky's "best work though an obvious and shameless imitation of Gogol's 'Nose.'"[14] Hermann too is quite aware of Gogol's "Nose." Holed up in a hotel after the murder, he listens to the wind, "now drawing noses in the margin of the page" (p. 15), describes a certain type of nose "*à la* Leo Tolstoy" (p. 51), and one night before the murder, intending to write "a bit of fine prose," finds that "all I managed to do was to beslobber my pen and draw a series of running noses" (p. 114). Hermann even gives us a detailed description of his own nose: "a big one of the northern type, with a hard bone somewhat arched and the fleshy part tipped up and almost rectangular" (p. 26). Felix's nose, he assures us, is an exact duplicate.

"The Nose" and Gogol generally are in the background of this novel; P. M. Bitsilli long ago pointed out similarities between Gogol and Nabokov, speculating in particular on Gogol's story "The Portrait" in relation to *Despair*.[15] More obviously in the foreground is Gogol's *Memoirs of a Madman* (as Nabokov translates it in the Gogol book), which was almost the title of Hermann's work: "assuredly I *had* at one time invented a title, something beginning with 'Memoirs of a —' of a what? I could not remember" (p. 211). We can well understand why Hermann would want to suppress the final word. In *Memoirs of a Madman* the final entry in Poprishchin's diary reads: "I can't stand this torture any more. My head is burning and everything is spinning round and round. Save me! Take me away! Give me a troika with horses swift as the whirlwind! Climb up, driver, and let the bells ring! Soar away, horses, and carry me from this world! Further, further, where nothing can be seen, nothing at all!"[16] The last chapter of *Despair* expresses a similar wish. After discovering his error, Hermann lapses into a diary and calls, not for a troika, but for a getaway car: "French crowd! I want you to make a free passage . . . from door to car. Remove its driver! Start the motor! Hold those policemen, knock them down, sit on them . . . I want a clean getaway" (p. 222). Moreover, Hermann's diary ends on 1 April, among other things Gogol's birthday.

Still another proposed title, also rejected, for his manuscript is "'Crime and Pun'? Not bad—a little crude, though" (p. 211). Hermann even finds himself quoting from Dostoevsky: "'Mist, vapor . . . in the mist a chord that quivers.' No, that's not verse, that's from old Dusty's great book, *Crime and Slime*. Sorry: *Schuld und Sühne* (German edition)" (p. 187, ellipsis in original). It turns out, and we are beginning to expect such "coincidences," that in *Crime and Punishment* Raskolnikov's words are themselves an allusion to the final pages of *Memoirs of a Madman*.[17] Finally, when faking some "Dusty-and-Dusky charm of hysterics" (p. 198) to deceive the doctor in the hotel, Hermann says to himself, "In spite of a grotesque resemblance to Rascalnikov—No, that's wrong. Cancelled. What came next? Yes, I decided that the very first thing to do was to obtain as many newspapers as possible" (p. 199). Hermann's initial impulse was correct, for the resemblance is there—Raskolnikov too riffled through the newspapers to read of his own crime.[18] Pushkin, Gogol, Dostoevsky, Nabokov: the connections are everywhere and inescapable. Hermann summons up a world of failed criminals and madmen, but refuses to learn anything from them.

Another extensive network of allusions, specifically focused on doppelgänger themes, involves Oscar Wilde. Hermann at one point offers as evidence of his literary prowess a "little story in the Oscar Wilde style" (p. 118), about a Mr. X. Y., weak and seedy, and Mario, strong and sunburned. In spite of these physical dissimilarities, they are said to be doubles. A few pages later, Hermann tells Lydia an elaborate Wildean story of his long-lost "brother," who has been corrupted. According to Hermann, his imagined brother has committed "murder: he poisoned the woman who kept him. I learned of the latter affair from his own lips; he had not even been suspected—so cunningly had the evil deed been concealed" (p. 149). This fantasy may be an echo of Dorian Gray's initial evil—provoking the suicide, by poison, of Sibyl Vane.[19] Nabokov, moreover, makes Hermann a self-conscious fop who can only aspire to but not possess the elegance and wit of Wilde and his characters. Among Hermann's trademarks are "new yellow gloves" (p. 16), and he describes himself as "a smartly dressed fellow, slashing his knee with a yellow glove" (p. 21; cf. pp. 173, 180). In *Dorian Gray* Wilde has Lord Henry "sinking into a chair and slowly pulling off his yellow gloves."[20] More than once, Hermann offers us a portrait of himself as foppish dandy: "what I like is to display expensive fawn gloves, spreading my fingers and swinging my arms freely, as I saunter along and turn out the glistening toes of my handsomely shod feet, which are small for my size and very smart in their mouse-grey spats, for spats are similar to gloves in that they lend a man mellow elegance akin to the special cachet of high-class traveling articles" (pp. 75–76). Hermann tries to sound like Oscar Wilde as well as look like him. After asking a little girl to mail a letter, Hermann "did not wait to see the rest, and crossed the street, slitting my eyes (that ought to be noted) as if I really did not see well: art for art's sake, for there was no one about" (p. 135).[21] Lord Henry argues to Dorian Gray that "crime was to [the lower orders] what art is to us, simply a method of procuring extraordinary sensations,"[22] and Hermann, a petit bourgeois who ludicrously aspires to nobility, asks "let us discuss crime, crime as an art" (p. 131) and convinces himself that "if the deed is planned and performed correctly, then the force of creative art is such, that were the criminal to give himself up on the very next morning, none would believe him, the invention of art containing far more intrinsical truth than life's reality" (p. 132). Hermann goes on to argue that "every work of art is a deception" and boasts, "Oh, yes, I was the pure artist of romance" (p. 188). But for both Dorian Gray and Hermann "life's reality" proves more potent than their circumscribed "art."

Hermann also has apparently picked up an extraordinary fondness for lilacs from Wilde: "a languid lady in lilac silks" (p. 14) is supposed to be a description of Hermann's mother but is only a transfiguration of his company's trademark, "a lady in lilac, with a fan" (p. 15). Hermann's favorite piece of clothing appears to be "a lilac tie flecked with black" (p. 102) which he gives to Mr. X. Y. in the Wildean story (p. 117), puts on before his last encounter with Felix (p. 162), and finally, with his spats, gives to Felix to wear (p. 179). The number of lilac allusions in *Dorian Gray* is quite large, beginning in the first paragraph with "the heavy scent of the lilac."[23] But perhaps the main reason for the lilac in *Despair* is that in Russian the word is *siren'yu*—an echo of Sirin, Nabokov's pen name in the 1930s.

Yet the real point of comparison between *Dorian Gray* and *Despair* is the portrait in each. It is for Dorian Gray a "visible symbol of the degradation of sin," at first identical with his appearance but then growing old and ugly while he remains young and beautiful. In *Despair* Ardalion ironically takes Basil Hallward's role, but Hermann will never admit that there is any resemblance between himself and the portrait. Ardalion begins sketching him at the lake, remarking that he has "a tricky face . . . All your lines sort of slip from under my pencil, slip and are gone" (pp. 49–50). In a dream, Hermann sees the "trembling travesty of my face; which, as I noticed with a shock, was eyeless. 'I always leave the eyes to the last,' said Ardalion self-approvingly" (p. 61), as he completes the portrait. It is in the eyes, of course, that Hermann feels he and Felix are not quite identical (p. 39).

When Ardalion finishes the portrait, a parallel between it and the crime begins, as in Wilde, for Hermann has set the date of Ardalion's finishing the portrait as his own time limit for writing Felix and thus beginning the murder plot. But when the painting is revealed, Hermann is horrified to see "the ruddy horror of my face. I do not know why he had lent my cheeks that fruity hue; they are really as pale as death. Look as one might, none could see the ghost of a likeness! How utterly ridiculous, for instance, that crimson point in the canthus, or that glimpse of eyetooth from under a curled, snarly lip" (p. 66). Wilde's readers will also recall Dorian Gray's horror at discovering "a touch of cruelty in the mouth" of his portrait: "The quivering ardent sunlight showed him the lines of cruelty round the mouth as clearly as if he had been looking into a mirror after he had done some dreadful thing." Like Hermann, Dorian finds no resemblance: "no line like that warped his red lips. What did it mean?" What it obviously means for both Hermann and Dorian Gray is that the portraits reveal their moral natures, to which they remain blind. Hermann's "hideous portrait" (p. 74) looms through the rest of the novel (pp. 122, 190, 217) as a reminder of what he is. The allusions to Wilde, then, are ironic in the same way as those to the Russian authors. Hermann's partial recognitions never quite extend far enough to be self-recognitions.

The doppelgänger allusions also pose important aesthetic questions, and we should note how Nabokov's allusions work more ingeniously than as mere parallel or contrast. Hermann would undoubtedly have agreed, for example, with Wilde's Lord Henry that "one should absorb the colour of life, but one should never remember its details. Details are always vulgar." The details of life—sticks and pictures—continuously elude and trip up Hermann, who prizes not variety but repetition, not the Many but the One, not others but himself. After remarking on Hermann's "tricky face," Ardalion goes on to say, "Every face is unique," a position which Hermann cannot accept: "Well, now, really—unique! . . . Isn't that going too far? Take for instance the definite types of human faces that exist in the world; say, zoological types. There are people with the features of apes; there is also the rat type, the swine type. Then take the resemblance to celebrities—Napoleons among men, Queen Victorias among women. People have told me I reminded them of Amundsen" (pp. 50–51, ellipsis in original). Here the philosophical consequences of the doppelgänger allusions have a far-reaching import. They remind us of some general assumptions in Nabokov's fiction. When we recall Nabokov's public pronouncements on such matters ("Caress the details," he would tell his classes, "the divine details!"),[24] we can predict Ardalion's response to Hermann: "you'll say next that all Chinamen are alike. You forget, my good man, that what the artist perceives is, primarily, the *difference* between things. It is the vulgar who note their resemblance. Haven't we heard Lydia exclaim at the talkies: 'Oo! Isn't she just like our maid?'" The naive level of Lydia's aesthetic appreciation is an unrecognized analogue to Hermann's. His grandiose claims as an artist are simply another manifestation of the delusions of grandeur he suffers elsewhere. To prove the point, Nabokov concludes the dialogue with Ardalion most ironically: "'But you must concede,' I went on, 'that sometimes it is the resemblance that matters.' 'When buying a second candlestick,' said Ardalion." Exactly the point: the "stick," echoing at the end of the line, is the central detail Hermann neglects in his masterpiece (he leaves the walking stick engraved with Felix's name at the scene of the crime).[25] But it is only one of many errors of detail. Ardalion will hammer the lesson home in his letter to Hermann at the end of the novel: "It is not enough, however, to kill a man and clothe him adequately. A single additional detail is wanted and that is: resemblance between the two; but in the whole world there are not and cannot be, two men alike, however well you disguise them" (p. 215). So much for the possibility of doppelgänger fiction: the very idea of it violates Nabokov's central aesthetic assumptions.

A similar conversation occurs in *Pale Fire*. Kinbote (or Botkin) replies to the suggestions that he resembles King Charles: "I negligently observed that all bearded Zemblans resembled one another—and that, in fact, the name Zembla is a corruption not of the Russian *zemlya*, but of Semblerland, a land of reflections, of 'resemblers.'"[26] Thus Kinbote, by apparently denying a specific resemblance, argues for a generic one, just as he believes that Shade's poem is a reflection of him. Shade delivers an important rebuttal to Kinbote's theory of resemblance, one that recalls Ardalion's in several ways: "Nay, sir . . . there is no resemblance at all. I have seen the King in newsreels, and there is no resemblance. Resemblances are the shadows of differences. Different people see different similarities and similar differences." Thus for Shade and Ardalion, but not for Kinbote and Hermann, the shadow of a difference is all that's necessary to destroy a total resemblance.

When Hermann tells Lydia the story of his long-lost "brother," and of his elaborate plan for collecting his life insurance, Lydia replies, "I've just been reading a story like that" (p. 151). Hermann tells her that he has "been trying to make myself believe that it was purely an invention of mine or some story I had read somewhere . . . the hero of this cheap mystery story demands the following measures" (pp. 153–54). He begins to explain the string around the gun's trigger, but Lydia interrupts: "I've remembered something: he somehow fixed the revolver to the bridge . . . No, that's wrong: he first tied a stone with a string . . . let me see, how did it go? Oh, I've got it: he tied a big stone to one end and the revolver to the other, and then shot himself. And the stone fell in the water, and the string followed across the parapet, and the revolver came next—all splash into the water. Only I can't remember why it was necessary" (p. 154, ellipsis in original). Hermann dismisses her recollection of "some Sherlock Holmes adventure" (p. 154), because the conclusion of the story, in which the scheme does not succeed as planned, is as dangerous as the context of the Turgenev refrain. Lydia has in fact dimly recalled, and Hermann has plagiarized from, Arthur Conan Doyle's story "The Problem of Thor Bridge," in which the would-be suicide Mrs. Gibson tries to pin a murder on Miss Dunbar, whom she jealously takes to be her husband's mistress. For Luzhin in *The Defense*, the appeal of Holmes is the fascination of an "exact and relentlessly unfolding pattern," with "Sherlock endowing logic with the glamour of a daydream . . . progressing through a crystal labyrinth of possible deductions to the one radiant conclusion."[27] That the "one radiant conclusion" forever eludes Hermann is obvious; he has endowed a daydream with spurious logic. In fact he inverts the Holmesian scheme, imagining a final story "concluding the whole Sherlock Holmes epic; one last episode beautifully setting off the rest: the murderer in that tale should have turned out to be not the one-legged bookkeeper, not the Chinaman Ching and not the woman in crimson, but the very chronicler of the crime stories, Dr. Watson himself—Watson, who, so to speak, knew what was Whatson. A staggering surprise for the reader" (pp. 131–32). Stumbling further into the labyrinth rather than escaping it, Hermann is in the end far more surprised than the reader, who has played Holmes to his Watson. In some mystery stories, as Humbert Humbert tells us, "the clues were actually in italics,"[28] but that is hardly possible here, for the narrator doesn't see them.

Dostoevsky, Gogol, Wilde, Doyle—all exponents, to some degree, of the doppelgänger motif, a literary theme that is now a "frightful bore" to Nabokov,[29] yet one that he uses and parodies throughout his fiction. Many of these works appear to date from Nabokov's reading as a youth, and he has a lurking fondness for such stories, like Mayne Reid's *The Headless Horseman*, a novel which Van Veen read at age ten,[30] though in his world it is a poem by Pushkin ("The Bronze Horseman"). Nabokov and his cousin Yuri acted out key scenes as teenagers, and he devotes several pages of *Speak, Memory* to recounting its convoluted and fantastic plot, summarizing it thus: "Two friends swap clothes, hats, mounts, and the wrong man gets murdered—this is the main whorl of its intricate plot."[31] Hermann's plan is identical but, once again, he will not succeed and get the girl as Maurice the Mustanger does. The clichés of romance and fantasy are invoked by Hermann again and again, but never are they successfully completed, nor does Hermann ever allow himself to remember an unhappy ending. He has a severe case of memoria interrupta.

Behind *Despair* stands a nexus of allusions so dense, so rich, that progressing through their labyrinth would require another Holmes. Some of Nabokov's novels have comparable range (*Lolita* and *Ada* certainly surpass it), but no earlier novel, I think, reaches as far or as frequently as this one does. As a final illustration, I would recall again Hermann's proposed title—"something beginning with 'Memoirs of a—' of a what? I could not remember; and, anyway, 'Memoirs' seemed dreadfully dull and commonplace" (p. 211). Later, under the heading "March 31st. Night," Hermann complains, "Alas, my tale degenerates into a diary. There is nothing to be done, though; for I have grown so used to writing, that now I am unable to desist. A diary, I admit, is the lowest form of literature!" (p. 218). Most readers have assumed, as I did earlier, that the title Hermann cannot remember is Gogol's *Memoirs of a Madman* (in Nabokov's translation, but often glossed as "Diary"), and many parallels are at work on this level, as we have seen. But the diary/memoirs/notes genre is not only the "lowest form of literature" but also one of the most popular, at least in Russian literature, and if Gogol's work is in the foreground, a number of other examples seem to be in the background. There is, for example, Tolstoy's "Notes of a Madman," in which the supposedly "mad" narrator suddenly one night becomes aware of death: "Horror at my perishing life overwhelmed everything. I had to sleep. I lay down. But no sooner had I done so than I leapt up, horrified. And despair, despair, such spiritual despair—the sensation before you retch, only spiritual."[32] This narrator's "despair" is a far cry from Hermann's, however, for Tolstoy's religious solution is completely at odds with Hermann's absolute atheism. Nabokov, it would seem, prefers neither.

Still another diary analogue is Dostoevsky's *Notes from Underground* (or, in Nabokov's memorable putdown, "memoirs from a mousehole").[33] We have already seen much of the "dark Dostoevskian stuff" (p. 215) Hermann invokes and dismisses, commenting that soon "we should hear that sibilant whisper of false humility, that catch in the breath, those repetitions of incantatory adverbs— and then all the rest of it would come, the mystical trimming dear to that famous writer of Russian thrillers" (p. 98). If this is not a description specifically of the famous opening lines of *Notes from Underground*, we can at least recognize a general similarity to the words of Dostoevsky's most hysterical narrator.

The notion of the impotent diarist recalls one of the most famous diaries in Russian literature: Turgenev's *The Diary of a Superfluous Man.*[34] Turgenev's Chulkaturin learns he is to die, and begins a diary on 20 March (about the time Hermann's diary begins; it is 20 March in chapter 5, p. 91). Like Hermann, he sometimes doubts his literary abilities—"I have read over what I wrote yesterday, and was all but tearing up the whole manuscript. I think my story's too spun out and too sentimental."[35] When Hermann decides "that before penning the two or three final sentences [of the manuscript] I would read it over from beginning to end" (p. 210), he too discovers that his work is flawed, that there is a fatal error concealed in it somewhere. Turgenev's narrator is unlucky in love, of course, and at one point, with his "attention centered anxiously about [his] nose" in Gogolian fashion,[36] becomes more frantic as his life ebbs away, until he openly links his own fate with that of Gogol's madman: "Yesterday I had not the strength to go on with my diary; like Poprishtchin, I lay, for the most part, on my bed, and talked to Terentyevna." As Chulkaturin gives up all hope of Liza, he fades quickly, with anticipations of Dostoevsky ("I'm in a bad way. I am writing these lines in bed . . . I am very ill, I feel that I am breaking up") and of Tolstoy ("Death, death is coming. I can hear her menacing *crescendo*. The time is come . . . the time is come! . . . And indeed, what does it matter? Isn't it all the same whatever I write?"—ellipsis in original). Chulkaturin remarks that "It's as though I were writing a sentimental novel and ending up a despairing letter." His despair ends, as does Hermann's, with a final entry dated 1 April: "It is over . . . life is over. I shall certainly die today. It's hot outside . . . almost suffocating . . . or is it that my lungs are already refusing to breathe? My little comedy is played out. The curtain is falling" (ellipsis in original). Hermann also resorts to theatrical metaphors at the end: "This is a rehearsal. . . . A famous film actor will presently come running out of this house. . . . This is part of the plot" (p. 222).

Still more analogies for the "Memoirs of a—" genre are available by writers well known to Nabokov, such as Mikhail Saltykov's *The Diary of a Provincial in Petersburg* (Bitsilli compared its style to that of *Invitation to a Beheading*),[37] and Andrey Bely's *The Memoirs of a Crank* (or *Eccentric*), published in 1922.[38] Resemblances are the shadows of differences, however, and every book is unique. I can claim only some of those analogous works as direct, conscious allusions by Nabokov; many he makes overt, others are unvoiced. Taken altogether, they form a web of circumstance and failure that is palpable to every reader.

Nabokov's parody in *Despair* is, in the now famous phrase from *The Real Life of Sebastian Knight*, a "springboard for leaping into the highest region of serious emotion." In burlesquing the old forms of narration and theme, Nabokov has, paradoxically, given them new life. Rather than being merely ornamental, or serving as analogues, Nabokov's allusions provide the very structure of Hermann's world. They spin a web of significance entrapping Hermann, though he steadfastly denies that any external force controls him. The overall irony implies another world beyond this one, another power beyond the feeble human will.

But Hermann is an atheist, and both he and Nabokov make much of it. Lamenting "our eternal subjection to the circle in which we are all imprisoned," Hermann resolutely ignores the implied active agent in his passive construction. His fate, like that of most of Nabokov's characters, is to be a "galley slave"[39] or prisoner of type. But while Kinbote, for example, blissfully welcomes the comforting

hand of the Divine, Hermann resists the idea that he is in the control of a higher power. At a particularly bad moment, Hermann exclaims "Please, God!" but then "failed to understand, myself, why I
said so; for did not the sense of my whole life consist now in my
possessing a live reflection? So why then did I mention the name of a
nonexistent God, why did there flash through my mind the foolish
hope that my reflection had been distorted?" (p. 77). In chapter 6,
Hermann confronts the problem directly: "The nonexistence of God
is simple to prove. Impossible to concede, for example, that a serious
Jah, all wise and almighty, could employ his time in such inane fashion as playing with manikins, and—what is still more incongruous
—should restrict his game to the dreadfully trite laws of mechanics,
chemistry, mathematics, and never—mind you, never!—show his
face, but allow himself surreptitious peeps and circumlocutions, and
the sneaky whispering (revelations, indeed!) of contentious truths
from behind the back of some gentle hysteric" (p. 111). It must be
admitted that on the surface Hermann's objections to the existence
of God are not only plausible but conventional. The triviality of
human actions, the existence of evil—these are genuine questions.
Yet the paranoid Hermann quickly resorts, as we might have expected, to a theory of conspiracy: "The idea of God was invented in
the small hours of history by a scamp who had genius; it somehow
reeks too much of humanity, that idea, to make its azure origin
plausible; by which I do not mean that it is the fruit of crass ignorance; that scamp of mine was skilled in celestial lore—and really I
wonder which variation of Heaven is best: that dazzle of argus-eyed
angels fanning their wings, or that curved mirror in which a self-
complacent professor of physics recedes, getting ever smaller and
smaller" (p. 111). The non-sequiturs lead us astray, as they have led
the speaker, but that "scamp who had genius" differs little from Hermann's working conception of divinity itself. But whichever variation of heaven Hermann prefers, both are characterized by the delusions of paranoia: external observation (by "argus-eyed angels") or
narcissistic self-reflection (the human image receding in a "curved
mirror" toward nothingness).

The rationale behind Hermann's atheism becomes increasingly
revealing (pp. 111–12):

> There is yet another reason why I cannot, nor wish to, believe
> in God: the fairy tale about him is not really mine, it belongs
> to strangers, to all men; it is soaked through by the evil-smell-
> ing effluvia of millions of other souls that have spun about a
> little under the sun and then burst; it swarms with primordial

fears; there echoes in it a confused choir of numberless voices striving to drown one another; I hear in it the boom and pant of the organ, the roar of the orthodox deacon, the croon of the cantor, Negroes wailing, the flowing eloquence of the Protestant preacher, gongs, thunderclaps, spasms of epileptic women; I see shining through it the pallid pages of all philosophies like the foam of long-spent waves; it is foreign to me, and odious and absolutely useless.

Straightforward snobbery and elitism here degenerate into an oblique revelation of the "primordial fears," "numberless voices," and other sounds and diseases which, we are learning, exist principally in Hermann's mind.

What Hermann most strongly defends in his rejection of divine existence is his own sense of human freedom—and here we begin to see something of our own anxieties and fears: "If I am not master of my life, not sultan of my own being, then no man's logic and no man's ecstatic fits may force me to find less silly my impossibly silly position: that of God's slave; no, not his slave even, but just a match which is aimlessly struck and then blown out by some inquisitive child, the terror of his toys. There are, however, no grounds for anxiety; God does not exist, as neither does our hereafter, that second bogey being as easily disposed of as the first" (p. 112). What makes Hermann's speculations so ironic for the reader is our increasingly complete knowledge of the "bogey" who has created and manipulated him. The presumed "editor" of this manuscript (still another hoary narrative device) is of course a parodic stand-in for Nabokov himself. Hermann refers to "that Russian author . . . the well-known author of psychological novels," most of them "very artificial, though not badly constructed" (pp. 90–91). This "penetrating novelist" (p. 167), as we soon learn, is an émigré "whose books cannot possibly appear in the U.S.S.R." (p. 168). In Hermann's fantasy about his future happiness, "a Russian author who lives in the neighborhood highly praises my style and vivid imagination" (p. 189). But this is a delusion of grandeur, for on its paranoiac side lie fears that the "crafty and experienced imagination" of the editor will turn to plagiarism: "you may use my termless removal to give out my stuff for your own" (p. 91), though of course his name on the book "will deceive nobody" (p. 168). Nabokov the local author represents only the first of a receding series of "gods" who deny Hermann the ability to be "master of my life . . . sultan of my own being" (p. 112). The reader is still another, for both reader and author have collaborated in unfolding the ironic allusions. A universe of linear allusions has been drawn into a tight, self-enclosed circle, isolating Hermann and singling him out for unwelcome attention. His paranoia is not only intense but to some extent justified.

Speculating on the nature of the dead who would welcome us to the afterlife, Hermann raises a final argument (pp. 112–13):

> Now tell me, please, what guarantee do you possess that those beloved ghosts are genuine; that it is really your dear dead mother and not some petty demon mystifying you, masked as your mother and impersonating her with consummate art and naturalness? There is the rub, there is the horror; the more so as the acting will go on and on, endlessly; never, never, never, never, never will your soul in that other world be quite sure that the sweet gentle spirits crowding about it are not fiends in disguise, and forever, and forever, and forever shall your soul remain in doubt, expecting every moment some awful change, some diabolical sneer to disfigure the dear face bending over you.

Here he offers no argument against God's existence, but rather a naked exposure of pure fear—that "God" might turn out to be evil, that "some petty demon" or, more generally, "fiends in disguise" will deceive us even in paradise. The origins of this fear are obvious. Nabokov has condemned Hermann to live in a symbolic world where literary allusions form a constricting and menacing web, in which sneers and whispers are perceived but not identified, and in which all is deceit. This is the same world inhabited by the boy in the short story "Signs and Symbols." It is the typical Nabokovian realm of terror, in which even so genial a character as Pnin is trapped (though he escapes). The reader inhabits a similar world, or so seems the implication, and collaborates in the creation of this one, for only by the reader's recognition do Hermann's speeches turn toward irony. Author and reader are therefore co-conspirators, "playing with manikins," allowing only "surreptitious peeps and circumlocutions." *We* are the "fiends in disguise" that bring forth Hermann's primordial fears. Hermann can sense our presence, hear our breathing. He knows we're there.

This typical symbolic world may best be described as a Cartesian nightmare. Hermann begins to sense that indeed there is a "God," but that he is no other than the "evil demon" about whom Descartes wrote as follows: "I shall then suppose, not that God who is supremely good and the fountain of truth, but some evil genius not less powerful than deceitful, has employed his whole energies in deceiving me: I shall consider that the heavens, the earth, colors, figures, sound, and all other external things are nought but illusions and dreams of which this genius has availed himself in order to lay traps for my credulity."[40] Hermann is the logical heir of this position; all of his arguments against God's existence, all of his fears, begin from the belief that the controlling agent of destiny is malevolent. To deny such evil is to help preserve the self, whose identity is already so precarious that it must be duplicated in a stranger, as though it were looking for strength in numbers. But success eludes Hermann because every fantasy must evaporate. In a remarkable scene, Hermann tries to re-read the manuscript he has written, but something keeps going wrong until "the delicious foretaste with which I had just been penetrated, now changed to something like pain—to a horrible apprehension, as if an evil imp were promising to disclose to me more and more blunders and nothing but blunders" (p. 211).

The pain increases during Hermann's final hours until, when his narrative has turned into a diary, ontological despair overwhelms him: "There is, thank God, no mirror in the room, no more than there is the God I am thanking. All is dark, all is dreadful, and I do not see any special reason for my lingering in the dark, vainly invented world" (p. 220). Again, the implied active agent of the passive construction betrays the prior assertion; equally telling is the reiterated link between Hermann's rejection of God and the presence of a mirror. He will not kill himself, he assures us later, but we have long since witnessed his psychological death. In his final entry on "April 1st." he becomes most explicit: "Maybe it is all mock existence, an evil dream; and presently I shall wake up somewhere; on a patch of grass near Prague" (p. 221)—thus beginning the cycle all over again as Felix. When Hermann peeps out the window, he sees confirmed what he has sensed all along: "The street is full of people who stand there and gape; a hundred heads, I should say, gaping at my window" (p. 221). These are not the "argus-eyed angels" (p. 111) of heaven, but gaping gargoyles welcoming Hermann to a new hell: "I have peeped again. Standing and staring. There are hundreds of them—men in blue, women in black, butcher boys, flower girls, a priest, two nuns, soldiers, carpenters, glaziers, postmen, clerks, shopkeepers . . . But absolute quiet; only the swish of their breathing" (p. 221, ellipsis in original). The elusive shadow and sensed presence have become his entire world, a panorama of society watching and judging. And surely no one is more objectionable than those "glaziers," creators of so many of Hermann's most treacherous objects. Mirrors have been the focus of his greatest fears and fantasies, at once a screen between two realms and a polished reflecting surface giving Hermann back nothing but himself. The lack of sound here, moreover, is only fitting for phantasms. In the "swish of their breathing" he hears a telltale heart, as much his as it may be ours.

The appeal to the Cartesian nightmare is habitual in Nabokov's fiction. In *Bend Sinister*, the philosopher Adam Krug—of all Nabokov's characters the one who should be the most familiar with the idea—remarks that "so suddenly did his guards disappear that, had he been a character in fiction, he might well have wondered whether the strange doings and so on had not been some evil vision, and so forth."[41] Shortly afterward, when a dream grants Krug a glimpse of "the mind behind the mirror," the narrator/demon who has caused the "evil vision" shifts his stance: "it was then," the narrator says, "that I felt a pang of pity for Adam and slid towards him along an inclined beam of pale light—causing instantaneous madness, but at least saving him from the senseless agony of his logical fate." A few pages later, the narrator stops the story just before a bullet will kill Krug.

The "mind behind the mirror" is the presence felt by virtually all of Nabokov's protagonists, and their search for or flight from this mind forms a central movement in the novels. Whether that mind is described as "God" (by Kinbote) or, much more frequently, as an evil demon, its powers remain oppressive. The protagonists have only their senses to guide them, and inevitably see not the "mind" but only the "mirror"—that is, they see only their own projections. No wonder the boy in "Signs and Symbols" tries to "tear a hole in his world and escape."[42] No wonder Hermann, among others, is so drawn toward and yet frightened of mirrors, for they throw back at him only his own inner turmoil.

Some of Nabokov's protagonists escape the nightmare—Pnin even drives off into his freedom. And in *Invitation to a Beheading* Cincinnatus finds, like the boy of "Signs and Symbols," the hole in this world through which to escape: "I have discovered it. I have discovered the little crack in life, where it broke off, where it had once been soldered to something else, something genuinely alive, important and vast."[43] At the end of the novel, as the ax descends, Cincinnatus gets up, looks around, and the nightmare world begins to collapse: "Everything was coming apart. Everything was falling. A spinning wind was picking up and whirling: dust, rags, chips of painted wood, bits of gilded plaster, pasteboard bricks, posters; an arid gloom fleeted; and amidst the dust, and the falling things, and the flapping scenery, Cincinnatus made his way in that direction where, to judge by the voices, stood beings akin to him." Such an optimistic reunion with the "voices," the minds behind the mirror, is rare in Nabokov. The more usual escape, if that is what it is, comes through death: Humbert dies in prison, the boy in "Signs and Symbols" perhaps kills himself, Kinbote hints at suicide, Albinus in *Laughter in the Dark* dies alone in his hellish *camera obscura*, Luzhin of *The Defense* commits a "suicide-mate,"[44] and on it goes. The mortality rate in Nabokov's fiction approaches pandemic proportions. The major alternative to death is madness—Vadim, Krug, Kinbote, possibly Van Veen,[45] and certainly, to come full circle, Hermann.

Hermann fancies himself a brilliant artist, makes strong claims for the autonomy of the artist and his integrity, and describes his carefully plotted crime as if it were a portrait. Felix himself is part of the raw materials. It is easy to see how this allegory continues through the novel, and also easy to see how Hermann's failure reflects ironically on Nabokov's success. We can go further, however, and distinguish between Hermann's conscious and unconscious creations. The crime doesn't succeed, but the creation of resemblance in Felix works all too well. In one way at least, Felix is one of Hermann's triumphs, perhaps his only one. Someone is actually there, but that is not the point. On this level of creation, we can see that Hermann is to Felix as Nabokov is to Hermann—both are in the process of creating a character who is a projection, distorted in varying degrees, of himself. In forming Felix, Hermann attempts the same transformation of recalcitrant "reality" as any artist—though it is difficult to say at what level of consciousness or intention this act occurs. The obvious analogy within the novel is Ardalion's portrait of Hermann, whose tricky face resists easy capture and must go through a change of medium from "the honest slog of charcoal . . . to the petty knavishness of pastel" (p. 65).

Hermann has tried to become the evil demon for Felix, to assume the role of creator and destroyer. He has created an elaborate "plot," in both senses of the word, in which Felix is willingly to act out one role (playing Hermann's stand-in for a movie scene) while Hermann has secretly provided a far different role beneath the deceptive appearances (sacrificial "double" for the insurance scheme). The scheme offers a close analogy to the plot in which Hermann is himself trapped, and reminds us again of all those characters who lead their lives on one level of "reality" but suspect and fear that they are unwittingly assuming some other role on a quite different, unknown level. This is the world in which a paranoid or outright lunatic lives; but it is very similar to the world anyone with imagination must inhabit. The protagonists who live in such worlds are engaged in a constant discovery of signs and symbols; the interpretations come later, if at all. The power of imagination has run amok in these characters, and almost every object around them achieves a local habitation and a name. Paranoia, then, is Nabokov's emblem for the imagination.

Personification is the major stylistic device for rendering the feeling of this world. Given the belief that "all is deceit, a low conjuring trick" (p. 113), it is only logical that deceivers and conjurers be found everywhere. Even astronomical events take on malevolent implications. Thus, "a cloud every now and then palmed the sun, which reappeared like a conjurer's coin" (pp. 15–16). Even smoking in the woods can be a prelude to terror: "I smoked a cigarette there. I looked at the little puff of smoke that slowly stretched out in midair, was folded by ghostly fingers, and melted away. I felt a spasm in my throat" (pp. 64–65). But the mysterious, changing wind—its true origin one of the mysteries of the novel—presents the greatest variety of faces to Hermann: frolicsome ("the wind roughly upturning the several petticoats of the olive trees which it tumbled"—p. 192); violent ("that murderous mountain draft"—p. 192); cruel ("a brutal wind was blowing and chasing leaves—scurry, cripples!—athwart the street"—p. 78); deceitful ("I stopped, trying to light my cigarette, but the wind kept filching my light until I took shelter under a porch, thus blasting the blast—what a pun!"—p. 79); and, inevitably, sexual ("their [the pines'] green fur which the wind was stroking the wrong way"—p. 46). It is difficult to describe the effects of such a menacing world, and even more difficult to describe how these effects are created. Personification is only one of the devices so masterfully employed. The texture of ironic allusion is another, as is the insistent use of syntax to suggest psychic collapse. It is the *felt* experience of reading, collaborating, and therefore living imaginatively in this world that represents Nabokov's great achievement in *Despair*. He even makes readers co-conspirators, not opponents, by making them complete the allusions, correct the errors, and become unseen accomplices in "crime as an art." This world exists because we are made to feel it.

NOTES
1. Nabokov, *Despair*, p. 220 (ellipsis in original). Hereafter cited in text.
2. Vladislav Khodasevich, "On Sirin," in *Nabokov*, ed. Appel and Newman, p. 99; cf. Vladimir Weidle: "Everyone who has not yet lost his sensitivity to literary innovation and freshness in Russian prose will acknowledge the enormous giftedness of [*Despair's*] author" (cited in Andrew Field, *Nabokov: His Life in Art*, p. 235).
3. There are two studies of the revisions in translation of this novel: Carl R. Proffer, "From *Otchaianie* to *Despair*," *Slavic Review* 28 (1968),

258–67; and Jane Grayson, *Nabokov Translated*, pp. 59–82.

4. Field, *Life in Art*, p. 235.

5. This is Nabokov's own description of Gogol's fiction: "in Gogol's books the real plots are behind the obvious ones. . . . His stories only mimic stories with plots. It is like a rare moth that departs from a moth-like appearance to mimic the superficial pattern of a structurally quite different thing—some popular butterfly, say" (Nabokov, *Nikolai Gogol*, p. 152).

6. Stephen Suagee, "An Artist's Memory Beats All Other Kinds: An Essay on *Despair*," in *A Book of Things about Vladimir Nabokov*, ed. Proffer, pp. 55, 60.

7. Clarence Brown, "Nabokov's Pushkin and Nabokov's Nabokov," in *Nabokov*, ed. Dembo, p. 207.

8. Proffer, "From *Otchaianie*," p. 264.

9. See Nabokov's edition of *Eugene Onegin*, III, 284.

10. Walter Arndt, *Pushkin Threefold* (New York: Dutton, 1972), p. 197.

11. A. S. Pushkin, *The Complete Prose Tales of Aleksandr Sergeyevitch Pushkin*, trans. Gillon R. Aitken (New York: Norton, 1966), pp. 305, 301.

12. Ivan Turgenev, *Dream Tales and Prose Poems*, trans. Constance Garnett (London: Heinemann, 1899), pp. 315, 317 (ellipsis in original). The Turgenev refrain and a link with Pushkin appear again in Nabokov's *Pnin*, p. 42.

13. Nabokov, *Strong Opinions*, p. 84.

14. Ibid.

15. P. M. Bitsilli, "The Revival of Allegory," in *Nabokov*, ed. Appel and Newman, p. 106.

16. Nikolay Gogol, *Diary of a Madman and Other Stories*, trans. Ronald Wilks (Baltimore: Penguin, 1972), pp. 40–41.

17. Raskolnikov's quotation is in part 6, chapter 2 of F. M. Dostoevsky, *Crime and Punishment*, ed. George Gibian (New York: Norton, 1975), p. 381.

18. Ibid., pp. 135–36.

19. Nabokov elsewhere uses her name for one of the sisters in his short story "The Vanc Sisters." See the recent article by Isobel Murray, "'Plagiatisme': Nabokov's 'The Vane Sisters' and *The Picture of Dorian Gray*," *Durham University Journal* 39 (1977), 69–72.

20. Oscar Wilde, *The Picture of Dorian Gray* (New York: New American Library, 1962), p. 110.

21. Cf. Nabokov, *Strong Opinions*, p. 33.

22. Wilde, *Dorian Gray*, p. 224.

23. See also ibid., pp. 23, 37, 40, 227, 229, etc. Succeeding quotations are from pp. 110, 104, 115.

24. Ross Wetzsteon, "Nabokov as Teacher," in *Nabokov*, ed. Appel and Newman, p. 245.

25. Proffer has shown how Nabokov carefully revised *Otchayanie* to throw even more emphasis on the "stick" throughout.

26. Nabokov, *Pale Fire*, p. 265.
27. Nabokov, *The Defense*, p. 34.
28. Nabokov, *The Annotated Lolita*, p. 213.
29. Nabokov, *Strong Opinions*, p. 83.
30. Nabokov, *Ada*, p. 171.
31. Nabokov, *Speak, Memory*, p. 195.
32. Lev Tolstoy, "Notes of a Madman," *RLT* 10 (1974), 96.
33. Wetzsteon, "Nabokov as Teacher," p. 243.
34. Clarence Brown has found Nabokov's Smurov (in *The Eye*), Kinbote, Sebastian Knight's half-brother V., and Fyodor Godunov-Cherdyntsev (*The Gift*) to be the direct descendants of this tradition which dates back to Pushkin's Onegin (Brown, "Nabokov's Pushkin," p. 204). I would of course add Hermann to the list. G. M. Hyde, in *Vladimir Nabokov*, discusses Smurov, Hermann, and Humbert in relation to the "superfluous man" convention (pp. 99–128); he also calls *Despair* "the most 'Dostoyevskian' of Nabokov's novels" (p. 113).
35. Ivan Turgenev, *The Diary of a Superfluous Man and Other Stories*, trans. Constance Garnett (London: Heinemann, 1899), p. 36.
36. Ibid., p. 40; cf. p. 54. Further quotations are from pp. 75, 93, 93, 95, 97.
37. Bitsilli, "The Revival of Allegory," p. 111.
38. See Nabokov's comments on Saltykov (*Eugene Onegin*, I, 85) and on Bely (*Strong Opinions*, p. 57; *Eugene Onegin*, III, 459).
39. Nabokov, *Strong Opinions*, p. 95.
40. René Descartes, *The Philosophical Works of Descartes*, trans. E. S. Haldane and G. R. T. Ross (Cambridge: Cambridge University Press, 1968), I, 148. I have expounded on this theme in relation to *Pnin* and "Signs and Symbols" in "Nabokov's Signs and Symbols," in *A Book of Things about Vladimir Nabokov*, ed. Proffer, pp. 203–17. Nabokov shows considerable familiarity with Descartes in his works: Gradus, after all, "started as a maker of Cartesian devils—imps of bottle glass bobbing up and down in methylate-filled tubes" (*Pale Fire*, p. 151); and devils and demons may also be found frequently, as in "In Memory of L. I. Shigaev" (*Tyrants Destroyed and Other Stories*, pp. 158, 161). See also Vadim's belief that "A demon . . . was forcing me to impersonate that other man, that other writer who was and would always be incomparably greater, healthier, and crueler than your obedient servant" (*Look at the Harlequins!*, p. 89).
41. Nabokov, *Bend Sinister* (1973), p. 210. Further quotations are from p. 233.
42. Nabokov, *Nabokov's Dozen*, p. 69.
43. Nabokov, *Invitation to a Beheading*, p. 205. The further quotation is from p. 223.
44. Field, *Life in Art*, p. 176.
45. In *Nabokov's Garden* Bobbie Ann Mason argues that Van is "a madman of sorts" (p. 12).

Invitation to a Beheading and the Many Shades of Kafka

MARGARET BYRD BOEGEMAN

Invitation to a Beheading has always been an anomaly in the Nabokov canon. Nabokov has called it his most esteemed novel,[1] but that is a judgment that stands alone in critical estimation. A major problem in giving the book an objective evaluation has been the long shadow of Kafka in which it stands. The book has been dogged both by the possibility of actual borrowings and also by the exegetical anticipations of critics reared to see Kafka's presence everywhere. Nabokov himself has denied the charge of borrowing from Kafka or anyone else. While Nabokov has been all too quick to deny influence of any sort, with the result that he seems to protest too much, if one looks at *Invitation to a Beheading* from the perspective of its place in the Nabokov canon, and its timing in the history of literary criticism, Nabokov's denials seem justified at least in spirit. Whether or not such a reading raises the critical view of the book to the "esteem" of Nabokov's opinion, it may allow us to see the novel as playing an integral part in the development of Nabokov's artistry.

Nabokov originally wrote *Invitation to a Beheading* as *Priglashenie na kazn'* in Berlin in 1934 and published it serially in the émigré journal *Sovremennye Zapiski* in 1935–1936. Two years later (1938) the book appeared in Paris and Berlin. In the foreword to his English translation (1959), Nabokov discusses the reception of the Russian original: "Émigré reviewers, who were puzzled but liked it, thought they distinguished in it a 'Kafkaesque' strain, not knowing that I had no German, was completely ignorant of modern German literature, and had not yet read any French or English translation of Kafka's works."[2] Nabokov's ignorance of Kafka in 1934 cannot be disproved, but certain details of his denial must at least be considered exaggerations—for example, the statement "I had no German." Nabokov lived in Berlin for fourteen years, from 1923 to 1937, and by his own account earned his bread by giving lessons in tennis and English to the Berliners.[3] It would seem therefore that he had at least a minimal knowledge of spoken German. His reading knowledge of

German was probably more than adequate, since his bibliography lists a 1932 translation of the "Prologue" of *Faust* from German to Russian.[4]

In the years when Nabokov lived in Berlin, the city was a whirl-pool of cultural ferment, not only politically, but artistically as well, though Nabokov's biographer Andrew Field emphasizes the isolation of the Russian émigrés. "The Russians lived with each other in Berlin and marked time, hoping that history would allow them to go back even if it was not on a White steed."[5] Nabokov may have been aloof, but Field also demonstrates clearly that he was no émigré isolate, as if that were not already implicit in his multilingual, widely traveled upbringing. Though he was disdainful of the German society in which he lived, he did not confine himself to the émigré community or to Berlin. Field documents Nabokov's appearances during the thirties at literary readings across the European continent, in Paris, Brussels, Antwerp, Prague, and Dresden as well as Berlin. Paris was the second center of émigré life, and it was there that Nabokov had the opportunity to mingle with those émigré critics who had recognized and written on his talents. One of these, Vladimir Weidle, also had written a book on the state of contemporary literature, *Les Abeilles d'Aristée* (Paris, 1936), which contained some incisive criticism of Kafka. In the same year this book was published, Weidle was one of several critics who shared Nabokov's table in a Parisian cafe, after a reading by Nabokov.[6] Mingling with the literary avant-garde in Paris, sharing often heated discussions of literary merit, Nabokov could hardly have failed to be aware of Kafka's name, even if, as he has claimed, he had not read his works.

But the probability of foreknowledge is not sufficient to substantiate influence. We need to look more closely to see not only if influence could have existed, but where and how, and with what consequences. And we need to consider not only the literary activity around Nabokov during the thirties but the literary activity around Kafka.

The thirties were a crucial decade for both authors. Kafka, who had died in 1924, was being "discovered" during the thirties by a larger and more sophisticated readership than he had ever enjoyed during his lifetime. His works were first published in Germany but were quickly translated, particularly into French and English, and his reputation grew because of critical acclaim in those languages. *Der Prozess*, the book with which *Invitation to a Beheading* most often has been compared, appeared posthumously in Berlin in 1925; by 1933 it had been translated into French as *Le Procès* and was being reviewed by the major critics in France (including Weidle).

Also available in French by this year were eight of Kafka's major stories, including "Die Verwandlung" ("La Métamorphose"). All had appeared in France's prestigious contemporary literature periodical *La Nouvelle Revue Française.*[7]

The early criticism of Kafka, in French as well as in German and English, was heavily influenced by the views of Kafka's friend and literary executor Max Brod, who interpreted Kafka from a religious perspective. The now dominant view of Kafka as prophet of social dehumanization and political repression did not appear until late in the thirties and did not reach its peak until around 1945, just after the end of World War II.[8] Once that change occurred, Kafka's name became a commonplace and his influence ubiquitous. But in 1934, when Nabokov first composed *Invitation*, this change in critical perspective was still in the offing. Even in 1937, when Nabokov was revising his serial version of *Invitation* for book publication, the picture of Kafka as a social allegorist and literary cult object was just beginning to emerge. During the early thirties, Kafka was admired and respected by the literary avant-garde, but his reputation was not yet large, and no popular interpretation of his work had yet appeared.

Assuming, for the sake of argument, that Nabokov did know Kafka's work in 1934, he could not have been aware that Kafka would soon be considered a twentieth-century literary touchstone or spokesman for the individual persecuted by the State. Hence, neither the magnitude of Kafka's name nor the politics of Kafka's interpretations would have stood in Nabokov's way, had he found it convenient to appropriate any literary material he admired, as he borrowed, for example, from Lewis Carroll for the ending of *Invitation*.

If we consider what aspects of *The Trial* might have been used in *Invitation*, we can clarify the relationship between the two authors and perhaps see *Invitation* as having a different relationship to Kafka than has been previously assumed. The suspected "borrowings" fall into three categories: incidentals that are strikingly similar but not very important, parallels that are probably coincidental, and similarities that are central and probably copied but used by Nabokov for a purpose quite different from Kafka's.

In the category of incidental parallels, we can note such details as that Joseph K. and Cincinnatus C. are both thirty years old, are referred to as children, are emotionally dependent on women (Leni and Marthe) and count on them for succor, when in fact the women are of no help whatsoever. Both women actually suggest that the men repent and give up trying to maintain their innocence. Even in the description of the two women one hears a remarkable echo. "Leni had a doll-like rounded face; not only were her pale cheeks and her chin quite round in their modeling, but her temples and the line of her forehead as well."[9] Marthe's face appears to Cincinnatus "as in a locket; her doll-like rosiness; her shiny forehead with its childlike convexity; her thin eyebrows, slanting upward, high above her round hazel eyes" (p. 20). Both of these doll-like, appealing women are also promiscuous. These parallels are interesting insofar as they suggest that both Kafka and Nabokov have rejected the hallowed (and hackneyed) tradition of woman as pure and noble intercessor, but this hardly gets us to the heart of either novel.

Two other similarities between *Invitation* and *The Trial* are probably coincidental, but an examination of them can nevertheless demonstrate the different fictional intentions of the two authors. One such similarity is the doubling of minor characters who are agents of containment—warders, jailers, or escorts to the execution. Both Cincinnatus C. and Joseph K. are marched to their doom by identical, noncommittal automatons; Joseph K. faces another pair when he is arrested. That two writers, both portraying humans at the mercy of vast and unapproachable powers, should see the agents of these powers as faceless, interchangeable dummies requires no great exercise of the imagination. The image is almost impossible to avoid. It is an indictment of the banality of evil and of the idea of humans as replaceable cogs in an assembly-line machine. In *The Trial*, the doubles serve to illustrate the impersonality of the power that persecutes Joseph K., who cannot reach these faceless robots with any plea of logic or justice. In *Invitation*, the doubles show the shoddiness of the social values, which attempt to reduce all people to one person, to a bland uniformity which fears the outstanding and the original. Kafka uses the double to show the protagonist's radical "otherness" and leave him isolated and powerless. Nabokov uses the double to show his contempt for the society where anyone can be replaced by anyone else.

Another minor and probably coincidental parallel between Kafka and Nabokov is that in both *Invitation* and *The Trial* a theatrical metaphor accompanies the execution. However, the sources of the imagery are different, as is the aesthetic effect. In *The Trial*, the reference is brief but notable in a book virtually devoid of metaphor. Joseph K. calls his executioners "tenth rate actors" and asks them, "What theater are you playing at?" (p. 280). The theatrical imagery is much more fully integrated into *Invitation* than into *The Trial*, where it strikes a meretricious note strangely at odds with the towering, archetypal imagery of the cathedral scene in the preceding chapter. Heinz Politzer has observed the tendency in Kafka to end in some form of theatricality and suggests that such endings are a way of distancing the author from the excruciating dilemmas in which he repeatedly involves his characters. "Kafka is . . . well aware of the incompatibility existing between these stage effects and his artistic integrity; therefore he detaches himself from the show by turning it into a parody."[10]

This same tone of a comic-opera performance is especially well suited to the scene in *Invitation*, where the problems are aesthetic rather than moral. The shabbiness of the theater, its flimsy pretensions to reality, the studied gaiety of its deception, all underscore Nabokov's contempt for the artifice of conformity. Indeed, images of theatricality abound in *Invitation*. Every chapter reveals another tawdry deception, from the makeup worn by the prosecutor and the defense counsel so that they look alike to the phony rescues effected by Emmie and M. Pierre. The theatrical imagery culminates in the final scene. But the collapsing sets of Thriller Square derive from Lewis Carroll, not Kafka. The final scene in *Invitation* strongly suggests the last scene in *Alice's Adventures in Wonderland*, where the Queen of Hearts issues her "invitation to a beheading" by shouting, "Off with her head!"[11] But Alice, who has been throughout the book as intimidated as Cincinnatus, now asserts herself. "'Who cares for you?' said Alice (she had grown to her full size by this time). 'You're nothing but a pack of cards!' At this, the whole pack rose up into the air, and came flying down upon her."[12] The same unexpected size changes, the same sudden whirl and collapse of the cardboard world occur in the last scene of *Invitation*. Like Alice, Cincinnatus is rescued from this nightmare by an act of will. Like *Alice*, *Invitation* has horrors that are only painted. The sense of dislocation is genuine but not inescapable. We know that Cincinnatus and Alice will live happily ever after. Carroll and Nabokov manipulate and mitigate their horrors in cheerful conclusions. This buffo affirmation of human control over destiny is a striking contrast to the monotone of impasse in Kafka. The tonal contrast in finales points up the justness of the theatrical metaphor in Nabokov and its arbitrary imposition in Kafka, whose horrors cannot be dispelled by ringing down the curtain.

More pervasive and fundamental parallels are those of plot, and these parallels first drew critics' attention to the connection between *Invitation* and *The Trial*. Joseph K. and Cincinnatus C., initialed characters of uncertain ancestry, are accused of crimes, the nature of which is unclear. They are tried by powerful courts, against which there is no appeal. The characters are allowed no legal defense for what seems to be their inherent guilt. Once they have fallen under suspicion, they can only resort to ingenious evasive tactics in order to put off the inevitable execution. Joseph K., for example, ponders whether to try to have his case infinitely delayed or to seek "ostensible acquittal." Cincinnatus C. postpones his arrest by disguising through mirrors and shadows his criminal "opacity."

Both characters try to fit into a society which singles them out as oddities and rejects them as anomalies. But the attitude of the two authors regarding this expulsion from the community is vastly different. For Nabokov, a recurrent theme is the oppressiveness of belonging to any society. Cincinnatus is better than his fellow citizens, more sensitive, more independent in thought and will and action than they. The society of crass mediocrity (*poshlost'*) punishes the superior individual in its midst for betraying its shabby standards. Persecution (like prosecution) is here a form of compliment, a recognition that there are standards higher than the least common denominator. To belong to any society would be to diminish one's own independence and the integrity of one's personal standards.

For Kafka, on the other hand, to belong, to be a member of a community, is a desirable objective, one which his characters pursue in vain. They are outsiders, trying to insist on their right to belong, trying to insinuate themselves into a society closed to them. Arrest or persecution means the expulsion from union with other members of society, or exposure of the character's basic "otherness," and a cause for despair.

Another parallel between *Invitation* and *The Trial*, the initialed name, is a detail unusual enough to suggest at least a passing acquaintance with Kafka, but the difference in intention again renders the influence negligible. Cincinnatus' initial C. hints at the mystery of his origins, in the tradition of spy novels and changeling fables. His anonymity is a romantic secret; he is the child of a legend. K., on the other hand, is not romantic in the least. K.'s is the anonymity of Everyman, and of Kafka's self-abnegating literary self shrunk to a single letter.[13] K. is the name of a man who scarcely exists. Nabokov sets Cincinnatus C. apart from and above his society by his initial; Kafka sets K. apart from and outside of society with his. The use of initials is merely a detail in building two very different characterizations, again based on the author's attitude toward the role of the individual in society.

Further, while both Cincinnatus C. and Joseph K. accept the accusations of their societies regarding their crime, they differ dramatically in their assumption of personal guilt. Cincinnatus' crime is "gnostical turpitude"; literally, "knowledgeable vileness"—the state of being consciously different from his fellow citizens. Of this he is certainly guilty, but at the same time he is not responsible. His condition is a consequence of his unusual heredity. (The hint of divine parentage reinforces the superiority of his "differences.") He is paradoxically a "guilty innocent." While he regards himself as a victim, he never regards himself as a sinner in any sense. And he never stops trying to escape his victimization.

Joseph K.'s crime is never named, but his guilt is assumed. Though he insists upon his innocence, he uses this term to mean that he is innocent of violating any law. But an agent of the court tells him that the court's officials "never go hunting for crime in the populace, but as the Law decrees, are drawn toward the guilty and must then send out us warders. That is the Law" (p. 10). A distinction is made between mere criminals and "the guilty," a distinction which apparently never registers with Joseph K. He is guilty in another sense than being a transgressor of a legal statute. His guilt, like Cincinnatus', is a consequence of his metaphysical state. But K. is not a "guilty innocent"; he is a "guilty responsible." His metaphysical state is not, like Cincinnatus', an accident of personal heredity but a state of conscience. While K. protests his innocence, he accepts his guilt. He does not finally deny the justice of the court's claims as Cincinnatus does.

Both are self-propelled victims: K. is caught by his own fascination with examining his guilt, Cincinnatus by his refusal to pretend any longer that he is just like all the other transparent dummies in his society. But Cincinnatus is condemned only by his society, not by himself. Kafka says that one is caught by one's own mind; Nabokov that one is freed by the same instrument. K.'s is a descent into the depths of conscience; Cincinnatus' is an ascent into the reaches of imagination. Thus the two authors have used the same frame for opposing messages.

Even comparisons of these major structural patterns have shown only differences between the two authors in attitude and intention. Nabokov seems to have borrowed a great deal from Kafka but not Kafka's themes or teleology. What appears to be borrowed is superficial and cosmetic, not fundamental.

Beyond these similarities of text, similar political interpretations have also been imposed on the two authors, first on Kafka, then on Nabokov through Kafka. Here it is important to consider the timing of the two books. *Invitation* appeared in 1938, a time when Hitler's designs were becoming apparent to the larger Western world. The magnitude of this political phenomenon caused a groundswell of sociopolitical literary criticism unparalleled in this century, a movement which affected Kafka's reputation with an impact immediate, overwhelming, and permanent. Within a few years after the beginning of World War II, critics had all but forgotten the metaphysical interpretations initially attached to Kafka's works and were concentrating almost exclusively on the works as political paradigms, seeing in them the powerless individual persecuted by the malign and unreachable powers of the State. Kafka suddenly became a "classic" in France, England, and the United States. No writer could construct imaginary societies without being read in his shadow and the shadow of his critics.

This politicization of criticism has constrained the interpretations of *Invitation* as well as those of Kafka, for if one reads the novel politically, one must agree that Nabokov has falsified the political situation by robbing it of the brutality and terror which cannot in fact be wished away by the imagination. Even if we consider *Invitation* in the light (or shadow) of Kafka, relying on the earlier metaphysical interpretation, *Invitation* still suffers, since on a humanistic scale of values spiritual crisis weighs heavier than aesthetic crisis. Thus, reading *Invitation* through *The Trial* has trivialized the book and has kept it from being considered on its own terms. Nabokov's intentions were never to write a weighty spiritual, political, or ethical tract. He repudiates such an attempt even within the pages of *Invitation*. "I do not get all hot wrestling with my soul in a darkened room," Cincinnatus says, "I have no desires, save the desire to express myself—in defiance of all the world's muteness" (p. 91). Nabokov's denial of influence thus seems true to the spirit of his novel, even if not circumstantially accurate.

However, a subtler connection with Kafka, made by Nabokov himself, may suggest an additional thematic ripple in *Invitation*, as well as a reason for the use of an exigent physical vehicle to express an ethereal aesthetic tenor. This clue may also lead us to an idea of the novel's place in Nabokov's artistic development. To follow this path we must first examine the formal properties of the literary genre Nabokov is using.

Invitation also has been associated with *The Trial*, though in a more general way, on the basis of its fantastic mode. Nabokov has played games with the tradition of social realism in all of his novels, but *Invitation* is the one most completely disengaged from that central tradition which he mocks. The book is a fantasy, with no pretensions to being located in any historical matrix. Fantasy is rare enough in the novelistic tradition to cause its critics some discomfort, and it is on this basis as well as on the particulars of plot that *Invitation* has been linked to Kafka. But here, too, misguided expectations lead to a blurring of terms.

Fantasy in Kafka's work is the fantasy of nightmare, and the evocation of an emotional state (usually anxiety) is the defining component. There is no Aristotelian structure in nightmare, no beginning, no middle, and especially no end. There is no sense of proportion among its elements, no connection between its incidents, and no termination to its oppressive terrors. And any message that exists is so thoroughly sublimated in code as to be undecipherable, even to the dreamer. This form was radically different from traditional fiction, and Kafka's critics tended to read it as allegory—hence the predominant emphasis on Kafka's "message."

Invitation to a Beheading is not nightmare but fable, and the difference extends far beyond the difference in tone implied by the two terms. Fable is a well-established literary tradition, and indigenous to it is deliberate design and explicit instruction, exactly the contrary of nightmare. A recent literary handbook defines fable as "a brief tale, either in prose or verse, told to point a moral." A better phrase would be, "told to demonstrate a lesson," rather than a "moral," since even among the better-known fables the lessons are not always moral. But this is not the point here. Rather, it is that a message of some kind is the raison d'être of the form. This implies a structure with a definite terminus out of which comes the lesson; in other words, a beginning, a middle, and an end. Further, the object lesson of the fable is almost always conveyed by a simplified story of two opposing forces contending for superiority, the winner gaining a triumph by some virtue or skill we are meant to emulate. Hence the fable is prescriptive in intention, and carefully but simply structured so as to convey the message in a clear and memorable way. In the interest of dramatizing, and perhaps exaggerating, the opposition of the forces in question, realism is usually bypassed for the greater power of myth or the supernatural. All of these defining qualities are found in *Invitation to a Beheading*, and only one has been a problem for its critics—its exemplary message.

Anyone who has read Nabokov even casually has noted his refusal to assign a socially redeeming message to his fictions, which are usually peopled by an unregenerate assortment of perverts, loonies, murderers, and social misfits of many minor stripes. Nabokov appears to enjoy working against the expectations of his readers that they will be instructed as well as delighted. This antipathy to moralizing is consistent in his criticism and his literary tastes as well as his own work. Friend and critic Gleb Struve notes only what Nabokov himself has said over and over again, "his outspoken contempt for any kind of 'message' in literature, be it social, moral or religious-philosophical."[14] Yet the fable structure of *Invitation* demands that there be a message. Andrew Field very sensibly sees the message as an aesthetic one, with Cincinnatus as the artist imprisoned in the realm of "dead, ready-made art." Field goes on to say that the "politics" (i.e., the message) of the novel is "the inevitable and natural exile that is the fate of all culture—especially in Russia."[15] The condemnation of cheap art and the liberation of the individual through the power of the imagination are two themes that recur consistently throughout Nabokov's work. Given Nabokov's persistence in treating these themes and practically no others, one wonders why their presence in *Invitation* has not been considered a sufficient resolution for the fable structure. But the book has been a problem for critics since its first appearance. Early émigré critics disliked its divorce from reality, its frivolity and disjointed plot.[16] While critics in English have shown a bit more sophistication in dealing with the fantasy, they still have had difficulty reconciling the political vehicle with the aesthetic tenor. The reviews of the 1959 English translation, in particular, were hard on the book, citing its escapist mood, its lack of causality, and its facile ending.[17] There is, moreover, a certain illogic within the book itself (beyond that intended by the author) which distracts from the aesthetic message.

Cincinnatus, proponent of the creative imagination, is condemned to death by his society. His only crime lies in being different—different in aesthetic standards and different in refusing to appreciate *poshlost'* art. For this he is condemned to death—not exile, not incarceration, not torture, but what seems to be real, physical death. It would seem that there is a disproportion between Cincinnatus' crime and his punishment: that is, his crime is imaginative while his punishment is material. The two forces contending in this fable are both aesthetic, but one side seems to have all the physical power. In the contest between a sharp ax and a sharp wit, the ax usually wins. And yet, in this case, it doesn't. As fable, the message is clear: the imagination can rescue one from even the most dire circumstances. But as metaphor, the image of a beheading is so strong as to distract us from the mental state and imaginative powers of poor little Cincinnatus. Such heavy equipment is brought to bear against such a lightweight threat—or as one reviewer put it, Nabokov finds it necessary to break a butterfly upon a wheel.[18]

We find ourselves asking, if Cincinnatus can escape through an exercise of his imagination, why doesn't he do it earlier? The parallel comes from *Alice in Wonderland*: the threat has to be formidable, even life threatening, before the mind is jolted out of its state of fear, stupor, or simple amazement to rescue itself. Had Cincinnatus been confined in one of those other clichés of the fantastic, a nut house or a fun house, an ancient myth or a futuristic planet, there would have been neither the immediate material threat nor the urgency that prompts Cincinnatus into reluctantly exercising his imaginative powers and completing the fable structure.

The execution, which forces the exemplary action of the conclusion, is imminent in the text from the beginning. The twenty chapters correspond to the number of days from Cincinnatus' arrest until the day of his execution, and the pencil with which he writes wears away at the same rate as the days. When the novel opens, the pencil is described as "long as the life of any man except Cincinnatus," but in chapter 8, on the eighth day, Cincinnatus is writing with the same pencil, "which had lost more than a third of its length" (pp. 12, 89).

So the extremity of situation that Cincinnatus faces is planned by Nabokov, not accidental. If beheading seems to command excessive attention here, and not in *Alice in Wonderland*, it is perhaps due to its threat throughout the book, not just at the end, as in *Alice*. Though the threat is imminent throughout in order to force Cincinnatus to make his great leap, and so solve the requirements of the form, it may also be present for another reason, more personal to the author's own artistic development.

If fable's main function is to offer the reader a cautionary tale, the message in *Invitation* would seem to have small application to a general readership in a prosaic world. Yet the fable may be an exemplum not to the world but to the author.[19] A reflexive message is perfectly appropriate to the kind of closed system found in Nabokov's crystal worlds of the imagination. The novel was written at a crucial juncture in his life and with an ease that would seem to suggest a great release of tension and energy. "The first draft [of *Invitation to a Beheading*]," he has said, "I wrote in one fortnight of wonderful excitement and sustained inspiration."[20]

Hints such as this are as close as we ever get to self-revelation by our cleverly reticent author, but a few clues to the problems occupying Nabokov during the thirties exist in a later novel. In 1974, Nabokov published a parodic biography of himself—*Look at the Harlequins!*—in which the details of his human relationships are mostly invented, but the details of his artistic career are fairly accurate. In this book, he refers to *Invitation to a Beheading* as *The Red Top Hat* or *The Red Topper*. The imagery which pervades the discussion of *The Red Topper* is provocative, for one reason, because it alludes to Kafka, in a context absolutely unforced. He says, "During those months of correcting and partly rewriting *The Red Topper* . . . I began to experience the pangs of a strange transformation. I did not wake up one Central European morning as a great scarab with more legs than any beetle can have, but certain excruciating tearings of secret tissues did take place in me."[21] The allusion can only be to Kafka's "The Metamorphosis," one of Nabokov's favorite works of fiction, and it is very appropriate in this context. The "strange transformation" is, of course, Nabokov's decision to switch from Russian to English as his language of composition. "The Russian typewriter was closed like a coffin," he writes (p. 120). This change of languages (metamorphosis) is central to Nabokov's artistic career, and that career is the real subject of *Harlequins!*. Given the facts that the major themes in Nabokov's novels are aesthetic ones and that his continuous preoccupation, both in his own writing and in his writing about others, has been with quality of language, the switch from Russian to English must be considered an enormous decision in his career, a change more fundamental to his life than any of the many changes in domicile, passports, or economic condition to which he was subjected. Such a metamorphosis would have been every bit as terrifying as that made by Cincinnatus, and only enacted under similarly extreme conditions, for it meant leaping a chasm both of language and of fears. On the success of this metamorphosis would depend his very artistic existence.

For a writer, the dilemma of beginning to compose in a new language could be a form of extinction in several ways. If Nabokov had continued to write in Russian, to be read only by an émigré audience, neither would he have been able to keep himself and his family "alive" (in the sense of supporting them), nor would he have been "alive" artistically to that much larger Western literary world with which he himself was very much in contact. But if he switched to English in the middle of his career, he would be consigning to extinction his former artistic achievements, no small oeuvre in terms of either volume or quality. This same metamorphosis might also lose him the readers and critics he had already reached, and, far worse, might lose him a language that had worked magic for him and replace it with one that would not. He wrote in *Harlequins!* that "the question confronting me in Paris, in the late Thirties, was precisely could I fight off the formula and rip up the readymade, and switch from my glorious self-developed Russian, not to the dead leaden English of the high seas with dummies in sailor suits, but an English I alone would be responsible for, in all its new ripples and changing light?" (p. 124). Nabokov had no guarantee that his effort would succeed; he could have ended up merely a different kind of dead writer, without audience and without a language of his own.

He notes in *Harlequins!* the satisfaction he received from praise by English critics for his style in English translations of his Russian works but says, "It was, however, quite a different matter 'to work without net' (as Russian acrobats say), when attempting to compose a novel straight in English, for now there was no Russian safety net spread below, between me and the lighted circlet of the arena" (p. 120). It cannot have escaped the eye of the acute reader that most of Nabokov's metaphors in *Harlequins!* surrounding this intended transformation are images of danger, death, and metamorphosis. "I daresay the description of my literary troubles will be skipped by the common reader; yet for *my* sake, rather than his, I wish to dwell mercilessly on a situation that was bad enough before I left Europe but *almost killed me during the crossing*" (p. 124, italics mine). Since Nabokov does not go on to describe any particularly hazardous experience during his transatlantic voyage, we might assume "the crossing" to mean a crossing of another sort, especially since the following sentence reads, "Russian and English had existed for years in my minds as two worlds detached from one another."

This entire cluster of images speaks to the urgency and daring of the artistic attempt and perhaps helps to explain the exaggerated situation in which Nabokov places Cincinnatus, who is so secure in the comfort of his disguise that he does not take his imaginative leap until threatened with extinction. "My head is so comfortable," Cincinnatus laments (p. 22).

The imagery of metamorphosis also suggests a different and deeper link with Kafka than those noted by the critics reviewing *Invitation*. That the book was connected in Nabokov's mind with Kafka is indicated not only by the frequency of his denials, which in fact serve only to draw attention to the connection, but also by the reference in *Harlequins!*, since no one would have recalled that *Invitation* had been linked with Kafka without this allusion to "The Metamorphosis."[22] The story appeared in the *N.R.F.* (1928), a periodical which published some things by Nabokov during the thirties, and Nabokov was probably familiar with the French translation. (In another reference to the same story, in *Bend Sinister* [1947], Nabokov used the French form of the hero's name, Gregoire.) Like Cincinnatus, Gregor Samsa (or Gregoire) withdraws from society by an act of the imagination—though it is the unconscious rather than the conscious mind acting here—at a point when the pressures to continue in the same state simply become too great to be endured. That his story too was a fable of personal crisis, concluding in an enigmatic message to himself, is borne out by Kafka's diaries, letters, and conversations.[23] He told one friend, "The dream [of the story] reveals

the reality, which conception lags behind. That is the horror of life—
the terror of art."[24] For Nabokov, too, the dream reveals the reality,
though if life is a horror, art certainly is not. Rather, art is the salva-
tion from the horror.

I do not wish to suggest that the book is an allegory, a mode
which Nabokov has always abhorred. But I do believe that a kind of
transformation which is relevant to Nabokov's own artistic development ripples behind the dominant metamorphosis and escape from
a *poshlost'* society. Nabokov was too careful an artist to allow any of
his novels to become merely commentary on his life—even *Harlequins!*—and he has derided biographical as well as Freudian interpretation. But he used what he found convenient, and one finds
pieces of himself in nearly every book, from the émigré professor in
Pnin to the "old, happy, healthy, heterosexual Russian, a writer in
exile" of *Pale Fire*. In *Invitation*, if one listens carefully to the laments of Cincinnatus, one can also hear the doubts of a writer arguing himself into a new medium of expression (pp. 95, 90, 93, second
ellipsis mine):

> No, I have as yet said nothing, or rather, said only bookish
> words . . . and in the end the logical thing would be to give up
> and I would give up if I were laboring for a reader existing to-
> day, but as there is in the world not a single human who can
> speak my language . . . I must think only of myself, of that
> force which urges me to express myself.

> Or will nothing come of what I am trying to tell, its only ves-
> tiges being the corpses of strangled words, like hanged
> men. . . .

> Sensing with my criminal intuition how words are combined,
> what one must do for a commonplace word to come alive and
> to share its neighbor's sheen, heat, shadow, while reflecting it-
> self in its neighbor and renewing the neighboring word in the
> process, so that the whole line is live iridescence; while I sense
> the nature of this kind of word propinquity, I am nevertheless
> unable to achieve it, yet that is what is indispensable to me for
> my task, a task of not now and not here.

In this way, the book can be seen as a hortatory rather than an
exemplary fable, and prescriptive in a very personal way. Nabokov
constructed, among other things, a wish-fulfillment, a dream vision,
and encouraged himself to follow it. *Invitation* thus can be seen as
pivotal in the Nabokov canon.

Nabokov did not immediately plunge into English upon finishing this book; in fact, he was working simultaneously on his longest and, some feel, his most brilliant Russian novel, *The Gift*, which took him four long years to complete.[25] In the preface to his English translation, Nabokov "explains" this book to a degree unusual for him. "The world of *The Gift* being at present as much of a phantasm as most of my other worlds, I can speak of this book with a certain degree of detachment. It is the last novel I wrote, or ever shall write, in Russian. Its heroine is not Zina, but Russian literature."[26] Nabokov goes on to list, chapter by chapter, the Russian literary styles and stylists he has used. In a very fundamental way, this book is Nabokov's farewell to Russian language and literature, and there is a finality even in this preface. The novel itself is a monument—big, carefully constructed, and full of ornament. It is a parody and a settling of scores, but at the same time it is also a kind of homage and valediction. In it, Nabokov sets himself apart from this Russian literature he is leaving, finally and definitively.

With *The Real Life of Sebastian Knight* (1941) Nabokov began composing in English. The narrator in the novel—not surprisingly named V.—is self-consciously unsure of his English, and registers in a writing class to bolster himself. Nabokov's parody here is not of others, as in *The Gift*, but of himself, as a writer hesitant about his talents in a new medium. This clever device shielded Nabokov from the demands of the perfection he expected of himself stylistically and also shielded him from the same expectations from critics. It was a shrewd and cautious step born from the egotism of a great talent.

Taken together, the three novels form a commentary on a critical period of Nabokov's artistic development. All are concerned with making the transition from one language and state of thought to another. *Invitation* can be seen in this series as the dream vision of Nabokov's initial impulse to make the change, a fable with a triumphant and programmatic outcome. *The Gift* is an elegiac farewell, a final sorting of literary values, both homage to and parody of that rich literary land he was leaving. *Sebastian Knight* represents the first, somewhat tentative tryout of the new medium, carefully structured to buffer the sensitive ego and metamorphosed talent, with mockery as insurance against anyone's great expectations. Thus, these very differently designed works of art have a continuity emanating from the life of the artist himself. If we are to make sense of Nabokov's work in a developmental perspective, links of this kind allow us to see the artistry and patternings in his life's work as well as within each individual piece.

When Nabokov called *Invitation to a Beheading* his most esteemed novel, he did not explain why he felt this way. He did claim that it was the easiest to compose, a "spectacular" exception to his usual slow pace.[27] The book is also freer than any of his other novels from the constraints of realistic convention, which Nabokov always looked upon with some disdain. But there might in addition be an affection for the novel as a well-fulfilled prophecy, the prototype of a metamorphosis which Nabokov then determined to follow and achieve. And regardless of his frequent but formulaic laments for his abandoned Russian, he did break through to a language and style even richer than that which he commanded in his earlier novels. He became a stylist in English so dazzling that he is without peer and might well be considered in another realm of language from the common sphere of English prose. *Invitation* might have been the author's invitation to himself, an invitation he later held in esteem because, by then, he had fulfilled and surpassed his own dream wish.

NOTES

1. Nabokov, *Strong Opinions*, p. 92.
2. Nabokov, *Invitation to a Beheading*, p. 6. Hereafter cited in text.
3. Nabokov, *Speak, Memory*, p. 283.
4. Andrew Field, *Nabokov: A Bibliography*, p. 163.
5. Andrew Field, *Nabokov: His Life in Part*, p. 171.
6. Field, *Life in Part*, p. 193.
7. The stories include "La Métamorphose" (1928); "Bucéphale," "Le Nouvel Avocat," "Devant la loi," "Un Message impérial," "Le Plus Proche Village," "Il tue son frère" (all 1929); and "Le Terrier" (1933).
8. For a thoroughly documented study of this subject, see Margaret Byrd Boegeman, "Paradox Gained: Kafka's Reception in English from 1930 to 1949, and His Influence on the Early Fiction of Borges, Beckett, and Nabokov."
9. Franz Kafka, *The Trial*, trans. Edwin Muir (New York: Modern Library, 1964), p. 124. Hereafter cited in text.
10. Heinz Politzer, *Franz Kafka: Parable and Paradox* (Ithaca: Cornell University Press, 1966), pp. 212–13.
11. Nabokov translated this book into Russian in 1923.
12. Charles Dodgson [Lewis Carroll], *Alice in Wonderland* (Belmont, Calif.: Wadsworth, 1969), p. 209.
13. Kafka wrote in his diary, "I find the letter K. offensive, almost nauseating, and yet I write it down, it must be characteristic of me."—*The Diaries of Franz Kafka, 1914–1923*, trans. Martin Greenberg (New York: Schocken, 1965), pp. 33–34.
14. Gleb Struve, "Notes on Nabokov as a Russian Writer," in *Nabokov*, ed. Dembo, p. 54.
15. Andrew Field, *Nabokov: His Life in Art*, p. 195.

16. See Ludmila A. Foster, "Nabokov in Russian Émigré Criticism," in *A Book of Things about Vladimir Nabokov*, ed. Proffer, pp. 47–48.

17. See especially Maurice Richardson, "New Novels," *New Statesman* 59 (1960), 832; R. G. G. Price, "New Novels," *Punch* 238 (15 June 1960), 854; and "The Dream of Cincinnatus," *Time* 74 (26 October 1959), 110.

18. Burns Singer, "Utopia and Reality," *Encounter* 14 (1961), 79.

19. Andrew Field, for example, has made a subtle identification of Cincinnatus with Nabokov, in glossing the classical name: "The hero's name seems to refer not to Lucius Quinctius Cincinnatus, who is generally the model of the simple and virtuous statesman, but rather to the statesman's son . . . who was censored in 461 B.C. *for his extraordinary oratory and excessive pride* by a Tribune of the People and *forced to go into exile*" (italics mine), *Life in Art*, p. 195.

20. Nabokov, *Strong Opinions*, p. 68.

21. Nabokov, *Look at the Harlequins!*, p. 120. Hereafter cited in text.

22. Nabokov denies *Invitation* was influenced by Kafka in the prefaces to *Invitation* and *Bend Sinister*, in an interview with Appel (see note 1 above), and in an interview with the BBC (*Strong Opinions*, p. 152).

23. For concise documentation of the relevant sources, see Franz Kafka, *The Metamorphosis*, ed. Stanley Corngold (New York: Bantam, 1972), pp. 105–12.

24. Gustav Janouch, *Conversations with Kafka*, trans. Goronwy Rees (New York: New Directions, 1971), p. 32.

25. The exact dating here is unclear. Field says in his biography that from 1929 to 1936 many of Nabokov's writing projects overlapped (in composition, not necessarily in theme). In his book of criticism, Field dates the composition of *The Gift* from 1934 to 1937 and calls *Invitation* Nabokov's "major 1935 novel" (p. 185). But in *Harlequins!* Nabokov says he wrote *The Red Topper* at the beginning of 1934 but revised and rewrote it in 1937, while he claims dates of 1934 to 1938 for *The Dare* (*The Gift*). In spite of the confusion, it seems clear that both novels were under way at roughly the same time, though *Invitation* was substantially completed by 1935.

26. Nabokov, *The Gift*, no page number.

27. Nabokov, *Strong Opinions*, pp. 92, 68.

Part 3

The Third Arc

1940: Vladimir Nabokov arrives in America.

1941: *The Real Life of Sebastian Knight*

1941–1948: Teaches at Wellesley College.

1942–1948: Also works as a research fellow in lepidopterology at Museum of Comparative Zoology, Harvard University.

1944: *Nikolai Gogol*

1945: Becomes an American citizen.

1947: *Bend Sinister*

1948: "Signs and Symbols" published in the *New Yorker.*

1948–1959: Teaches at Cornell University.

1951: *Conclusive Evidence*

1951–1952: Guest lecturer at Harvard.

1954: *Drugie berega* (Russian version of *Conclusive Evidence*)

1955: *Lolita* published in Paris.

1957: *Pnin*

1958: *Lolita* published in the United States.
Nabokov's Dozen, containing "Signs and Symbols"

Focus Pocus:
Film Imagery in *Bend Sinister*

BEVERLY GRAY BIENSTOCK

From his moviegoing boyhood in St. Petersburg to his days as a tux-
edoed extra in German films up through the Hollywood sojourn
connected with his *Lolita* screenplay, Vladimir Nabokov was always
vitally interested in the motion picture medium. *Nabokov's Dark
Cinema* (1974) by Alfred Appel, Jr., chronicles this interest, particularly examining Nabokov's use of movie references to satirize the
expectations of the bourgeoisie. *Lolita*, for instance, "stands alone
among postwar American novels in its uncompromising yet controlled dramatization of the manner in which the iconography of
popular culture forms or twists its consumers."[1] The nymphet, her
imagination shaped by comic strips and movie magazines, is seduced away from Humbert's loving care by Clare Quilty's promises
of Hollywood stardom. Nor did Nabokov begin to write about the
lures of movieland only on coming to America. Such early Russian-
language novels as *Laughter in the Dark* (originally *Kamera obskura*, 1932) and *Despair* (*Otchayanie*, 1936) feature characters who
envision themselves as screen heroes and heroines. Appel takes
pains to show that virtually every Nabokov novel contains sly allusions to that mass culture which movies have helped to foster.

Yet Appel leaves one area almost untouched. In detailing the
impact on Nabokov's writings of the cinema as cultural phenomenon, Appel largely neglects the metaphorical implications of film.
Nabokov, though, has often used a cinematic motif to suggest something about the workings of the human mind. *Ada* (1969), written
after Nabokov's own Hollywood experience, naturally pokes fun at
the *poshlost'* of the movie industry and at the helpless author whose
novel is transformed beyond recognition during the filmic process.[2]
But, more importantly, *Ada* relies on film images to convey the
forces of memory and nostalgia. Thus Marina, looking back on her
own turbulent life, muses that someday "one's past must be put in
order. Retouched, retaken. Certain 'wipes' and 'inserts' will have to
be made in the picture; certain telltale abrasions in the emulsion

will have to be corrected; 'dissolves' in the sequence discreetly combined with the trimming out of unwanted, embarrassing 'footage,'
and definite guarantees obtained; yes, someday—before death with
its clapstick closes the scene."[3] And Van, separated from Ada, pursues from flick-house to flick-house the filmed image which pre-
serves her as she once was (pp. 481, 488–89). These cinematic references are noted, in passing, by Appel, but he never tries to relate
them to the novel's concern for the texture of time. Neither does he
discuss the elaborate pattern of film imagery in the lovely, much-
neglected *Bend Sinister*.

Bend Sinister (1947), the first of Nabokov's novels to be written
in the United States and the second written in English, is best
known as a companion piece for *Invitation to a Beheading* (*Priglashenie na kazn'*, 1938). Both deal with totalitarian regimes and with
the fate of a hapless citizen caught in the State's clutches. But
though Cincinnatus C., the protagonist of the earlier book, remains
a cartoon figure among cartoon figures, Adam Krug of *Bend Sinister*
is one of Nabokov's most human creations. An eminent philosopher, a man of deep and tender feelings, Krug is hemmed in on all
sides by the pressures of authoritarianism. While trying to cope with
the fact of his wife's recent death, Krug battles to preserve his young
son's innocence and his own intellectual integrity. In this intensely
charged atmosphere, Nabokov has made distinctive use of the devices and the symbolic implications of the cinema.

As might be expected by a reader of Appel, moviegoing is used
in *Bend Sinister* to convey the banality of the new regime and its
supporters. The hero of a politically influential comic strip finds one
of his chief quotidian pleasures in visits to the movies;[4] the seductive young governess who turns out to be a government spy claims
to spend her days off quite wholesomely at "the pictures" (p. 162).
But film is not merely seen here as a source of mindless entertain-
ment: in conjunction with other types of mass media it serves to
keep the citizenry under control. The State, having discovered the
charms of the reproduced human voice, spreads its message via
megaphone and loudspeaker (pp. 96, 125, 168, 227),[5] while also congratulating itself publicly in the "homogeneous press" and in endless
mimeographed circulars (pp. 165–68). The single device, though,
that most effectively symbolizes the new regime is the padograph.
This ingenious contrivance, invented by the father of the current
dictator, is a sort of portable typewriter "made to reproduce with repellent perfection the hand of its owner" (p. 69). Thus something as
intimate as one's handwriting can easily be mimicked by a foe who
gains control of the correct padograph. Yet the citizenry as a whole is

not perturbed by this potential invasion of privacy. In contrast to Krug, who writes his works in longhand and reserves his signature for special occasions (p. 56), the average citizen enjoys "seeing the essence of his incomplex personality distilled by the magic of an elaborate instrument"; the State's ability to undermine individual expression is based on a shrewd awareness that "devices which in some curious new way imitate nature are attractive to simple minds" (p. 69). Ultimately, the padograph comes to represent the grotesque "Ekwilist" philosophy of the regime, since it exists "as a proof of the fact that a mechanical device can reproduce personality, and that Quality is merely the distributional aspect of Quantity" (pp. 69–70).

Photography, first cousin to the film, is still one more tool through which the State maintains its ascendancy. It can, for instance, serve to keep track of individuals: all bus passengers are required to submit a photo to the conductor when they board (p. 179). And photography is equally useful in verifying the official point of view. The regime's leaders, looking toward the capitulation of Adam Krug to the State, envision the worldwide publicity to be gained in photographically documenting such a moment: "Tentatively scheduled to take place in three months' time, the opening of the new University was to be a most ceremonious and widely publicized affair, with a host of reporters from foreign countries, ignorant overpaid correspondents, with noiseless little typewriters in their laps, and photographers with souls as cheap as dried figs. And the one great thinker in the country would appear in scarlet robes (click) beside the chief and symbol of the State (click, click, click, click, click, click) and proclaim in a thundering voice that the State was bigger and wiser than any mortal could be" (pp. 151–52).

By means of mass media, then, the State asserts its power over the body and mind of the individual. But in one crucial instance a State-sponsored film serves to point up the State's own fallibility and ultimate powerlessness. This occurs when Krug, desperate to be reunited with his kidnapped son, succumbs at last to the regime's demands. He is driven to an Institute for Abnormal Children where the reunion is scheduled to take place; once there, he is ushered into a projection hall and shown a home movie. To Krug's horror and everyone else's embarrassed surprise, the film—complete with comical subtitles—neatly documents young David's being led to his death as part of a therapy program for criminal inmates. The screen image of his son's death turns Krug irretrievably away from the State. No matter how it cajoles, haggles, finally threatens, it can no longer touch him. So in the moment when film becomes not an imitation of life but a recording of life, not a fantasy for public consumption but an unexpurgated documentary, the State loses its hold on the citizen it most wants to win over.

Film, it seems, has two contradictory dimensions. It is both an artificial construct and a momentary capturing of reality. Even in the most conventional movie, the characters may be fictive but the actors, undeniably, are real. The same holds true, of course, for theater, but the acute realism of the cinematic closeup, when played off against our sense of a film as a made object, helps us to feel the paradox more keenly. This very paradox between life and art, between the cinema of fact and the cinema of fiction, impinges strongly on *Bend Sinister*'s narrative structure.

Though the outline of its basic plot is grounded in the realities of totalitarianism, *Bend Sinister* is not meant to be taken as literally true. Nabokov ensures against this by setting himself up, as author figure, in cosmic opposition to the powers of the State. Thus Krug's life is shown to be shaped, on the one hand, by the demands of a political system, on the other, by the exigencies of his creator. In the former case he functions as a sentient human being; in the latter he is no more than a part of "the puppet show going on in my mind," as Nabokov says in the autobiographical *Speak, Memory* (p. 281). By making his authorial presence felt, Nabokov functions quite explicitly as an impresario. He has done this in other works, appearing in *Speak, Memory*, for instance, as both puppet master and magic lantern projectionist (pp. 153, 155), and hinting at the close of *The Real Life of Sebastian Knight* that he might be a conjuror hidden in the wings.[6] In *Bend Sinister*, Nabokov steps into the role of producer-director, thus anticipating the thwarted ambitions he will reveal in the foreword to his *Lolita* screenplay twenty-six years later: "By nature I am no dramatist; I am not even a hack scenarist; but if I had given as much of myself to the stage or the screen as I have to the kind of writing which serves a triumphant life sentence between the covers of a book, I would have advocated and applied a system of total tyranny, directing the play or the picture myself, choosing settings and costumes, terrorizing the actors, mingling with them in the bit part of guest, or ghost, prompting them, and, in a word, pervading the entire show with the will and art of one individual."[7]

It should be noted here that Nabokov seems to see the rival media of cinema and theater as interchangeable. Within *Bend Sinister*, too, many of his metaphors can apply either to stage or screen. But his vision of himself as artistic tyrant—as *auteur*, to use the fashionable term—is more appropriate to film, wherein the director has control over the finished product. Nabokov recognizes this distinction in *Ada* by making the two lovers agree that "the talking screen was certainly preferable to the live theater for the simple reason that with the former a director could attain, and maintain, his own standards of perfection throughout an unlimited number of performances" (p. 425). We might also acknowledge that the ideal dictator-director as outlined in the foreword to the *Lolita* screenplay comes close to being a portrait of the filmmaker Alfred Hitchcock, who shared with Nabokov a hearty mutual admiration.[8] Hitchcock is known for his iron grip on the reins of a production, and for a distinctive, baroque style somewhat akin to Nabokov's own. His famous walk-ons—in the bit part of guest, or ghost—further suggest Nabokov's own predilection for personal appearances in his fiction. Nabokov shows up in several of his novels and gives himself the cameo role of a butterfly hunter in his (as opposed to Stanley Kubrick's) screenplay of *Lolita*. It is not wrong, then, to see Nabokov as a filmmaker *manqué* in the Hitchcock mold.

Within *Bend Sinister*, the Nabokovian director-producer uses his powers to confute the power of the politicians. This can be seen most vividly in the chapter in which Krug visits Paduk, once an obnoxious schoolmate nicknamed the "Toad" and now Head of State. In this sequence, the solemn bureaucracy of the regime is played off against monkeyshines reminiscent of Nabokov's much-beloved Marx Brothers.[9] And Nabokov here, for the first time in the novel and more explicitly than in any of his other works, comes out from behind the scenes to direct the action. Following a hideous description of the dictator, he pauses to remark, "In a word, he was a little too repulsive to be credible, so let us ring the bell (held by a bronze eagle) and have him beautified by a mortician" (p. 143). The ensuing makeup process is then described in detail. Further on, Nabokov shifts his camera angle so that we see Krug and Paduk in new visual terms: "Photographed from above, they would have come out in Chinese perspective, doll-like, a little limp but possibly with a hard wooden core under their plausible clothes." It is Nabokov at his most godlike who points out that "the secret spectator (some anthropomorphic deity, for example), surely would be amused by the shape of human heads seen from above" (p. 147). Elsewhere in the sequence, Nabokov gives clearcut directions to his performers: "The actor playing the recipient should be taught not to look at his hand while he takes the papers *very slowly* (keeping those lateral lower-jaw muscles in movement, please) but to stare straight at the giver: in short, look at the giver first, *then* lower your eyes to the gift" (p. 151). It appears in all this that Krug has been reduced from a suffering human being to simply "my favorite character" (p. 151), a figment impersonated by an actor for the sake of art.

As Krug's troubles multiply, his human reality is reaffirmed. The Nabokovian director here recedes into the background, leaving Krug to cope as best he can. But the death of his son provokes in Krug an unbearable strain. When he lashes out at the State and is condemned to prison, Nabokov again intervenes, less as director than as sympathetic God: "It was then that I felt a pang of pity for Adam and slid towards him along an inclined beam of pale light— causing instantaneous madness, but at least saving him from the senseless agony of his logical fate" (p. 233). From this point onward, Nabokov's directorial impulses reassert themselves, and the expected horror of the firing squad is diminished into movie footage. To establish the scene, Nabokov first takes a verbal still photograph (p. 237) which captures (with wide-angle lens, certainly) the assembled extras in their costumes as well as a bit of sloppy set-dressing. This long descriptive paragraph ends with his words to cast and crew: "You can move again" (p. 238).

The key moment comes, though, when Krug madly charges the dictator, prompting Nabokov to step in one final time: "He saw the Toad crouching at the foot of the wall, shaking, dissolving, speeding up his shrill incantations, protecting his dimming face with his transparent arm, and Krug ran towards him, and just a fraction of an instant before another and better bullet hit him, he shouted again: You, you—and the wall vanished, like a rapidly withdrawn slide, and I stretched myself and got up from among the chaos of written and rewritten pages, to investigate the sudden twang that something had made in striking the wire netting of my window" (p. 240). This climactic passage is rich in implications. It renders the Toad helpless by dealing with him in language reminiscent of cinematic techniques: "dissolving," "speeding up," "dimming," "transparent." The comparison of the vanishing wall to a withdrawn slide reminds us of Nabokov in his magic lantern days, controlling an imaginary destiny by casting images on a screen.[10] And by plucking Krug out of a seemingly realistic situation, Nabokov confirms Krug's status as a mere creature of his own fancy, a refugee from a fictive world coming to rest within the writer's larger reality.

But despite quiet hints throughout the novel, Krug is slow to realize that he is merely fictional. His sufferings are for him extremely real, and they must be dealt with as such. Significantly, he tries to relieve his troubled mind by resorting to his own brand of mental moviemaking. This occurs mostly while he sleeps, since for Nabokov a dream is closely related to a film. As Krug shuts off his conscious mind, his memory assembles a cast of characters, hires a third-rate "orchestra of the senses" (p. 64), and improvises a set out of the odds and ends available. The resulting dream-film may be a casual rerun of past events or a projection of suppressed desires, as when the sleeping Krug plays out his secret seduction of the governess (p. 178). At times, though, dreams may explode into nightmare. Krug's recurrent dream-image of his wife removing her jewels is transformed (pp. 81–82) into a grotesque striptease in which, accompanied by the click of a flash-camera, she sheds bones and flesh along with her clothing.

The waking mind, too, is prone to moviemaking. As an expert in these matters, Nabokov can tell us that "the script of daytime memory is far more subtle in regard to factual details, since a good deal of cutting and trimming and conventional recombination has to be done by the dream producers (of whom there are usually several, mostly illiterate and middle-class and pressed by time); but a show is always a show" (p. 63). In daylight hours, Krug's mental movie tends toward hope rather than horror. Thus he envisions his son as a happy young man in America, playing baseball, frequenting soda parlors, "crossing a technicoloured campus" (p. 188). But the fully awake Krug uses film most poignantly as a vain attempt at halting the onward rush of time.

This trait is common to several other Nabokov characters. Van sees in Ada's filmed image a chance to return to their common past. Humbert, remembering the beauty of Lolita's tennis game, aches for cinematic comfort: "I could have filmed her! I would have had her now with me, before my eyes, in the projection room of my pain and despair! . . . That I could have had all her strokes, all her enchantments, immortalized in segments of celluloid, makes me moan today with frustration."[11] Faced with a comparable loss, Krug too longs to freeze bygone happiness into a tangible permanence. Soon after Olga's death he stops to caress, ritualistically, the knob of a parapet, thinking, "This moment of conscious contact holds a drop of solace. The emergency brake of time. Whatever the present moment is, I have stopped it. Too late. In the course of our, let me see, twelve, twelve and three months, years of life together, I ought to have immobilized by this simple method millions of moments; paying perhaps terrific fines, but stopping the train" (pp. 12–13). Krug's feelings here are much like those of Nabokov himself in *Speak, Memory*'s most tender passage, directed toward his own wife and son: "I have to have all space and all time participate in my emotion, in my mortal love, so that the edge of its mortality is taken off, thus helping me to fight the utter degradation, ridicule, and horror of having developed an infinity of sensation and thought within a finite existence" (p. 297). For both Nabokov and Krug, death is an obscenity which the mind must somehow challenge.

Krug tries to challenge death as an artist would, fabricating pretty mental pictures of a wife not dead but convalescent in some remote storybook village. And yet mind cannot defeat mortality: "The picture is pretty, but how long can it stay on the screen? We expect the next slide, but the magic-lantern man has none left" (p. 98). Still Krug presses on, turning to the past as a means of making the present bearable. He would probably share with Van Veen the hopeful belief that "our modest Present is, then, the time span that one is directly and actually aware of, with the lingering freshness of the Past still perceived as part of the nowness" (p. 550). But whereas Van pursues an old movie as a way of infusing the past into the present, Krug turns movie director. One long passage in *Bend Sinister* watches him in action, directing and redirecting a half-remembered, half-invented sequence from Olga's girlhood. Seeking to make time and space work in his favor, he seizes on the ability of cinema to move both forward and back: "I think I want to have the whole scene repeated. Yes, from the beginning. . . . I think I shall have you go through your act a third time, but in reverse—carrying that hawk moth back into the orchard where you found it" (pp. 133–34). By means of a mental film, then, Krug seeks to stop, and even to reverse, the direction and the forward motion of his own life.

The cinema of the mind, though, is finally not enough. It contrasts painfully with the instant when Krug sees David on the screen. For this is one film that Krug cannot direct; the filmed image will not respond to his commands or even to his presence: "David had his warmest overcoat on, but his legs were bare and he wore his bedroom slippers. The whole thing lasted a moment: he turned his face up to the nurse, his eyelashes beat, his hair caught a gleam of lambent light; then he looked around, met Krug's eyes, showed no sign of recognition and uncertainly went down the few steps that remained" (p. 223). Here Krug is totally helpless. Even if he were to set the film running in reverse, he could not undo the reality that film merely reproduces. No wonder that Krug, his last mental resource gone, is ripe for madness.

Meanwhile the agent of this madness, the director who works Krug's insanity into his scenario, can be seen in another light. From Krug's perspective he is an all-powerful figure, capable of superseding as if by magic the forces of the State. And yet he is no god, not even a Hitchcock, but rather a worker in words whose bouts with language are similar to those of Krug himself. Krug turns to mind-pictures partly because words fail him in his moment of grief. Unable to write, he can only re-create in visual terms the images of his loss. The Nabokovian narrator need contend with no such sorrow, but he is faced with the task of trying to render in verbal form the flights of his imagination. His basic problem is not far from that of Krug: "And then, thought Krug, on top of everything, I am a slave of images. We speak of one thing being like some other thing when what we are really craving to do is to describe something that is like nothing on earth" (p. 174). Nabokov, of course, is a gifted artist, one whose verbal felicities are widely recognized. But in *Bend Sinister* we see the narrator he associates with himself (in his 1963 introduction and elsewhere) struggling at times to suit his words to his meaning. Early on, this narrator hesitates in describing his hero: "He had thick (let me see) clumsy (there) fingers which always trembled slightly" (p. 6). And later he vainly tries to hold back the flow of the narrative by reminding himself, "Last chance of describing the bedroom" (p. 107). In one of the now-insane Krug's precious transcendent moments he seems to hear, from his prison cell, "the cautious crackling of a page which had been viciously crumpled and thrown into the wastebasket and was making a pitiful effort to uncrumple itself and live just a little longer" (pp. 233–34). As the introduction hints, the discarded page represents Nabokov wrestling with his first draft in his flat in Cambridge, Massachusetts (pp. v, xii–xiii).

Bend Sinister, in many ways, is a book about the limitations of language. The debased, cliché-ridden language of the State, the thwarted language of Adam Krug, the graceful yet self-questioning language of the author-narrator: all serve to undermine our sense of the supremacy of words. Krug, as we have seen, tries to escape from the burden of language by retreating into cinematic images. Curiously, the narrative format of *Bend Sinister* seems at times an attempt to render verbally the techniques of the cinema. The shifting camera angles of the interview sequence and the stop-action in the last scene have already been detailed, but other examples abound. The novel opens cinematically with a lingering pan of the sunlight and shadow observed by Krug from Olga's hospital window. The style here is close to the subjective camera technique in which we look temporarily through the eyes of a given person before returning to the normal objectivity of film. Krug's later raising of a handkerchief to his spectacles to wipe not the lenses themselves but "the dark sky and amorphous houses" (p. 7) exemplifies this technique once more. When Krug in his apartment undertakes to telephone a friend, the abrupt spatial transition is similar to a jump cut: "He found his spare glasses and then the familiar number with the six in the middle resembling Ember's Persian nose, and Ember put down his pen, removed the long amber cigarette holder from his thickly pursed lips and listened" (p. 28). There is also an explicitly labeled close-up (p. 60), and one key passage illustrates the town's "Painted Days" by means of a long tracking shot which takes in muddy curbs, gleaming house fronts, freshly painted benches, a toy balloon, busy cafes, and a man's rubber overshoe and blood-stained cuff lying in the middle of a sidewalk (p. 129). Elsewhere the perceptive reader can find slow motion, speed-ups, flashbacks, and other familiar film devices. One might also note that the rebel leader who remains unseen throughout the novel is named Phokus, a word strongly reminiscent of camera focus.

The frequent use of techniques borrowed from the cinema, when coupled with Krug's mental movies and the intervention of Nabokov in the guise of film director, suggests that the novel has one more fertile thematic dimension. This concerns the tension between written language and film. Like Krug, the narrator of *Bend Sinister* appears determined at times to shape his thoughts and observations into the purely visual vocabulary of cinema. He is no more fully successful at this than Krug is, though for a rather different reason. As a writer he must rely upon words, and while words can describe a picture, they are fundamentally unable to *be* a picture. With words, it seems, the mind always intrudes: in the opening chapter, for instance, strictly visual impressions soon give rise to memory and wordplay. Though Alain Robbe-Grillet experiments with language as photography in his *Snapshots* (*Instantanés*, 1962) and though Pound and others have made extravagant claims for the pictorial aspect of the Chinese ideogram, the fact remains that words are linked to an abstract meaning in a way that a picture or film is not. In choosing language rather than film as the basic mode of expression, the novelist assuredly gains some key artistic advantages—far more control over cast and crew, for example, than any *auteur* director could wish for.[12] But the novelist also unavoidably is cut off from certain effects which words can only approximate.

By distilling film techniques into language, Nabokov explores the gulf between the two media. The bridging of this gulf can be seen as part of the problem of the translator, as set forth in that portion of *Bend Sinister* wherein Krug and Ember discuss both the translation of Shakespeare's plays into foreign tongues and the transferring of *Hamlet* from page to screen. In Krug's mind, the task of rendering the rhythms and metaphors of Shakespeare in a different language is bound to be fruitless. He compares it to the man who, having seen a certain unique oak tree, proceeds to erect in his garden "a prodigiously intricate piece of machinery which in itself was as unlike that or any other tree as the translator's inspiration and language were unlike those of the original author, but which, by means of in-genious combinations of parts, light effects, breeze-engendering en-gines, would, when completed, cast a shadow exactly similar to that" of the tree in question (pp. 119–20). Is not such an act, specu-lates Krug, simply "an exaggerated and spiritualized replica of Pa-duk's writing machine?" (p. 120). Presumably, the wind machines and light effects which would help to translate Hamlet's Denmark to the movie screen merely contribute to a shadow play which is one more glorified padograph. So verbal language cannot be transformed into cinematic visuals without the loss of its own artistic reality. And the same applies to visual artistry when we try to pin it down in words. Translation inevitably means debasement.

The same axiom holds true when external reality is translated into art. In Krug's case this signifies that his delicate re-creations of his life with Olga are merely poor copies of the actual life he once knew. And the writer, like the filmmaker, is aware that his finished product is always one step removed from that reality existing within his mind. Of course, the artificiality of art is one of its greatest charms. Nabokov often reminds us, too, that all reality is merely subjective and hence not to be treated too solemnly.[13] But special problems are posed when, as in *Bend Sinister*, the apparent reality established by an artist within the framework of artifice is juxta-posed against the artist's own world.

The transfiguration of Krug at the end of *Bend Sinister* com-pletes his slide into non-being. The State works to deprive him of his soul, but Nabokov himself does this far more efficiently by convinc-ing him that "he and his son and his wife and everybody else are merely my whims and megrims." This passage from Nabokov's 1963 introduction speaks of Krug, in his state of "blessed madness," as coming to perceive "the simple reality of things" (p. viii). But it is a reality which has no place for Krug except as someone else's char-acter. In the moment that Krug's life is saved, his life is also lost; the free will he strove to preserve within the movie scenario has been emphatically denied him.

Nabokov surely realizes that in rescuing his "favorite character" he is taking from him the traits that made him worthy of affection. He knows that "the immortality I had conferred on the poor fellow was a slippery sophism, a play upon words" (p. 241). Perhaps it is for this reason that we are conscious, in the last page of the novel, of a moth fluttering outside Nabokov's window. This, we learn in the in-troduction, is Olga, her rosy soul bombinating "in the damp dark at the bright window of my room" (p. xiii). On the far side of the window screen (as in the far-off world of the novel), Olga retains a reality of her own. If the screen were taken down, though, she would end up as a prized but wholly inert specimen in a collection of butterflies: "A good night for mothing," says Nabokov to conclude the novel (p. 241).[14] Whereas Olga had once been alive, not least in the memories of those who knew her, in this new reality she would now be merely an object. Similarly Krug, when whisked off the movie screen by his director-turned-projectionist, leaves his sentient self behind. In the wider, brighter world he enters, preservation means paralysis. Yet only by such radical means can Krug be saved from that literal death which the logic of his script demands. In our own more strictly *cinéma vérité* experience, we have not even this chance of eluding the reality we face. In this, as in so much else, art and life are worlds apart.

To understand the film imagery of *Bend Sinister* is to hold the key to the novel's multiple meanings. Along with other forms of mass media, film is used both to convey the banality of the totalitarian regime and to suggest the State's attempts to control popular opinion. But film, as a recording (as well as a reshaping) of life, also serves to unveil the horror which the State is determined to keep hidden. Film references, moreover, effectively delineate the role of the novelist within *Bend Sinister*: in putting himself forth as an *auteur* filmmaker, the Nabokovian author-narrator reveals his power over his fictive world. This contrasts with the main character's reliance on mental movies in a hopeless attempt to regain control over a life molded both by the State and by the demands of his author.

For Krug, film provides an alternative to words as a mode of expression. The author too tries to avail himself of film techniques but finds that language cannot quite approximate the purely visual cinematic image. This discovery underscores the basic aesthetic gap between literature and film, a gap which is of profound interest to Nabokov. He broadens this topic to include the whole futile issue of translation—from page to screen, from one language to another—and, by analogy, the equally vain translation of a character from one form of reality to another, from the reality of art (to put it simply) into the reality of life. Here we see, however subtly, the limitation of an author's power. Though he can act toward his characters with the hauteur of a deity or of a Hitchcockian director, he himself is curbed by the boundaries of his medium. He cannot solve the problems of one art form with the devices of another; nor can he, in deus-ex-machina fashion, rescue a character from a fictive environment without destroying the validity both of the environment and of the character. It is proof of Nabokov's artistic greatness that he can break these rules for the sake of an aesthetic point and still give us a thoroughly compelling novel.

NOTES

1. Alfred Appel, Jr., *Nabokov's Dark Cinema*, p. 107.
2. Nabokov spent six months in Hollywood preparing a screenplay of *Lolita* for director Stanley Kubrick. The completed film, though, altered much of what he had written. In an interview with Herbert Gold, Nabokov had this to say about the film: "I do not wish to imply that Kubrick's film is mediocre; in its own right, it is first-rate, but it is not what I wrote. A tinge of *poshlost* [*sic*] is often given by the cinema to the novel it distorts and coarsens in its crooked glass. Kubrick, I think, avoided this fault in his version, but I shall never understand why he did not follow my directions and dreams" (*Strong Opinions*, pp. 105–6). *Poshlost'*, of course, is Nabokov's favorite Russian word for vulgarity.
3. Nabokov, *Ada*, pp. 253–54. Hereafter cited in text. *Ada* contains Nabokov's use of the term "fokus-pokus" in referring to film themes (p. 426).
4. Nabokov, *Bend Sinister* (1973), p. 78. Hereafter cited in text. The 1973 McGraw-Hill edition contains both the original text (New York: Holt, 1947) and the later introduction (dated 9 September 1963) to the Time Reading Program Special Edition (New York: Time, Inc., 1964).
5. Nabokov is surely remembering here his own years in Hitler's Germany, where one's ears were constantly bombarded by "the multiplied roar of a dictator." See Nabokov, *Speak, Memory*, p. 300. Hereafter cited in text.
6. Nabokov, *The Real Life of Sebastian Knight*, p. 205. I take "the old conjuror [who] waits in the wings with his hidden rabbit" to be an avatar of Nabokov, the author behind the several authors visible within the novel.
7. Nabokov, foreword to *Lolita: A Screenplay*, pp. ix–x.
8. Appel, *Nabokov's Dark Cinema*, pp. 129–30, documents the mutual admiration between Nabokov and Hitchcock. During the winter of 1970, Hitchcock asked Nabokov to write an original screenplay, but the latter declined because of his commitment to the novel *Transparent Things*.
9. Nabokov, *Strong Opinions*, p. 163. Nabokov here speaks of his affectionate memories of Marx Brothers movies, particularly the famous stateroom sequence from *A Night at the Opera*. During this same interview (p. 161) he mentions his appearance as an émigré extra in long-forgotten German motion pictures.
10. See Nabokov, *Speak, Memory*, pp. 164–65, 153, 155.
11. Nabokov, *The Annotated Lolita*, pp. 233–34.
12. Nabokov seems to be voicing his own opinion in *Ada* when he says of Van: "For him the written word existed only in its abstract purity, in its

unrepeatable appeal to an equally ideal mind. It belonged solely to its creator and could not be spoken or enacted by a mime (as Ada insisted) without letting the deadly stab of another's mind destroy the artist in the very lair of his art. A written play was intrinsically superior to the best performance of it, even if directed by the author himself" (p. 425).

13. In a BBC television interview originally taped in 1962 and reprinted in *Strong Opinions,* Nabokov is quoted as saying, "You can get nearer and nearer, so to speak, to reality; but you never get near enough because reality is an infinite succession of steps, levels of perception, false bottoms, and hence unquenchable, unattainable" (p. 11). He has restated this position in several other well-known interviews.

14. Susan Fromberg Schaeffer sees this incident differently in her *"Bend Sinister* and the Novelist as Anthropomorphic Deity," *Centennial Review* 17 (1973), 115–51. This article, though it does not deal with the film element per se, is certainly the best and most complete study of *Bend Sinister* to date.

Deciphering "Signs and Symbols"

LARRY R. ANDREWS

In his little story about a family of émigré Russian Jews called "Signs and Symbols" (1948), Vladimir Nabokov suggests that the son is destroyed by the very forces he fears in his "referential mania." At least he tantalizes us with this possibility, yet all the while he is chuckling at us, and particularly if we are symbol-hunting critics, for momentarily believing in it. It is the intention of this study to demonstrate how Nabokov foreshadows by hidden clues an ending he does not reveal explicitly—the mad son's suicide, perhaps by defenestration. It will conclude by exposing the irony that makes these clues ultimately false.[1]

On a first reading we may find the story superficial, with its shameless exploitation of suspense and clichéd, indeterminate ending. Can the author be *serious*? Yet the tone is quiet and unsensational. The characters' situation is compelling. Something leaves us vaguely uneasy. Upon further examination we perceive the narrator's wayward, Gogolesque eye for seemingly trivial and insignificant details. We notice the odd focus at both the opening and close of the story on the parents' birthday present of jellies for their insane son.

In the first paragraph of the story, Nabokov emphasizes the difficulty of finding the son a "safe" birthday present in view of his "referential mania": "For the fourth time in as many years they were confronted with the problem of what birthday present to bring a young man who was incurably deranged in his mind. He had no desires. Man-made objects were to him either hives of evil, vibrant with a malignant activity that he alone could perceive, or gross comforts for which no use could be found in his abstract world."[2] The parents, however, are confident that they have found a proper gift: "After eliminating a number of articles that might offend him or frighten him (anything in the gadget line for instance was taboo), his parents chose a dainty and innocent trifle: a basket with ten different fruit jellies in ten little jars." The jellies will come to seem anything but innocent, as we shall see, and Nabokov's emphasis on them here (end of sentence, end of paragraph, repetition of number) helps to establish their important role in the story.

Nabokov slyly reminds us of the jellies twice again in the middle of the story. When the parents are turned away from the sanitarium after learning of their son's latest suicide attempt, they bring the present back with them to save for the next visit, because "the place was so miserably understaffed, and things got mislaid or mixed up so easily." And later, on the way home, the mother gives the father the basket of jellies to take home, while she stops to buy fish. Then in the last paragraph the jellies loom large again. At the couple's "festive midnight tea" celebrating their decision to take their son out of the institution and care for him at home, "the birthday present stood on the table." The father is in the act of fondling the jars and spelling out the names of the jellies, when the telephone rings for the third time. With the third ring of the telephone the story breaks off, raising the possibility—but leaving it only a possibility—that the call is from the sanitarium and brings the news that the son has finally succeeded in killing himself. At the same time that Nabokov seems to be treating the jellies as "innocent," he has carefully linked them in the structure of the story to the son's fears, to his unsuccessful suicide attempt, and to the possibility of a final, successful suicide.

We do not know whether the late phone call at the end will be a wrong number again, a death notice from the sanitarium, or some other call. It could be either trivial or ominous. Yet the parents are frightened by the first call: "it was an unusual hour for their telephone to ring," the husband gapes in suspense at his wife, and the wife clutches "her old tired heart" and says, "It frightened me." Clearly they fear that their son has succeeded in killing himself. When the second call comes, the wife is much more matter-of-fact about it. By the third call they are completely relaxed over the pleasure of the tea and the "luminous" little jars. Their confidence makes them ripe for disaster. Nabokov has emphasized this confidence in the opening and closing paragraphs in order to make the reader suspect dramatic irony and conclude that the final call will report the son's death. The proof is that in both scenes he links the *jellies* to the parents' feelings of self-assurance. He thus leads us to suspect that the jellies are not "innocent" but are in some mysterious way a *cause* of the supposed death. An overwhelming irony becomes apparent in what appeared to be a rather plotless and inconsequential story: the parents, who have tried to please their son with a birthday gift, and who have decided to bring him back home to *save* him from suicide, may in fact have helped to cause his death. They may have been used unwittingly as part of the conspiracy of mysterious forces which the son has long feared and attempted to escape by suicide. But suicide in this context would, of course, be a self-defeating gesture, less a liberation than an ultimate entrapment signaling the triumph of the hostile forces.

Other details of the story support this view. The jellies are part of an intricate system of images and symbols which add a second dimension to Nabokov's title. On one level, the signs and symbols of the title are those mysterious sources of apparent meaning that afflict the son in his referential mania. On another level, they are the literary signs and symbols which the reader or critic must interpret in order to find meaning in the story. One cluster of such signs—in both senses—is the tree images. Trees are among the elements of "phenomenal nature" which supposedly conspire against the son in his delusions: "His inmost thoughts are discussed at nightfall, in manual alphabet, by darkly gesticulating trees." "Groaning firs" on mountainsides also participate. The jellies are an indirect extension of this tree imagery—they come from fruit trees—and can be seen as insidiously infiltrating the relatively treeless city and sterile sanitarium walls in the hands of the well-meaning parents. The names of the jellies are singled out for special emphasis at the end, as the old man's "clumsy moist lips spelled out their eloquent labels: apricot, grape, beech plum, quince." The stress on "eloquent" and the focus on the words themselves recall the "manual alphabet" of the trees. The father's act of pronouncing the words may in fact signal the son's death. Certainly the emphasis on external forces as bearers of secret coded messages puts us on the alert as to Nabokov's own tricks of language and imagery in the story.

The imagery of sinister trees is echoed elsewhere in the story. Immediately after leaving the sanitarium, the parents encounter a "swaying and dripping tree" with "a tiny half-dead unfledged bird" under it (the bird image will also soon prove momentous). The "swaying" motion here recalls the "manual alphabet" of the "gesticulating trees" mentioned above as well as the general description of the hostile forces as an "undulation of things." An unpleasant tree also figures prominently in the exposition of the son's increasingly phobic childhood. At the age of eight, he was "afraid of a certain picture in a book which merely showed an idyllic landscape with rocks on a hillside and an old cart wheel hanging from the branch of a leafless tree." Since leaflessness suggests lifelessness, this tree is perhaps intended to foreshadow the son's death. The tree images may even be reflected in the metaphor of "a dense tangle of logically interacting illusions" (jungle?) and in the references to the "swollen veins" in the old man's hands and the prominent vein on his head (leaf venation? roots?). Several other key objects in the story with sinister overtones are also products ("man-made objects") of trees— the Russian newspaper, the playing cards, the album and photographs, the wallpaper, the picture book, the cart wheel, and even the labels on the jelly jars (not to mention the paper on which the story itself is printed). Finally, the only animal life mentioned in the story occurs in passages on the son's mania and consists, with perhaps the exception of the bees suggested in "hives of evil," of species that inhabit trees: the squirrel in the park which the four-year-old boy was "looking away from" in the photograph; the primate in the metaphor of the scything farmer's brutal "simian stoop"; and, most importantly, the numerous references to birds.

While the tree images tend to be negatively colored and to function as hostile forces, the bird images that pervade the story are ambivalent and may suggest either freedom or entrapment. A bird image with the former connotation appears in the description of one of the son's recent suicide attempts. Nabokov tantalizingly refuses to elaborate on this attempt, saying only that it was a "masterpiece of inventiveness" and that an "envious" inmate interpreted it as an attempt to fly. That it was indeed an attempt to fly—to escape from persecution by emulating a bird's freedom—is suggested by the later reference to the son's drawings of "wonderful birds with human hands and feet." This image, combined with the "envious" inmate's interpretation of the suicide attempt, hints that the son's final, successful suicide, if it occurred, also took the form of some ingenious emulation of flight. (The father's concern to keep knives locked up after their son returns to them shows the parents' misunderstanding of him.)

A conspicuously negative bird image, suggesting death and entrapment, occurs in close conjunction with the sanitarium. After failing to see their distraught son, the old couple encounter the "tiny half-dead unfledged bird . . . helplessly twitching in a puddle" cited earlier. Clearly this bird is a symbol of the son himself, who has never properly grown up and who is at the mercy of the sinister forces represented by the "swaying and dripping tree" overhead and the inescapable puddle. It also refers to the recent suicide attempt and foreshadows the possibility of successful suicide at the end. The son does not have wings and cannot escape, yet he perhaps tries to fly out a window at the sanitarium and is destroyed in the attempt.

Still more bird references infiltrate the story in clever disguises. On the bus from the sanitarium the boy's mother notices "a girl with dark hair and grubby red toenails . . . weeping on the shoulder of an older woman. Whom did that woman resemble? She resembled Rebecca Borisovna, whose daughter had married one of the Soloveichiks—in Minsk, years ago." The name "Soloveichik" is a diminutive of the Russian word for nightingale, *solovey*, subject of many popular songs, poems, and legends, in which it connotes persecution and sorrow. This nightingale reference is echoed in the names of the doctor ("Solov," a truncated form of the same word) and next-door neighbor (Mrs. "Sol," a still further shortened form of the word which may refer simultaneously to "sun," as we shall see).

In addition to the tree and bird images there is a host of other "signs and symbols" seemingly at work in the story. The suggestion that the son in the sanitarium is like a caged bird is related to a whole series of claustral images, which in turn reinforce the idea of a sinister conspiracy directed against and enclosing the son. The sanitarium, the parents' flat, and the building that contains the flat are oppressive enclosures. The son has tried to flee the institution. The flat is small and will seem even smaller if the son moves in, and it has a "narrow yard." The power failure in the subway causes temporary enclosure and entrapment and is the first example following the foreboding statement, "That Friday everything went wrong." The crowded bus, the hard rain, the umbrella, the bus-stop shelter, the puddle with the struggling bird, the landing on which the old man waits ten minutes, and the "unswept corners" of neglected children also serve to circumscribe and hem in. Even the jellies are imprisoned in jars, which in turn are enclosed in a basket. All of these images, besides commenting on the stifling and dehumanizing atmosphere of the city, reflect the son's mania: to him the whole world is an enclosure he wants to "tear a hole in . . . and escape."

Death images form another branch of the conspiracy and also serve as foreshadowing devices in the plot. The mother wears "black dresses"; the stalled subway is described as having "lost its life current"; the bird in the puddle is "half-dead"; the anonymous neighbor seen through the window is a "black-trousered man," lying, in a deathlike posture, "supine on an untidy bed"; Aunt Rosa was obsessed with death and catastrophe and was herself put to death; and the old father comes out of the bedroom saying, "I can't sleep because I am dying." The midnight hour and the crucial zero of the telephone number also intimate death. And in general, the imminence of death and decay pervades the old people's lives, from her heavy "trudging" up the stairs to his swollen head vein and the "horrible masklike grimace" in the mirror when he removes his dentures.

Another persistent pattern in the complex conspiracy of the

story is the parent-child relationship, stressing an element of parental responsibility for the offspring's unhappiness or death. Was it right to place the son in the caged institution that "was so miserably understaffed," where "things got mislaid or mixed up so easily"? This innocent language refers to the jellies but obliquely suggests that the son himself has become a "thing" that the parents have "mislaid" and is now even more "mixed up" than before. The father suddenly decides to bring the son home, because he feels guilty over the latter's suicide attempts: " 'We must get him out of there quick. Otherwise we'll be responsible. Responsible!' he repeated and hurled himself into a sitting position, both feet on the floor, thumping his forehead with his clenched fist." The parents *are* indirectly responsible for the son's condition, not just because they have put him in an asylum or have been unable to understand him but because the jellies and every other object they come into contact with seem to use them to persecute him. This responsibility is implicit in the distance between parents and son. They were unusually old when he was born, and now twenty years later they are aged. They are also physically separated from the son. No direct communication between them and their son occurs in the story or even in the snippets of exposition from the past (photographs mingled with reminiscence). The budding child prodigy had become not only "difficult to understand" at eight but "totally inaccessible to normal minds" in his teens. The sanitarium nurse turns the parents away for fear that their "visit might disturb him." Even their various migrations through Europe and America in flight from revolution, world war, and pogrom must have had a disturbing effect on the child.

Again there are concealed clues to reinforce the monstrous suspicion that the story's end portends a suicide for which the parents are responsible. The story is filled with images of parental distance and neglect. The "unfledged bird" that symbolizes the son has been neglected by its parents—neither guarded closely nor trained for survival in the world on its own. The raven-haired girl on the bus is weeping on an older woman's shoulder and reminds the mother of another mother and daughter from the past. The girl here is unhappy and unkempt, with "grubby red toenails." Earlier the "garrulous high-school children" on the bus exist in isolation from parents and are annoying to the old couple. Later the mother muses on the "neglected children" of the world with impotent sorrow. The reference to the father's prosperous brother Isaac recalls the similar prosperity of the Biblical Isaac and underscores two other parallels with that story: (1) the extreme age of Abraham and Sarah when Isaac was born is a parallel to the age of the father and mother in the story; (2) the divine test in which Abraham nearly slew his son as a sacrifice is a parallel to the parents' implicit responsibility for their son's condition and his attempted suicides. The son's tragic wish to fly also reminds us of the Icarus myth, in which the father, Daedalus, is responsible for his son's death, while the father survives.

Other, less conspicuous symbolic patterns arise through the use of doubling.[3] We have seen that the black-trousered man is the son's double, because he is used to foreshadow the son's death. The son's cousin also serves as a double. This cousin is a "famous chess player" and is perhaps a projection of Luzhin in Nabokov's *The Defense*, who is also a victim of referential mania and who commits suicide by defenestration. There are other doubles for the parents and son in addition to the parallel sets of parents and children mentioned in the preceding paragraph. The insensitive nurse at the sanitarium is yet another reflection of the "irresponsible" mother. And two pairs of details link the son with the father: (1) at age six the son is described as having "insomnia like a grown-up man," and in the last scene we see that the father is unable to sleep for anxiety over his son; (2) the son is referred to as "ill-shaven," and one of the last details in the story shows that "although [the father] had shaved that morning, a silvery bristle showed on his chin." Furthermore, both the father and the son are imprisoned and dying. These details suggest that the son's condition is partly due to his similarity to his father, thus again implying the father's responsibility for the son's possible death.

Doubling is not only applied to character: there is also a doubling of images, such as those of trees and birds discussed earlier. In fact, almost every hostile image in the long paragraph describing the son's referential mania is doubled elsewhere in the story. Below is a list of such images:

Description of mania	*References elsewhere*
"clouds in the staring sky"	the cloudy, rainy day, "rain tinkled in the dark," "monstrous darkness"
"pebbles," "granite," "mountains"	"rocks on a hillside"
"stains"	"blotched with acne," "brown-spotted skin," "soiled cards," "large birthmark"
"sun flecks"	"Mrs. Sol," "fault-finding light of spring days"

Description of mania	*References elsewhere*
"glass surfaces"	the mirror the father uses, "his raised glass," "his spectacles," the jelly jars
"still pools"	the puddle, the tea
"coats"	"old overcoat"
"store windows"	"windows were blandly alight and in one of them a black-trousered man could be seen," allusion to window in description of son's suicide attempt
"lynchers at heart"	"cart wheel hanging from the branch of a leafless tree," "one could hear nothing but the dutiful beating of one's heart," "her hand went to her old tired heart," "knave of hearts"
"running water," "torrents"	"raining hard," "dripping," "circular motion" of the tea
"storms"	"raining hard," "thunder"
"undulation of things"	"swaying," "waves of pain"
"air he exhales is indexed and filed away"	"foul air of the subway," "pneumonia"
"groaning"	"moan"

Other pairs of images include the newspapers rustling on the subway echoed in the father's Russian newspaper at home and the "twitching" of the bird echoed in the "twitching" of the father's old hands. The sinister implications here are again monstrous. The real world of the parents and even the language of the story seem to be infiltrated by the hostile elements of the son's mania. Furthermore, the extraordinary emphasis on images of language codes ("veiled reference," "transmit," "alphabet," "messages," "cipher," "decoding") invites us to consider the story itself as a code with a sinister meaning.

Another pattern emerges from the numerological symbolism of the story, which brings us to the deck of cards and the telephone number. The numbers that dominate the story tend to be even:

2—"two-room flat," "twice a week"
4—"fourth time in as many years," "quarter of an hour," "four years old"

6—"age six," father reading sixth label when phone rings at end

8—"aged about eight"

10—"ten different fruit jellies in ten little jars," "ten minutes later," "aged ten"

12—"scientific monthly," "midnight"

20—"a score of years," age of son

40—"American of almost forty years standing"

Yet a few odd numbers infiltrate with particular suspiciousness. The mystic number three shows in the three sections of the story, three landings on the stairs, three cards on the floor, three telephone calls at the end, and three suicide attempts specifically mentioned or suggested. The knave of hearts and the nine and ace of spades, the cards that accidentally fall to the floor with the picture of Elsa and her beau, are also suspicious, since Nabokov's careful eye selects them for naming. The nine is yet another mystic number, the square of the mystic number three, which occurs regularly in the story. The ace of spades is a traditional omen of death. The knave of hearts contains at least three allusions, all of them relevant to the concerns of the story: (1) an allusion to guilt, since the knave of hearts is the stealer of tarts in Lewis Carroll's *Alice's Adventures in Wonderland*, which Nabokov translated into Russian and published in Germany in 1923; (2) an allusion to conspiracy and death, since in Nabokov's early novel *King, Queen, Knave* the "knave" conspires to murder his lover's husband; (3) an allusion to the rainy, claustrophobic setting of Baudelaire's first "Spleen" poem and to its description of an old deck of cards with dirty odors:

> Héritage fatal d'une vieille hydropique,
> Le beau valet de coeur et la dame de pique
> Causent sinistrement de leurs amours défunts.

> Fatal inheritance from a dropsical crone,
> The handsome knave of hearts and the queen of spades
> Chat sinisterly of their dead loves.

These lines echo the story's pervasive imagery of death and decay and also the son's fantasy that things are communicating with each other in sinister ways about him.

When we hear of the "wrong number" on the first two phone calls, we are suddenly convinced that the texture of numbers in the story is part of the conspiracy against the son. All we know about the wrong number is that the girl is "turning the letter O instead of the zero." On the third try, presumably the girl dials the correct number, the zero. If so, the third ring is not hers and is perhaps the sanitarium's. Zero is a death omen as well as a "veiled reference" to the "cipher" of the referential mania: "cipher" can mean "zero" as well as "code" and "symbolic image." The zero is thus a part of the son's mania, and all the numbers seem to be a part of the code used by the hostile forces. The telephone itself becomes a sinister threat because of the numbers on its dial, because of the prominence of zero among those numbers in the story's final episode, and also because it is the most obvious example in the story of the sort of man-made "gadget" mentioned in the first paragraph as "malignant" and hence "taboo" as a birthday gift.

Another important detail in the phone call is the mention of the name "Charlie." It seems strange that Nabokov refuses to name the three leading characters in the story but gladly offers up the names of minor characters who do not even appear (Mrs. Sol, Herman Brink) and finally names a seemingly irrelevant "Charlie," who is asked for by someone dialing a wrong number! The namelessness of the main characters has, however, at least two purposes: it suggests their lack of clear identity, especially in the case of the son; and it also suggests, when set in the context of the extensive naming of others, that the world outside is strong and threatening and that names are a part of its sinister code. As in the case of the numbers, however, the hostile significance of the names is not always clear. By now we have surely come to see the story as a gothic tale.

The images that have symbolic overtones in the story sometimes occur with similar overtones in Nabokov's other work: Humbert fears the conspiracies of poplar trees and lovebirds in a cage; and Pnin is paranoiac about his oak-leaved wallpaper. The conspiracy finally extends beyond the world of this particular story to include characters in earlier novels (such as Luzhin) and also, proleptically, characters in the later novels as well. We are implicitly invited to read those novels in terms of this story and this story in terms of those novels, so that Nabokov's entire career gradually takes on the appearance of an elaborate code with an intricate symbolic meaning.

As we perceive the intricate system of hidden clues in the story, apparently planted by Nabokov to convince us that the son's paranoia is justified and the conspiracy real, we momentarily suspend our disbelief and see the world through the son's eyes, the sane and insane visions now reversed. The dull, gray world of the parents now seems impossible, unreal, insane, and tainted by mortality, while the son's imaginary world is intensely alive.[4] The fictive world viewed by the son has taken over the "real" world of the parents in our eyes and in the fabric of the story. Everything in the story seems to corroborate the son's feeling of total vulnerability. The world has become a projection of his self turned inside out ("The silhouettes of his blood corpuscles, magnified a million times, flit over vast plains"). It is astonishing how Nabokov has involved us in this vision in so short a space. Yet, in retrospect, such a paranoiac view of the world seems preposterous, no matter how plausibly the fiction justifies it. The suggestion that occult influences have affected even the linguistic texture of the story seems, in retrospect, particularly absurd. The idea is slightly more credible in "The Vane Sisters" and "Scenes from the Life of a Double Monster," because of their first-person point of view. But here, after being momentarily mesmerized by Nabokov's skillful imagery, we emerge from the trance realizing that the sly author has played a joke on us again. Not only do we realize that the son is, after all, mad and the "conspiracy" his delusion, but we also realize that the question of which world (the son's or the parents') is real has become irrelevant, since both are equally unreal fictions of the author.

The artificiality of the ending, with its suggestive withholding of the story's climax, reminds us of the artificiality of the whole. Furthermore, there are many crucial elements of the plot that are either denied us by the artifice of the story or filtered through secondary, unreliable sources, thus calling further attention to the story's receding levels of artifice. The narrator seems objective, yet he withholds a great deal of straightforward information we are sure he possesses. Exactly what was the "masterpiece of inventiveness" of the son's recent suicide attempt? We are told only that "an envious fellow patient thought he was learning to fly—and stopped him." The son himself never appears in person. We go to visit him with the parents but are turned away. His childhood is glimpsed only in impressionistic fragments through the medium of photographs. Most of the details of the story are seen through the eyes of the parents: the jellies, sanitarium, rain, bird, people on the bus, neighbors, cards, photographs, and telephone (e.g., "she glanced at his old hands"; "she . . . examined the photographs"; "he put on his spectacles and re-examined . . . the . . . little jars"). The description of the son's mania, which is central to the image patterns, is itself of doubtful "reality." His symptoms and the term "referential mania" are not related directly by the narrator but through the medium of "an elaborate paper in a scientific monthly." Undercutting the seriousness with which we may take the article is the light mockery of its author as a comic stereotype of a German psychiatrist in the adjective "elaborate" and in the name Herman Brink, with its reminder of the thin borderline between sanity and madness, reasonable and arbitrary interpretations, fiction and "reality." Further undercutting the authority of the report is the fact that the parents had "puzzled it out for themselves" long before (but this puzzling out produces, of course, still another subjective view). Finally, much of the mania is described in imagery of art, making us aware of the artifice of the scientific paper and of the story itself ("reference," "alphabet," "patterns," "messages," "theme," "misinterpret," "indexed and filed," "silhouettes," "sum up . . . the ultimate truth of his being," in addition to the similar terms cited earlier). Brink's scholarly article can be seen as a fiction about the son, just as Nabokov's story is a fiction about Brink and the son, and just as this essay is a fiction about Nabokov's story. Where lies "reality"?

In his essay on the story William Carroll argues that "a 'cipher' can be a nullity just as easily as it can be a key, but most readers will see it as a key; we will conclude that the third call is from the hospital. In so doing, we will have assigned a meaning to the signs based on something outside the closed system; we will have, in effect, participated with Nabokov in killing the boy."[5] Carroll also points out that it is "just as plausible to argue . . . that the signs and symbols of death have no logically inherent and inescapable conclusion." He nonetheless insists that "most readers" (and this presumably includes Carroll himself) automatically complete the pattern of symbols, assume that the third call is from the sanitarium, and therefore "kill" the boy by mentally writing their own ending to the story. Such a view does not take full account of the story's aesthetic implications. As soon as we appreciate that the story is a fiction and that all its clues are therefore false, the "reality" of the boy and his mania is shattered, and it is no longer possible to speak of our participation in his "world." There is no ambiguity left at the end about the significance or meaninglessness of the symbols in the story, and speculation about the boy's possible suicide is irrelevant, since the world of the story has ceased to exist with the story's final punctuation mark. It has been translated, so to speak, from our perspective to the higher sphere of the artist's fictive world (in which we are characters too) and ultimately to a configuration of black marks on the page. The reliability of *all* the information about the boy is questionable. Carroll's argument to the contrary notwithstanding, we *are* ultimately distanced from the story and hence even from what Carroll calls an "esthetic responsibility" for the boy's death.[6]

This is the final stage of deciphering "Signs and Symbols," the stage that goes one step beyond Carroll's otherwise convincing interpretation. This stage reminds us of the "Hegelian syllogism of humor" practiced by Axel Rex in *Laughter in the Dark*:

Uncle alone in the house with the children said he'd dress up to amuse them. After a long wait, as he did not appear, they went down and saw a masked man putting the table silver into a bag. "Oh, Uncle," they cried in delight. "Yes, isn't my make-up good?" said Uncle, taking his mask off. Thus goes the Hegelian syllogism of humor. Thesis: Uncle made himself up as a burglar (a laugh for the children); antithesis: it *was* a burglar (a laugh for the reader); synthesis: it still was Uncle (fooling the reader).[7]

William Woodin Rowe uses this passage to illustrate his contention that in Nabokov's works "the reader is often subtly induced to draw premature, erroneous conclusions about *what* is taking place."[8] In "Signs and Symbols" the parents at first seem innocent. Then they appear to be implicated in their son's condition and perhaps his death; finally, we sense the hoax: the story is a fiction, and nobody is responsible. Yet the joke is a serious one. Nabokov is not simply playing an empty game at our expense. He is affirming art as sacred play. In calling our attention to the artifice of his story, he reminds us of the superior vision of the artist. As a private world of the imagination the story shares something with the son's mania. But unlike the latter it is redeemed by an act of freedom—the artistic expression that consciously creates the fictive world of the story and the playful configuration of its language. Nabokov succeeds in capturing both our belief and our disbelief. We relish the irony after the terror of momentary belief. And in so doing we are rescued from the foul air of mortality by the pleasure and vivifying force of art.

NOTES

1. I agree with William Carroll ("Nabokov's Signs and Symbols," in *A Book of Things about Vladimir Nabokov*, ed. Proffer, pp. 203–17) on the deceptive nature of the symbols and omens in the story though not entirely on the ultimate relation of the reader to the author and the work. Furthermore, I attempt to give a fuller analysis of the story's image patterns and false clues than does Carroll.
2. The text of the story will be found in Nabokov, *Nabokov's Dozen*, pp. 67–74.
3. Cf. L. L. Lee, "Duplexity in Vladimir Nabokov's Short Stories," *Studies in Short Fiction* 2 (1965), 307–15.
4. As Douglas Fowler puts it, "The mad young fantasts of the stories 'Lance' and 'Signs and Symbols' and Luzhin in *The Defense* create complicated second worlds—wholly subjective, yet both terrible and wonderful in the completeness and energy with which they are endowed"; and later, "In Nabokov's world, fact kills, fantasy gives life" (*Reading*

Nabokov, pp. 161, 172). We note that the son has brilliant mental powers and considers himself superior to all other people.

5. Carroll, "Nabokov's Signs and Symbols," p. 214.
6. Ibid., p. 215.
7. Nabokov, *Laughter in the Dark*, p. 143.
8. William Woodin Rowe, *Nabokov's Deceptive World*, p. 82.

Humbert Humbert
and the Limits of Artistic License

GLADYS M. CLIFTON

Humbert Humbert frequently insists on his status as a poet, especially in the first part of *Lolita*. While this can be taken as a bit of seductiveness toward the readers (the "ladies and gentlemen of the jury,"[1] to whom he addresses his self-justification), he soon abandons the originally stated purpose for writing his story, which was to produce a document that might be used in his defense at his trial for the murder of Quilty; instead, he becomes caught up in re-creating the past he has shared with Lolita, and with the attempt to get the reader to view it—statutory rape notwithstanding—in the same tragic and romantic light as he does. Distracted by his charm, his wit, his intelligence, and—yes—his murderer's fancy prose style, we may momentarily forget that he is indeed the monster he says he is.

But whenever Humbert begins to describe the actual details of his life under the influence of "the perilous magic of nymphets," a grotesque gap appears between his fantasy of "bliss" and his life with a flesh-and-blood American teen angel. It is a gap filled with comedy and irony at his own expense (p. 131, italics mine):

> I decided I might risk getting a little closer to that lovely and maddening glimmer; but hardly had I moved into its warm purlieus than her breathing was suspended, and I had the odious feeling that little Dolores was wide awake and would explode in screams if I touched her with any part of my wretchedness. Please, reader: no matter your exasperation with the tenderhearted, morbidly sensitive, infinitely circumspect hero of my book, do not skip these essential pages! Imagine me; I shall not exist if you do not imagine me; try to discern the doe in me, trembling in the forest of my own iniquity; *let's even smile a little.*

That final invitation is surely Nabokov's as well as Humbert's. And if one has indeed fully imagined Humbert's plight, it is impossible not to smile at its ludicrous aspect, especially when his grumbling continues, "I had no place to rest my head, and a fit of heartburn (they call those fries 'French,' *grand Dieu!*) was added to my discomfort."

Humbert's dream seems to become a nightmare during this long and sleepless night in the "loud American hotel" with its clattering elevator gates, cascading toilets, chattering guests in the corridor, retching guests just beyond his wall. He describes lying all night, rigid with suspense on the edge of the bed, "burning with desire and dyspepsia" (p. 132). Then, in a comic reversal sure to catch the uninitiated off guard, Humbert abruptly announces to his readers: "Frigid gentlewomen of the jury! I had thought that months, perhaps years, would elapse before I dared to reveal myself to Dolores Haze; but by six she was wide awake, and by six fifteen we were technically lovers. I am going to tell you something very strange: it was she who seduced me" (p. 134).

Although Humbert does spare us the literal details of this first coupling—claiming, "I am not concerned with so-called 'sex' at all. Anybody can imagine those elements of animality" (p. 136)—we do get a rather unsettling sense of his pleasure and her pain in the two paragraphs that comprise chapter 30. Humbert confides that, had the management of the Enchanted Hunters allowed him to alter the conventional hunting murals of the hotel dining room, he would have substituted the following (pp. 136–37):

> There would have been a lake. There would have been an arbor in flame-flower. There would have been nature studies—a tiger pursuing a bird of paradise, a choking snake sheathing whole the flayed trunk of a shoat. There would have been a sultan, his face expressing great agony (belied, as it were, by his molding caress), helping a callypygean slave child to climb a column of onyx. There would have been those luminous globules of gonadal glow that travel up the opalescent sides of juke boxes. There would have been all kinds of camp activities . . . Canoeing, Coranting, Combing Curls . . . There would have been poplars, apples, a suburban Sunday. There would have been a fire opal dissolving within a ripple-ringed pool, a last throb, a last dab of color, stinging red, smarting pink, a sigh, a wincing child.

This mural, a metaphorical representation of Humbert's sexual transport, shimmers with his self-indulgent feasting of the senses. But there is something slightly repellent and off-color about the violence with which pleasure is taken by the tiger, the snake, and the sultan; and we see Humbert in these, just as surely as we see Lolita in the wincing child who won't quite fit in with the stylized mural because she exists independent of his fantasy. This passage is an emphatic reminder that while we may be invited to smile at Humbert's situation and find it comical, this is not true for Lolita, even though she is part of the same situation. It is an important paradox.

This is why Humbert's self-serving announcement that he did not even "deprive her of her flower" carries so little weight. It cannot overcome the images of pain and loss just cited. Furthermore, Lolita obviously had little more in mind in seducing Humbert than a bit of glamorous adventure with an older man (mentally, as Humbert says, she has been "hopelessly depraved" by movies, teen magazines, the "campfire racket"). Since Charlotte has been sexually jealous of her daughter and cruel to her, vengeful mischief at her mother's expense is another of Lolita's motives; however, she has no doubt that she is on her way home to this same mother, and is secure in this knowledge even as she naughtily beds down with Mummy's Hummy, whom she has just ironically called "Dad." Establishing a lasting sexual tie with Humbert is certainly the farthest thing from her mind.

When Humbert finally does break the news of her mother's death to Lo shortly after they leave the Enchanted Hunters, she feels betrayed and angrily rejects him. He attempts to bribe her with more gifts, but she remains alienated: "we had separate rooms, but in the middle of the night she came sobbing into mine, and we made it up very gently. You see, she had absolutely nowhere else to go" (p. 144).

A very delicate fictional balance has been achieved at this point in the novel. There are few comic subjects less likely than child molesting or incest (even "parody" incest); yet Nabokov has managed to write a great comedy on just these subjects, because Lolita is finally defiantly resilient, whatever she may suffer; and Humbert, her tormentor, convinces us that he suffers as much as the most punitive moralist could wish.

Among early readers and reviewers of *Lolita*, few were more perceptive on this point than Howard Nemerov:

> Nabokov's own artistic concern, here as elsewhere . . . has no more to do with morality than with sex . . . His subject is always the inner insanity and how it may match or fail to match the outer absurdity, and this problem he sees as susceptible of only *artistic* solutions. . . . *Lolita* is nevertheless a moral work, if by morality in literature we are to understand the illustration of a usurious rate of exchange between our naughty desires and virtuous pains, of the process whereby pleasures

become punishments . . . Humbert Humbert . . . gets punished
. . . in the end. Also in the middle. And at the beginning.[2]

Yet many early readers and critics did find the book objectionable on
moral grounds, and its publication was delayed in the United States
and in England for several years. Such readers must have seen only
the stereotypes they brought to their reading, not the unique creations that Humbert and Lolita are in their fictional world.

Far from remaining a helpless victim, Lolita learns to assert herself in spite of Humbert's hold over her as the blackmailing official
guardian whose potent threat is that he will turn her over to the
even worse alternative of official guardianship by judges, juvenile
authorities, and orphanages, if she does not cooperate with his demands. A great comic irony is that the demands that she most bit-
terly resents are *not* the ones for which Humbert might be sent to
jail, the demands of a lover on a child mistress; they are the demands
of a strict parent on a rebellious teen-age child. Of course these are
not unconnected to what Humbert himself calls the relationship, "a
parody of incest." Humbert is never seen as more comically helpless
than when he tries to deal with Lolita as a daughter; fatherhood is, of
course, the public social role he must assume in order to live with
Lolita unmolested by the law.

In the first chapter of part 2 Humbert records some of his tra-
vails in the quasi-parental role during their first year together on the
road (p. 160):

> We had rows, minor and major. The biggest ones we had took
> place: at Lacework Cabins, Virginia; on Park Avenue, Little
> Rock, near a school; on Milner Pass, 10,759 feet high, in Colo-
> rado; at the corner of Seventh Street and Central Avenue in
> Phoenix, Arizona; on Third Street, Los Angeles, because the
> tickets to some studio or other were sold out; at a motel called
> Poplar Shade in Utah, . . . where she asked, *à propos de rien*,
> how long did I think we were going to live in stuffy cabins,
> doing filthy things together and never behaving like ordinary
> people? On N. Broadway, Burns, Oregon, corner of W. Wash-
> ington, facing Safeway, a grocery.

The list continues; Humbert acknowledges that most of the con-
flicts were over her sociable urges to be with other people, especially
young people. He is not only fearful of discovery through such con-
tacts, but pathologically jealous. In his desire to secure her to him
absolutely, he fantasizes flight to Mexico, where he feels he might

safely breed with her a little "Lolita the Second"; and the possibility of compound incest with a "supremely lovely Lolita the Third" is not dismissed by Humbert at his maddest. After sharing this particular fantasy, Humbert soberly concedes, "In the days of that wild journey of ours, I doubted not that as father to Lolita the First I was a ridiculous failure. I did my best; I read and reread a book with the unintentionally biblical title *Know Your Own Daughter*" (p. 176). His best indeed: this juxtaposition of a madman's logic and an appeal to conventional pieties shows Humbert's style at its most characteristic.

Humbert's decision to try a more settled and domestic routine is made in an effort to improve their relationship, to give Lo a chance to resume her formal schooling, and to replenish Humbert's funds, greatly depleted by the year on the road. He secures a position in Beardsley College through an old friend, Gaston Godin, a fellow European, whose sexual tastes are a mirror-image of Humbert's (Gaston prefers young boys). But when Humbert informs Lolita of his determination to enroll her in dayschool at Beardsley, "a rather high-class, non-coeducational one, with no modern nonsense" (p. 173), Lo begins "one of those furious harangues of hers" which nearly results in the arrest of the distracted Humbert by a traffic policeman.

It is, of course, a joke on Humbert that Beardsley School for girls is not as he wishfully describes it but replete with "modern nonsense" of the sort that will eventually lead Lolita to plot her escape from him. Headmistress Pratt, a fatuous proponent of vaguely "progressive" educational theories, is sketched with malicious glee by Nabokov in Humbert's first interview with her—an interview which bears out Gaston's warning that the school might be one where young girls are taught "not to spell very well, but to smell very well" (p. 179). Here is Pratt's complacent outline of the curriculum: "We are not so much concerned, Mr. Humbird, with having our students become bookworms or be able to reel off all the capitals of Europe which nobody knows anyway, or learn by heart the dates of forgotten battles. What we are concerned with is the adjustment of the child to group life. This is why we stress the four D's: Dramatics, Dance, Debating and Dating" (p. 179).

Humbert is disappointed in other respects. That outwardly serene European gentleman is as morbidly beset by fear of detection at 14 Thayer Street, Beardsley, as at the motels, especially by the "east-door neighbor . . . a sharp-nosed character" (p. 181). Lolita is more estranged than ever, resentful of his interdictions against dating and other teen-age activities. Because her sulkiness carries over into school, where her indifference baffles her teachers, Humbert must face Pratt again. He fortifies himself with gin. (He appears to be a near-alcoholic by the end of the story.)

In the second interview Pratt is on the Freudian hobbyhorse in a hilariously wide-of-the-mark analysis of Dolores Haze's retarded sexual development and difficult "latency adjustment." Then, while Humbert squirms, she confidently explains that "Beardsley School does not believe in bees and blossoms, and storks and love birds, but it does believe very strongly in preparing its students for mutually satisfactory mating and successful child rearing" (p. 197). Faced with Pratt's attack on him as "an old-fashioned Continental father," he is forced to give ground, not on dating, the one of the four D's he finds most threatening, but on dramatics, mostly to end the interview and Pratt's prying into the "home situation." He consents grudgingly: "You win. She can take part in that play. Provided male parts are taken by female parts" (p. 198). This bit of suggestive wordplay is not merely playful but prefigures Lolita's acceptance of the playwright Clare Quilty as a lover during the rehearsal period.

Humbert credits himself with other concessions: he allows Lo to attend a heavily chaperoned formal dance at the nearby boys' academy, later attempting to pump her friend Mona about her behavior; and he allows her to give a boy-girl party, a dismal failure because Humbert hovers over it like a vulture (he has been drinking again), and also because there are few friends that she will risk inviting to Humbert's lair (he does not acknowledge this directly).

Humbert makes it a point to recount instances of his parental generosity and concern: tennis rackets and instruction, music lessons, a beautiful birthday bicycle; he nurses her when she is ill (though he shamelessly admits that he could not resist her "exquisite caloricity" at the outset of her fever).

There are some hints by Humbert that Lolita finds certain of his sexual demands on her especially distasteful, and that raising her allowance is a concession to her dislike of providing him with oral sexual stimulation. Here is a deliciously perverse passage in which he is sorry to record a "drop in Lolita's morals." He is deadpan serious, as Nabokov of course is not (pp. 185–86):

> If her share in the ardors she kindled had never amounted to much, neither had pure lucre ever come to the fore. But I was weak, I was not wise, my schoolgirl nymphet had me in thrall. . . . of this she took advantage. . . . Only very listlessly did she earn her three pennies—or three nickels—per day; and she

proved to be a cruel negotiator whenever it was in her power to deny me certain life-wrecking, strange, slow, paradisal philters without which I could not live more than a few days in a row, and which, because of the very nature of love's languor, I could not obtain by force. Knowing the magic and might of her own soft mouth, she managed—during one school year!—to raise the bonus price of a fancy embrace to three, and even four bucks. O Reader! Laugh not, as you imagine me, on the very rack of joy noisily emitting dimes and quarters, and great big silver dollars like some sonorous, jingly, and wholly demented machine vomiting riches. . . .

This is both sordid and humorous; we cannot help applauding Lolita's toughness. Merely sordid is Humbert's further admission that he would search out and confiscate the money she had thus squeezed out of him, "because what I feared most was not that she might ruin me, but that she might accumulate sufficient cash to run away. I believe the poor fierce-eyed child had figured out that with a mere fifty dollars in her purse she might somehow reach Broadway or Hollywood—or the foul kitchen of a diner (Help Wanted) in a dismal ex-prairie state, with the wind blowing, and the stars blinking, and the cars, and the bars, and the barmen, and everything soiled, torn, dead" (p. 187). This sad echo of the jaunty "Little Carmen" refrain (Nabokov's parody of banal popular tune lyrics) looks ahead to what actually becomes of Lolita when she has run away from both Humbert and Hollywood, that is, Quilty.

Most of *Lolita*, part 2, is dominated by Humbert's loss of and agonized search for his nymphet, who escapes him both physically and spiritually. We become more and more aware that poet-manipulator Humbert is not entirely in control, bowing as he must to the whims of "McFate" (or the exigencies of a plot devised by someone else). On the road again with Lolita, Humbert is stricken with panic when he perceives he is being tailed from state to state. He alternates between terror of literal pursuit and terror of the phantoms of his own mind. Little wonder that he has the first of a series of heart attacks (the last one occurs shortly after he completes his manuscript). Humbert's "quest for ecstasy"—to use Bader's phrase[3]—leads him instead into nightmarish paranoia.

Humbert, after a violent quarrel with Lolita over some unexplained absences during the rehearsal period of the play, is delighted when she suggests they leave Beardsley—abandoning the play, school, friends, everything that he has felt to be a threat. The reader is allowed to guess, as Humbert cannot at the time, that she has an ulterior motive. The itinerary she plans for their trip coincides with that of playwright Clare Quilty.

In Quilty the motif of the double comes into play, as several critics have noted and documented.[4] Quilty is indeed something of a coarse parody of Humbert, like him a middle-aged nympholept and self-indulgent sensualist; he too has pretensions as an artist and a fairly highbrow education in literature. But Quilty only appears to be as obsessed with Lolita as Humbert is. Once he has had the fun of harassing Humbert and stealing her from him, he proves to be less "enchanted," less the monomaniac—as well as less the artist. In fact, he kicks Lolita out of his entourage as soon as she becomes uncooperative, something Humbert could never conceive of doing. Still, there is little question that he is a figure whom Humbert perceives as a mocking distortion of himself. When a frantic Humbert confronts the nurse who has helped Lolita sign out of the Elphinstone hospital with her "uncle," she is only literally mistaken in informing him, "He is your brother" (p. 251). Humbert angrily snatches back the offered bribe, but he himself, after apologizing to the hospital authorities for a very violent outburst, leaves congratulating himself on still being free—"free to trace the fugitive, free to destroy my brother" (p. 249).

And since they are also brothers in crime, Humbert's murder of Quilty is morally gratuitous, not "justice" on any level, as Appel notes: "By making Clare Quilty too clearly guilty [here Appel credits Stegner for first detecting the pun], Nabokov is assaulting the convention of the good and evil 'dual selves' found in the traditional Double tale. Humbert would let some of us believe that . . . the good poet has exorcised the bad monster, but the two are finally not to be clearly distinguished: when Humbert and Quilty wrestle, 'I rolled over him. We rolled over me. They rolled over him. We rolled over us'" (p. lxiv). Andrew Field has called attention to Humbert's wearing black, heretofore Quilty's color, in this climactic scene, and noted that Quilty appears in a purple robe that Humbert sees as resembling one of his. Field goes on perceptively to characterize Humbert's murder of Quilty as a "partial suicide or auto-assassination."[5]

It does appear that Humbert is punishing and destroying himself in Quilty. To punish Quilty is a histrionic gesture, epitomized by the histrionic and maudlin verse with which he accuses the cowering playwright of being a heartless debaucher and implies his own innocence: "because of all you did / because of all I did not / you have to die" (p. 302). Fittingly, if one takes Quilty as Humbert's sinister side, he is very hard to destroy. The carnage at Pavor Manor is rendered with almost cartoon violence: Quilty shows cartoon-figure resiliency as Humbert pumps bullet after bullet into him, and he keeps getting up to offer fresh pleas and bribes in preposterous accents. The effect is grotesquely comic, in spite of the gore; the scene comes off as a burlesque of B-movie violence—as it also did in Stanley Kubrick's film.

But Humbert's spectacular effort to avenge Lolita and revenge himself is finally hollow and self-indulgent. He has already acknowledged his own greater guilt, his having robbed her of her childhood and turned her into an idealized object of desire. Before confronting Quilty he has found Lolita again and discovered in himself a genuine love for the person she has become, a drab, pregnant Dolly Schiller who resembles neither a nymphet nor any other idealized sex object. His pity and even his repentant generosity show that he is redeemed as far as redemption is possible for incurables (pp. 279–80):

> She was only the faint violet whiff and dead leaf echo of the nymphet I had rolled myself upon with such cries in the past; an echo on the brink of a russet ravine . . . but thank God it was not that echo alone that I worshiped. What I used to pamper among the tangled vines of my heart, *mon grand péché radieux*, had dwindled to its essence: sterile and selfish vice, all *that* I canceled and cursed. You may jeer at me, and threaten to clear the court, but until I am gagged and half-throttled, I will shout my poor truth. I insist the world know how much I loved my Lolita, *this* Lolita, pale and polluted, and big with another's child, but still gray-eyed, still sooty-lashed, still auburn and almond, still Carmencita, still mine. . . .

This is very persuasive. Still, at the very moment of parting and renunciation, Humbert tells us that it is with the greatest difficulty that he restrains an impulse to ask her if she knows what has become of "the little McCoo girl"—this prompted by a sudden vision of "radiant" Lolita at twelve, when he first saw her.

And when Humbert leaves the Schillers on his errand of assassination, he cannot resist a sentimental side trip to 342 Lawn Street, Ramsdale, before looking up Quilty's uncle to get Quilty's address. Humbert listens to a "torrent of Italian music" as he stands before his old residence in some very old clothes he has worn all the previous night, indulging himself in nostalgia: "All at once I noticed that from the lawn I had mown a golden-skinned, brown-haired nymphet of nine or ten, in white shorts, was looking at me with wild fascination in her large blue-black eyes. I said something pleasant to her, meaning no harm, an old-world compliment, what nice eyes you have, but she retreated in haste and the music stopped abruptly, and a violent-looking dark man, glistening with sweat, came out and glared at me" (p. 290). This scene casts considerable doubt on Field's reading of *Lolita*, which takes Humbert's announced reform as a "daring and abrupt breakthrough . . . into normalcy."[6]

Nor is the two-year liaison with Rita by any means conclusive evidence that Humbert has overcome his desire for nymphets, for he admits to still pursuing occasional voyeuristic satisfactions during this period. Rita is agreeable as a companion because she makes no grownup demands on him, in spite of being twice Lolita's age. She is "a good sport," absolutely compliant, unquestioning, and stupid. In comparing her to his first two wives, Humbert asserts: "In comparison to her, Valechka was a Schlegel, and Charlotte a Hegel" (p. 261). Actually, he picks her up after a brief spell in a psychiatric institution, having had a breakdown after his fruitless search for the runaway Lolita. He admits he could still be aroused by glimpses of nymphet flesh across a courtyard at sunset, but maintains: "one essential vision in me had withered: never did I dwell now on possibilities of bliss with a little maiden, specific or synthetic, in some out-of-the-way place; never did my fancy sink its fangs into Lolita's sisters, far far away, in the coves of evoked islands. *That* was all over, *for the time being at least*" (p. 259, second italics mine).

Rita distracts Humbert from his obsession and serves as willing ministrant to his acquired "habits of lust." But when she strays off occasionally in a drunken fog with someone else—and since she is a free spirit, totally irresponsible and amoral, this happens fairly frequently—Humbert is not frantic in searching her out and rescuing her from whatever ludicrous scrape she has gotten into. When Humbert receives the totally unexpected "Dear Dad" letter from Lolita, he abandons Rita without hesitation—leaving a grateful good-bye note taped to her navel but not looking back. Obviously, any commitment to "normalcy" embodied by the Rita relationship is a very shallow one in comparison to the commitment to revenge in his mind as he arms himself and sets out to find and destroy the person responsible for ending his satisfactions.

His posturing parody of the wronged lover undermines his self-justification; this nicely struck balance encourages the reader to respond ambivalently, still believing in Humbert's charm, his intelligence, his capacity for genuine emotion, and, above all, his art, but seeing also his core of self-indulgence and insanity. Moreover, Nabokov has scattered passages throughout Humbert's narrative giving indications that even for Humbert the cost of pursuing his vision of bliss cannot be justified. We have already interpreted the ambivalent imagery of the imaginary Enchanted Hunters mural as Humbert's veiled criticism of his own self-indulgence. But Humbert lets the reader know directly that he is aware of willfully inflicting pain on the child: "We had been everywhere. We had really seen nothing. And I catch myself thinking today that our long journey had only defiled with a sinuous trail of slime the lovely, trustful, dreamy, enormous country that by then, in retrospect, was no more to us than a collection of dog-eared maps, ruined tour books, old tires, and her sobs in the night—every night, every night—the moment I feigned sleep" (pp. 177–78). Later in Beardsley Humbert recalls overhearing Lolita in serious conversation with a young friend (p. 286):

> "You know, what's so dreadful about dying is that you are completely on your own"; and it struck me . . . that I simply did not know a thing about my darling's mind and that quite possibly, behind the awful juvenile clichés, there was in her a garden and a twilight, and a palace gate . . . I often noticed that living as we did, she and I, in a world of total evil, we would become strangely embarrassed whenever I tried to discuss something she and an older friend, she and a parent, she and a real healthy sweetheart . . . might have discussed—an abstract idea, a painting, stippled Hopkins or shorn Baudelaire, God or Shakespeare. . . . She would mail her vulnerability in trite brashness and boredom, whereas I, using for my desperately detached comments an artificial tone of voice that set my own last teeth on edge, provoked my audience to such outbursts of rudeness as made any further conversation impossible, oh my poor, bruised child.

Humbert also records Lolita's obvious pain in watching an ordinary exchange of father-daughter affection between her friend Avis and her father—"Avis who had such a wonderful fat pink dad and a small chubby brother, and a brand new baby sister, and a home, and two grinning dogs, and Lolita had nothing" (p. 288). This is indeed her view of her situation, and Humbert acknowledges that he may have "relied too much on the abnormally chill relations between Charlotte and her daughter" in supposing that Lolita would happily adapt to life with him. He knows his error: "It had become gradually clear to my conventional Lolita during our singular and bestial cohabitation that even the most miserable of family lives was better than the parody of incest, which, in the long run, was the best I could offer the waif" (p. 289).

It is little wonder, then, that Humbert's urgent plea to Lolita at their last meeting—that she leave her shabby life with her husband

and come away with him—is met with an emphatic rejection, a rejection that confirms the magnitude of his culpability: "'No,' she said, 'it is quite out of the question. I would sooner go back to Cue. I mean—' She groped for words. I supplied them mentally ('*He* broke my heart. *You* merely broke my life')" (p. 281). Quite so. Obviously her two months' exposure to the flamboyant lifestyle of Quilty, replete with orgies, was far less damaging to her than the two years of furtive vice she was forced to endure with Humbert behind a façade of boring respectability. Little wonder, too, that all Humbert is able to achieve in his grotesque revenge is to cover himself with Quilty— that is, guilt (his pun).

Yet there are a surprising number of readers who have been misled here, interpreting Lolita's expressed preference for Quilty as something more than the choice of lesser evils, which is certainly all that it is. Field, usually more astute, distorts her answer thus: "In their last meeting Lolita tells Humbert that she really loves not him or her husband Dick but the perverse Quilty."[7] This she does not; she does say that Quilty is the only man she was ever really "crazy about"—but she is not crazy about him in the present tense. In fact, she found life with him disillusioning: "all drink and drugs. And, of course, he was a complete freak in sex matters" (p. 278). She has refused to take part in filming group-sex pornographic movies at Quilty's ranch, and she now refuses "to go into particulars with that baby inside her" (p. 279).

G. D. Josipovici has also written of Lolita's relationship to Quilty that "he remains the one man Lolita ever really loves."[8] It is, of course, probable that a fourteen-year-old girl's crush on a movie-magazine celebrity might seem like "love" to her at the time. However, Lolita, in looking back, never says "love." Josipovici joins other readers who have, I think, overvalued Humbert's perspective and undervalued Lolita's. (Granted we get only infrequent indications of hers filtered through Humbert's narrative.) His tone is very condescending: "Neither her education nor her imagination allow her to distinguish between the truly perverted and nature's faithful hounds. Or rather, she does distinguish, but wrongly, seeing in Humbert only a 'dirty old man' and in Quilty a genius whose superior qualities render necessary a slightly eccentric way of life."[9] This seems a bit obtuse; after all, what side of Humbert, other than that of the dirty old man, is she really familiar with from her period of nymphet thralldom, from age twelve to age fourteen? Quilty may be a trashy artist, but she has no basis to compare Humbert with him— she will never read the book we are reading. And, as a companion, Quilty was at least chosen by her, at least showed her a good time (up to a point), and finally caused her less pain than Humbert. How then can she be said to "distinguish wrongly" in preferring Quilty, who merely broke her heart, to Humbert, who broke her life?

Even more distortion is found in Douglas Fowler's attempt to fit Humbert into his category of "Nabokovian favorites," those fictional creations whom he sees as authorial equivalents, who stand for values we are intended to admire. In the following passage Humbert is rather unpersuasively championed as the unequivocal moral center of *Lolita*: "If the novel included no Quilty, Humbert would still be less than fully criminal in our minds. He is, after all, the most attractive character in it."[10] This is at least debatable. Fowler further misplaces, as well as misreads, the passage which relates Humbert's moment of insight above a mountain village at evening. It happens as he is recovering from one of his heart seizures, becoming aware of lovely sounds: "What I heard was but the melody of children at play, nothing but that. . . . I knew that the hopelessly poignant thing was not Lolita's absence from my side, but the absence of her voice from that concord" (p. 310). This experience takes place during the period of Humbert's frantic search for Lolita in the Western mountains shortly after her disappearance, not, as Fowler claims, while Humbert stands on the Appalachian embankment, waiting to be arrested after killing Quilty and driving off on the wrong side of the road, ultimately wrecking the car. It is at that point that the experience is *relived* in flashback and first shared with the reader.

But in any case, there is little basis for Fowler's claim that this passage shows that Humbert's "final vision of his crime is of a moral sensitivity completely beyond Lolita's capabilities."[11] Any doubt of Fowler's male-chauvinist bias is soon resolved by the following: "The poignancy of this loss afflicts only Humbert. Mrs. Richard Schiller, who finds Quilty a 'genius,' who finds Humbert only some 'dry mud caking her childhood,' and who is busy incubating a philistine fetus in her stretched belly, is not given this sensitivity."[12] Philistine fetus? What can one say of such "sensitivity" as Fowler's? Neither any authorial intrusion nor Humbert himself has directed the reader to view Humbert as morally superior to Lolita.

Finally, there is the author's own word to be weighed. Here is a pertinent exchange between interviewer Herbert Gold and interviewee Vladimir Nabokov. Gold: "A third critic has said that you 'diminish' your characters 'to the point where they become ciphers in a cosmic farce.' I disagree; Humbert, while comic, retains a touching and insistent quality—that of the spoiled artist." Nabokov: "I would put it differently: Humbert Humbert is a vain and cruel wretch who manages to appear 'touching.' That epithet, in its true, tear-iridized sense, can only apply to my poor little girl. Besides, how can I 'diminish' to the level of ciphers, et cetera, characters that I have invented myself? One can 'diminish' a biographee, but not an eidolon."[13]

As early as 1937, Vladimir Khodasevich, Nabokov's most perceptive early critic, recognized that almost without exception the heroes of Nabokov's fiction are artists or artists manqué.[14] It is of course true that Humbert too is an artist and that Nabokov is at least always on the side of art. Bader has argued, following Khodasevich (and Page Stegner in *Escape into Aesthetics*) that Nabokov's novels are mainly concerned with the artistic imagination and consciousness.[15] This fits the early Russian novels without doubt, especially *The Gift* and *Invitation to a Beheading*, and it applies in a very obvious way to *Pale Fire*. But the formula is applied with considerable strain to *Lolita*, which Bader has given a totally allegorical reading; she interprets Humbert's obsession with Lolita as a brilliant aberration of the imagination through which Humbert creates her as the mythic nymphet type—and may even be said to possess her only at that level.

Further developing this idea, Bader writes: "His unquenchable desire for Lolita is identified with his search for a mode of expression which is mysterious, tender, alluring, at the same time that it is growing up into the conventional commonplace, for the use of pseudo-artists like Quilty."[16] We can grant all this—that Humbert's presentation is dazzling enough to make us accept as authentic his myth of the nymphet, his passion, and even his humanized love at the end; but can we also assent to the demonstrable human cost of his pursuit of his "ecstasy," his "aesthetic bliss"? Bader tries to forestall this question by moving entirely into abstraction: "Whether or not we are to 'believe' Humbert's final conversion and declaration of love does not seem to me to be an issue in the novel. The element of surprise . . . becomes metaphoric of the artist's relation to his material. Humbert's unconventional obsession is a necessary aspect of imaginative transformation, and his acceptance of his love for the grown-up Lolita provides for his moral apotheosis into the realm of art."[17] This claim has a grandiose ring, but it is distressingly vague and unsatisfying.

Richard Poirier has written a perceptive essay on self-parody in twentieth-century fiction that goes to the heart of the trouble with such formulaic readings:

> While Nabokov's parody is of an extraordinarily compassionate kind, resisting all but the most delicate translation into interpretive language, nearly all of his interpreters continue to

insist on irrelevant distinctions between art and life, fiction and reality. Humbert is not an example of a man victimized by mistaking art for reality or for living in a relationship that violates the limitations of time and physical nature. These things may be said, of course, and they are true, just as it is true that King Lear had a bad temper. It is possible to be right and vapid, and such a way of being right about Humbert thwarts precisely those responses of fascination, affection, bewilderment, and awe that Humbert and Nabokov call for.[18]

We can, then, accept Bader's assertions that the questions raised by *Lolita* are artistic and aesthetic and that in the novel we find moral questions treated in aesthetic terms, without conceding that this is all there is to the novel. To declare Humbert's vice is merely "the inexpert artist's brutal treatment of a tantalizingly undeveloped subject" and further to insist that "the grossest violation is Quilty's, the commercial artist's"[19]—this is to push the formula of the artist as pervert ("pervert" here defined as one capable of originality, the prime artistic virtue) too far.

Humbert's originality in creating a mythology around the idea of the "nymphet" can be appreciated without succumbing to his vision entirely. After all, Humbert's vision is immature and susceptible, on that count, to irony. Here, for example, is Humbert taking us into the world of park-bench ecstasy: "Rope-skipping, hopscotch. That old woman in black who sat down next to me on my bench, on my rack of joy (a nymphet was groping under me for a lost marble), and asked if I had stomachache, the insolent hag. Ah, leave me alone in my pubescent park, in my mossy garden. Let them play around me forever. *Never grow up*" (pp. 22–23, italics mine). Not only the nymphets, but Humbert himself, need never grow up in his fantast's dream-world.

We have seen that many of Humbert's troubles in life are connected with his refusal of adult roles or failure to fit into them: for example, husband, father. Moreover, in looking back over the novel as a whole, there is one final, oddly pathetic irony to be perceived, namely, that the most convincingly erotic passage is not one in which Humbert actually possesses Lolita but one which involves masturbation. It involves Lolita too, but unknowingly and inactively. Humbert draws out his account for more than three pages, seeming to relive each sensuous detail with rapture (pp. 62–63):

> I entered a plane of being where nothing mattered, save the infusion of joy brewed within my body. What had begun as a delicious distension of my innermost roots became a glowing

tingle which *now* had reached that state of absolute security, confidence and reliance not found elsewhere in conscious life. . . . I felt I could slow down in order to prolong the glow. Lolita had been safely solipsized. The implied sun pulsated in the supplied poplars. . . . In my self-made seraglio, I was a radiant and robust Turk. . . . Suspended on the brink of that voluptuous abyss . . . her teeth rested on her glistening underlip as she half-turned away, and my moaning mouth, gentlemen of the jury, almost reached her bare neck, while I crushed out against her left buttock the last throb of the longest ecstasy man or monster had ever known.

It is fitting and funny that Humbert's one flight into erotic writing is couched mainly in a beautiful parody of the florid prose style of Victorian pornographers. Humbert acknowledges that he has possessed not Lolita herself, "but my own creation, another, fanciful Lolita—perhaps, more real than Lolita; overlapping, encasing her; floating between me and her, and having no will, no consciousness—indeed, no life of her own" (p. 64). Humbert will never achieve such a peak in his two years of sexual cohabitation with the Lolita who does have a will, consciousness, and life of her own.

Humbert's error in attempting to live his fantasies is finally understood even by him. The barrier between fantasy and reality cannot be crossed, as he acknowledges in one of his more sober passages of self-analysis. In speaking of the delights of voyeurism—even those involving his arousal by a deceptive illusion in a distant window that only seems to hold an undressed nymphet (she turns into an old man in his undershirt when the light comes on)—he writes: "There was in the fiery phantasm a perfection which made my wild delight also perfect, just because the vision was out of reach, with no possibility of attainment to spoil it by the awareness of an appended taboo; indeed, it may well be that the very attraction immaturity has for me lies not so much in the limpidity of pure young forbidden fairy child beauty as in the security of a situation where infinite perfections fill the gap between the little given and the great promised—the great rosegray never-to-be-had" (p. 266).

Humbert has salvaged something from the destruction wreaked by his pursuit of never-to-be-had phantasms of delight with the living Lolita. He has imbued his vision (madman and pervert's though it may be) with such persuasive and passionate hues of art that we accept it as authentic. He has created a balance of interest between the fantastic and the real Lolita and allowed the latter finally to triumph in escaping him. His narrative dignifies her triumph and offers her the only restitution he can make—immortality in art. This is what restores his dignity too. The closing *envoi*, which he knows she will never read, establishes this delicate equipoise: "And do not pity C. Q. One had to choose between him and H. H., and one wanted H. H. to exist at least a couple of months longer, so as to have him make you live in the minds of later generations. I am thinking of aurochs and angels, the secret of durable pigments, prophetic sonnets, the refuge of art. And this is the only immortality you and I may share, my Lolita" (p. 311).

Nabokov's narrative persona has indeed given to both himself and Lolita a shared immortality. She has become not only the prototype of the elusive, mythic nymphet (as Humbert intended), but a prototype of American youth, the teenager (as such, no part of Humbert's myth). Nabokov's great success is in his having made both the mythic and the human Lolita plausible, even while undermining the credibility of her mythmaker-biographer, who is also, perhaps first, an unreliable autobiographer. Humbert's self-portrait is a fascinating combination of artistic triumph (as he intended) and moral failure (as Nabokov intended). These balanced oppositions, more than anything else, account for the appearance of *Lolita* on so many lists of masterpieces of fiction.

NOTES

1. Nabokov, *The Annotated Lolita*, p. 11. Hereafter cited in text.
2. Howard Nemerov, "The Morality of Art," *Kenyon Review* 19 (1957), 320.
3. See Julia Bader, *Crystal Land*, chapter 4 ("The Quest for Ecstasy"), for an interesting, if not entirely persuasive, reading of *Lolita* as a pure fable of artistic creation.
4. Appel's introduction to *The Annotated Lolita* summarizes this aspect of the novel in detail (see pp. lxiii–lxvii).
5. Andrew Field, *Nabokov: His Life in Art*, p. 347.
6. Ibid., p. 345.
7. Ibid., p. 344.
8. G. D. Josipovici, "*Lolita*: Parody and the Pursuit of Beauty," *Critical Quarterly* 6 (1964), 43.
9. Ibid., p. 43.
10. Douglas Fowler, *Reading Nabokov*, p. 153.
11. Ibid., p. 165.
12. Ibid.
13. Nabokov, *Strong Opinions*, p. 94.
14. See Khodasevich's essay "On Sirin," in *Nabokov*, ed. Appel and Newman, pp. 96–101.
15. Bader, *Crystal Land*, pp. 2–4.

16. Ibid., p. 64.
17. Ibid., p. 79.
18. Richard Poirier, "The Politics of Self Parody," in his *The Performing Self*, pp. 40–41.
19. Bader, *Crystal Land*, p. 80.

Parody and Authenticity in *Lolita*

THOMAS R. FROSCH

It has been said that *Lolita* is simultaneously "a love story and a parody of love stories" and that its parody and its pathos are "always congruent."[1] In this article I wish to explore what such a condition—that of being both parodic and authentic at the same time—may mean.

First, however, I suggest that we best describe *Lolita* generically not as a love story or a novel of pathos but as a romance. The plot itself is composed of a series of typical romance structures, each one a version of the quest or hunt and each one an embodiment of a specific type of suspense or anxiety. We begin with the pursuit of Lolita, and the anxiety of overcoming sexual obstacles. Next, once Humbert and Lolita are lovers, we have a story of jealousy and possessiveness, as Humbert is beset by fears of rivals and by Lolita's own resistance. Finally, in Humbert's dealings with Quilty, we have a third and fourth type, each with its attendant style and anxiety: the double story and the revenge story. Furthermore, these plot structures are infused with the daimonic (that is, a quality of uncanny power possessed originally by beings, whether good or evil, midway between gods and people), which is a primary characteristic of romance as a literary mode. Lolita is an inherently unpossessable object; her appeal consists partly in her transiency—she will only be a nymphet for a brief time—and partly in her status as a daimonic visitor to the common world. The quest is thus an impossible one from the outset; it is variously presented as a quest for Arcadia, for the past, for the unattainable itself; it is nympholepsy. Even in the rare moments when Humbert is free from his typical anxieties, he is not totally satisfied; he wants to "turn my Lolita inside out and apply voracious lips to her young matrix, her unknown heart, her nacreous liver, the sea-grapes of her lungs, her comely twin kidneys" (p. 167). Humbert is a believer in the enchanted and the marvelous. Like Spenser's Red Cross Knight, he rides forth on his quest adorned by the image of his guiding principle, in his case a blue cornflower on the back of his pajamas—the blue cornflower being Novalis' symbol of infinite desire. *Lolita* contains numerous parodic allusions to other literary works, especially to Mérimée's *Carmen* and Poe's "Annabel Lee," but the real anti-text implied by the allusions and parodies together is the romantic sensibility in general from Rousseau to Proust.

But exactly how seriously are we meant to take Humbert and his quest? The book's complexity of tone and the question of Humbert's reliability as a narrator are the first issues in an investigation of the relationship between the parodic and the authentic.

Nabokov takes great delight in rapid and unpredictable changes in tone; we are never permitted to rest for long in the pathetic, the farcical, the rapturous, or the mocking. One of the clearest examples of tonal complexity is the novel's "primal scene," the seaside love scene with Annabel Leigh. After a buildup of high erotic suspense during which the two children are repeatedly frustrated in their sexual attempts, the famous episode concludes as follows: "I was on my knees, and on the point of possessing my darling, when two bearded bathers, the old man of the sea and his brother, came out of the sea with exclamations of ribald encouragement, and four months later she died of typhus in Corfu" (p. 15). We misread this little rollercoaster ride from the impassioned to the hilarious to the poignant if we take any one of its tonalities as definitive. Certainly this is not simply a satire of the romantic; its effect comes rather from the coexistence of its three tonalities in a single moment. In such a passage, we might expect the romantic to go under, partly because of its inherent vulnerability and partly because, as the dominant tone of the long buildup, it is apparently punctured by the intrusion of the burlesque. Yet the paragraphs that follow return to a tone of erotic rapture in a scene that is chronologically earlier than the seaside scene. The second scene, describing another frustrated tryst, concludes as follows: "That mimosa grove—the haze of stars, the tingle, the flame, the honeydew, and the ache remained with me, and that little girl with her seaside limbs and ardent tongue haunted me ever since—until at last, twenty-four years later, I broke her spell by incarnating her in another" (p. 17). If Nabokov had intended to puncture Humbert's rhapsody, it would have been more appropriate for him to arrange the two scenes chronologically so that the ribald bathers would appear at the end of the entire sequence, instead of in the middle. As it is, nothing is punctured; if anything, the romantic has found a new energy after the interruption. It is as if, in the following paragraphs, the romantic has been given the bolstering it needs to be able to hold its own with the jocular.

The novel's narrative point of view is as elusive as its tone. Clearly, when Humbert tells us, as he does repeatedly, that he has an essentially gentle nature and that "poets never kill" (p. 90), he is belied by the destruction he wreaks on Charlotte, Quilty, and Lolita. And when Humbert accuses Lolita of "a childish lack of sympathy for other people's whims," because she complains about being forced to caress him while he is spying on schoolchildren, Nabokov is being sarcastic (p. 163). Humbert also fails to see things that the reader can pick up; for example, he misses the name Quilty ("Qu'il t'y") concealed in a friend's letter to Lolita (p. 225). Just as clearly, though, Humbert is sometimes Nabokov's champion, as for example in Humbert's satirical comments about psychoanalysis and progressive education. At other points, Nabokov's attitude toward his persona is quite intricate: Humbert says of his relationship with Annabel that "the spiritual and the physical had been blended in us with a perfection that must remain incomprehensible to the matter-of-fact, crude, standard-brained youngsters of today" (p. 16); and Humbert does serve as a serious critic of modern love from the standpoint of a romantic exuberance of feeling, even if his criticism is undercut by his own divided love, in which what he calls his "tenderness" is always being sabotaged by what he calls his "lust" (p. 287).

But if we compare Humbert to another demented storyteller in Nabokov, Hermann in *Despair*, we see how Nabokov operates when he really wants to make a dupe out of his narrator. *Despair* is a take-off on the doppelgänger theme, in which the hero, Hermann, takes out an insurance policy on himself and then murders his double in order to collect; it doesn't work, however, because he's the only one who sees the resemblance. Hermann is among other things a Marxist, a sure sign that Nabokov is using him ironically, and Nabokov puts into his mouth frequent and obvious reminders of his unreliability. "I do not trust anything or anyone," he tells us.[2] His wife's hero-worship of him is one of his constant themes, and yet his self-satisfaction and blindness are such that he can find her undressed in the apartment of a man who is her constant companion and not experience a moment's doubt of her fidelity. Nabokov himself, calling both Humbert and Hermann "neurotic scoundrels," does make an important distinction between them, when he writes that "there is a green lane in Paradise where Humbert is permitted to wander at dusk once a year; but Hell shall never parole Hermann."[3]

Even Hermann, however, at times seems a stand-in for Nabokov, as, for instance, whenever he speaks of outwitting or playing games with the reader. Much has been written of Nabokov's own fondness for game-playing, such as the use of the *Carmen* parallel in *Lolita* to tease the reader into believing that Humbert will kill his nymphet.[4] In fact, it's difficult to find a Nabokov hero or narrator, however antipathetic, who doesn't at times sound like the author in his non-fiction. Even John Ray, the fool who introduces *Lolita*, asserts a prime Nabokov theme when he says that every great work of art is original and "should come as a more or less shocking surprise" (p. 7). And many readers have noticed the relationship between the desperate nostalgia of Humbert or that of the crazed Kinbote in *Pale Fire* and Nabokov's own commitment to the theme of remembrance. Conversely, Van Veen in *Ada*—who is the Liberated Byronic Hero, among other things, as Humbert is the Enchanted Quester and Hermann the Metaphysical Criminal—although he has been taken as almost a mouthpiece for Nabokov himself, has been condemned by his creator as a horrible creature.[5] The fact seems to be that Nabokov in his fictional and non-fictional utterances has created a composite literary persona, just as Norman Mailer has. His heroes, like Mailer's D. J. and Rojack, tend to be more or less perverse or absurd inflections of his own voice. In two of his own favorite works, *Don Juan* and *Eugene Onegin*, we have narrators who keep intruding on their heroes to deliver speeches and who also are at pains to differentiate themselves from those heroes. Nabokov behaves similarly, except that he does so within the range of the single voice. As in the case of tone, we discover an interplay of engagement and detachment, an interplay that is most active and subtle in the most memorable of the characters, like Humbert and Kinbote.

With this general sense of the status of tone and narrator in *Lolita*, we can turn now to consider what Humbert actually says. Humbert subtitles his story a confession. More accurately, it is a defense. Portraying himself as a man on trial, Humbert repeatedly refers to his readers as his jury. "Oh, winged gentlemen of the jury!" he cries, or, "Frigid gentlewomen of the jury!" (pp. 127, 134). But he also frequently addresses us directly as readers; in the middle of a torrid sequence he speculates that the eyebrows of his "learned reader . . . have by now traveled all the way to the back of his bald head" (p. 50). And late in the book, in a parody of Baudelaire's "Au lecteur," he addresses the reader as his double: "Reader! *Bruder!*" (p. 264). The reader is sitting in judgment on Humbert; the purpose of his story is to defend what he calls his "inner essential innocence" (p. 302); and the rhetoric of the book as a whole, its strategy of defense, is proleptic, an answering of objections in advance. Humbert's self-mockery, for example, has to be understood as a proleptic device, and, indeed, to follow the style of *Lolita* is to track the adventures of a voice as it attempts to clear itself of certain potential charges. As we will see, in many ways the defense is Nabokov's, even more than Humbert's.

At the end of the novel, Humbert sums up his defense by passing judgment on himself; he would give himself "at least thirty-five years for rape" and dismiss the other charges, meaning chiefly the murder of Quilty (p. 310). But there are further accusations that the novel strives to evade. As a whole, the book defends itself against a utilitarian concept of art. This charge is rather easily evaded by the use of John Ray, who introduces the novel as an object-lesson in the necessity of moral watchfulness on the part of "parents, social workers, educators" (p. 8). Nabokov's obvious satire here is intended to remove the allegation of his having a conventional moral purpose. Other accusations are handled within the text itself. In addition to conventional moralists, Nabokov detests psychiatrists and literary critics, and it is against these types of readers—or these metaphors for the Reader—that Humbert wages constant war. Anti-Freudianism is one of Nabokov's pet themes, and Humbert is a man who, in his periodic vacations in insane asylums, loves nothing more than to take on a psychiatrist in a battle of wits. His chief defense against a psychoanalytic interpretation of *Lolita* is to admit it readily and dismiss it as trite and unhelpful. When he describes his gun, he says, "We must remember that a pistol is the Freudian symbol of the Urfather's central forelimb" (p. 218); Humbert beats the analysts to the draw and says, in effect, "So what?" At another point, he anticipates a Freudian prediction that he will try to complete his fantasy by having intercourse with Lolita on a beach. Of course he tried, Humbert says; in fact, he went out of his way to look for a suitable beach, not in the grip of unconscious forces but in "rational pursuit of a purely theoretical thrill"; and when he found his beach, it was so damp, stony, and uncomfortable that "for the first time in my life I had as little desire for her as for a manatee" (p. 169).

Ultimately, we have to understand Nabokov's anti-Freudianism in the context of a hatred for allegory and symbolism in general. In *Ada*, Van Veen says of two objects that both "are real, they are not interchangeable, not tokens of something else."[6] Nabokov is against interpretation; an image has no depth, nothing beneath or behind or beyond; it is itself. Discussing Hieronymus Bosch, Van tells us, "I mean I don't give a hoot for the esoteric meaning, for the myth behind the moth, for the masterpiece-baiter who makes Bosch express some bosh of his time, I'm allergic to allegory and am quite sure he was just enjoying himself by crossbreeding casual fancies just for the fun of the contour and color" (p. 437). Another of Nabokov's heroes, Cincinnatus in *Invitation to a Beheading*, is a man whose mortal crime is to be opaque, or inexplicable, while everyone else is transparent. To be inexplicable is to be unrelatable to anything else; Humbert refers to the "standardized symbols" of psychoanalysis (p. 287), and Hermann, a bad literary critic, points out a resemblance that nobody else can see. Nabokov's hero-villains are often allegorists, like Humbert, who imposes his fantasy of Annabel Leigh on Lolita and turns her into a symbol of his monomania.

Allegory, as Angus Fletcher has shown, is daimonic and compulsive; it is a spell, enchanted discourse.[7] Nabokov, on the contrary, tries to create structures that defy interpretation and transcend the reader's allegorism, Freudian or otherwise; like Mallarmé, he dreams of a literature that will be allegorical only of itself. Thus, Humbert evades our attempts to explain him according to prior codes or assumptions. First of all, he insists that women find his "gloomy good looks" irresistible (p. 106); therefore, we can't pigeonhole him as someone forced into perversion by his inability to attract adult women. Then, too, Lolita is not "the fragile child of a feminine novel" (p. 46) but a child vamp, who, furthermore, is not a virgin and who, even further, Humbert claims, actually seduces him—a claim that is at least arguable. And finally, when we are forced to compare Humbert to Quilty, a sick, decadent, and cynical man, a man who is immune to enchantment, it becomes impossible simply to categorize Humbert as a pervert like all others. In all these ways, Humbert is not only made to look better than he otherwise would; he is also made difficult to explain and classify, and his uniqueness is a crucial theme of his defense. In *Ada*, Van Veen acclaims the "individual vagaries" without which "no art and no genius would exist" (p. 237). In *Despair*, Hermann the Marxist longs for the "ideal sameness" of a classless society, where one person is replaceable by another, while his rival, the artist Ardalion, believes that "every face is unique" (pp. 168–69, 50). In fact, even Hermann admits that his double resembles him only in sleep or death; vitality is individuation. It is a favorite theme of Nabokov. We are told in *Pnin* that schools of art do not count and that "Genius is non-conformity."[8] The author himself always hates being compared to other writers: "Spiritual affinities have no place in my concept of literary criticism," he has said.[9] In light of this, it is worth noting that the alienation and linguistic eccentricity of a character like Pnin are, in addition to being poignant and comical, the valuable signs of his singularity. Whatever else they are, heroes like Pnin, Humbert, and Kinbote are recognizable; they are rare birds. Humbert tells us that he is even singular physiologically in that he has the faculty of shedding tears during orgasm.

Humbert's chief line of defense is that he is no "brutal scoundrel" but a poet (p. 133). Nympholepsy is aesthetic as well as sexual; the nymphet in the child is perceived by the mind. Humbert does not wish merely to tell us about sex, which anyone can do; he wants "to fix once for all the perilous magic of nymphets" (p. 136); he wants to fix the borderline between "the beastly and beautiful" in nymphet love (p. 137). He calls himself "an artist and a madman, a creature of infinite melancholy" (p. 19); he is an explorer of that special romantic domain of sensation, the feeling of being in paradise and hell simultaneously; and he is a sentimentalist who revokes the anti-romantic bias of modernism in a sentimental parody of Eliot's "Ash Wednesday." The problem is that in portraying himself as a romantic dreamer and enchanted poet, rather than as a brutal scoundrel, he leaves himself open to another charge: literary banality. He recognizes his position as a spokesman for values that no one takes seriously anymore and says that his judges will regard his lyrical outbursts and rhapsodic interpretations as "mummery," so much hot air to glorify his perversion (p. 42). His nymphet, on the other hand, is at best bored by his mummery, and the two often operate as a vaudeville team, in which he is the alazon and she the eiron (p. 114):

> "Some day, Lo, you will understand many emotions and situations, such as for example the harmony, the beauty of spiritual relationship."
> "Bah!" said the cynical nymphet.

Humbert fears Lolita's "accusation of mawkishness" (p. 202), and his madcap and mocking humor defends him against any such accusation by the reader. So too does the presence of Charlotte, a trite sentimentalist whose mode of expression he mocks and against which his own appears unimpeachable. Yet he says, "Oh, let me be mawkish for the nonce. I am so tired of being cynical" (p. 111).

If the book's central rhetorical figure is prolepsis, its central structural figure is displacement, or incongruity. Often cultural or geographical, incongruity appears in such local details as Charlotte's calling her patio a "piazza" and speaking French with an American accent; but more generally it appears in Humbert's old-world, European manner—aristocratic, starchy, and genteel—set in a brassy America of motels and movie magazines, and in his formal, elegant style of speaking posed against Lolita's slang. But Humbert is not only out of place; he is also out of time, since he is still pursuing the ghost of that long-lost summer with Annabel Leigh. The incongruity is also erotic, in the sexual pairing of a child and an adult, and, in the application of romantic rhetoric to child-molesting, it appears as a problematic relation between word and thing. The geographical, linguistic, and temporal aspects of Humbert's dislocation are often related to Nabokov's own exile; but I wish to emphasize here another primal displacement, Humbert's status as a nineteenth-century hero out of his age. In this literary dislocation, a romantic style is placed in a setting in which it must appear alien and incongruous. Humbert's problem is to defend his romanticism in a de-idealizing, debunking, demythologizing time.

In *Eugene Onegin* Tatiana wonders if Onegin is a mere copy of a Byronic hero:

> who's he then? Can it be—an imitation,
> an insignificant phantasm, or else
> a Muscovite in Harold's mantle,
> a glossary of other people's megrims,
> a complete lexicon of words in vogue? . . .
> Might he not be, in fact, a parody?[10]

Humbert, in his displaced and belated romanticism, must prove that he is not an imitation. Nabokov's use throughout his work of various doubles, mirrors, anti-worlds, and reflections has been much documented and explored. His heroes are typically set in a matrix of doubleness: the condemned man Cincinnatus in *Invitation to a Beheading*, for example, is doubled both by his secret inner self—his freedom or his imagination—and by his executioner. Among its many functions, the double serves as a second-order reality, or parody. The double Quilty parodies Humbert who parodies Edgar Allan Poe. Humbert is referred to many times as an ape, and an ape is not only a beast but an imitator.[11] Nabokov has written that the inspiration of *Lolita* was a story of an ape who, when taught to draw, produced a picture of the bars of his cage.[12] So Humbert, the ape, the parody, gives us a picture of his emotional and moral imprisonment and enchantment. To be free is to be original, not to be a parody.

"I am writing under observation," says the jailed Humbert (p. 12). Once upon a time, observers walked out of the sea to destroy the best moment of his life; before their arrival, he and Annabel had "somebody's lost pair of sunglasses for only witness" (p. 15). Fear of discovery is Humbert's constant anxiety; he feels that he lives in a "lighted house of glass" (p. 182). The observer, the jury, the brother in the mirror represent the reader and also the self-consciousness of the writer. Robert Alter has pointed out in his excellent study *Partial Magic* that an entire tradition of the "self-conscious novel," stemming from *Don Quixote*, employs a "proliferation of doubles" and mirror-images to present a fiction's awareness of itself as fiction and to speculate on the relation between fiction and reality.[13] *Lolita* certainly participates in this tradition, but the sense of time expressed by its displacements and its literary allusions suggests that we understand its self-consciousness as specifically historical, as in the theories of Walter Jackson Bate and Harold Bloom. Humbert's jury is the literary past, which sits in judgment over his story. Humbert is both a mad criminal and a gentleman with an "inherent sense of the *comme il faut*" (p. 249); self-consciousness figures here as the gentleman in the artist, his taste or critical faculty, his estimation of what he can get away with without being condemned as an imitator, a sentimentalist, or an absurdly displaced romantic.

What is on trial, then, is Humbert's uniqueness and originality, his success in an imaginative enterprise. To what judgment of him does the book force us? Quilty is the embodiment of his limitations and his final failure. He first appears to Humbert in the hotel where the affair is consummated; thus as soon as the affair begins in actuality, Humbert splits in two; and later, practicing to kill Quilty, he uses his own sweater for target practice. Described as the American Maeterlinck, Quilty is a *fin-de-siècle* decadent and thus the final, weak form of Humbert's romanticism; his plays reduce the themes of the novel to the sentimental and the banal: the message of one of them is that "mirage and reality merge in love" (p. 203). Quilty, who is worshipped by Lolita and who couldn't care less about her, incarnates the ironies of Humbert's quest: to possess is to be possessed; to hunt is to be hunted. In addition, to be a parody, as Humbert is of a romantic Quester, is to be defeated by doubleness: Quilty is an ape who calls Humbert an ape.[14]

In relation to Lolita, Humbert accepts complete guilt. The end of the book is filled with outbursts against himself for depriving her of her childhood. A poet and a lover of beauty, he finishes as a destroyer of beauty. At one point, learning how to shoot, Humbert admires the marksmanship of John Farlow, who hits a hummingbird, although "not much of it could be retrieved for proof—only a little iridescent fluff" (p. 218); the incident aptly characterizes Humbert's actual relationship to his own ideal. At the end, he recognizes that "even the most miserable of family lives was better than the parody of incest, which, in the long run, was the best I could offer the waif" (p. 289). All he can achieve is parody. When he calls himself a poet, the point is not that he's shamming but that he fails. Authenticity eludes him, and he loses out to history. What he accomplishes is solipsism, a destructive caricature of uniqueness and originality, and he succeeds in creating only a renewed sense of loss wherever he turns: of his first voyage across America with Lolita, he says: "We had been everywhere. We had really seen nothing. And I catch myself thinking today that our long journey had only defiled with a sinuous trail of slime the lovely, trustful, dreamy, enormous country . . ." (pp. 177–78).

Humbert is finally apprehended driving down the wrong side of the road, "that queer mirror side" (p. 308). This is his last dislocation and is symbolic of all of them. We can now address one further form of displacement in Humbert's quest, the displacement of the imagination into reality. The mirror side of the road is fantasy, and Humbert has crossed over. Lolita was a mental image, which Humbert translated into actuality and in so doing destroyed her life and his; but his guilt is to know that she has a reality apart from his fantasy. The narrator of Nabokov's story " 'That in Aleppo Once . . . ,' " measuring himself against Pushkin, describes himself as indulging in "that kind of retrospective romanticism which finds pleasure in imitating the destiny of a unique genius . . . even if one cannot imitate his verse."[15] So Humbert is proud to inform us that Dante and Poe loved little girls. Hermann, in *Despair*, treats the artist and the criminal as parallels in that both strive to create masterpieces of deception that will outwit observers and pursuers; it is Hermann's failure not only to be found out but to be told that his crime, an insurance caper, was hopelessly hackneyed. Kinbote too confuses imagination and reality in *Pale Fire*, for he thinks he has written a critique and a factual autobiography, whereas he has really produced a poem of his own.[16] Crime and mythomania are parodies of art; Humbert parodies the novelist who attempts to displace the imagination into actuality, and this would seem to be the judgment of him handed down by the novel itself. Note, however, that this is the way romantic heroes—for example, Raskolnikov, Frankenstein, Ahab—typically fail. Perhaps it is Humbert's deeper failure to think, not that he could succeed, but that he could achieve the same kind of high romantic failure as those heroes of a lost age.

In any case, at the end, Humbert—who was a failed artist early in his career, who tried to translate art into life and again failed, and who then turned a third time to art, now as a refuge, a sad compensation, and a "very local palliative" (p. 285)—sees art as a way to "the only immortality" he and Lolita may share (p. 311). Having in effect destroyed her, he now wants to make her "live in the minds of later generations" (p. 311). A new idea of art does begin for him in his own imaginative failures. Then, too, he now claims to love Lolita just as she is, no longer a nymphet and now possessing an identity, dim and gray as it may be, that is separate from his private mythology. Thus, unlike Hermann, who will never be paroled from Hell, Humbert is finally able to see beyond the prison of his solipsism.

At this point I wish to turn from Humbert's engagement with the parodic and the romantic to Nabokov's, and I will begin with several points about parody in general.[17] Parody is representation of representation, a confrontation with a prior text or type of text. The mood of the confrontation varies with the instance. We can have parody for its own sake; for example, in *TLS* (21 January 1977), Gawain Ewart translated an obscene limerick into two prose passages, one in the style of the *OED*, the second in the style of Dr. Johnson's dictionary. Then we can have parody for the purpose of critique—satirical parody, such as J. K. Stephen's famous takeoff on Wordsworth and his "two voices": "one is of the deep . . . And one is of an old half-witted sheep." *Lolita* includes examples of both types: for instance, the roster of Lolita's class with its delightful names (Stella Fantazia, Vivian McCrystal, Oleg Sherva, Edgar Talbot, Edwin Talbot . . . [p. 54]) and the Beardsley headmistress' spiel about her progressive school ("We stress the four D's: Dramatics, Dance, Debating and Dating" [p. 179]). But as a whole the novel participates in a third type, parody that seeks its own originality, what Robert Alter would call metaparody: parody that moves through and beyond parody.[18]

When Alter calls parody "the literary mode that fuses creation with critique," he is saying something that is strictly true only of satirical parody.[19] What is common to all three types is that they fuse creation with differentiation. Parodists use a voice different from their own in such a way as to call attention to themselves. Parody is at once an impersonation and an affirmation of identity, both an identification with and a detachment from the other. This sense of displaced recognition, this incongruous simultaneity of closeness and distance, is a primary source of the delight and humor of parody, although it should be noted that parody is not inevitably comic, as in the case of John Fowles's *The French Lieutenant's Woman*, for example. Some parody, such as Stephen's, emphasizes the distance, but we also need to remember John Ashbery's idea of parody to "revitalize some way of expression that might have fallen into disrepute."[20] It may be true that some aggression is inherent in all parody, no matter how loving, but it is an aggression that is more primal than intellectual critique: it is the kind of aggression that says, "This is me. This is mine."

Page Stegner has said that Nabokov uses parody to get rid of the stock and conventional,[21] and Alfred Appel, Jr., that he uses parody and self-parody to exorcise the trite and "to re-investigate the fundamental problems of his art."[22] I think it is finally more accurate to say that he uses parody to evade the accusation of triteness and to elude the literary past in the hope of achieving singularity. Nabokov's parodism is an attempt to control literary relations, a way of telling his jury that he already knows how his book is related to prior work. More than that, it is a way of taking possession of the literary past, of internalizing it. Nabokov has repeatedly noted and critics—most vividly, George Steiner[23]—have often stressed the idea that he writes in a borrowed language. But in his difficult condition of personal and linguistic exile, Nabokov also points to another, more general kind of displacement. Irving Massey has suggested that many works of literature deal with the problem that *"parole* is never ours,"* that we all speak a borrowed idiom in expressing ourselves in the public medium of language.[24] It is also relevant that a writer inevitably speaks in the borrowed language of literary convention. Like so many other writers of the nineteenth and twentieth centuries, Nabokov dreams of detaching his representation from the history of representations, of creating a *parole* that transcends *langue.*

In relation to romance, parody acts in *Lolita* in a defensive and proleptic way. It doesn't criticize the romance mode, although it criticizes Humbert; it renders romance acceptable by anticipating our mockery and beating us to the draw. It is what Empson calls "pseudo-parody to disarm criticism."[25] I am suggesting, then, that *Lolita* can only be a love story through being a parody of love stories. The most valuable insight about *Lolita* that I know is John Hollander's idea of the book as a "record of Mr. Nabokov's love-affair with the romantic novel, a today-unattainable literary object as short-lived of beauty as it is long of memory."[26] I would add that parody is Nabokov's way of getting as close to the romantic novel as possible and, more, that he actually does succeed in re-creating it in a new form, one that is contemporary and original, not anachronistic and imitative. Further, it is the book's triumph that it avoids simply re-creating the romantic novel in its old form; for Nabokov to do so would be to lose his own personal, twentieth-century identity.[27]

Nabokov has tried to refine Hollander's "elegant formula" by applying it to his love affair with the English language.[28] His displacement of the formula from the literary to the linguistic is instructive. Indeed, both in theory and practice, he is always moving the linguistic, the stylistic, and the artificial to center-stage. "Originality of literary style . . . constitutes the only real honesty of a writer," says Van Veen, who characterizes his own literary activities as "buoyant and bellicose exercises in literary style" (pp. 471, 578).

Language that calls attention to itself relates to romance in one of two ways. Either it becomes—as in Spenser or Keats—a magical way of intensifying the romance atmosphere, or—as in Byron with his comical rhymes and his farcical self-consciousness—it demystifies that atmosphere. As in *Don Juan*, language in *Lolita* is used to empty out myth and romance. The novel opens with Humbert trilling Lolita's name for a paragraph in a parody of incantatory or enchanted romance language and proceeds through a dazzling panorama of wordplay, usually more Byronic than Joycean: zeugmas, like "burning with desire and dyspepsia" (p. 132); puns, such as "We'll grill the soda jerk" (p. 227); alliterations, such as "a pinkish cozy, coyly covering the toilet lid" (p. 40); unexpected and inappropriate condensations, such as the parenthetical comment "(picnic, lightning)" following Humbert's first mention of his mother's death (p. 12); instances of language breaking loose and running on mechanically by itself, as in "drumlins, and gremlins, and kremlins" (pp. 35–36); monomaniacal distortions of diction: "adults one dollar, pubescents sixty cents" (p. 157).

Certainly, verbal playfulness for its own sake is an important feature of Nabokov's art; certainly, too, we ought not underestimate the way in which Nabokov's linguistic exile has contributed to his sense of language as an objective presence, not merely a vehicle. It may also be that wordplay is used to overcome language. In *Despair*, Hermann says that he likes "to make words look self-conscious and foolish, to bind them by the mock marriage of a pun, to turn them inside out, to come upon them unawares" (p. 56). But I would suggest that language is finally a false clue in Nabokov's work unless we see that his centering of language and style chiefly has the value of a poetic myth. A literature of pure language and convention is a dream, congruent with the dream of a literature beyond interpretation; it is a dream of literature as a word game with no depth, a manipulation of conventions, a kind of super-Scrabble. The function of this poetic myth, or "bellicose exercise," is here proleptic; it detaches the writer from the romantic so that he may then gain for the romantic an ultimate acceptability.

This is also true of the idea of games in Nabokov and of all the devices of self-consciousness that Alfred Appel, Jr., has valuably described, such as the kind of coincidental patterning that runs the number 342 into the novel in different contexts to emphasize the artificiality of the fiction.[29] Humbert and Quilty share with their creator a love for the magic of games, as do so many other of Nabokov's characters; and sometimes that magic can assume diabolical form, as it does in the case of Axel, a forger of paintings and checks in

Laughter in the Dark. The vicious Axel completely identifies creativity with game-playing; for him, "everything that had ever been created in the domain of art, science or sentiment, was only a more or less clever trick."[30] Parody, Nabokov has said, is a game, while satire is a lesson.[31] A game is a matter of manipulating conventions; it is also a matter of play, a little Arcadia; and it is also a matter of competition. We can look at the idea of the game as a trope, a clinamen in Harold Bloom's sense, by which Nabokov swerves from the dead-seriousness of typical romance. But I see it ultimately, like parody and the centering of style, as an enabling poetic myth, the I-was-only-joking that permits us to get away with shocking utterances, like romantic rhapsodies in the mouth of an urbane, sophisticated, literate person like Humbert. It is the fiction that permits fiction to occur.

We might say that Nabokov must kill off a bad romantic and a bad artist in Humbert in order for his own brand of enchantment to exist. Nabokov's recurrent fascinations are romantic ones; he writes about passion, Arcadia, memory, individualism, the ephemeral, the enchanted, imagination, and the power of art. Indeed, his problem in *Lolita* is essentially the same as Humbert's: first, to be a romantic and still be original, and, second, to get away with being a romantic. *Lolita* has been taken as a critique of romanticism, and I am not arguing that it should be read as a romantic work. Rather, in its final form it is a work of complex relationship to romanticism, a dialectic of identification and differentiation. Like Byron in *Don Juan*, Nabokov in *Lolita* is divided against himself, although in a different way: Byron is a poet struggling against his own romantic temperament, while in Nabokov we see a romantic temperament trying to achieve a perilous balance in an unfriendly setting. But the results do illuminate each other: in *Don Juan* a romantic lyricism and melancholy are achieved through mocking parody and farce; in somewhat similar fashion, Nabokov uses the energies of his style—its parody, its centering of language, its flamboyant self-consciousness—first against the spirit of romance and then in behalf of it. This, then, is the status of style in *Lolita*, and this is why style is elevated to such prominence; perhaps this is even why it must be a comic style: it functions as a defensive strategy both against the romanticism of the material and against the anti-romanticism of the "jury."

Indeed, the tradition of romance continues most interestingly and convincingly today in writers, such as Thomas Pynchon and John Fowles, who are ambivalent about it and often present it negatively. In such teasing and parodic works as *V.* and *The Magus* we see an attempt to gain the literary power of romance without falling under its spell. These are romances for a demythologizing age. The phenomenon of the romantic anti-romance is hardly new; *Don Quixote, The Odyssey,* and *Huckleberry Finn,* in addition to *Don Juan,* are also works of enchantment that simultaneously reject enchantment. All of them create a language which, in Marthe Robert's description of *Don Quixote,* is both "invocation and critique"—indeed, Alter applies this phrase to the self-conscious novel as a tradition.[32] What may be new, however, is the anxiety created by novels like *V.* and *The Magus* in their skeptical and modernistic perspective on the daimonic. That anxiety—our uncertainty about how we are meant to take the daimonic—is the source of the suspense in such works. In *Lolita,* the comedy considerably mitigates this anxiety; it is, however, produced to an extent by the dizzying narcissism of Kinbote in *Pale Fire* and, even more, by the celebratory tone of *Ada,* that incestuous love story with a happy ending.

Writing of Spenser, Harry Berger, Jr., has said that advertised artificiality in Renaissance art functioned to mark off an area in which artist and audience could legitimately indulge their imaginations.[33] Today similar techniques of self-consciousness serve to keep our imaginations in check by telling us that what we are offered is only a fiction, merely a myth. Yet these cautionary measures, even when—as in *V.*—they seem to constitute the major theme of the work, may, once again, serve chiefly to allow us to enter a daimonic universe with a minimum of guilt and embarrassment. In sophisticated art we can consent to romance only after it has been debunked for us.

In *The Magus,* Fowles tells a fable of a young man who learns that the only way to avoid being victimized by magical illusions is to be a magician oneself. This is also true of Nabokov. In *Invitation to a Beheading,* everyone in Cincinnatus' totalitarian society appears to him to be a parody, a shadow of a reality, a copy. To be a parodist is one way of not being a parody. In *Despair,* Hermann, who seeks originality and hates and shuns mirrors, falls prey to a fake doubleness; Kinbote and Humbert are also trapped by reflections and doubles. But uniqueness resides in being able to manipulate doubleness; the inability to do this seems to be one of Nabokov's central criticisms of his failed artists. As for *Lolita* itself, it does beyond a doubt achieve singularity; however, singularity is not, as Nabokov would have it, to transcend literary relations but to be able to hold one's own among them.

Appel points out that Jakob Gradus, the assassin of *Pale Fire,* is an anagrammatic mirror-reversal of another character in that novel, Sudarg of Bokay, described as a "mirror-maker of genius," or artist.[34] Both death and the artist create doubles of life, and each struggles against the other. For the writer the assassin comes from many directions: previous literature, current critical standards, the expectations of the audience, the resistance of language, the writer's own self-consciousness. Nabokov has spoken of the artist as an illusionist trying to "transcend the heritage" with his bag of tricks.[35] This is the magic of sleight-of-hand, and Nabokov is referring to matters of style, technique, and language. But we are really dealing in works such as *Lolita* with the magic of the shaman, and, in this case, parody—together with the other features of a proleptic comic style—is perhaps his most powerful spell.

NOTES

1. Alfred Appel, Jr., introduction and notes, *The Annotated Lolita*, pp. 395, liv (same pagination as the 1958 Putnam's edition). Hereafter cited in text.
2. Nabokov, *Despair*, p. 113.
3. Nabokov, foreword, *Despair*, p. 9.
4. Carl R. Proffer, *Keys to "Lolita,"* pp. 45–53.
5. Alfred Appel, Jr., "*Ada* Described," in *Nabokov*, ed. Appel and Newman, p. 182.
6. Nabokov, *Ada*, p. 363. Hereafter cited in text.
7. Angus Fletcher, *Allegory: The Theory of a Symbolic Mode* (Ithaca, N.Y.: Cornell University Press, 1964).
8. Nabokov, *Pnin*, pp. 96, 89.
9. Nabokov, foreword, *Invitation to a Beheading*, p. 6.
10. Nabokov, trans., *Eugene Onegin*, I, 262 (ellipsis in original).
11. Appel notes that the ape metaphor is common in double stories, introduction, *The Annotated Lolita*, p. lxiv.
12. Nabokov, "On a Book Entitled *Lolita*," in *The Annotated Lolita*, p. 313.
13. Robert Alter, *Partial Magic*, pp. 21 ff.
14. Appel, introduction, *The Annotated Lolita*, p. lxiv.
15. Nabokov, *The Portable Nabokov*, ed. Stegner, p. 146.
16. See Alter's fine discussion of *Pale Fire* in *Partial Magic*, pp. 180–217. See also G. D. Josipovici's discussion of the confusion of imagination and reality in *Lolita* and in Nabokov's other works, "*Lolita*: Parody and the Pursuit of Beauty," *Critical Quarterly* 6 (1964), 35–48.
17. Some of the points in this section are discussed in greater detail in my article "Parody and the Contemporary Imagination," *Soundings* 56 (1973), 371–92.
18. Alter, *Partial Magic*, p. 215.
19. Ibid., p. 25.
20. "Craft Interview with John Ashbery," *New York Quarterly*, no. 9 (1972), 30.
21. Stegner, editor's introduction, *The Portable Nabokov*, pp. xix–xxi.
22. Appel, "*Ada* Described," pp. 174, 171.

23. George Steiner, "Extraterritorial," in *Nabokov*, ed. Appel and Newman, pp. 119–27.

24. Irving Massey, *The Gaping Pig: Literature and Metamorphosis* (Berkeley: University of California Press, 1976), p. 30.

25. William Empson, *Some Versions of Pastoral* (Harmondsworth, England: Penguin, 1966), p. 52.

26. John Hollander, "The Perilous Magic of Nymphets," in *On Contemporary Literature*, ed. Richard Kostelanetz, p. 480.

27. Both Lionel Trilling and G. D. Josipovici have approached the same general understanding of the book as a serious engagement with the romantic, although in ways different from my own. Trilling sees Humbert as the last exponent of "passion-love," which, although traditionally finding its setting in the story of adultery, now requires a more extreme vehicle, like child-molesting, for adequate shock value. Trilling calls *Lolita* a "regressive book": "although it strikes all the approved modern postures and attitudes, it is concerned to restore a foredone mode of feeling" ("The Last Lover—Vladimir Nabokov's *Lolita*," *Encounter* 11 [1958], 9–19). For Josipovici, in "*Lolita*: Parody and the Pursuit of Beauty," Humbert fails to capture Lolita in life, but he does capture her in his memoir, that is, in and as language. His ability to do so depends upon his learning to distinguish reality from imagination and understand words as arbitrary signs, not objects. Parody, as the mode that treats convention as convention rather than as reality, becomes the medium through which Humbert can successfully conduct his quest for beauty that is otherwise unattainable. Trilling and Josipovici are far more accurate guides to the novel than those who read it as a satire, but neither accounts for the interplay of the romantic and the comical, which constitutes the book's special impact.

28. Nabokov, "On a Book Entitled *Lolita*," *The Annotated Lolita*, p. 318.

29. Appel, introduction, *The Annotated Lolita*, especially pp. xxvii–xxxi and lviii–lxxi.

30. Nabokov, *Laughter in the Dark*, p. 182.

31. Nabokov, *Strong Opinions*, p. 75.

32. Alter, *Partial Magic*, p. 11.

33. Harry Berger, Jr., introduction, *Spenser: A Collection of Critical Essays*, Twentieth Century Views (Englewood Cliffs, N.J.: Prentice-Hall, 1968), pp. 3–5.

34. Alfred Appel, Jr., "*Lolita*: The Springboard of Parody," in Dembo, ed., *Nabokov*, p. 108.

35. Nabokov, "On a Book Entitled *Lolita*," in *The Annotated Lolita*, p. 319.

Postscript to the Russian Edition of *Lolita*

VLADIMIR NABOKOV

TRANSLATED BY EARL D. SAMPSON

Translator's note: Lolita was first published in 1955 in Paris, by
Olympia Press, with a preface from the publisher but without any
authorial comment. The first American edition (New York: Putnam's, 1958) included an author's afterword, "On a Book Entitled
Lolita," which was also included in the English edition (London:
Weidenfeld and Nicolson, 1959) and in the many translations mentioned in Nabokov's text below. When Nabokov translated *Lolita*
into Russian (New York: Phaedra, 1967), he included a translation of
that afterword and added a "Postscript to the Russian Edition."

Nabokov's translation into Russian of "On a Book Entitled *Lolita*" is scrupulous, but there are a few interesting discrepancies between the two texts. For example, "Suave John Ray" of the first sentence becomes in the Russian "John Ray, pleasant in every respect,"
a borrowing from *Dead Souls*, where Gogol distinguishes between
two unnamed female personages as "a lady simply pleasant" and "a
lady pleasant in every respect." In the fourth paragraph, Nabokov
adds German blood to the Irish blood in Lolita's lineage (presumably
from her father's side: Nabokov has indicated that "Haze" is derived
from the German *Hase*, "hare"). In the sixth paragraph, he adds the
American Museum of Natural History in New York to the list of lepidopterological collections to which he has contributed specimens
and comments that Humbert Humbert wrote *Lolita* thirty times
faster than did Nabokov: Humbert took fifty-six days and Nabokov
about four and a half years. (In this paragraph's list of localities
where Nabokov hunted butterflies and worked on *Lolita*, Ashland,
Oregon, is mistakenly given as "Ashton"—possibly a printer's error
influenced by Afton, Wyoming, earlier in the list.) In the fourteenth
paragraph, "the tinkling sounds of the valley town coming up the
mountain trail (on which I caught the first known female of
Lycaeides sublivens Nabokov)" is expanded to "the mountain trail
(in Telluride [Colorado], where I caught the heretofore undiscovered

female of the blue *Lycaeides sublivens* Nabokov, which I had described myself on the basis of the male)."

Perhaps the most interesting interpolation occurs in the seventh paragraph. In the original, the paragraph begins with the two sentences "At first, on the advice of a wary old friend, I was meek enough to stipulate that the book be brought out anonymously. I doubt that I shall ever regret that soon afterwards, realizing how likely a mask was to betray my own cause, I decided to sign *Lolita*." The Russian text inserts between these two sentences the following: "The anagram of my name and surname in the name and surname of one of my characters is a memorial of that hidden authorship." The reference is to Clare Quilty's friend Vivian Darkbloom, whose role in the novel, though minor, gives every appearance of being preplanned, so the implication that she was inserted after the work's completion for the sole purpose of leaving a thumbprint should not be taken at face value (nor, on the other hand, should it be summarily dismissed). But there is another implication here: that the anagrammatical characters that occur in so many of Nabokov's Russian novels were not just the result of linguistic playfulness but also a means of insuring that Sirin's novels would be identified with Vladimir Nabokov.

There are a number of other discrepancies between the English and Russian versions, small differences in wording or phrasing, often a matter of stylistic equivalencies vs. lexical literalness. But there is at least one single-word interpolation in the Russian text that deserves further comment. It occurs in the significant, often-quoted passage on aesthetic bliss (pp. 316–17 in the American edition). The English text reads: "For me a work of fiction exists only in so far as it affords me what I shall bluntly call aesthetic bliss, that is a sense of being somehow, somewhere, connected with other states of being where art (curiosity, tenderness, kindness, ecstasy) is the norm." The Russian text translates exactly those four words in parentheses, but adds, between kindness and ecstasy, "harmony" (*stroynost'*), apparently another essential element of art that occurred to Nabokov after the original publication of the essay. It is interesting, in light of the accusation often leveled at Nabokov of being a "formalist," ostensibly unconcerned with the moral content of his fiction, that he at first defined art exclusively in terms of moral categories and only added a formal category as an afterthought.

Nabokov's "Postscript" to the Russian edition of *Lolita* extends and amplifies both the English and the Russian versions of his afterword. Nabokov devoted a good deal of time in his last years to making his Russian writings available to readers of English, so it seems appropriate now to make this late Russian text, with its witty, perceptive, and touching commentary, likewise available. Here, then, is an English rendering of the Russian "Postscript." The endnotes are supplied by the translator, who wishes to record his gratitude to Véra Nabokov for reading the manuscript and proofs of the translation, making various suggestions for improvement, and ultimately approving the text and the notes.—E. D. S.

Scholarly scruples prompted me to retain the last paragraph of the American afterword in the Russian text, in spite of the fact that it can only confound the Russian reader who does not remember, or didn't understand, or never even read "V. Sirin's"[1] books, published in Europe in the twenties and thirties. I so fervently stress to my American readers the superiority of my Russian style over my English that some Slavists might really think that my translation of *Lolita* is a hundred times better than the original, but the rattle of my rusty Russian strings only nauseates me now. The history of this translation is a history of disillusionment. Alas, that "wondrous Russian tongue" that, it seemed to me, was waiting for me somewhere, was flowering like a faithful springtime behind a tightly locked gate, whose key I had held in safekeeping for so many years, proved to be nonexistent, and there is nothing behind the gate but charred stumps and a hopeless autumnal distance, and the key in my hand is more like a skeleton key.

I console myself, first of all, with the thought that the fault for the clumsiness of the translation offered here lies not only with the translator's loss of touch with his native speech but also with the spirit of the language into which the work is being translated. In the course of a half year's labor over the Russian *Lolita*, I not only recognized the loss of a number of personal trifles and irretrievable linguistic skills and treasures but also came to certain general conclusions regarding the mutual translatability of two amazing languages.

Gestures, grimaces, landscapes, the torpor of trees, odors, rains, the melting and iridescent hues of nature, everything tenderly human (strange as it may seem!), but also everything coarse and crude, juicy and bawdy, comes out no worse in Russian than in English, perhaps better; but the subtle reticence so peculiar to English, the poetry of thought, the instantaneous resonance between the most abstract concepts, the swarming of monosyllabic epithets—all this, and also everything relating to technology, fashion, sports, the natural sciences, and the unnatural passions—in Russian become clumsy, prolix, and often repulsive in terms of style and rhythm. This discrepancy reflects a basic historical difference between the green Russian literary language and English, ripe as a bursting fig: between a youth of genius, but not yet sufficiently well educated and at times rather tasteless, and a venerable genius who combines a motley erudition with absolute freedom of spirit. Freedom of spirit! All the breath of humanity lies in that conjunction of words.

The bibliographical information cited in the afterword to the American edition (Putnam, 1958) can now be amplified. The first edition, published with copious misprints in two small volumes in Paris (Olympia Press, 1955), sold rather sluggishly to English tourists until it came to the attention of Graham Greene, who praised the book in a London newspaper. He and *Lolita* were attacked in another London newspaper by a reactionary columnist, a certain John Gordon, and it was his virtuous horror that attracted general attention to *Lolita*. As to her fate in the United States, it should be noted that she was never banned there (as she is still banned in some countries). The first copies of the Paris edition of *Lolita* that private individuals had ordered were held and read at American customs, but my unknown friend and reader in the customs service pronounced my *Lolita* legal literature, and the copies were forwarded to their addressees. This settled the doubts of the cautious American publishers, and now I could select from among them the one most suitable to me. The success of the Putnam edition (1958) exceeded, as they say, all expectations. Paradoxically, though, the first English-language edition, which had been published in Paris in 1955, now suddenly fell under a ban. I often wonder what I would have done at the time of the initial negotiations with Olympia Press if I had learned then that alongside talented, albeit immodest, literary works, the publisher gained his main income from vulgar little books that he commissioned from meretricious nonentities, books of exactly the same nature as the pictures hawked on dark corners of a nun with a St. Bernard, or a sailor with a sailor. Be that as it may, the English customs had long since, in the stern and sober fog that greets homebound vacationers, been confiscating that pornographic trash—in the same grass-green covers as my *Lolita*. And now, the English Home Secretary had asked his French colleague, as ignorant as he was obliging, to forbid the sale of the entire Olympia catalog, and for a time *Lolita* in Paris shared the fate of Olympia's obscene publications.

Meanwhile a London publisher had turned up who wanted to publish it. This coincided with the discussion of a new censorship law (1958–59), in which *Lolita* served as an argument for both liberals and conservatives. Parliament ordered a number of copies from

America, and the MP's familiarized themselves with the book. The law passed, and *Lolita* was published in London by Weidenfeld and Nicolson in 1959. Simultaneously Gallimard in Paris published it in French—and Olympia Press's ill-starred first English edition appeared again in the bookstands, dusting its lapels with a businesslike and indignant air.

Since then *Lolita* has been translated into many languages: it has appeared in separate editions in the Arabic lands, Argentina, Brazil, China,[2] Denmark, Finland, France, Germany, Greece, Holland, India, Israel, Italy, Japan, Mexico, Norway, Sweden, Turkey, and Uruguay. Its sale has just been permitted in Australia, but it is still banned in Spain and South Africa. Nor has it appeared in the puritan countries behind the Iron Curtain. Of all these translations, I can answer, as to accuracy and completeness, only for the French one, which I checked myself prior to publication. I can imagine what the Egyptians and the Chinese did with the poor thing, and I imagine still more vividly what that "displaced lady" who had recently learned English would have done with it, if I had permitted it, or the American who had "taken" Russian at the university. But the question of for whom, in fact, I translate *Lolita* belongs to the sphere of metaphysics and humor. I find it difficult to imagine the regime in my prim homeland, whether liberal or totalitarian, under which the censorship would pass *Lolita*. I don't know, by the way, who is held in special esteem in Russia today—Hemingway, I think, that contemporary replacement for Mayne Reid,[3] and the nonentities Faulkner and Sartre, those darlings of the Western bourgeoisie. Russian émigrés, on the other hand, avidly read Soviet novels, enthralled by cardboard Quiet Don Cossacks[4] on their cardboard horses, rearing back on their cardboard tails; or by that lyrical doctor[5] with his inclinations toward a vulgar mysticism, his philistine locutions and his charmer out of Charskaya,[6] who brought in so much hard foreign currency for the Soviet government.

In publishing *Lolita* in Russian, I am pursuing a very simple aim: I want my best English book—or, let us say more modestly, one of my best English books—to be translated correctly into my native language. It's the whim of a bibliophile, no more. As a writer, I have grown all too accustomed to the fact that a blind spot has loomed black on the eastern horizon of my consciousness for nearly half a century now: I don't have to worry about any Soviet editions of *Lolita*! As a translator, I am not vain, I'm indifferent to the experts' corrections, and pride myself only on the iron hand with which I checked the demons who incited me to deletions and additions. As a reader, I have the ability to multiply without end and could easily pack a huge sympathetic auditorium with my doubles, spokesmen, extras, and those stooges who without a second's hesitation go up on stage from various rows, the moment the magician invites the audience to make certain he is not cheating. But what can I say about the other, normal, readers? In my magic crystal rainbows play, my glasses are reflected obliquely, a miniature scene of festive illumination begins to take shape—but I see precious few people there: a few old friends, a group of émigrés (who on the whole prefer Leskov),[7] a visiting poet from the land of the Soviets, the makeup man from a traveling troupe, three Polish or Serbian delegates in a mirrored café, and far at the back—the beginnings of a vague movement, signs of enthusiasm, the approaching figures of young people waving their hands . . . but they're just asking me to move aside—they're about to photograph the arrival of some president in Moscow.

Vladimir Nabokov
7 November 1965
Palermo

NOTES

1. "V. Sirin" (or "Vladimir Sirin") is the *nom de plume* under which Nabokov published his Russian writings in the 1920s and 1930s.
2. Nationalist China, of course. A Chinese translation (*Lo li t'ai*) was published in Formosa in 1960. Nabokov's list of translations runs from the first to the last letter of the Russian alphabet, but since no translation has yet appeared in, say, Zaire or Zambia, the list could not be made to stretch to the end of the English alphabet.
3. Captain (Thomas) Mayne Reid, an Irish-born adventure novelist whose works, with settings in America, Africa, and so forth, were extremely popular in Russia from the 1860s on into this century. All his many novels and stories were translated into Russian, and even today he is better known in Russia than in Britain or America. A six-volume selection of his works was published in the USSR as recently as 1958. Nabokov recalls his boyhood acquaintance with him in chapter 10 of *Speak, Memory*: "The Wild West fiction of Captain Mayne Reid (1818–1883), translated and simplified, was tremendously popular with Russian children at the beginning of this century, long after his American fame had faded. Knowing English, I could savor his *Headless Horseman* in the unabridged original." The 1866 novel that Nabokov mentions has seen at least two translations into Russian a century apart (1868 and 1968).
4. The reference is to the novel *The Quiet Don* (translated in two parts as *And Quiet Flows the Don* and *The Don Flows Home to the Sea*), by 1964 Nobel laureate Mikhail Sholokhov (1905–).
5. *Doctor Zhivago*, by 1958 Nobel laureate Boris Pasternak (1890–1960).
6. Lidiya Charskaya (1875–1937), children's author who enjoyed a great vogue in the early part of this century, in particular among schoolgirls.

Many of her heroines are schoolgirls. The critic Korney Chukovsky called her a "genius of vulgarity" (*geniy poshlosti*).

7. Nikolay Leskov (1831–1895), a prosaist, like Nabokov, of remarkable verbal and narrative inventiveness, but in just about every other respect very unlike Nabokov.

Pnin: The Wonder of Recurrence and Transformation

JULIAN W. CONNOLLY

Many critics regard *Pnin* as the most accessible and straightforward of the novels that Vladimir Nabokov wrote in English, finding it both more realistic and less complex than *Lolita* and *Pale Fire*, for example. This opinion extends to the design of the work as well, and several critics have commented on the novel's loose construction. Douglas Fowler writes, "in its final form the work seems in many ways to be more a series of sketches than a novel."[1] Similarly, Howard Nemerov has written that "as a novel, the book looks somewhat accidental."[2] Yet this appearance of looseness is perhaps deceiving; other readers have found the work to possess a considerable degree of cohesiveness arising from a delicately balanced patterning of repeated images and events, beginning with the narrator's account of Pnin's trip to Cremona and concluding with Jack Cockerell's version of the same episode. Indeed, a close reading of the book reveals that *Pnin* is not simply a string of sketches linked primarily by the figure of the main character, but rather that the novel is organized along the lines of one of Nabokov's famous spirals: events, images, and associations recur over the course of the novel in a tightly controlled pattern in which external repetition is accompanied by internal transformation. The reader, like the Nabokovian artist, must be attuned to the differences in recurring events as well as to the similarities.

To see this spiral design in effect, one must first consider the fact that the novel consists of seven chapters, with chapter 4 as the central, pivotal chapter of the work, dividing it into two sections of three chapters apiece. Significantly, chapter 4 is devoted to the character of Victor Wind and is the only chapter in which the reader, with Pnin, meets this character. As more than one critic has observed, Victor is a "Nabokovian favorite," and shares deep affinities with his creator.[3] His artistic genius is a rare and precious gift, and his respect for Pnin is a credit to the old professor. His appearance in the *middle* chapter of the novel is not accidental, for his gifted nature, coupled with his warm attitude toward Pnin, has a considerable effect on the old man, even if Pnin himself is unaware of it. The clearest emblem of Victor's effect on Pnin is their shared dream. Chapter 4 begins with Victor's dream of his father, "the King," forced to flee his throne to await rescue by motorboat from a lonely beach at the seashore. Near the conclusion of the chapter, Pnin is shown having a similar dream, with Pnin himself in the role of the refugee, awaiting rescue by a motorboat from a "desolate strand." This overlapping of dreams suggests that some kind of spiritual or psychic transference has occurred between Victor and Pnin, and that Pnin possibly has gained something of Victor's special aura of genius and magic.

This suggestion is proven true over the rest of the novel, for one notes that when events or images that were prominent in the first three chapters recur in the last three chapters, their effect on Pnin and his life is recognizably different. He reveals a new resilience and ability to cope with misfortune over the last three chapters, and there is an indication that fate or chance itself has taken a special, protective interest in the man. Appreciation of Nabokov's design is enhanced when one realizes not only that chapter 4 divides the novel into two halves, but that on the basis of the plot, key imagery, and theme, each chapter in the first half can be directly paired with a corresponding chapter in the second half in a mirrorlike fashion. Thus chapter 1 can be paired with chapter 7, chapter 2 with chapter 6, and chapter 3 with chapter 5, as in the following "spiral" scheme:

$$
\begin{array}{cccc}
7 & & & \\
 & 6 & & \\
 & & 5 & \\
 & & & 4 \\
 & & 3 & \\
 & 2 & & \\
1 & & &
\end{array}
$$

To verify this pattern of recurrence (and transformation) in *Pnin*, it will be useful to go through the novel chapter by chapter, pointing out in the first three chapters the significant images and incidents that are to recur later, and delineating in the last three chapters the direction and extent of their repetition and transformation.[4]

Chapter 1 begins with the narrator describing Pnin on his journey to Cremona to deliver a lecture to a women's club. After a brief description of Pnin, the reader is told of Pnin's love of timetables, and his unfortunate mistake of relying on a timetable five years out of date. Thus Pnin finds himself on the wrong train. Eventually, he does arrive at Cremona in time to give his lecture, but not without first experiencing an attack of severe anxiety and dislocation that leads to a strange sensation of dissolution and delirium. In this, the central episode of the chapter, Pnin is sitting on a park bench in Whitchurch when suddenly he "found himself sliding back into his own childhood."[5] The vision that follows is a recollection of childhood illness and fever mixed with a dim awareness of the surrounding reality. Most troubling to Pnin is his sensation of re-experiencing his childhood efforts to make out or decipher an intricate design on the wallpaper of his sickroom. Every time that he was about to distinguish the design's pattern of recurrence, his mind would become lost again in a "meaningless tangle of rhododendron and oak": "It stood to reason that if the evil designer—the destroyer of minds, the friend of fever—had concealed the key of the pattern with such monstrous care, that key must be as precious as life itself. . . ." (p. 23).

At one point in his struggle, Pnin is on the verge of the solution, and has "the sensation of holding at last the key he had sought" (p. 24). However, a sudden breeze disrupts the foliage in the park, and the pattern is again blurred. Yet, as Nabokov writes, Pnin is comforted: "He was alive and that was sufficient."

In this passage, Nabokov makes two important statements, one about patterns, and the other about life. After describing how Pnin suspects that there are patterns created by an "evil designer" which one must decipher in order to recover one's health and sanity, Nabokov notes that Pnin doesn't find any pattern and states that to be alive is sufficient, implying that such patterns, if they exist, need not be a central concern for Pnin. Indeed, as Julia Bader has pointed out, the very fact that Pnin is alive allows him to escape the pattern which "the author is on the verge of imposing on Pnin's life."[6] Yet although this escape is significant and tangible at the end of the novel, no less significant and tangible is the pattern of repetition or recurrence that is established over the course of the novel not by an "evil designer," but by Nabokov himself. One finds in *Pnin* the reverse of the situation in *The Defense*, where Luzhin became so paranoid about the pattern of recurrence he perceived in his life that he killed himself. Pnin is nearly oblivious to such patterns, and his naive innocence serves as a counterpoint to the complex sequence of repetition and transformation that develops around him. However, recurring images are present even in the first chapter: one of the first objects that Pnin sees upon coming out of his spell of delirium is a gray squirrel sitting on the ground in front of him (p. 24), a striking reflection of the mysterious squirrel depicted on the screen that stood near his childhood bed.[7]

This first chapter concludes with a further instance of Pnin's childhood past surging up into the present. As the professor surveys the faces of the Cremona Women's Club, he suddenly sees his parents, relatives, and sweethearts in the crowd: "Murdered, forgotten, unrevenged, incorrupt, immortal, many old friends were scattered throughout the dim hall among more recent people . . ." (p. 27). Like the earlier vision, this one also passes, and the present returns to Pnin with grotesque clarity: "while from behind . . . another twinkling old party was thrusting into her field of vision a pair of withered, soundlessly clapping hands" (p. 28). The fading of the past is succeeded by a grim view of the present.

In chapter 1, then, the reader is introduced to Professor Pnin and finds him not only somewhat absentminded and disorganized, but also a passive, helpless victim of profoundly moving childhood memories. One notes that these memories come unbidden, and that Pnin is powerless to dismiss or counter them. Similar confrontations with childhood memories will occur later in the novel, but their effect on Pnin, and his reaction to them, will be different. Behind these differences, as will be seen below, one can perceive the magic power of transformation in the novel.

In chapter 2, Nabokov shifts his setting from Cremona to Waindell, the town in which Pnin teaches and resides. The opening scenes describe Joan and Lawrence Clements' plans for a party, and Pnin's search for a new home. Pnin, like Nabokov himself, displays a peripatetic life-style, regularly moving from one set of lodgings to another. At the Clements' house he finds an environment more congenial than any since his arrival in Waindell years earlier. Not only is the physical setting comfortable, but his landlords are able to appreciate the man "at his unique Pninian worth" (p. 39).

The real focus of the chapter, though, is not Pnin's discovery of a new home, but the visit of his ex-wife, Liza Wind, to this new home. As the narrator describes her, Liza Wind is a physically attractive woman of shallow character, a mediocre, imitative poet. Most damning of all in Nabokov's world is the fact that she is a psychologist who, along with her latest husband, Eric Wind, is an advocate of Freudian and group therapy. Unlike Pnin, she cannot perceive or appreciate the individual, the unique in life. Thus, as they pass the Waindell campus in a taxi she exclaims, "Yes, I see, *vizhu, vizhu, kampus kak kampus*: The usual kind of thing" (p. 53).

Anticipating her visit, Pnin experienced a great sense of expectation, as well as some trepidation, and the latter mood proves to be more prescient. After telling Pnin that her relationship with her husband has disintegrated, Liza explains that her real problem is their son, Victor. The boy's father dislikes him, and sees himself only as his "land father." Pnin, in Eric's view, is Victor's "water father" (p. 55). The association of Pnin with water, made explicit here, is suggested in the previous chapter when Pnin undergoes his attack of dissolution and recollection; there his experience is compared to that of a drowning sailor (p. 21). Similar images connecting Pnin with water will recur repeatedly throughout the novel, forming one strand of the complex web of repetition that surrounds his life.

The point of Liza's visit is only made as she is about to leave. She wants Pnin to assume a certain financial responsibility for Victor's education, sending him "a small sum now and then, as if coming from his mother" (p. 57). As she did years earlier in Paris, Liza has returned to Pnin to take advantage of his kindness and generosity, and she leaves him as before, without any indication of gratitude. Nabokov underscores this point as he describes Pnin returning from the bus station after seeing Liza off. Walking through the park, Pnin stops to give water to a thirsty squirrel, who eyes him "with contempt" (p. 58). After drinking its fill, "the squirrel departed without the least sign of gratitude" (p. 58). Although the squirrel here obviously echoes Liza's attitude toward Pnin, the image itself has greater significance. Like the squirrel on Pnin's screen in chapter 1, the animal represents an ominous and unsettling element in Pnin's environment, and it will appear again in the next chapter with a similar resonance.

Disappointed by both Liza and the squirrel, Pnin is shown at the end of chapter 2 deep in sorrow, resisting Joan Clements' attempts at consolation. She shows him a cartoon in which a shipwrecked mariner and a cat dream longingly about a nearby mermaid. This cartoon and Pnin's reaction to it are significant. Both the cat and the sailor dream in vain that the mermaid is a creature who is compatible with their needs. The mermaid, however, remains aloof, much like Liza in her relationship with Pnin. Pnin's first comment on the cartoon and its water images expresses his own feelings at the moment: "Impossible isolation," he says (p. 60). Then he ignores Joan Clements' attempt to explain the cartoon and comments despondently, "Lermontov . . . has expressed everything about mermaids in only two poems" (p. 61).

The poems to which he is referring are quite likely "Rusalka" ("The Mermaid") and "Morskaya tsarevna" ("The Sea Princess"). In the latter poem, the title figure seems at first to be a seductive beauty who calls invitingly from the sea to a passing prince (in Russian, *tsarevich*). Yet when the prince grabs the maiden by the hair and pulls her from the water, he discovers that she is in fact a supernatural creature with a green tail, covered in serpent's scales, that writhes and shudders in the throes of impending death. The prince's discovery of unsuspected horror under a façade of seeming beauty finds a reflection in *Pnin* in the reader's discovery that under Liza Wind's "animated, elemental" beauty (p. 44) lies a vulgar and insensitive soul. The association is strengthened when one recalls that the narrator has characterized Liza as a "limpid mermaid" (p. 44). One further notes that the very process of debasement or fall in fortune experienced by the fantastic creature in Lermontov's poetic fable stands in sharp contrast to the fairy-tale *elevation* that takes place in the Cinderella story, a tale which, as Charles Nicol has persuasively shown, is utilized by Nabokov later in the novel to link the characters of Pnin and Victor.[8]

The weight of Pnin's despair at the end of the chapter finally causes him to break down in tears. His composure shattered, he pounds the table with "his loosely clenched fist," and he wails in broken English, "I haf nofing. . . . I haf nofing left, nofing, nofing!" (p. 61). Pnin, as chapter 2 ends, is driven by the anguish of failed dreams and loss into a state of helpless despair. Yet, as one discovers at the end of chapter 6, such a state is not the inevitable product of misfortune in Pnin's life. Again, transformation will accompany repetition in the latter half of the novel.

The events described in chapter 3, occurring about a year after those of chapter 2, depict Pnin on the Waindell campus, in his classroom discussing Pushkin's poem "Whether I wander along noisy streets," at the library doing research for his *Petite Histoire* of Russian culture, and finally at a movie program that features three Charlie Chaplin shorts and a Soviet propaganda film. The central theme of this chapter is Pnin's love for old Russia—his personal interest in Pushkin the man as well as Pushkin the poet, his fascination with old books and Russian folk festivals, and the nostalgia for the Russian countryside that wells up within him after viewing a scene in the Soviet film.

The chapter also contains a large number of recurring elements. Among the most important of these is the third appearance of the squirrel, once again an animate creature, who, while scolding and chattering at some unseen delinquents, presides over Pnin's fall on an icy path. Also significant is the image of the floating maidens of a Russian folk ritual who appear to Pnin as Slavic embodiments of Shakespeare's Ophelia and who foreshadow the "handsome, unkempt girls" who march in an "immemorial Spring Festival with banners bearing snatches of old Russian ballads such as '*Ruki proch ot Korei*' ['Hands off Korea']" (p. 81). One notes that the Soviet version of the ancient Slavic ritual is corrupt, politicized, and anything but timeless in its focus.

A final theme that recurs significantly in this chapter is the theme of death, introduced in Pnin's discussion of Pushkin and echoed repeatedly throughout the chapter: the pencil sharpener in Pnin's office feeds on "sweet wood, and ends up in a kind of soundlessly spinning ethereal void as we all must" (p. 69); Pnin thinks of Pushkin's poem as he slips on the ice on his way to the Waindell library "to his paradise of Russian lore" (p. 73); he recalls Ophelia's death in Hamlet (p. 79); and, as he dreams of Stalin's participation in the election of governmental pallbearers, he once again recalls Pushkin's poem about death with his own personal emendation—"In fight, in travel . . . waves or Waindell" (p. 82, ellipsis in original).

Pnin's dream at the end of chapter 3 concludes with his vision that "groaning and clutching at its brow, a statue was making an extravagant fuss over a broken bronze wheel . . ." (p. 82). The figure appearing in this dream is very likely a bizarre reflection of the bronze statue on the Waindell campus that depicts Alpheus Frieze mounting a bicycle (pp. 72–73). One perceives, however, that Pnin's consciousness has reshaped the statue, adding to it a strange blend of fragmentary elements from Pushkin's narrative poem *The Bronze Horseman* and Tolstoy's *Anna Karenina*. In Pushkin's work, a poor inhabitant of St. Petersburg is driven mad by the death of his fiancée in a flood and has visions of being pursued by Falconet's bronze statue of Peter the Great. Anna Karenina, of course, has a terrible nightmare in which an old peasant mutters incomprehensibly as he bends over a piece of iron; shortly before she throws herself under the wheels of a train she sees a grimy, deformed peasant bending over the train's wheels. In both works, the main character is stricken with a delirium leading to death.

In *Pnin*, the ominous forebodings of the dream do not lead to death, but they are followed by an unsettling experience nonetheless. At the very end of the chapter, Pnin, "in fear and helplessness, toothless" (p. 83), hears the arrival of Isabel Clements, returning home from Arizona in flight from a broken marriage. Under the spell of "the automatic revival of happy homecomings from dismal summer camps" (p. 83), Isabel is on the verge of kicking open the door to her old room, now occupied by Pnin, when her mother halts her. Pnin, forewarned of the eventuality by Mrs. Thayer (p. 74), is still not prepared for Isabel's intrusion, and once again he faces a new round of dislocation and unrest.

Following Pnin's uneasy sleep and his rude awakening, and as if in answer to it, comes Victor's tranquilizing reverie described at the outset of chapter 4. The central figure in Victor's dream is "the King," seen by Victor as his father—not his real father, Eric Wind, but his "more plausible father" (p. 85). Like Pnin, Victor's "water father," this father figure is associated with water. In Victor's dream the King stands alone on a beach awaiting an American adventurer who "had promised to meet him with a powerful motorboat" (p. 86). Unlike the shipwrecked sailor in Joan Clements' cartoon, the King is not marooned—for him the possibility of escape is genuine.

This scene, termed a "crucial" episode by the narrator, also appears in Pnin's dream at the end of the chapter when Pnin sees himself "fantastically cloaked, fleeing . . . from a chimerical palace, and then pacing a desolate strand with his dead friend Ilya Isidorovich Polyanski as they waited for some mysterious deliverance to arrive in a throbbing boat from beyond the hopeless sea" (pp. 109–10). Despite the differences in detail between the dreams, an enigmatic transference from Victor's inner world to Pnin's clearly has occurred. There is no indication that Victor has told Pnin of his dream; Pnin's appropriation of it remains one of those mysterious "coincidences" that appear without warning in Nabokov's fictional world. Moreover, in this dream, which Pnin has taken over from Victor, one perceives the embryonic transformation of the water image in *Pnin* from an emblem of death or isolation to a portent of escape and freedom.

Victor, unlike the other main characters in *Pnin*, makes an appearance only in chapter 4, and Nabokov treats him to what some might feel is an inordinate degree of description for a character with so small a role. However, although his active role in the novel is minor, his ideological impact is highly significant. As Fowler puts it, "Victor Wind is perhaps Nabokov's most unflawed and precocious equivalent—at fourteen already the possessor of the taste, the political acumen, and the aloof superiority of such a genius as, say, Vladimir Nabokov."[9] Whether or not one wishes to go this far in defining Victor's "superiority," it is clear that Nabokov holds him up for special treatment. Free from all Freudian obsessions or neuroses, blessed with an IQ of 180, Victor possesses a special kind of genius: nonconformity.

His most precious gift is his artistic inclination. Able at three to draw his mother's shadow as it falls on the new refrigerator, Victor at six "already distinguished what so many adults never learn to see —the colors of shadows, the difference in tint between the shadow of an orange and that of a plum or of an avocado pear" (p. 90). Graced with such a sensitivity, Victor is one of the rare souls who can fully appreciate the color theory of his art teacher, Lake. According to Lake's theory, "the order of the solar spectrum is not a closed circle but a spiral of tints from cadmium red . . . to cobalt blues and violets, at which point the sequence does not grade into red again but passes into another spiral, which starts with a kind of lavender gray and goes on to Cinderella shades transcending human perception" (p. 96). Lake's color spiral, like Nabokov's own art, makes a quantum leap from the base colors of surrounding reality to the incredible colors of a fairy tale realm of the imagination. Victor, Nabokov stresses, is an initiate into this realm as well.

Pnin, on the other hand, as he writes to Liza while still in Paris, is no genius (p. 183). Nevertheless, his acquaintance with Victor brings him into contact with the aura of genius and magic that envelops the boy, and his life becomes charged with this aura too. Indeed, from the very first time that Victor learns of Pnin's existence, he endows Pnin with a kind of romantic charm, "a family resemblance to those Bulgarian kings or Mediterranean princes who used to be world-famous experts in butterflies or sea shells" (p. 88). As in the dream sequence, Pnin is associated with exotic royalty.

Furthermore, Nabokov tells us that Victor "experienced pleasure" when Pnin wrote to him. His second message from Pnin is on a postcard representing the Gray Squirrel, one of an educational series of such cards. Again the squirrel image appears, but now, it is not an animate, threatening creature, but rather a *picture* of a squirrel with an expressly educational or enlightening function. As with the water motif, in chapter 4 one can already detect the beginning of the process through which elements possessing a negative cast in the first three chapters are transformed in the last three into harmless or positive counterparts.

Chapter 4 concludes with a final image of artistic vision as the narrator draws the reader's attention to an unnoticed "luminous puddle, making of the telephone wires reflected in it illegible lines of black zigzags" (p. 110). This enigmatic image perhaps resonates with the image of the oblong puddle with which *Bend Sinister* begins and ends, described by Nabokov as evoking the writer's link to the character of Krug—"a rent in his world leading to another world of tenderness, brightness and beauty."[10] Awaiting Pnin, too, is another realm of brightness and beauty.

After the pivotal meeting of chapter 4, the narrative seems to begin anew, first with a journey on which Pnin becomes temporarily lost, as in chapter 1, and later with a recurrence of the attack of heart palpitations and its attendant recollections, again as in the first chapter. Yet there are other events and images that link chapter 5 not with the first chapter, but with chapter 3. Chief among these is the Russian atmosphere of the episode. In chapter 3, Pnin journeys to the library to do research on his cultural history of Russia and is deeply involved both in the scholarly aspect of the work and in the subject matter itself. In chapter 5, Pnin journeys to a summer colony of Russian émigrés, where he encounters both old Russian scholars and the essence of a Russian life-style. There is a clear correspondence between Pnin's activities in the library, where he discovers "Kostromskoy's voluminous work (Moscow, 1855)" (p. 77), and his conversations with such scholars as Count Poroshin, who would say "there is, by the way, an excellent monograph by Chistovich on the subject, published in 1833" (p. 119). Only at this Russian colony can Pnin find understanding listeners for his discourse on time in *Anna Karenina*. Cook's Castle is perhaps no "paradise of Russian lore," but it is a rare repository of Russian intellectual history and culture.

That Cook's Castle provides a compatible environment for Pnin is manifest in the description of his brief dip in the river. After noting that Pnin displays a "dignified" breast stroke, the narrator continues, "Around the natural basin, Pnin swam in state" (p. 129). Here one finds an echo of the image of Pnin as a member of royalty raised in the previous chapter. More importantly, though, the positive nature of this water scene contrasts vividly with the water images of chapter 3, where Pnin becomes obsessed with Pushkin's concern over the possibility of death "in waves," and where his research on Russian folk rituals leads him to dwell on Ophelia's death by drowning in *Hamlet*. The symbolic associations of this central water image have shifted from the negative to the positive, a shift that reflects the more general process of transformation at work throughout the last three chapters.

Also reflecting the general process of transformation is Pnin's second attack of the "frightening cardiac sensation" that makes him feel as if he were melting into the surrounding background. Physically similar to the attack in chapter 1, this event has a different psychological content. Swept into the past, Pnin is not returned to the sickbed and delirium of his childhood, but rather to the tranquil setting of a summerhouse owned by Dr. Yakov Belochkin, the father of Pnin's love, Mira Belochkin ("Belochkin," one notes, may be formed from a diminutive form of the Russian word for squirrel—*belka*). As in chapter 1, Pnin feels a sense of distress and anguish during this attack, but not because he confronts a strange pattern to unravel. Instead, he is faced with the image of Mira ruthlessly murdered by the Nazis at Buchenwald. Such a death, in his eyes, seems to deny the very possibility of conscience and consciousness in the world.

Coming as it does at the end of chapter 5, this vision of death at the hands of a cruel, tyrannical state resonates not only with a line from chapter 1—"Murdered, forgotten, unrevenged" (p. 27)—but also with the effect on Pnin produced by the Soviet documentary film at the end of chapter 3, where Pnin's dream of Stalin voting in the election of governmental pallbearers is followed in his sleep by the refrain about death in the Pushkin poem and the shreds of Anna Karenina's nightmare and death. Through a complex series of associations, both chapters 3 and 5 draw to an end with a reference to totalitarianism and human death, and the effect on Pnin in both cases is hard. However, one should note that the *final* scenes of the two chapters modify this effect in ways that are crucially different.

Chapter 3 ends with the imminent disruption of Pnin's life by a young girl fleeing a failed marriage, thus adding to his feelings of anxiety over death and loss. In chapter 5, though, the final scene is a description of a young couple silhouetted against an ember-red sky. The narrator does not know exactly who the two figures are, and asks whether it might be "merely an emblematic couple placed with easy art on the last page of Pnin's fading day" (p. 136). In any case, the image of young love softens the anguish of Pnin's attack with the promise of new life and generation. Again the transformation of unpleasant elements in Pnin's life in the last half of the novel operates here.

A more striking transformation occurs in chapter 6. Whereas the links between chapters 3 and 5 tend to be tenuous and ambiguous, the connections between this chapter and chapter 2 are clear and unmistakable. Like chapter 2, this chapter returns to the town of Waindell, and to characters other than Pnin at the outset. When Pnin *does* make his appearance in chapter 6, he is in roughly the same situation as in chapter 2: he has just found himself a new home. Earlier, it was a room in the Clements' house into which he moved; now, it is an entire house which he rents and makes his own. Earlier, the Clements' house was the best lodging he had lived in since coming to Waindell; now, his new house far surpasses the Clements' home. Indeed, Pnin is seduced by his new surroundings into a false sense of security and permanence; he tells the Clementses that he is thinking of buying the property. At one point he thinks to himself that "had there been no Russian Revolution, no exodus . . . everything . . . would have been much the same" had he remained in Russia (p. 144). Even the iridescent reflections of crystal candlesticks in the house recall to him similar effects in Russian country houses. This, of course, is a serious mistake: Pnin the émigré should know that the past cannot be resurrected materially; such physical ties to a dead Russia are only a painful illusion.

This false sense of security sets the stage for Pnin's disappointment later in the chapter. As in chapter 2, Pnin looks forward to a visit—not by Liza, but by his friends from the college—and he has high expectations of this visit. The occasion is a housewarming party, and one of the key guests is Dr. Hagen, his erstwhile protector in the German Department. It is Dr. Hagen who, like Liza, is in the position of bearing unexpected and unsettling news. As Fowler points out in *Reading Nabokov*, Hagen undergoes a metamorphosis during the party scene, at one point reminding Pnin of Eric Wind (p. 162).[11] Although Hagen's decision to inform Pnin that he will soon find himself jobless is intended as an act of kindness, Hagen displays a remarkable insensitivity to Pnin's distress, saying such things as, "Yes, we are in the same boat, in the same boat" (p. 170), and thinking to himself, "At least, I have sweetened the pill" (p. 171).

Hagen's brief communication, like Liza's, comes as a blow to Pnin, and he loses his composure. While cleaning the dishes after Hagen's departure, Pnin drops a nutcracker into the soapy water and hears the "excruciating crack of broken glass" (p. 172). The reader, with Pnin, immediately assumes that what has broken is a radiant bowl given to Pnin by Victor, and the effect on both the reader and Pnin is wrenching. Of Pnin, Nabokov writes, "He looked very old, with his toothless mouth half open and a film of tears dimming his blank, unblinking eyes. Then, with a moan of anguished anticipation, he went back to the sink, and bracing himself, dipped his hand deep into the foam" (p. 172). Miraculously, the bowl is intact; only a goblet has broken.

The preservation of the bowl is indeed a miracle, but one not entirely unexpected or unmotivated. The bowl is a present from Victor, and in previous descriptions Nabokov has shown it to be a wondrous object. For example, the bowl is first described as so striking that its tangible attributes are dissolved in the "pure inner blaze" of the delighted recipient. Yet these attributes "suddenly and forever leap into brilliant being when praised by an outsider to whom the true glory of the object is unknown" (p. 153). In addition, the greenish-blue tint of the crystal suggests to one of Pnin's guests the color of Cinderella's glass slippers. Although Pnin points out that Cinderella's slippers were actually shoes of squirrel fur (another transformation of the animate creature into an artistic work of beauty), the fairy-tale association established for the bowl remains. Further, the Cinderella reference connects the bowl to Lake's color theory, the spectrum of which "goes on to Cinderella shades transcending human perception." Clearly, Victor's bowl is cut from the magic glass of fairy tales and is thus impervious to the careless slips of humanity.[12]

Yet here the bowl also functions as a magic talisman preserving Pnin from harm. Its very survival bolsters his spirits: "He took a fresh dish towel and went on with his household work" (p. 173). As the bowl stands "aloof and serene" in the cupboard (aloofness is one of Victor's traits too; cf. p. 85), Pnin sits down to compose a letter: "'Dear Hagen,' he wrote in his clear, firm hand, 'permit me to recaputilate (crossed out) recapitulate the conversation we had to-night. It, I must confess, somewhat astonished me. If I had the honor to correctly understand you, you said—'" (p. 173). In marked contrast to the end of chapter 2, Pnin's misfortune and disillusionment here do not leave him in tears. Rather, the strength which he seems to draw from Victor's bowl allows him to regain his composure and control. The "clear, firm hand" of his letter contrasts with the loosely clenched fist of chapter 2, and the ability to write in an elevated, literate style, complete with the correction of a misspelling, vividly contrasts with the plaintive, simple, heavily accented "I haf nofing" that concludes chapter 2. In these last chapters, the transformation of events in Pnin's life and of Pnin himself is remarkable.

The final transformation occurs in chapter 7. Symmetrically mirroring chapter 1, this chapter begins with a view of Pnin's childhood (now from the narrator's perspective, not Pnin's) and concludes with Cockerell beginning his anecdote about Pnin's lectures. This is precisely the mirror-image, or reverse, of chapter 1, which begins with Pnin's journey to Cremona and only later turns to his childhood.

There is a shift in narrative perspective in the final chapter as well. The intrusive narrator finally moves to the center of the stage and treats the reader to an ample account of his own experience and virtues. However, his very narrative reveals him to be an unreliable, snobbish, and conceited character who is ultimately inferior to Pnin in nobility and kindness. One need not dwell on the narrator's flaws here; it is sufficient to point out his slipshod attitude toward dates: he states that in the spring of 1911 he was twelve (pp. 173–74), but then he says that five years later, in the summer, he was sixteen (pp. 177–78). Somewhere, he has lost a year, which would be a heinous error from Pnin's point of view. Pnin the pedant once exclaimed to the college librarian, "I put the year correctly, *that* is important!" (p. 75).

The narrator sets forth several recollections about Pnin's childhood in chapter 7, but they are fraught with prejudice and conjecture: "Perhaps because on my visits to schoolmates I had seen other middle-class apartments, I unconsciously retained a picture of the Pnin flat that probably corresponds to reality. I can report therefore that as likely as not it consisted of . . ." (p. 176). What follows is a series of observations, some of which may be accurate, others probably not. Among the objects that the narrator recalls seeing in Pnin's schoolroom is one that represents the final squirrel image of the novel—"a stuffed squirrel." That which previously was a source of anxiety to Pnin (as a mysterious image on a screen near his sickbed), or an ungrateful and threatening creature (in chapters 2 and 3), now has been transformed into an entirely harmless and innocuous object, a child's plaything.

Pnin's power, on the other hand, seems to grow in inverse relationship to the reduction of the squirrel image. In the first chapter, Pnin was a passive prey to childhood recollections; they came unbidden and nearly overwhelmed him. Now, in chapter 7, he is able to confront and refute pictures of his childhood and youth drawn by the narrator, and he does so with increasing vigor. The first time that the narrator tries to persuade Pnin of the accuracy of these memories, there is a neutral response: "he denied everything" (p. 180). On a later occasion, though, Pnin reacts heatedly to the narrator's anecdotes: "'Now, don't believe a word he says, Georgiy Aramovich. He makes up everything. . . . He is a dreadful inventor'" (p. 185). Here, gentle Pnin rises up against calumny and falsehood.

These scenes are important for two reasons. First, they indicate that Pnin is not doomed always to be a passive victim of childhood memories, and second, they reveal a side of Pnin's character that has not been fully exhibited before—they show him to be a strong and decisive battler. Although these scenes occur before the Victor episode in "real" time, they are presented *after* that episode in the novel's narrative and thus share in the positive aura that Pnin's contact with Victor has cast on other events.

This new image of Pnin leads directly into the final pages of the novel. Just as the narrator arrives at Waindell and enters into the sphere of Pnin's imitator, Jack Cockerell, Pnin manages to escape that very world. Cockerell's predilection for mimicry, as the narrator notes, has become for him "the kind of fatal obsession which substitutes its own victim for that of the initial ridicule" (p. 189). Although it bores the narrator, he too is trapped by it, while the original Pnin moves on. Nabokov intentionally employs the word "free" as he describes Pnin's car breaking out from the closed ranks of two identical beer trucks onto the open road: "Then the little sedan boldly swung past the front truck and, free at last, spurted up the shining road, which one could make out narrowing to a thread of gold in the soft mist where hill after hill made beauty of distance, and where there was simply no saying what miracle might happen" (p. 191). Pnin drives off toward a realm of possible miracles, a fairy-tale realm whose aura he has already felt in his contact with Victor and in his possession of the marvelous bowl. Behind him he leaves a world of lifeless imitation, smugness, and falsehood. Not only is the narrator's memory flawed, but Cockerell's version of the lecture incident is flawed too: according to him, Pnin took not the wrong train, but the wrong lecture.

Flawed or not, Cockerell's story returns the novel to its own beginning, closing a circle that is, like all ordinary circles in Nabokov's world, a vicious one. Yet this circular structure is vicious only for those characters unable to rise above it, figures such as Cockerell and the narrator. Pnin, in contrast, moves on to a higher plane—his path is that of the spiral, not the circle. At the end of his novel Pnin continues under the spell that transformed the threatening or disturbing events and images of the first three chapters into the less injurious and even innocent elements of the last three chapters. The crucial juncture on Pnin's path is his meeting with his spiritual son, Victor. The spirit of Victor's creative magic melds with Pnin's own irrepressible originality and life force to render him impervious to serious harm and capable of transforming hardship into moments of strength and courage. *Pnin*, then, is the story of this transference of grace, and it is far from being "accidental" in form. Rather, *Pnin* must be seen as a carefully crafted work whose patterns of recurrence and transformation can enchant and uplift its attentive readers.

NOTES

1. Douglas Fowler, *Reading Nabokov*, p. 122.
2. Howard Nemerov, "The Morality of Art," in his *Poetry and Fiction: Essays*, p. 261.
3. Fowler, *Reading Nabokov*, pp. 129–30. See also Ambrose Gordon, Jr., "The Double Pnin," in *Nabokov*, ed. Dembo, p. 152.
4. Nabokov told Alfred Appel, Jr., that he had originally planned to write an additional chapter which would fit in between the fourth and fifth chapters of the present book, but that "a combination of chance circumstances" prevented him from writing it. He continued, "it is only a mummy now" (Nabokov, *Strong Opinions*, pp. 84–85). Nabokov's decision never to write and add this missing chapter was perhaps based on

his perception that the novel as it stands is a self-contained, balanced whole and that an additional chapter would have upset its structural symmetry.

5. Nabokov, *Pnin*, p. 21. Hereafter cited in text.

6. Julia Bader, *Crystal Land*, p. 88.

7. Several critics have commented on the "series of uncanny squirrels" in *Pnin*. Charles Nicol's seminal article "Pnin's History," from which the above phrase is taken, traces in detail the recurring squirrel imagery in the novel and underscores its consistent association with Pnin and with such central motifs as the Cinderella story and "shadowgraphy" ("Pnin's History," *Novel* 4 [Spring 1971], 197–208). Expanding on Nicol's observations, William Woodin Rowe has suggested further implications for the squirrel imagery, finding, for example, that the squirrels in the tale are perhaps "fairy-tale-like reincarnations of Mira Belochkin" ("Pnin's Uncanny Looking Glass," in *A Book of Things about Vladimir Nabokov*, ed. Proffer, pp. 182–92). Both critics tend to view the squirrel images as generally beneficent throughout the novel, whereas the present article maintains that a transformation in the image's character occurs over the course of the work.

8. Nicol discusses the role of the fairy tale in *Pnin* in "Pnin's History," pp. 199–202.

9. Fowler, *Reading Nabokov*, pp. 129–30.

10. Nabokov, *Bend Sinister* (1973), p. ix.

11. Fowler, *Reading Nabokov*, pp. 141–42.

12. This reference to the Cinderella tale indicates that even on the level of fairy-tale associations, the process of recurrence and transformation is at work. Whereas the Lermontov mermaid poem to which Pnin refers in chapter 2 contains an unpleasant example of magical metamorphosis, the Cinderella tale to which reference is made in chapters 4 and 6 contains a metamorphosis in the opposite direction. Once again, negative images arising early in the novel give way to positive ones later in the work.

Part 4

The Fourth Arc

Pale Fire: The Art of Consciousness

MARILYN EDELSTEIN

Pale Fire is the supreme manifestation of the indivisibility of style and meaning in the work of Vladimir Nabokov. The novel's narrative consciousness, plot, and structure, as well as its ultimate significance, can only be discerned through the reader's own efforts; it thus becomes a paradigm of Roland Barthes's reader-created text. Critics uniformly recognize the playfulness of Nabokov's technique; few recognize the aesthetic and philosophical purpose of such literary sleight-of-hand. By placing the fictional process in the foreground of a novel, where the narrative human presence once was, Nabokov forces the reader to examine the similarity between fictional creation and self-creation.

In *Pale Fire* we are presented a poem with a critical commentary, including foreword and index. The poem was written by a homely American poet named John Shade, in largely autobiographical style. The commentary, we soon discover, is largely autobiographical too, with the "auto-" in this case somewhat harder to identify, ostensibly being one Charles Kinbote, who in reality is the exiled King Charles of Zembla, but who might also be V. Botkin, American scholar of Russian descent. Whoever the author of the commentary may be, on the very first page of the foreword the reader realizes that his work is not going to be an objective apparatus criticus. Kinbote is too personal, too anecdotal, and too absurd to be believed as a scholar. He constructs a complicated scenario for the events leading to Shade's demise, an almost paranoid plot that revolves around King Charles's overthrow in his kingdom of Zembla, a hired assassin named Jakob Gradus, and the murder of Shade— either as accidental victim of Gradus, out to kill King Charles (incognito in America as Charles Kinbote); or as accidental victim of Jack Grey, out for revenge on Judge Goldsworth, who sentenced Grey to the Institute for the Criminally Insane and whose house Kinbote is subletting. Soon one realizes that an integral component of the novel is this very confusion and multiplicity of plot, character, reality.

Pale Fire is concerned with "how each individual mind filters reality, recreates it."[1] We see the different patterns of sense that can be created out of the same set of events by different minds. Nabokov is aware of the reductionism necessary for people to perceive order in a chaotic world and of the further reductionism implicit in linguistic formulations of experience. Nabokov believes that seeing one static reality, perceiving facts without imagination, is like death (and like Gradus). Why should fictional characters be static and easily differentiable when life itself is not? Patterns of sense are personal creations, not universal givens. Nabokov constantly tricks the reader into believing in one possible interpretation of the facts, only to throw all "facts" into doubt, showing thereby that only individually created realities are possible. Nabokov constantly enters *Pale Fire* (with, for instance, his self-reflecting references to Hurricane Lolita, an émigré professor of Russian, and butterflies). These intrusions of the author's personality reinforce the artificiality of the fiction by emphasizing its maker's constant presence. They also stress that there is one undeniable human presence in the novel: the author himself. His is the controlling, unifying consciousness, and in that functional sense Nabokov's is the ultimate self of this book.

Each of the three main characters—Shade, Kinbote, and Gradus —can be seen as constituting one aspect of a whole human self. Gradus is the least conscious character. He can be seen as the repressed shadow of Shade, as the dark aspect of the unconscious, and, most importantly, as the darkness of death against which the artist struggles. He is almost a mechanical man, endowed with a sense of purpose (as assister of the plot) and little else. He is simply a killing device, a fictional tool; since he has no imagination, he cannot be a man in the Nabokovian schema. Charles Kinbote represents the solipsistic subjectivity of a not-quite-conscious self—like the surrealistic subconscious, where dreams, fantasy, and reality are indistinguishable. Yet he is also wildly imaginative, and thus creative, so he meets a basic Nabokovian criterion for humanity. Shade is objective and compassionate, as he presents himself in the poem and as he appears in Kinbote's commentary. He seems the most individuated and substantive character of the three. He is an artist, with the imaginative power to construct a reality and the awareness that reality *is* a construct: he is thus the most like his own author, Nabokov, and therefore the most like a man. Carol Williams has suggested that Shade, Kinbote, and Gradus are aspects of one whole artist who is centered in Shade.[2] Yet even he does not quite stand on his own as a fully developed fictional character or as the artistic equivalent of a fully realized human self. Shade's poem, the part of the book that manifests his identity, exists in the novel surrounded by the words of another man. Although critics point out that Shade's poem can stand alone, whereas Kinbote's commentary cannot, the fact remains that the poem *does not* stand alone. All the verbal elements in the book are interconnected in much the same way that the characters' identities are interlinked. Standing over all his inferior creations is the artificer-god Nabokov, playing a "game of worlds" with his creations.

One can clearly see the intermingling of the characters through an analysis of their respective names. "Gradus, Jakob, 1915–1959; alias Jack Degree, de Grey, d'Argus, Vinogradus, Leningradus, etc."[3] Bader tells us:

> Gradus in Latin means "step, *degree.*" A *Gradus ad Parnassum* is a dictionary used as an aid in writing poetry, and literally means "a step to the place where the Muses live." "Shade" is defined by the dictionary as "shadow, *degree* of darkness; a disembodied spirit; to undergo and exhibit difference or variation." There is thus a specific connection between Gradus and Shade, and the suggestion that the two characters are aspects of a single consciousness—that Gradus is a creation of the poet, a degree of Shade, or a step in the structure. Gradus, who is repeatedly identified with the inevitable ending of the poem—indeed he arrives at the very last line—may be the final tool used by the poet to complete his work and arrive at Parnassus.[4]

Shade has also written a poem called "The Sacred Tree" which Disa, exiled queen of Zembla, has translated. *Grados* means "tree" in Zemblan. Kinbote says that Shade "shared with the English masters the noble knack of transplanting trees into verse with their sap and shade" (p. 93). Kinbote is actually the one who transplants Gradus into the poem, through synchronizing his approach with the poem's progress. There is therefore an element of godlike power—over life and death—in Gradus' purpose in the story. Through Kinbote's eyes, we see Gradus arrive at the poem's completion, and we see him complete the *process* of the poem's growth by destroying its creator. Perhaps Shade is made to die in order to show the necessity of at least attempting to outwit the tyranny of death through art, or perhaps death comes to him simply to display the absolute authority of the novel's ultimate god—Nabokov—over him. Although both Gradus (Sudarg of Bokay) and Nabokov make mirrors, Gradus is anti-life,

anti-art, and he has the demonic power of unimaginative unconsciousness. Gradus awaits the end of Shade's artistic process just as
death awaits the end of Nabokov's deceitful illuminations. Both Degree and Gradus, as process, as steps toward something, are appropriate names for a character whose very being is viewed by Kinbote as
almost created by the processes of aesthetic motion (p. 78).

> We shall accompany Gradus in constant thought, as he makes
> his way from distant dim Zembla to green Appalachia [from Z
> to A, alphabetically], through the entire length of the poem,
> following the road of its rhythm, riding past in a rhyme, skid-
> ding around the corner of a run-on, breathing with the caesura,
> swinging down to the foot of the page from line to line as from
> branch to branch, hiding between two words . . . , reappearing
> on the horizon of a new canto, steadily marching nearer in
> iambic motion, crossing streets, moving up with his valise on
> the escalator of the pentameter, stepping off, boarding a new
> train of thought, entering the hall of a hotel, putting out the
> bedlight, while Shade blots out a word, and falling asleep as
> the poet lays down his pen for the night.

As Grey, Gradus not only represents the grayness of death, but also
the gray of the printed page, where black and white combine. He is
also a gray being, relatively unconscious, "endowed with a modicum
of self-awareness (with which he did not know what to do), some duration consciousness, and a good memory for faces, names, dates,
and the like. Spiritually he did not exist. Morally he was a dummy
pursuing another dummy" (p. 278). Gradus exists in a barely human,
pre-conscious state, where a creature can obtain faint sensual pleasure, of the sort appropriate to an "anticomedoist," from the extinction of a human life, from the murder of a fellow "dummy." He is a
fiction destroying another fiction within a fiction, and he is a degree
of the same shade that Shade is "most artistically caged" within—
the netherworld of fictional existence, subject to the whims of its
creator.

"Shade" and its related words, "umbra," "ombre," and "shadow,"
have various connotations relevant to this discussion. An "umbra"
is a ghost, a phantom, a shadow, a vestige. A shadow can be a
reflected image, or one who tags along with another, or watches
closely in a secret manner—much as Kinbote shadows (maintains
surveillance on) Shade through his window. "Shade" itself is partial
or relative darkness caused by the intervention of an opaque body
between the space contemplated and the source of light: absence of
complete illumination. Shade is not fully conscious, not fully il-

luminated, not totally aware of himself. Opacity is Cincinnatus C.'s "crime" in Nabokov's *Invitation to a Beheading*, since in his terrifyingly absurd society to be normal is to be transparent and without a self. Shade seeks self-knowledge, but he also seeks freedom from the dark knowledge of death. Though his imperfect creation of flesh—Hazel—dies, his beautiful linguistic creation will live on beyond even his own mortal existence. An "ombre" is a European *gray*ling, demonstrating yet another connection between Shade and Jack Grey/Gradus. The grayling called "ombre" is a type of fish; but "grayling" can also denote a butterfly of the family Satyridae, thus hinting at the controlling presence of Nabokov. "Ombre" is also a three-handed card game and the player in this game who elects to name the trump and oppose the other two players. There is certainly a three-handed game going on here, either with Shade calling the trump (in the sense of creating the aesthetic playing field), or with Nabokov calling the trump on all three of his characters. Shade is the closest thing we have to *un hombre*—a man—in the novel; we know far more about him *as* a man, through his poem and through the poem's distorted reflection in Kinbote's commentary, than we do about the other characters.

Kinbote/Botkin/King Charles is another multi-faceted character. The "-bote" in "Kinbote" seems to derive partly from the word "bot" or "botfly"—a parasite which lives in mammals. Shade's wife calls Kinbote "the monstrous parasite of a genius" (p, 172). A "kinbote" is also a bote given by a homicide to the kin of his victim—a bote being a compensation paid for a wrong done. This definition has intriguing implications, insofar as it appears to be a clue to Kinbote's contribution to Shade's death and to the subsequent "murder" of Shade's poem through the self-aggrandizing commentary. Gradus, Shade's shadow, has indirectly allowed Kinbote to acquire Shade's poem. Kinbote is thus compensated for the loss of a friend and potential Karlist court poet through his possession of Shade's poem and through his creation of a new hybrid literary entity from his friend's life and his own real or imagined life. Kinbote discusses suicide and speaks of "a bare botkin (note the correct spelling)" (p. 220). Apart from the intended meaning of a sharp dagger, there is "bodkin," the alternate spelling, which means a person wedged in between two others where there is proper room for only two. Kinbote attempts to wedge himself between Shade and Gradus' bullets; metaphorically, Kinbote's commentary stands between the created object and destruction. Kinbote lives somewhere between Nabokov, master-creator, and Shade, apprentice-creator. The story of Shade, Zembla, and King Charles is conveyed through Kinbote's eyes, filtered through his intermediary vision. A "bot," in addition to being a parasite, is an inveterate borrower or cadger, a sponger. Kinbote shines with the reflected glory of Shade's light through his own commentary, although Shade's poem is actually "pale and diaphanous" in imaginative power compared to Kinbote's story of Zembla. Kinbote is aware of "borrowing a kind of opalescent light from my poet's fiery orb" (p. 81). The relationship between Shade and Kinbote is more symbiotic than parasitic, suggesting once again that they are really facets of one *ur*-personality: Shade is orderly, rational, sublime; Kinbote is imaginative (to excess), fantastic, Dionysiac. Kinbote's commentary can be seen as the dark underside of the poem, just as Kinbote may be the dark underside of Shade. "Kinbote" also means regicide in Zemblan, which links Kinbote to Gradus. Of course, Gradus, as death and unconsciousness, awaits the madman as well as the poet.

There is also a set of surface connections among the three characters. All three have the same birthday (the day Nabokov—their artistic daddy—began the work). Shade and Kinbote both lost their fathers at the age of three, and neither boy knew his father (do characters ever really *know* their author?). And all three characters die at the end: Shade is shot by Gradus; Gradus takes his own life with a rusty razor; and, as Nabokov says in an interview, Kinbote commits suicide, too.[5] Kinbote knows: "My notes and self are petering out" (p. 300). They would necessarily end simultaneously, for even if Kinbote had not committed suicide, he would "die" at the end of the novel the same way he was "born" at its inception. His fictional self is only viable as long as his presence is aesthetically necessary. Aesthetic life, we are reminded, is artificial and at the whim of the author. The remark also seems to equate Kinbote's notes with his selfhood, and his selfhood with his writing and that of Nabokov. In fact, Kinbote and the other characters all exist merely as a series of written signs on paper.

We thus see each individual character as composite: Kinbote is also King Charles and Botkin the scholar; Shade looks like Samuel Johnson and an old hag who works in a cafeteria and Judge Goldsworth; Gradus is also Jack Grey, Jacques d'Argus, a Shadow, and a glass-maker.

The sense in which we should perceive these similarities and other "links and bobolinks" in the tale is rendered in a comment by Kinbote. He is considering the similarity between Shade's portrait of a younger Sybil and his own young Queen Disa; it seems a "strangeness" without whose full comprehension "there is no sense in writing poems, or notes to poems, or anything at all" (p. 207). One must perceive the integral relationship of events and people within the microcosmic world of the novel to understand the fundamental artifice of both nature and art. As Kinbote also says, "'reality' is neither the subject nor the object of true art which creates its own special reality having nothing to do with the average 'reality' perceived by the communal eye" (p. 130). Nabokov strips away layer after layer of reality, and beneath them all reside magic and artifice.

Even the title of the novel has multiple layers of meaning and importance. Though Kinbote fails to locate the phrase "pale fire" in his only volume of Shakespeare ("having no library in his Timonian cave," index, p. 308), and though he says that it would have been a "statistical monster" (p. 285) if the allusion *had* been in *Timon of Athens*, it is, indeed, there, in lines he quotes in a distorted and incomplete re-Englishing of a Zemblan translation. Such possibilities do come true in the world of *Pale Fire*: the "monstrous semblance of a novel" (p. 86) is actualized, and this staggering coincidence confirms the possibility of patterns in a chaotic world. The passage from *Timon* (in act 4, scene 3) describes the infinite reflection of objects upon each other, and implies that the borrowing of light and life is a cyclical process and a sign of interdependence:

> The sun's a thief, and with his great attraction
> Robs the vast sea: the moon's an arrant thief,
> And her pale fire she snatches from the sun:
> The sea's a thief, whose liquid surge resolves
> The moon into salt tears: the earth's a thief,
> That feeds and breeds by a composture stolen
> From general excrement: each thing's a thief. . . .

Timon of Athens is considered by some scholars to be unfinished and botched by a later hand. And we are told repeatedly, in the foreword and in the commentary, of various efforts by critics, editors, and even Shade's widow to extricate the poem from Kinbote's possession, lest it be botched by his hand. Ironically, the poem itself is left intact by Kinbote; he merely appends his wildly imaginative commentary to it. Some scholars regard Shakespeare's *Timon* as an incomplete rough draft, just as Shade's poem is regarded as an incomplete rough draft by its other potential editors and commentators, as Kinbote tells us in the foreword.[6] Still other critics think *Timon* was a rough draft for *King Lear*, just as Kinbote thinks "Pale Fire" a rough draft of the epic *Solus Rex* (itself an epic Nabokov once began). *Timon* falls naturally into two halves—the part before Timon's fall and the part after it; *Pale Fire* is essentially divided into the part written before Shade's death, by Shade, and the part written after his death, by Kinbote. Timon does not arrive at self-knowledge as Lear does; even at the end of the play he does not really know himself. Kinbote does not know himself either, and Shade has only partial self-knowledge. Furthermore, *Timon of Athens* may be a work that to some extent reveals Shakespeare's artistic *process*, since it is possibly a rough draft. And the artistic process is certainly a central concern in *Pale Fire*.

Analysis of *Pale Fire* which stops at the elucidation of the tricks and games and allusions within the novel is superficial, although not as fruitless as it might be with an author who, unlike Nabokov, does not place language in the foreground. The essential point about Nabokov's playful authorial omnipotence is that the trickery serves a function beyond mere aesthetic pleasure. Nabokov's incredibly rich use of language, his tricks of plot, his games with characterization, style, and structure act upon the reader. We are allowed to watch consciousness in action—the consciousness of two artists and a mad creative genius (Shade, Nabokov, and Kinbote, respectively) in the process of creating, and the consciousnesses of various "human" selves in the process of being created. The patterning that Shade seeks in life we discover in the book—but we must at least help to create it. The carpet may sometimes be pulled out from under us as it is pulled out from under Shade for a moment in the mountain/fountain episode. But such toppling of expectation is a medium for a message about the nature of reality. Since deception is an integral part of nature (as with Nabokov's beloved mimetic butterflies, who masquerade as bark), a writer who points out the deceptive potential of the world is doing the reader a service. If one adheres to a single version of reality, one runs the risk of being gravely misled. Nabokov demonstrates how different patterns are produced by different minds—Kinbote's, Shade's, Gradus', Nabokov's, each reader's—even when viewing the same events. This interplay of patterns, of processes of creation, of "webs of sense," shows that there is no one overriding pattern to be discerned; we must each create our own pattern, using our own imaginative consciousness. Awareness of the power of deception is necessary to understand this fluidity of reality; being allowed to watch the characters in the novel as they attempt to bring order out of chaos is also an important aid. Nabokov tricks us into believing temporarily in many different versions of reality and thus forces us to revise our perceptions, our presuppositions about fiction, reality, and language. To do this he must present a fiction which does not allow complacent reading and happy identification with safely human, substantive characters. Nabokov "assumes that the proper goal of an artist is to create timelessness; the realists err in thinking that they should recreate time by imitating real, or at least plausible actions."[7] He has said:

> A creative writer must study carefully the works of his rivals, including the Almighty. He must possess the inborn capacity not only of recombining but of re-creating the given world. In order to do this adequately, avoiding duplication of labor, the artist should *know* the given world. . . . Art is never simple. . . . Art at its greatest is fantastically deceitful and complex.

> The fake move in a chess problem, the illusion of a solution or the conjuror's magic: I used to be a little conjuror when I was a boy. I loved doing simple tricks—turning water into wine, that kind of thing [he has said elsewhere that "Vladimir" rhymes with "redeemer"]; but I think I'm in good company because all art is deception and so is nature; all is deception in that good cheat, from the insect that mimics a leaf to the popular enticements of procreation.[8]

As long as reality is a question of perception and interpretation by its beholder, deception will be possible. Some think of art as creating a static reality; Nabokov seems to think of it as an ongoing process that engages the reader in a revelatory hermeneutical event.

John Shade is the only character in *Pale Fire* conscious of the Nabokovian tenet that we each devise our own reality; thus, he is the most conscious character, and the artist figure in the novel. Shade learns that we cannot look to outside sources for the "correlated pattern"; if we do, we are tricked into mistaking "humdrummery" for reality. But Shade, in spite of all his attempts at creation of a perceptible pattern, is still at the mercy of his aesthetic captor/creator, Nabokov. Shade at least is aware that he is "artistically caged," and, as a practicing poet, he is of all the characters the most conscious of the power of art and artifice to shape reality. Reality, even if only *a* reality, is formed in the process of transmutation from event to word. The dark abyss of death and of meaninglessness (as manifested by Gradus) surrounds the attempt to achieve full consciousness; but the products of that attempt survive. "Dead is the mandible, alive the song" (p. 42). The instrument through which poetry passes is mortal; the poem is not. Shade converts life into art: he makes the rooms in which he, his wife, and his daughter sit into "a tryptich [*sic*] or a three-act play / In which portrayed events forever stay" (p. 46). Shade wants to carry the fruits of human consciousness with him into whatever lies beyond this life, a desire Nabokov has often expressed. Since Shade is an artist, he is aware, as is

Nabokov, of the power of imagination to make, or remake, a world. Yet, as F. W. Dupee has pointed out, "In *Pale Fire*, as so often in our author's work, it takes two men to make a proper Nabokovian man —two men who, however, rarely succeed in uniting."[9] Kinbote has the disordered power of pure imagination; this is necessary to the artist, but it must be tempered by insight, order, and lucid detachment, which Shade possesses. Together, Kinbote and Shade possess elements of the artist as Nabokov conceives, creates, and embodies him. Gradus lurks as the power of death, demonic unconsciousness, anti-imagination. Ironically, when Shade completes the poem, it does not fall into the hands of a dispassionate critic but into the hands of a fantasy-ridden, creative genius. But the mad genius and the sensitive poet are both dispensed with when Nabokov no longer needs them in his aesthetic process.

When Shade asks Kinbote how Kinbote can know intimate details about King Charles and how these details can be printed if they are true, Kinbote says, "Once transmuted by you into poetry, the stuff *will* be true, and the people *will* come alive" (p. 214). This statement seems applicable to the question of who is who, or who is "real" in the novel. It is ultimately irrelevant if "in fact" Kinbote has produced Shade and Zembla, as Stegner thinks, or if Shade has produced Kinbote and the rest, as Bader and Field think, or if any other possible permutation of the combinations might be "true."[10] Within the fiction, the characters are equally real, and they all only exist in words. If art and imagination are as real as facts in Nabokov's world, then these characters are also real. The characters' intermingling and interdependence are intentional, and the characters are definitely aesthetic tools of the author, made to combine and recombine for an aesthetic purpose. Nabokov created all of them, and he created them purposely to be difficult to differentiate.

Pale Fire is an assault on our "brutish routine acceptance" of the "miracle of a few written signs being able to contain immortal imagery, involutions of thought, new worlds with live people, speaking, weeping, laughing" (p. 289). Nabokov creates fragmented or schizophrenic narrators and characters precisely to inhibit an unthinking identification with the people of the book, thereby forcing the reader to grapple with the epistemological complexities of life. The idea of linear, discursive language and plot, of cause and effect, the whole set of Cartesian presuppositions that are the unconscious baggage of most of us are bombarded with refutation after refutation, in favor of a vision of correlations, patterns, and rhythms which each reader must discern for himself or herself. The novel makes the reader into an artist, an active participant in the creation of sense and meaning.

Just as *Finnegans Wake* uses "verbal pyrotechnics" as part of a thematic purpose—breaking down barriers between unconscious and conscious, between illusion and reality, and ultimately between individual and individual—so *Pale Fire*'s amazing articulateness is part of an aesthetic reordering and re-creation of reality through artifice. Both books make claims on the reader's consciousness and imagination, and both books are, finally, consciousness-expanding or consciousness-altering fictions. From notes rejected when writing *Pale Fire*, Nabokov reads: "Time without consciousness—lower animal world; time with consciousness—man; consciousness without time—some still higher state."[11] It may be this higher state that the fragmented self in *Pale Fire* attempts to find in the timeless, fluid realm of imagination.

NOTES

1. Robert Alter, *Partial Magic*, p. 215.
2. Carol T. Williams, "'Web of Sense': *Pale Fire* in the Nabokov Canon," *Critique* 6 (1963–1964), 29–45.
3. Nabokov, *Pale Fire*, p. 307. Hereafter cited in text.
4. Julia Bader, *Crystal Land*, p. 34.
5. Nabokov, *Strong Opinions*, p. 74.
6. There is, however, a reference to Shade's poem "The Nature of Electricity" (p. 192), wherein he refers to his fondness for the number 999 (the number of lines in "Pale Fire" as it stands), so there is some likelihood that the poem is after all complete. Even Kinbote thinks the poem is missing line 1000, which he believes was to be a repeat of the first line—a nice cyclical touch. Of course, Nabokov prefers spirals, with their open-endedness, to closed circles.
7. John O. Stark, *The Literature of Exhaustion*, p. 90.
8. Nabokov, *Strong Opinions*, pp. 32–33, 11.
9. F. W. Dupee, *The King of the Cats and Other Remarks on Writers and Writing*, p. 141.
10. Page Stegner, *Escape into Aesthetics*, pp. 129–30; Bader, *Crystal Land*, p. 35; Andrew Field, *Nabokov: His Life in Art*, pp. 316–17.
11. Nabokov, *Strong Opinions*, p. 30.

Speak, Memory:
The Aristocracy of Art

CAROL SHLOSS

In 1917 the Nabokov family left their St. Petersburg home for the south of Russia. What they thought would be a temporary perch, a prudent remove from spasmodic political violence, turned into permanent exile. The turbulence they avoided was caused by the new Soviet regime, and the Nabokovs, by virtue of their extraordinary wealth and liberal intellectual commitments, were central targets of that revolt.

These events are narrated in the thirteenth chapter of Vladimir Nabokov's autobiography *Speak, Memory*.[1] The book is composed of a series of short memoirs written erratically between 1936 and 1951 and revised in 1966. If the genesis of the text is seemingly disjointed, its completed themes are not. Nabokov remained imaginatively preoccupied with that great and final exile from Russia. Though it deprived him of opulence and aristocratic prerogatives, these losses were important not because they caused discomfort, but because they engendered a perspective: loss of childhood homeland became, for Nabokov, a model for all the losses of time, and his subsequent vulnerability a spur to re-examine the nature of wealth and the methods of recouping the tangible world's disintegration: "in regard to the power of hoarding up impressions, Russian children of my generation passed through a period of genius, as if destiny were loyally trying what it could for them by giving them more than their share, in view of the cataclysm that was to remove completely the world they had known" (p. 25). It is as if Nabokov's own creative sensibility were the continued voice of such children, his articulated memory the extension of aristocracy through art. What was lost, Nabokov would have us understand, was precisely what a person of his class and upbringing had been trained to spurn as bourgeois: the attachment to possessions. What he took with him was of more value: "I inherited an exquisite simulacrum—the beauty of intangible property, unreal estate—and this proved a splendid training" (p. 40).

In this context, Nabokov poses his observations about art and about autobiography. Though history might rob, it can only steal objects; one can, in return, "hoard impressions," "store" in memory, and arrange bright images in the "stacks of the mind." The material of art, being "unreal estate," is as portable as the valise which accompanied the Nabokovs into exile. His mother's jewels, stuffed in that suitcase and hidden in jars, paid for the family's life as European émigrés; for him, perception is an analogous wealth.

Figurative observations of this sort show the connection between the events of Nabokov's past life and his imaginative commitments as an artist: the birth of consciousness and the young child's growing wealth of perception are analogous to the author's creation of the book-world which narrates those same events. Both are exercises in building with intangibles; both are based upon, but ultimately free from, material circumstances. Because of this architectural analogy, Nabokov does not present his childhood in St. Petersburg or at the family's Vyra country estate, his butterfly hunting, schooling, or loves as continuous narrative but as a series of vignettes with little transition among them. "I see the awakening of consciousness as a series of spaced flashes . . . bright blocks of perception . . . affording memory a slippery hold" (p. 21). In the same way that a building is constructed, the text is built with these bright blocks of perception, and the self is re-created by discrete impressions: "[I saw] a handful of fabulous lights that beckoned to me from a distant hillside, and then slipped into a pocket of black velvet: diamonds that I later gave away to my characters to alleviate the burden of my wealth" (p. 24). Each increment in the narrative represents an acquisition of value. Perception may be a jewel and the artist, by extension, a philanthropist, a person of rich and cumbersome sensibility, who alleviates opulence by giving it away: "After I had bestowed on the characters in my novels some treasured item of my past, it would pine away in the artificial world where I had . . . placed it" (p. 95). "Somewhere, in the apartment house of a chapter, in the hired room of a paragraph, I have also placed that tilted mirror . . ." (p. 101). These are complex remarks, but through them we can see that Nabokov plays consistently with the analogy between building identity and building a text, and asserts in both instances his invulnerability to misfortune: memory and art are the repositories of inheritance—not those grand and leisurely country manors which the Soviet regime could and presumably did abolish.

Nabokov's topic, then, is art's ability to recoup the losses of the "real" world. But he does not view art and nature as antithetical. On the contrary, he insists that their procedures are analogous. Instead of positing nature as "real" and art as an "imitation of reality," he considers that his texts reflect the artifice and deception that exist in nature. "I discovered in nature the nonutilitarian delights that I sought in art. Both were a form of magic, both were a game of intricate enchantment and deception" (p. 125). Because nature itself is deceitful, and because nature provides the building blocks from which Nabokov creates his "unreal estate," he must, paradoxically, deceive his readers in order ultimately to reward them with the treasures of perception he has accumulated for himself. In order to be the architect of his own life, he must first be a magician, conjuring the illusions of nature and using these as the material from which he will then construct an identity and a past.

Nabokov's persona as a magician is another version of his personae as architect and as aristocrat. In all three guises he asserts his power not only to manipulate but to remold the natural world. Like the architect-aristocrat, the Nabokovian magician is ultimately philanthropic, a figure who conceals certain treasures in order to produce them at unexpected moments for the delight of others. From this triple persona—architect, aristocrat, and magician—issues the demiurgic power of *Speak, Memory* and of Nabokov's art generally. "A creative writer," he has said, "must study carefully the works of his rivals, including the Almighty."[2]

The deception in Nabokov's work often takes the form of a camouflage that art simultaneously creates and penetrates. Very often the initial camouflage is provided by time. To the undiscerning, time is a succession of undifferentiated days. To Nabokov, the matter is otherwise. To illustrate, he recounts a memory of General Kuropatkin, supreme commander of the Russian army in the Far East, who entertained him as a small boy with a handful of matches. Fifteen years later, when the family was in flight from Bolshevik-held St. Petersburg, they were accosted by an old man in a peasant's sheepskin coat who asked his father for a light. "The next moment each recognized the other. I hope old Kuropatkin, in his rustic disguise, managed to evade Soviet imprisonment, but that is not the point. What pleases me is the evolution of the match theme . . ." (p. 27). Nabokov continues by pointing out that this coincidence of detail, discerned among many unrelated events, is intrinsic to his method: "The following of such thematic designs through one's life should be, I think, the true purpose of autobiography" (p. 27). His intention here is to reveal life's pattern by violating chronology and, by so doing, to penetrate the camouflage of time.

Again and again he "folds" narrative time by juxtaposing events which were widely divergent in life: he points out that his father's assassination on 28 March 1922 followed by exactly eighteen years the death of another Nabokov relative, Dmitri, on 28 March 1904. With Yuri Van Trachtenberg, an elder cousin, Nabokov played a swinging game where ropes were adjusted to have the swingboard pass a few inches above the forehead and nose; three years from that remembered summer, Yuri was killed fighting the Reds in northern Crimea, the front of his skull pushed in by bullets, as it might have been in that daredevil swinging contest. The Cordigera, Sulphur, and Satyr butterflies pursued and lost in youth are chased around half the globe and caught by the fiftyish writer in Colorado. "I like to fold my magic carpet . . . in such a way as to superimpose one part of the pattern upon another" (p. 139).

Though it may seem that the autobiographer is exploiting random coincidence for the purposes of composition, artificially grouping events in the same plane of vision, Nabokov would argue that this technique is not only the prerogative of art—which constructs artifices—but also the procedure of nature, in whose patterns, arrangements, and formal structures he first found inspiration. He recalls sunsets, for instance, in terms of their construction, their "formidable . . . splendor," "changing amassments," "brightly stained structural details."

Such passages clearly show Nabokov's preoccupation with design both in nature and in art. But, as I have already suggested, Nabokov is not preoccupied with design for its own sake. He is fascinated with the design that encases something of value—the sort of design that is the province simultaneously of the aristocrat, the architect, and the magician. He remembers his mother as a lover of jigsaw puzzles and as a hunter of mushrooms. "Her main delight was in the quest, and this quest had its rules. . . . one had to poke and peer for a goodish while among the wet underwood before something really nice . . . could be discovered" (p. 43). His Uncle Ruka, an idle man who decoded ciphered messages for amusement, was similarly inclined to hunt for treasure obscured from easy view. Several other examples come from gamesmanship: one is Nabokov's memory of a chess problem he composed "for the delectation of the very expert solver." An unsophisticated player might discover right away the "fairly simple . . . solution without having passed through the pleasurable torments prepared for the sophisticated one." The sophisticated player, however, would "start by falling for an illusory pattern of play," which would lead him ultimately to "the simple key move" and to "a synthesis of poignant artistic delight" (pp. 291–92). Similarly, Nabokov remembers that one of his boyhood tutors could make a coin vanish under a glass by pasting a round piece of paper over its mouth. "The paper should be ruled (or otherwise patterned)—this will enhance the illusion" (p. 157). The coin, placed on a similarly ruled paper, "vanished" when the two paper patterns, placed one on top of the other, tallied.

The underlying parallel among these memories is the discernment of trickery. The delight in finding mushrooms, decoding messages, creating chess problems, or performing magic tricks comes from having seen through the ruse. In each instance Nabokov exposes the nature of the camouflage and shows that likeness is deceit, whether the mimicry be produced by a butterfly imitating a leaf or by a mimetic device of fiction. As Nabokov said in an interview about writing biography, "It is only the verisimilar and not the true that our spirit and mind perceives [sic]."[3] *Speak, Memory* is an assault on the verisimilar in order to arrive at the true.

The distinction between the verisimilar and the true has implications for the generic classification of *Speak, Memory*. The work is an autobiography, although the categories in which I have discussed it have been "fiction" and "reality," not "autobiography" and "reality." The method has been intentional, and, I believe, consonant with Nabokov's own view of his endeavor, for one of the covert messages of the text is the need for more flexible methods of classification of texts. Just as Nabokov in boyhood adjusted from an antiquated system of German classification of butterflies to an English system of nomenclature, so the autobiographer asks that readers become less concerned about the distinction between fiction and autobiography, between the "incidental appendages" of genre, and more aware of the "links between butterflies and the central problems of nature" (p. 124).

One of those links is that fact that artistic perfection occurs as surely in nature as in art. If verisimilitude is the province of each, then the problem of autobiography's categorization as "fiction" or "fact" is moot. An isolated memory may or may not be accurate and verifiable by other persons or documents. But a text that organizes isolated perceptions into a continuous narrative is inevitably a constructed pattern and therefore "true" by virtue of being carefully constructed around a particular body of individual perceptions. Nabokov paradoxically delineates the truth by using as his raw materials the intricate illusions of human perception and the elaborate deceptions of the natural world.

He thus retains his aristocratic allegiances throughout *Speak, Memory*. By constructing patterns, he not only shares a wealth of perception with his readers, just as he does with his invented characters: he also gives these readers potential access to the source and methods of his wealth. Camouflage challenges us to exercise the discernment that enabled Nabokov's mother to find mushrooms or the young Nabokov to see butterflies disguised against their backgrounds. It is as if reading enables one to re-experience, with Nabokov, something of greater value than the ownership of property—the birth of consciousness. We read the text of *Speak, Memory* in the same way that a bright child reads the natural world, finding "What the Sailor Has Hidden—that the finder cannot unsee once it has been seen" (p. 310).

NOTES
1. Nabokov, *Speak, Memory*, pp. 253–73. Hereafter cited in text.
2. Nabokov, *Strong Opinions*, p. 32.
3. Quoted by Andrew Field, *Nabokov, His Life in Art*, p. 14.

Ada or Disorder

CHARLES NICOL

Ada or Ardor is a disordered memoir that must be reorganized by the reader. Everything about it is in confusion, and while the confusion is of course deliberate on the part of Nabokov, it is also partially intentional on the part of Van Veen. Other people have added to the confusion: when the manuscript was left in a chaotic state at Van's death, Ronald Oranger took on the responsibility of editing the memoir; he chose to include not only the marginal notes scribbled by both Van and Ada, but even their oral corrections and annotations; further, he neglected to correct numerous errors of transmission made by the typist Violet Knox, and also made a few unauthorized deletions.[1] We cannot read *Ada* as an accurate recording of "reality" when even the text itself is disordered.

But the major disorder of *Ada* lies in the memory of Van Veen, since *Ada* is his re-creation of remembered reality. Van records events exactly as he remembers them, without recourse to any outside referent other than Ada, and his memory often plays tricks on him. Further, we are uncertain how far Van is aware of his distortions; a psychologist, Van has developed a theory concerning the texture of time that vindicates solipsism. Van is the most fiercely subjective of Nabokov's long list of subjective narrators; his enormous distortions and inaccuracies, while no doubt partially due to senility, seem primarily due to defiance—Van's intention to record *his* reality, and no other.

Some critics have assumed the accuracy of Van's memory and taken Antiterra at face value; starting with these premises, they have then logically concluded that Antiterra is a weakness in *Ada*, a pointless never-never-land created by a self-indulgent Nabokov for his own amusement.[2] I believe that no proper evaluation of *Ada* can be made until these initial premises are discarded. The purpose of this essay is to document Van's total unreliability as a narrator so that the façade of Antiterra can be torn away. When the density of Van's invention is established, I hope that he will no longer be

viewed as a transparent narrator with Nabokov hovering immediately over his shoulder; the games and playfulness will properly be
seen as part of Van's character, not his author's.

Van's mnemonic distortions fall into five interlocking categories: (1) simple forgetfulness, often compounded by the recurrence
of parallel situations and their resultant confusion; (2) a further,
similar confusion caused by parallels between life and art and Van's
inability to remember which is which; (3) the intrusion of remembered dreams into actual memories; (4) Van's tendency to make his
metaphors so concrete that we are unable to distinguish between his
descriptions of inscape and landscape—most notably, in his creation
of Antiterra; and (5) distortions in history, geography, and chronology caused by the psychological importance of certain pivotal events
in Van's life. The "game" in *Ada* is to create normal order out of
Van's disorder. But every step we take in demolishing Van's memoir
dramatizes the mind's ability to build its own past, and we celebrate
the combinational power of memory every time we challenge its factual accuracy.

Simple forgetfulness

Van's forgetfulness can easily be documented: merely consider his
arrivals at and departures from Ardis, where he continually, as it
were, changes horses in mid-timestream. For instance, at the end of
the summer of 1884 Van drives to the station in the "family motorcar"—one of those anachronistic technological details that makes
Antiterra credible.[3] He stops at Forest Fork for a farewell tryst with
Ada, while Bouteillan waits in the car (p. 157). After intimate good-
byes with Ada, "Van returned to the Forest Fork. Morio, his favorite
black horse, stood waiting for him, held by young Moore" (p. 159).
Van has confused two parallel incidents, forgetting which came first.
Either the horse or the motorcar is erroneous for this particular
memory; we may conclude that in 1884, Van leaves Ardis on a horse
and that the "family motorcar" is only an accidental anachronism
maintaining a phantom existence through his faulty memory.

A more elaborate confusion of transportation occurs when Van
first arrives at the Ardis station (pp. 34–35):

> In a miniature of the imagination, he had seen a saddled horse
> prepared for him; there was not even a trap. . . . Suddenly a
> hackney coach drove up to the platform and a red-haired lady,
> carrying her straw hat and laughing at her own haste, made for
> the train and just managed to board it before it moved. So Van
> agreed to use the means of transportation made available to

him by a chance crease in the texture of time, and seated himself in the old calèche. . . . Sunflecks and lacy shadows
skimmed over his legs and lent a green twinkle to the brass
button deprived of its twin on the back of the coachman's
coat. . . . The driver waved to an invisible friend and the sensitive runabout swerved slightly to match his gesture. They were
now spinning along a dusty country road between fields. The
road dipped and humped again, and at every ascent the old
clockwork taxi would slow up as if on the brink of sleep. . . .
They bounced on the cobblestones of Gamlet, a half-Russian
village, and the chauffeur waved again. . . . None of the family
was at home when Van arrived. A servant in waiting took his
horse.

Obviously a hackney coach is not a runabout is not a clockwork taxi
is not a horse. The runabout is anachronistic and impossible; the
lady in the hackney coach is also anachronistic, and we will look at
her later; the clockwork taxi is a mental stopgap that never existed,
confused with the clockwork baggage carts invented by Van's ancestor Erasmus Veen that are presumably used at the Ardis station. This
leaves us either with another horse, one that first exists in Van's
imagination, or with a totally unresolved, unremembered first transportation to the transports of Ardis.

These examples could be multiplied endlessly. Van is extremely
inaccurate about overlapping minor details. As a general rule, technological anachronisms have their origin in Van's faulty memory, as
do descriptive details such as a character's obviously dyed hair or
one minor character's resemblance to another. *Ada* is full of phantom candlesticks.

Parallels between life and art

Nabokov has frequently restated Oscar Wilde's dictum that "life imitates art," and countless book reviewers have borrowed it from Nabokov. In *Ada*, the dictum takes a new twist: "Memory replaces life
with art." Art—here, painting and literature—is more vivid than
life, and since memory is selective it chooses the liveliest details it
can get.

Van's memory frequently confuses art with life. A simple example is the recurrent appearance of a well-known Toulouse-Lautrec
poster and its confusion with Lucette. When Van visits Ada at her
school, he sees "a slender lady in black velvet, wearing a beautiful
black velvet picture hat, who sat with her back to them at a 'tonic
bar' and never once turned her head, but the thought brushed him

that she was a cocotte from Toulouse" (p. 169). A few years later, at a restaurant, "on one of the red stools of the burning bar, a graceful harlot in black—tight bodice, wide skirt, long black gloves, black-velvet picture hat—was sucking a golden drink through a straw" (p. 307). Much later still, Van has another encounter with the girl, but this time he catches his memory in the process of transformation (p. 460):

> He headed for the bar, and as he was in the act of wiping the lenses of his black-framed spectacles, made out, through the optical mist (Space's recent revenge!), the girl whose silhouette he recalled having seen now and then (much more distinctly!) ever since his pubescence, passing alone, drinking alone, always alone, like Blok's *Incognita*. It was a queer feeling—as of something replayed by mistake, part of a sentence misplaced on the proof sheet, a scene run prematurely, a repeated blemish, a wrong turn of time.

This time she turns on the bar stool and turns out to be Lucette. All of the details about Van's poor eyesight are relevant (even the black frame around the scene is deliberate), because it is precisely his inability accurately to visualize Lucette's appearance in his memory that allows the replacement mechanism to function. For a clear picture, his memory draws instead on the Toulouse-Lautrec poster, and having done so, is unable to avoid repeating the replacement elsewhere (where the reverse process apparently occurs: Van sees the poster but remembers seeing the girl).[4]

This confusion between paintings and life is frequent, and scholars have caught the allusions to a number of paintings.[5] Beyond noting references and their parallels to *Ada*'s plot, one should notice that Van's list of paintings is primarily a list of his confusions between art and life, indications of his inability to separate the two. This is why, for instance, Demon is frequently described as looking like a character from a painting by Bosch.

Incidentally, at the meeting with Lucette described above, Van makes something else clear as he reminisces: "The last time I saw you . . . was two years ago, at a railway station. You had just left Villa Armina and I had just arrived. You wore a flowery dress which got mixed with the flowers you carried because you moved so fast—jumping out of a green calèche and up into the Ausonian Express that had brought me to Nice" (p. 461). So the girl whose coach Van commandeers is Lucette, and he incorrectly places this minor event in the context of his first trip to Ardis, many years before its actual occurrence. The problem is one of "two or more impressions borrowing from one another and forming a compound image in the mind" (p. 546). This should be sufficient to demonstrate Van's consistently inaccurate memory.

But the present topic is the compound image formed when one impression comes from art, the other from life. These impressions come from literature as well as painting. Nearly everyone who has written about *Ada* has added to the list of literary allusions in its pages, and I intend to add a few more. However, too often these allusions have been regarded as a game in themselves rather than as purposeful references in the novel. As with the allusions to paintings, the primary purpose of Van's literary allusions is to cast doubt on the accuracy of his memory. Usually, he confuses art and life, merges the two impressions in his memory, and calls forth fragments of this multiple memory in a redintegrative process. (He also confuses art with other art.)[6]

In passing, the subsidiary theme of translation might be noted. Van continually notes the odd metamorphoses of literary works when they are translated from one language to another, or from one medium to another. The languages dealt with are English, Russian, and French, and in a larger sense all of these literary metamorphoses are metaphors for the translating power of the memory. The title of the novel, *Ada or Ardor*, is a pronunciation guide for the heroine's name in English and Russian, while the first sentence of the first chapter is a mistranslation from Tolstoy. Russian memories are translated by Van to America, and the peculiar version of *Eugene Onegin* Demon witnesses in the second chapter is not what Van says it is, "an American play based by some pretentious hack on a famous Russian romance" (p. 10), but Chaikovsky's opera. Demon's duel with a supposed Baron d'Onsky and Van's duel with Captain Tapper are both so loaded with references to *Onegin* that their very existence is doubtful.

Just as Ada's name in Russian sounds like the English "ardor," various alternate pronunciations of Van's name contribute confusion and add literary references. My own contribution to the literary allusions in *Ada* comes in the most prurient, sensual scene in the novel, the doubly incestuous + lesbian + three-a-bed lovemaking in book 2 (pp. 418–20). A look at Mallarmé demonstrates that naked Van, Ada, and Lucette on their hotel bed are borrowed from "L'Aprèsmidi d'un faune." There seem to be no hints in the text to direct us to the poem; our only clue is a pun that Nabokov doesn't even mention, the similarity between "faune" and one possible pronunciation of "Van." If this seems farfetched, consider another equally outrageous name-pun: at one point, Van's name is pronounced "Wann";

he then becomes a professor, or Don; finally, he sees, or remembers seeing, a film entitled *Don Juan's Last Fling*. Considering Van's probably exaggerated claims of sexual prowess, the Don Juan epithet is a natural one.[7]

Literary references in *Ada* also trace the evolution of the novel as a literary form, paralleling the evolution of the relationship of Van and Ada.[8] Other references to Chateaubriand and Byron relate to the theme of brother-and-sister incest—or perhaps the incest relates to romanticism. Although references to Tolstoy have been noted, I do not believe that scholars have fully appreciated the extent of Van's references to *War and Peace*, the final volumes of which were published in 1869, the year of Van's conception, 100 years before the publication of *Ada*. Van has read *War and Peace* not as a meditation on history but as a family chronicle, and many descriptions of young Ada can be traced to Tolstoy's Natasha. What interests Van most, presumably, is Tolstoy's concern with brother-and-sister incest between Anatole and Hélène, a concern more extensive in early drafts than in the completed novel (which may help account for the "L" disaster). Love between first cousins is also stressed early in *War and Peace*, and its twice-repeated adage, *cousinage—dangereux voisinage*, is repeated again in *Ada*. Not only Ada's initial appearance, but also her youthful affairs with Van's rivals, reflect and parallel the Tolstoy novel. Aqua's aural delusions—hearing voices in running water—seem to derive from Prince Andrew's aural hallucinations just before his death (a passage in Tolstoy that, according to Nabokov, is the first internal monologue in literature, long before Joyce). Again, this confusion of memory and literature casts doubt on the accuracy of Van's memory. Almost every scene in *Ada* is dubious in one way or another.

Dream memories

The intrusion of remembered dreams into actual memories is another source of confusion. Here it will suffice to point out that the chain of Villa Venus exists only in Van's dream (pp. 347–58). Within that chapter the brothels are called "an organized dream"—organized by a dead youth named Eric Veen—but clear evidence that the dream is actually Van's is that he falls asleep at the end of the preceding chapter. And if this is not enough, the following chapter opens with Van's categorical discussion of the dreams he has had over "the last nine decades" (p. 359). Incidentally, in that discussion he describes a dream where "under a nearby pine, his father, or his dress-coated mother, is trying to make a transatlantic call" (p. 361), which explains the telephone that "once" had been attached to a pine tree (p. 273); earlier still, Marina shows Van "the exact pine and the exact spot on its rugged red trunk where in old, very old days a magnetic telephone nested, communicating with Ardis Hall" (p. 83). Like the Villa Venus chain, that telephone never existed save in Van's dreams. Of course, Van dreams of telephones because one of the instruments is involved in the crucial moment of his life.

The concrete metaphor of Antiterra

Antiterra is, by itself, a simple concept: the external world. The real world is inside ourselves. What makes Antiterra seem other than Terra is the multiple series of geographical, chronological, historical, and technological confusions in *Ada*. The real world exists in Van's memory, in flashes of what he calls real time; as his chronicle approaches the present, his memory has not fully assimilated and transformed events, and Terra merges with Antiterra in book 5.

The theoretical basis for Van's division of the world is found in the fourth book, but hints are given when Antiterra is first introduced, in the third chapter of the first book, where it is described in parallel with Aqua's illness—of which Antiterra is a corollary: "Sick minds identified the notion of a Terra planet with that of another world and this 'Other World' got confused not only with the 'Next World' but with the Real World in us and beyond us" (p. 20). Healthy minds, then, would not sustain such an irreconcilable division between internal and external reality. Bobbie Ann Mason has suggested that Van's creation of Antiterra is the product of his own sickness, his abnormal, incestuous relationship with Ada.[9] The point is well taken.

Other hints that the Terra-Antiterra division is a purely subjective one are scattered throughout *Ada*. Marvell's "The Garden," referred to not only as a problem for translation but also as the key to Van and Ada's secret code, contains some highly revealing, relevant lines:

> Meanwhile the mind, from pleasure less,
> Withdraws into its happiness:
> The mind, that ocean where each kind
> Does straight its own resemblance find;
> Yet it creates, transcending these,
> Far other worlds and other seas,
> Annihilating all that's made
> To a green thought in a green shade.

When Aqua is described as "afflicted with her usual vernal migraine" (p. 4), the adjective "vernal" seems meaningless unless considered as a reference to "green thought"; the same is true for Van in the sentence "One such green resurrection he could particularize when replaying the past" (p. 74). And all the references to being "on Terra with Ada" demonstrate that Terra refers to the mind in its happiness, while Demonia, another frequent label for Antiterra, clearly identifies Antiterra with Van's forced separation from Ada. Terra is happiness, Antiterra pain, but Terra is also the world of duration, of real time, or "Veen's Time," while Antiterra is the forgettable surface of life.

Book 4 is the climax of *Ada*; it is also at least a portion, if not the whole text, of Van's lecture and later book, *The Texture of Time*. While writing *Ada*, Nabokov gave a filmed interview during which he called the whole work-in-progress *The Texture of Time* and described it in much the same words Van uses to summarize *his* book:[10] "My aim was to compose a kind of novella in the form of a treatise on the Texture of Time, an investigation of its veily substance, with illustrative metaphors gradually increasing, very gradually building up a logical love story, going from past to present, blossoming as a concrete story, and just as gradually reversing analogies and disintegrating again into bland abstraction" (pp. 562–563). Van's lecture actually does not quite follow this scenario; it indeed goes from abstractions to metaphors to a concrete story (Van's telephone call to Ada and their reunion), but it breaks off at this point, before returning to abstractions, when Ada says, "We can never know Time. Our senses are simply not meant to perceive it. It is like—" (p. 563). The metaphor remains incomplete, and we are meant to complete it for ourselves as follows: Time is like *Ada*. Van's book is an enormous, extended metaphor for our perception of time.[11]

For Van, real time is duration; it lasts only as long as we can keep aware of a continuous moment. Everything else is unreal, and Antiterra is the concrete metaphor for this unreality, "gradually reversing analogies and disintegrating again into bland abstraction."

Distortion caused by pivotal events

Although I have just challenged the existence of Antiterra as a separate planet, and in the previous sections on Van's faulty memory, his confusion of life with art, and his confusion of dreams with actual events I have challenged the actuality of a few specific anachronisms, the major delineation of Antiterra is as yet unscathed. The major dislocations of Antiterra are related to the major psychological events in the life of Van Veen, his most intense memories and his most intense awareness of real time.

Since book 4 is the climax of *Ada*, the explanation lies here, in the most important event of Van's life. On Monday, 14 July 1922, Van and Ada hold a telephone conversation that leads to spending the rest of their lives together. This conversation is the longest perceived continual, durational moment in Van's life, its greatest episode of real time: "That telephone voice, by resurrecting the past and linking it up with the present, with the darkening slate-blue mountains beyond the lake, with the spangles of the sun wake dancing through the poplar, formed the centerpiece in his deepest perception of tangible time, the glittering 'now' that was the only reality of Time's texture" (p. 556). This frozen moment explains much in *Ada*. Van's memories are clustered around this tableau like bees around honey; they have distorted external reality by their density, just as a large body in space bends light. Here, then, is the novel's major source of distortion. For instance, the continually destroyed and re-invented telephone of Antiterra makes no sense without Van's further comment on that conversation: "Now it so happened that she had never—never, at least, in adult life—spoken to him by phone; hence the phone had preserved the very essence, the bright vibration, of her vocal cords, the little 'leap' in her larynx, the laugh clinging to the contour of the phrase, as if afraid in girlish glee to slip off the quick words it rode" (p. 555). In Van's solipsistic universe, the power of that telephone call negates the existence of all other telephonic memories; since there are no previous telephones in Van's memory, no telephones existed before 1922. The substitution of "dorophones" is the memory's attempt to explain some otherwise inexplicable impressions, but an examination of such calls establishes their essential falsity. For instance, Van calls Ada on the dorophone on 25 July 1886 to suggest still another rendezvous at Forest Fork; however, the text states that "he called Ardis Hall from the Malahar post office" (p. 179), and the logical reconstruction would be that Van mailed Ada a note.

The freezing of time in an all-encompassing 1922 explains other anachronisms. When Van receives his telephone call, Warren Gamaliel Harding is the president of the United States of America. So in *Ada*, Gamaliel is almost always president; he maintains his office, apparently, from the time of Lincoln until the last few pages of the novel, where external reality intervenes.[12]

Van's knowledge of American history is extremely limited anyway, and extremely inaccurate. He cannot remember Lincoln's name, once referring to him as "Abraham Milton," a second time as "Milton Abraham," and when finally naming him correctly gives Lincoln an extremely attractive second wife (I wish I knew where that "Milton" came from). Van correctly recalls that Lincoln had something to do with the purchase of Alaska from Russia, but then confuses the two so that "Russia" is a "quaint synonym" for that "American province extending, from the Arctic no longer vicious Circle to the United States proper" (p. 17).

This brings us to Van's jumbled geography. His actual geographical knowledge is both limited and specialized. It comes from three sources: "a five-fold screen with bright paintings on its black panels reproducing the first maps of four and a half continents" (p. 43), "a large old globe" (p. 230), and "a botanical atlas" (p. 41). The old globe has provided "Tartary" as a substitute for the real Russia, the folding screen has been used to superimpose one continent on another, and the botanical atlas has provided Van's confusion between continents and climatic zones. Seeing the geography of the world through Ada's botanical and lepidopterous eyes, Van confuses his boyhood Russia with New England, and the Mediterranean coast with California. In *Speak, Memory* Nabokov has described his own experience of similar geographic congruities that eclipse time and establish a simultaneity and total identity between events actually separated by thousands of miles and many years; for instance, while chasing butterflies beyond the Oredezh around 1910, Nabokov sees Long's Peak in the distance.[13]

It should be remembered here that the flora and fauna of Antiterra are identical with those of Terra, because these are parts of the external world that have become internalized by Van and Ada; they are a part of the landscape that has become inscape. While Antiterra is a dream, a "wicked world which after all may have existed only oneirologically" (p. 15), "whose principal part is staged in a dream-bright America" (p. 588), the distortion does not extend to the botany and zoology of Ardis; these are known, and known accurately, to Van and Ada. Consequently, "reality and natural science are synonymous in the terms of this, and only this, dream" (p. 77). Their knowledge of the natural sciences has, however, added to their geographic distortions by providing a foundation on which to build an imaginary world.[14]

I have not attempted to exhaust the examples at any stage of my argument; to do so would be to write a book. However, I believe that any book written on *Ada* would have to agree with my premises, and, indeed, Bobbie Ann Mason's *Nabokov's Garden* is equally emphatic in denying Antiterra any existence outside the mind of Van Veen.

In place of a conclusion I would like to speculate briefly on what might result from a complete investigation of the anachronisms, distortions, and displacements in *Ada*. I would guess that such an investigation might completely overturn the tangled family relationships of the novel, and establish a radically different picture. *Either* Van and Ada might turn out to be cousins after all, because Van and Ada have created their own past so completely that they have imagined the baby-switch that made Marina Van's mother and the chronology of Marina's pregnancy that made Demon Ada's father; *or* they are indeed brother and sister because the two D. Veens are the same person seen from different perspectives (Van sees him as the stern father; Ada sees him as ineffectual), and Aquamarina is their mother, again seen from different perspectives. But since these speculations cancel each other out, and I can at present find no more evidence for one than the other, I mention them only to show that, in my opinion, the depths of *Ada* have not yet been plumbed.

NOTES

1. For some further details, see Alfred Appel, Jr., "Ada Described," in *Nabokov*, ed. Appel and Newman, p. 163.
2. A good statement of this position is in Douglas Fowler, *Reading Nabokov*, pp. 176–201. I agree with Fowler that *if* Antiterra is taken at face value, then *Ada* appears to be a weak, self-indulgent novel; I do not understand how Appel (on his p. 166) can be so delighted in *Ada* as "physics fiction." The best examination of SF elements in *Ada* is by Roy Arthur Swanson, "Nabokov's *Ada* as Science Fiction," *Science-Fiction Studies* 2, no. 1 (March 1975), 76–88. All of these critics take Antiterra seriously. The first critic to my knowledge unequivocally to deny the existence of Antiterra is Bobbie Ann Mason, *Nabokov's Garden*, p. 12.
3. Nabokov, *Ada*, p. 156. Hereafter cited in text.
4. While *Ada* was gestating, an advertisement that also employed the device of turning this particular poster by Toulouse-Lautrec into a "real" situation appeared frequently. See, for instance, the *New Yorker* for 23 March 1963, inside front cover (the issue includes an excerpt from *The Gift*).
5. Mason has been especially thorough.
6. Nabokov's "Notes to *Ada*" explicate a number of Van's portmanteau confusions of books and authors. These notes, ostensibly by Vivian Darkbloom, have been available in the Penguin edition of *Ada*, but not in the United States. They follow the present essay in this book.
7. As I noted in more detail in my review of *Ada*, "Don Juan Out of Hell," *Atlantic* (June 1969), 105–6.
8. Appel, "Ada Described," pp. 172–73; Appel also first pointed out the significance of the date of publication of *War and Peace*.
9. Mason, *Nabokov's Garden*, p. 12; Mason's discussion of Marvell's "The Garden" (her pp. 146–51) is relevant to my next paragraph.

10. See my "Don Juan Out of Hell" and Appel, "Ada Described," p. 164—or better, see the NET interview, which is on film and available for loan.
11. For a good discussion of the "texture of time" aspect of *Ada*, see Jeffrey Leonard, "In Place of Lost Time: *Ada*," in *Nabokov*, ed. Appel and Newman, pp. 136—46.
12. In "Notes to *Ada*," Nabokov annotated the first mention of Gamaliel as follows: "Gamaliel: a much more fortunate statesman than our W. G. Harding."
13. Nabokov, *Speak, Memory*, pp. 138—39; most methods of mnemonic distortion used by Van can be found in Nabokov's autobiography and its new foreword.
14. See Mason, *Nabokov's Garden*, for a detailed analysis of the extraordinary botany of Ardis.

Notes to *Ada* by Vivian Darkbloom

VLADIMIR NABOKOV

EDITED BY J. E. RIVERS AND WILLIAM WALKER

Editors' note: The British paperback edition of Nabokov's *Ada* (Harmondsworth, England: Penguin, 1970) contains a series of notes signed by Vivian Darkbloom (an anagram of Nabokov's own name). These notes have never appeared in the United States, and the book containing them is now out of print in Britain. Since these notes provide expert commentary on the novel's maze of languages and allusions, we believe they should be made available to Nabokov's American admirers and have therefore reprinted them below. The page references have been changed to refer to the three most widely available editions of *Ada*, all of which have the same pagination: the British and American hardback edition (New York: McGraw-Hill; London: Weidenfeld and Nicolson, 1969) and the most recent paperback edition (New York: McGraw-Hill, 1981).

In the following edition of Nabokov's text, the British conventions of punctuation have been retained. Punctuation, capitalization, and the use of italics have been made consistent. Misprints in the Penguin edition have been corrected as follows (first the error, then the correction): p. 5, Phieeas: Phileas; p. 27, Joe's: Jo's; p. 46, *Descanso en jardin* and his *El otono: isla*): *Descanso en jardín* and his *El otoño: isla*; p. 55, Rostopchin: Rostopchine; p. 83, *grand: grande*; p. 138, *Abencerage: Abencérage*; p. 140, *vendage: vendange*; p. 171, Mayn: Mayne; p. 228, *qui: que*; p. 243, *filius aqua: filius aquae*; p. 342, Abencerage: Abencérage; p. 375, *coigner: cogner*; p. 384, Rostopchin: Rostopchine; p. 403, O'Neil: O'Neill; p. 536, *trève: trêve*; p. 553, *a: à.* Véra Nabokov read and approved the edited text.—J. E. R. and W. W.

p. 3. All happy families, etc.: mistranslations of Russian classics are ridiculed here. The opening sentence of Tolstoy's novel is turned inside out and Anna Arkadievna's patronymic given an absurd masculine ending, while an incorrect feminine one is added to her surname. 'Mount Tabor' and 'Pontius' allude to the transfigurations (Mr G. Steiner's term, I believe) and betrayals to which great texts are subjected by pretentious and ignorant versionists.

p. 3. Severnïya Territorii: Northern Territories. Here and elsewhere transliteration is based on the old Russian orthography.

p. 3. granoblastically: in a tesselar (mosaic) jumble.

p. 4. Tofana: allusion to 'aqua tofana' (see any good dictionary).

p. 4. sur-royally: fully antlered, with terminal prongs.

p. 4. Durak: 'fool' in Russian.

p. 5. Lake Kitezh: allusion to the legendary town of Kitezh which shines at the bottom of a lake in a Russian fairytale.

p. 5. Mr Eliot: we shall meet him again, on pages 459 and 505, in company of the author of 'The Waistline' and 'Agonic Lines'.

p. 5. Counter-Fogg: Phileas Fogg, Jules Verne's globetrotter, travelled from West to East.

p. 6. Goodnight Kids: their names are borrowed, with distortions, from a comic strip for French-speaking children.

p. 7. Dr. Lapiner: for some obscure but not unattractive reason, most of the physicians in the book turn out to bear names connected with rabbits. The French *'lapin'* in Lapiner is matched by the Russian *'Krolik'*, the name of Ada's beloved lepidopterist (p. 8, *et passim*) and the Russian *'zayats'* (hare) sounds like *'Seitz'* (the German gynecologist on page 230); there is a Latin *'cuniculus'* in *'Nikulin'* ('grandson of the great rodentiologist Kunikulinov', p. 433), and a Greek *'lagos'* in *'Lagosse'* (the doctor who attends Van in his old age). Note also Coniglietto, the Italian cancer-of-the-blood specialist, p. 379.

p. 7. *mizernoe:* Franco-Russian form of 'miserable' in the sense of 'paltry'.

p. 8. *c'est bien le cas de le dire*: and no mistake.

p. 8. *lieu de naissance*: birthplace.

p. 8. *pour ainsi dire*: so to say.

p. 8. Jane Austen: allusion to rapid narrative information imparted through dialogue, in *Mansfield Park*.

p. 8. 'Bear-Foot', not 'bare foot': both children are naked.

p. 8. Stabian flower girl: allusion to the celebrated mural painting (the so-called 'Spring') from Stabiae in the National Museum of Naples: a maiden scattering blossoms.

p. 11. Raspberries; ribbon: allusions to ludicrous blunders in Lowell's versions of Mandelshtam's poems (in the *N.Y. Review*, 23 December 1965).

p. 11. Belokonsk: the Russian twin of 'Whitehorse' (city in N.W. Canada).

p. 13. *en connaissance de cause*: knowing what it was all about (Fr.).

p. 14. Aardvark: apparently, a university town in New England.

p. 14. Gamaliel: a much more fortunate statesman than our W. G. Harding.

p. 15. interesting condition: family way.

p. 16. Lolita, Texas: this town exists, or, rather, existed, for it has been renamed, I believe, after the appearance of the notorious novel.

p. 16. *penyuar*: Russ., peignoir.

p. 17. *beau milieu*: right in the middle.

p. 17. Faragod: apparently, the god of electricity.

p. 17. braques: allusion to a bric-à-brac painter.

p. 21. *entendons-nous*: let's have it clear (Fr.).

p. 21. *Yukonets*: inhabitant of Yukon (Russ.).

p. 23. lammer: amber (Fr.: *l'ambre*), allusion to electricity.

p. 23. my lad, my pretty, etc.: paraphrase of a verse in Housman.

p. 23. ballatetta: fragmentation and distortion of a passage in a 'little ballad' by the Italian poet Guido Cavalcanti (1255–1300). The relevant lines are: 'you frightened and weak little voice that comes weeping from my woeful heart, go with my soul and that ditty, telling of a destroyed mind'.

p. 25. Nuss: German for 'nut'.

p. 26. *Khristosik*: little Christ (Russ.).

p. 26. *rukuliruyushchiy*: Russ., from Fr. *roucoulant*, cooing.

p. 27. horsepittle: 'hospital', borrowed from a passage in Dickens' *Bleak House*. Poor Jo's pun, not a poor Joycean one.

p. 29. *aujourd'hui, heute*: to-day (Fr., Germ.).

p. 29. *Princesse Lointaine*: Distant Princess, title of a French play.

p. 32. *pour attraper le client*: to fool the customer.

p. 36. *Je parie*, etc.: I bet you do not recognize me, Sir.

p. 36. *tour du jardin*: a stroll in the garden.

p. 37. Lady Amherst: confused in the child's mind with the learned lady after whom a popular pheasant is named.

p. 38. with a slight smile: a pet formula of Tolstoy's denoting cool superiority, if not smugness, in a character's manner of speech.

p. 39. *pollice verso*: Lat., thumbs down.

p. 43. Sumerechnikov: the name is derived from '*sumerki*' ('dusk' in Russian).

p. 46. lovely Spanish poem: really *two* poems—Jorge Guillén's *Descanso en jardín* and his *El otoño: isla*.

p. 49. *Monsieur a quinze ans*, etc.: You are fifteen, Sir, I believe, and I am nineteen, I know. . . . You, Sir, have known town girls no doubt; as to me, I'm a virgin, or almost one. Moreover . . .

p. 49. *rien qu'une petite fois*: just once.

p. 50. *mais va donc jouer avec lui*: come on, go and play with him.

p. 50. *se morfondre*: mope.

p. 50. *au fond*: actually.

p. 50. *Je l'ignore*: I don't know.

p. 51. *cache-cache*: hide-and-seek.

p. 52. *infusion de tilleul*: lime tea.

p. 53. *Les Amours du Dr Mertvago*: play on 'Zhivago' ('zhiv' means in Russian 'alive' and 'mertv' dead).

p. 53. *grand chêne*: big oak.

p. 54. *quelle idée*: the idea!

p. 55. *Les Malheurs de Swann*: cross between *Les Malheurs de Sophie* by Mme de Ségur (née Countess Rostopchine) and Proust's *Un Amour de Swann*.

p. 61. *monologue intérieur*: the so-called 'stream-of-consciousness' device, used by Leo Tolstoy (in describing, for instance, Anna's last impressions whilst her carriage rolls through the streets of Moscow).

p. 64. Mr Fowlie: see Wallace Fowlie, *Rimbaud* (1946).

p. 64. *soi-disant*: would-be.

p. 64. *les robes vertes*, etc.: the green and washed-out frocks of the little girls.

p. 64. *angel moy*: Russ., 'my angel'.

p. 65. *en vain*, etc.: In vain, one gains in play

The Oka river and Palm Bay . . .

p. 66. *bambin angélique*: angelic little lad.

p. 69. *groote*: Dutch, 'great'.

p. 69. *un machin*, etc.: a thing as long as this that almost wounded the child in the buttock.

p. 71. pensive reeds: Pascal's metaphor of man, *un roseau pensant*.

p. 72. horsecart: an old anagram. It leads here to a skit on Freudian dream charades ('symbols in an orchal orchestra'), p. 73.

p. 72. *buvard*: blotting pad.

p. 73. *Kamargsky*: La Camargue, a marshy region in S. France combined with *Komar*, 'mosquito', in Russian and *moustique* in French.

p. 74. *sa petite collation du matin*: light breakfast.

p. 75. *tartine au miel*: bread-and-butter with honey.

p. 77. Osberg: another good-natured anagram, scrambling the name of a writer with whom the author of *Lolita* has been rather comically compared. Incidentally, that title's pronunciation has nothing to do with English or Russian (*pace* an anonymous owl in a recent issue of *TLS*).

p. 77. *mais ne te*, etc.: now don't fidget like that when you put on your skirt! A well-bred little girl . . .

p. 78. *très en beauté*: looking very pretty.

p. 78. *calèche*: victoria.

p. 79. *pecheneg*: a savage.

p. 80. *grande fille*: girl who has reached puberty.

p. 83. *La Rivière de diamants*: Maupassant and his '*La Parure*' (p. 87) did not exist on Antiterra.

p. 83. *copie*, etc.: copying in their garret.

p. 83. *à grande eau*: swilling the floors.

p. 83. *désinvolture*: uninhibitedness.

p. 83. *vibgyor*: violet-indigo-blue-green-yellow-orange-red.

p. 85. *sans façons*: unceremoniously.

p. 86. *strapontin*: folding seat in front.

p. 87. *décharné*: emaciated.

p. 87. *cabane*: hut.

p. 87. *allons donc*: oh, come.

p. 87. *pointe assassine*: the point (of a story or poem) that murders artistic merit.

p. 87. *quitte à tout dire*, etc.: even telling it all to the widow if need be.

p. 88. *il pue*: he stinks.

p. 89. *Atala*: a short novel by Chateaubriand.

p. 90. *un juif*: a Jew.

p. 91. *et pourtant*: and yet.

p. 92. *ce beau jardin*, etc.: This beautiful garden blooms in May, but in Winter never, never, never, never, never is green, etc.

p. 96. *chort!*: Russ., 'devil'.

p. 102. *mileyshiy*: Russ., 'dearest'.

p. 102. *partie*, etc.: exterior fleshy part that frames the mouth . . . the two edges of a simple wound . . . it is the member that licks.

p. 103. *pascaltrezza*: in this pun, which combines Pascal with *caltrezza* (Ital., 'sharp wit') and *treza* (a Provençal word for 'tressed stalks'), the French '*pas*' negates the '*pensant*' of the '*roseau*' in his famous phrase 'man is a thinking reed'.

p. 105. *Katya*: the ingénue in Turgenev's 'Fathers and Children'.

p. 106. a *trouvaille*: a felicitous find.

p. 106. Ada who liked crossing orchids: she crosses here two

French authors, Baudelaire and Chateaubriand.

p. 106. *mon enfant*, etc.: my child, my sister, think of the thickness of the big oak at Tagne, think of the mountain, think of the tenderness—

p. 107. *recueilli*: concentrated, rapt.

p. 107. canteen: a reference to the 'scrumpets' (crumpets) provided by school canteens.

p. 112. *puisqu'on*, etc.: since we broach this subject.

p. 113. *hument*: inhale.

p. 113. *tout le reste*: all the rest.

p. 113. *zdravstvuyte*, etc.: Russ., lo and behold: the apotheosis.

p. 114. Mlle Stopchin: a representative of Mme de Ségur, née Rostopchine, author of *Les Malheurs de Sophie* (nomenclatorially occupied on Antiterra by *Les Malheurs de Swann*).

p. 114. *au feu!*: fire!

p. 114. *flambait*: was in flames.

p. 114. Ashette: 'Cendrillon' in the French original.

p. 115. *en croupe*: riding pillion.

p. 117. *à reculons*: backwards.

p. 120. The Nile is settled: a famous telegram sent by an African explorer.

p. 120. *parlez pour vous*: speak for yourself.

p. 120. *trempée*. soaked.

p. 125. *je l'ai vu*, etc.: 'I saw it in one of the wastepaper-baskets of the library'.

p. 125. *aussitôt après*: immediately after.

p. 127. *ménagez*, etc.: go easy on your Americanisms.

p. 127. *leur chute*, etc.: their fall is slow . . . one can follow them with one's eyes, recognizing—

p. 127. Lowden: a portmanteau name combining two contemporary bards.

p. 128. *baguenaudier*: French name of bladder senna.

p. 128. Floeberg: Flaubert's style is mimicked in this pseudo quotation.

p. 130. *pour ne pas*, etc.: so as not to put any ideas in her head.

p. 130. *en lecture*: 'out'.

p. 131. *cher, trop cher René*: dear, too dear (his sister's words in Chateaubriand's *René*).

p. 132. *Chiron*: doctor among centaurs: an allusion to Updike's best novel.

p. 132. London Weekly: a reference to Alan Brien's *New Statesman* column.

p. 132. *Höhensonne*: ultra-violet lamp.

p. 132. *bobo*: little hurt.

pp. 132–133. *démission*, etc.: tearful notice.

p. 133. *les deux enfants*, etc.: 'therefore the two children could make love without any fear'.

p. 134. *fait divers*: news item.

p. 135. *blin*: Russ., pancake.

p. 135. *qui le sait*: who knows.

p. 136. Heinrich Müller: author of *Poxus*, etc.

p. 138. *Ma soeur te souvient-il encore*: first line of the third sextet of Chateaubriand's *Romance à Hélène* ('Combien j'ai douce souvenance') composed to an Auvergne tune that he heard during a trip to Mont Dore in 1805 and later inserted in his novella *Le Dernier Abencérage*. The final (fifth) sextet begins with '*Oh! qui me rendra mon Hélène. Et ma montagne, et le grand chêne*'—one of the leitmotivs of the present novel.

p. 138. *sestra moya*, etc.: my sister, do you remember the mountain, and the tall oak, and the Ladore?

p. 138. *oh! qui me rendra*, etc.: oh who will give back my Aline, and the big oak, and my hill?

p. 139. Lucile: the name of Chateaubriand's actual sister.

p. 139. la Dore, etc.: the Dore and the agile swallow.

p. 140. *vendange*: vine-harvest.

p. 142. Rockette: corresponds to Maupassant's *La Petite Rocque*.

p. 142. *chaleur du lit*: bed warmth.

p. 143. *horosho*: Russ., all right.

p. 145. *mironton*, etc.: burden of a popular song.

p. 147. Lettrocalamity: a play on Ital. *elettrocalamita*, electromagnet.

p. 150. Bagrov's grandson: allusion to *Childhood Years of Bagrov's Grandson* by the minor writer Sergey Aksakov (A.D. 1791–1859).

p. 151. *hobereaux*: country squires.

p. 152. *biryul'ki proshlago*: Russ., the Past's baubles.

p. 154. *traktir*: Russ., pub.

p. 154. (avoir le) *vin triste*: to be melancholy in one's cups.

p. 154. *au cou rouge*, etc.: with the ruddy and stout neck of a widower still full of sap.

p. 155. *gloutonnerie*: gourmandise.

p. 155. *tant pis*: too bad.

p. 155. *je rêve*, etc.: I must be dreaming. It cannot be that anyone should spread butter on top of all that indigestible and vile British dough.

p. 155. *et ce n'est que*, etc.: and it is only the first slice.

p. 155. *lait caillé*: curds and whey.

p. 156. *shlafrok*: Russ., from Germ. *Schlafrock*, dressing gown.

p. 157. *tous les*, etc.: all the tires are new.

p. 157. *tel un*: thus a wild lily entrusting the wilderness.

p. 157. *non*, etc.: no, Sir, I simply am very fond of you, Sir, and of your young lady.

p. 158. *qu'y puis-je?*: what can I do about it?

p. 159. Stumbling on melons . . . arrogant fennels: allusions to passages in Marvell's 'Garden' and Rimbaud's 'Mémoire'.

p. 164. *d'accord*: Okay.

p. 167. *la bonne surprise*: what a good surprise.

p. 168. *amour propre, sale amour*: pun borrowed from Tolstoy's 'Resurrection'.

p. 169. *quelque petite*, etc.: some little laundress.

p. 169. Toulouse: Toulouse-Lautrec.

p. 170. *dura*: Russ., fool (fem.).

p. 171. *The Headless Horseman*: Mayne Reid's title is ascribed here to Pushkin, author of *The Bronze Horseman*.

p. 171. Lermontov: author of *The Demon*.

p. 171. Tolstoy, etc.: Tolstoy's hero, Haji Murad (a Caucasian chieftain) is blended here with General Murat, Napoleon's brother-in-law, and with the French revolutionary leader Marat assassinated in his bath by Charlotte Corday.

p. 173. Lute: from 'Lutèce', ancient name of Paris.

p. 175. *constatait*, etc.: noted with pleasure.

p. 176. Shivering aurora, laborious old Chose: a touch of Baudelaire.

p. 178. *golubyanka*: Russ., small blue butterfly.

p. 178. *petit bleu*: Parisian slang for pneumatic post (an express message on blue paper).

p. 179. *cousin*: mosquito.

p. 180. *mademoiselle*, etc.: the young lady has a pretty bad pneumonia, I regret to say, Sir.

p. 180. Granial Maza: a perfume named after Mt Kazbek's *'gran' almaza'* (diamond's facet) of Lermontov's *The Demon*.

p. 183. *inquiétante*: disturbing.

p. 187. Yellow-blue Vass: the phrase is consonant with *ya lyublyu vas* ('I love you' in Russian).

p. 190. *mais, ma pauvre amie*, etc.: but, my poor friend, it was imitation jewelry.

p. 190. *nichego ne podelaesh'*: Russ., nothing to be done.

p. 191. *elle le mangeait*, etc.: she devoured him with her eyes.

p. 192. *petits vers*, etc.: fugitive poetry and silk worms.

p. 193. Uncle Van: allusion to a line in Chekhov's play *Uncle Vanya*: We shall see the sky swarming with diamonds.

p. 198. *Les Enfants maudits*: the accursed children.

p. 199. *du sollst*, etc.: Germ., you must not listen.

p. 199. *on ne parle pas*, etc.: one does not speak like that in front of a dog.

p. 200. *que voulez-vous dire*: what do you mean.

p. 202. Forestday: Rack's pronunciation of 'Thursday'.

p. 202. *furchtbar*: Germ., dreadful.

p. 203. Ero: thus the h-dropping policeman in Wells' *Invisible Man* defined the latter's treacherous friend.

p. 206. *mais qu'est-ce*, etc.: but what did your cousin do to you?

p. 210. *petit-beurre*: a tea biscuit.

p. 217. *unschicklich*: Germ., improper (understood as 'not chic' by Ada).

p. 219. *ogon'*: Russ., fire.

p. 220. Microgalaxies: known on Terra as *Les Enfants du Capitaine Grant*, by Jules Verne.

p. 220. *ailleurs*: elsewhere.

p. 222. *alfavit*: Russ., alphabet.

p. 224. *particule*: 'de' or 'd''.

p. 224. Pat Rishin: a play on 'patrician'. One may recall Podgoretz (Russ. 'underhill') applying that epithet to a popular critic, would-be expert in Russian as spoken in Minsk and elsewhere. Minsk and Chess also figure in Chapter Six of *Speak, Memory* (p. 133, N.Y. ed. 1966).

p. 225. Gerschizhevsky: a Slavist's name gets mixed here with that of Chizhevki, another Slavist.

p. 227. *Je ne peux*, etc.: I can do nothing, but nothing.

p. 227. *Buchstaben*: Germ., letters of the alphabet.

p. 227. *c'est tout simple*: it's quite simple.

p. 227. *pas facile*: not easy.

p. 228. *Cendrillon*: Cinderella.

p. 228. *mon petit . . . que dis-je*: darling . . . in fact.

p. 231. *elle est folle*, etc.: she is insane and evil.

p. 231. Beer Tower: pun on 'Tourbière'.

p. 232. *chayku*: Russ., tea (diminutive).

p. 232. Ivanilich: a pouf plays a marvelous part in Tolstoy's *The Death of Ivan Ilyich*, where it sighs deeply under a friend of the widow's.

p. 232. *cousinage*: cousinhood is dangerous neighborhood.

p. 232. *on s'embrassait*: kissing went on in every corner.

p. 232. *erunda*: Russ., nonsense.

p. 232. *hier und da*: Germ., here and there.

p. 233. *raffolait*, etc.: was crazy about one of his mares.

p. 235. *tout est bien*: everything is all right.

p. 235. *tant mieux*: so much the better.

p. 235. Tuzenbakh: Van recites the last words of the unfortunate Baron in Chekhov's *Three Sisters* who does not know what to say but feels urged to say something to Irina before going to fight his fatal duel.

p. 237. *kontretan*: Russian mispronunciation of *contretemps*.

p. 238. *kameristochka*: Russ., young chambermaid.

p. 239. *en effet*: indeed.

p. 239. *petit nègre*: little Negro in the flowering field.

p. 240. *ce sera*, etc.: it will be a dinner for four.

p. 240. Wagging his left forefinger: that gene did not miss his daughter (see p. 227, where the name of the cream is also prefigured).

p. 240. Lyovka: derogative or folksy diminutive of Lyov (Leo).

p. 243. *antranou*, etc.: Russian mispronunciation of Fr. *entre nous soit dit*, between you and me.

p. 243. *filius aquae*: 'son of water', bad pun on *filum aquae*, the middle way, 'the thread of the stream'.

p. 244. *une petite juive*, etc.: a very aristocratic little Jewess.

p. 245. *ça va*: it goes.

p. 245. *seins durs*: mispronunciation of *sans dire* 'without saying'.

p. 245. *passe encore*: may still pass muster.

p. 246. *Lorsque*, etc.: When her fiancé had gone to war, the unfortunate and noble maiden closed her piano, sold her elephant.

p. 247. *Klubsessel*: Germ., easy chair.

p. 247. By chance preserved: The verses are by chance preserved
                    I have them, here they are:
                    (*Eugene Onegin*, Six: XXI: 1–2)

p. 248. *devant les gens*: in front of the servants.

p. 249. Fanny Price: the heroine of Jane Austen's *Mansfield Park*.

p. 249. *grib*: Russ., mushroom.

p. 249. *vodochki*: Russ., pl. of *vodochka*, diminutive of *vodka*.

p. 251. *zakusochnïy*, etc.: Russ., table with hors-d'oeuvres.

p. 251. *petits soupers*: intimate suppers.

p. 251. Persty: Evidently Pushkin's *vinograd*:
                    as elongated and transparent
                    as are the fingers of a girl.
                    (*devï molodoy, jeune fille*)

p. 251. *ciel-étoilé*: starry sky.

p. 255. *ne pïkhtite*: Russ., do not wheeze.

p. 256. *vous me comblez*: you overwhelm me with kindness.

p. 256. *pravda*: Russ., it's true.

p. 256. *gelinotte*: hazel-hen.

p. 257. *le feu*, etc.: the so delicate fire of virginity
that on her brow . . .

p. 257. *po razschyotu po moemu*: an allusion to Famusov (in Griboedov's *Gore ot yma*), calculating the pregnancy of a lady friend.

p. 257. *protestuyu*: Russ., I protest.

p. 257. *seriozno*: Russ., seriously.

p. 257. *quoi que ce soit*: whatever it might be.

p. 257. *en accuse*, etc.: . . . brings out its beauty.

p. 258. certicle: anagram of 'electric'.

p. 258. *Tetrastes*, etc.: Latin name of the imaginary 'Peterson's Grouse' from Wind River Range, Wyo.

p. 259. Great good man: a phrase that Winston Churchill, the British politician, enthusiastically applied to Stalin.

p. 260. *voulu*: intentional.

p. 261. *echt*, etc.: Germ., a genuine German.

p. 261. *Kegelkugel*: Germ., skittle-ball.

p. 261. *partir*, etc.: to go away is to die a little, and to die is to go away a little too much.

p. 263. tangelo: a cross between the tangerine and the pomelo (grapefruit).

p. 263. *fal'shivo*: Russ., false.

p. 264. *rozï . . . beryozï*: Russ., roses . . . birches.

p. 265. *ou comme ça?*: or like that?

p. 270. *sale*, etc.: dirty little Philistine.

p. 270. *d'accord*: Okay.

p. 271. *zhe*, etc.: Russ., distortion of *je t'en prie*.

p. 272. Trigorin, etc.: a reference to a scene in *The Seagull*.

p. 273. Houssaie: French, 'hollywood'. *Gollivud-tozh* means in Russian 'known also as Hollywood'.

p. 273. *enfin*: at last.

p. 274. *passati*: pseudo-Russian pun on 'pass water'.

p. 274. *coeur de boeuf*: bull's heart (in shape).

p. 277. *quand tu voudras*, etc.: any time, my lad.

p. 278. *la maudite*, etc.: the confounded (governess).

p. 279. *vos*, etc.: Franco-Russ., your expressions are rather free.

p. 279. *qui tâchait*, etc.: who was trying to turn her head.

p. 280. *ombres*, etc.: shadows and colors.

p. 285. *qu'on la coiffe*, etc.: to have her hair done in the open.

p. 285. *un air entendu*: a knowing look.

p. 288. *ne sais quand*, etc.: knows not when he'll come back.

p. 289. *mon beau page*: my pretty page.

p. 292. *c'est ma dernière*: this is my last night in the manor.

p. 293. *je suis*, etc.: I'm yours, it's soon dawn.

p. 293. *parlez pour vous*: speak for yourself.

p. 293. *immonde*: unspeakable.

p. 293–294. *il la mangeait*, etc.: he devoured her with disgusting kisses.

p. 296. *qu'on vous culbute*: that they tumble you.

p. 300. *marais noir*: black tide.

p. 303. *j'ai des ennuis*: I have worries.

p. 303. *topinambour*: tuber of the girasole; pun on 'pun' ('calembour').

p. 304. *on n'est pas*, etc.: what scurvy behavior.

p. 304. Tapper: 'Wild Violet', as well as 'Birdfoot' (p. 306), reflects the 'pansy' character of Van's adversary and of the two seconds.

p. 306. Rafin, Esq.: pun on 'Rafinesque', after whom a violet is named.

p. 306. Do-Re-La: 'Ladore' musically jumbled.

p. 308. *partie*, etc.: picnic.

p. 311. *palata*: Russ., ward.

p. 314. *tvoyu mat'*: Russ., 'Thy mother': the end of a popular Russian oath.

p. 315. *Ich bin*, etc.: Germ., I'm an incorrigible joker.

p. 317. uncle: 'my uncle has most honest principles'.
(*Eug. Onegin*, One: I: 1)

p. 321. *encore un*, etc.: one more 'baby ghost' (pun).

p. 325. the last paragraph of Part One imitates, in significant brevity of intonation (as if spoken by an outside voice), a famous Tolstoyan ending, with Van in the role of Kitty Lyovin.

p. 330. *poule*: tart.

p. 331. *komsi*, etc.: *comme-ci comme-ça* in Russ. mispronunciation: so-so.

p. 331. *mestechko*: Russ., little place.

p. 331. *bateau ivre*: 'sottish ship', title of Rimbaud's poem here used instead of 'ship of fools'.

p. 332. *poshlïy*: Russ., vulgar.

p. 333. *da*: Russ., yes.

p. 334. *ce qui*, etc.: which amounts to the same thing.

p. 334. *maux*: aches.

p. 334. aril: coating of certain seeds.

p. 334. Grant, etc.: Jules Verne in *Captain Grant's Children* has *'agonie'* (in a discovered message) turn out to be part of 'Patagonie'.

p. 339. Cyraniana: allusion to Cyrano de Bergerac's *Histoire comique des Etats de la Lune.*

p. 339. *Nekto*: Russ., quidam.

p. 339. *romanchik*: Russ., novelette.

p. 340. Sig Leymanski: anagram of the name of a waggish British novelist keenly interested in physics fiction.

p. 342. Abencérage, Zegris: Families of Granada Moors (their feud inspired Chateaubriand).

p. 344. *fille de joie*: whore.

p. 350. *maison close*: brothel.

p. 351. *vyshibala*: Russ., bouncer.

p. 353. *Künstlerpostkarte*: Germ., art picture postcards.

p. 354. *la gosse*: the little girl.

p. 355. *subsidunt*, etc.: mountains subside and heights deteriorate.

p. 358. *smorchiama*: let us snuff out the candle.

p. 360. Marmlad in Dickens: or rather Marmeladov in Dostoevsky, whom Dickens (in translation) greatly influenced.

p. 361. *frôlements*: light touchings.

p. 365. *sturb*: pun on Germ. *sterben*, to die.

p. 367. *qui prend*, etc.: that takes wing.

p. 367. all our old, etc.: Swinburne.

p. 368. Larousse: pun: *rousse*, 'redhair' in French.

p. 368. *pourtant*: yet.

p. 369. *cesse*: cease.

p. 369. *Glanz*: Germ., luster.

p. 369. *Mädel*: Germ., girl.

p. 370. *vsyo sdelali*: Russ., had done everything.

p. 372. relanced: from Fr. *relancer*, to go after.

p. 375. *cogner*, etc.: pun ('to coin a phrase').

p. 375. *fraise*: strawberry red.

p. 375. *krestik*: Anglo-Russian, little crest.

p. 375. *vanouissements*: 'Swooning in Van's arms'.

p. 378. I have not art, etc.: Hamlet.

p. 379. *si je puis*, etc.: if I may put it that way.

p. 379. *la plus laide*, etc.: the ugliest girl in the world can give more than she has.

p. 380. *Wattebausch*: Germ., piece of cottonwool.

p. 381. *à la queue*, etc.: in Indian file.

p. 382. making follies: Fr. 'faire des folies', living it up.

p. 383. *komondi*: Russian French: 'comme on dit', as they say.

p. 384. *Vieux-Rose*, etc.: Ségur-Rostopchine's books in the *Bibliothèque Rose* edition.

p. 386. *l'ivresse*, etc.: the intoxication of speed, conceptions on Sundays.

p. 387. *un baiser*, etc.: one single kiss.

p. 391. *shuba*: Russ., furcoat.

p. 395. *ébats*: frolics.

p. 396. *mossio*, etc.: *monsieur* your cousin.

p. 397. *jolies*: pretty.

p. 397. *n'aurait*, etc.: should never have received that scoundrel.

p. 397. Ashettes: Cinderellas.

p. 399. Sumerechnikov: His name comes from Russ., *sumerki*, twilight; see also p. 43.

p. 399. *zdraste*: abbrev. form of *zdravstvuyte*, the ordinary Russian greeting.

p. 400. *lit*, etc.: pun on 'eider-down bed'.

p. 401. *d'ailleurs*: anyhow.

p. 401. *pétard*: Mr Ben Wright, a poet in his own right, is associated throughout with *pets* (farts).

p. 402. *bayronka*: from Bayron, Russ., Byron.

p. 402. *réjouissants*: hilarious.

p. 403. Beckstein: transposed syllables.

p. 403. *Love under the Lindens*: O'Neill, Thomas Mann, and his translator tangle in this paragraph.

p. 403. vanishing, etc.: allusion to 'vanishing cream'.

p. 404. *auch*: Germ., also.

p. 405. *éventail*: fan.

p. 405. *fotochki*: Russ., little photos.

p. 406. *foute*: French swear word made to sound 'foot'.

p. 406. *ars*: Lat., art.

p. 406. *Carte du Tendre*: 'Map of Tender Love', sentimental allegory of the seventeenth century.

p. 408. *Knabenkräuter*: Germ., orchids (and testicles).

p. 408. *perron*: porch.

p. 410. *romances, tsiganshchina*: Russ., pseudo-Tsigan ballads.

p. 413. *vinocherpiy*: Russ., the 'wine-pourer'.

p. 413. *zernistaya ikra*: 'large-grained' caviar (Russ.).

p. 413. *uzh gasli*, etc.: Russ., the lights were already going out in the rooms.

p. 415. *Nikak-s net*: Russ., certainly not.

p. 416. famous fly: see p. 135, *Serromyia*.

p. 416. *Vorschmacks*: Germ., hors-d'oeuvres.

p. 419. *et pour cause*: and no wonder.

p. 419. *karavanchik*: small caravan of camels (Russ.).

p. 420. *oberart*, etc.: Germ., superspecies, subspecies.

p. 421. *spazmochka*: Russ., little spasm.

p. 422. *bretteur*: duelling bravo.

p. 422. *au fond*: actually.

p. 426. *fokus-pokus*: Russ., bogus magic.

p. 427. *au dire*, etc.: according to the reviewers.

p. 428. *finestra, sestra*: Ital., window, sister.

p. 428. *Arinushka*: Russ., folksy diminutive of 'Irina'.

p. 428. *oh qui me rendra*, etc.: Oh, who'll give me back
my hill and the big oak.

p. 430. *sekundant*: Russ., second.

p. 430. *puerulus*: Lat., little lad.

p. 430. *matovaya*: Russ., dull-toned.

p. 430. *en robe*, etc.: in a pink and green dress.

p. 434. R 4: 'rook four', a chess indication of position (pun on the woman's name).

p. 436. *c'est le mot*: that's the right word.

p. 437. *pleureuses*: widow's weeds.

p. 438. *Bozhe moy*: Russ., good Heavens.

p. 443. ridge: money.

p. 445. *secondes pensées*, etc.: second thoughts are the good ones.

p. 445. *bonne*: housemaid.

p. 451. *dyakon*: deacon.

p. 452. *désolé*, etc.: distressed at being unable to be with you.

p. 454. So you are married, etc.: see *Eugene Onegin*, Eight: XVIII: 1–4.

p. 455. *za tvoyo*, etc.: Russ., your health.

p. 456. *guvernantka*, etc.: Russ., governess-novelist.

p. 457. *moue*: little grimace.

p. 459. *affalés*, etc.: sprawling in their armchairs.

p. 460. *bouffant*: puffed up.

p. 461. *gueule*, etc.: simian facial angle.

p. 461. *grustnoe*, etc.: Russ., she addresses him as 'my sad bliss'.

p. 462. *troués*: with a hole or holes.

p. 463. engripped: from *prendre en grippe*, to conceive a dislike.

p. 463. *pravoslavnaya*: Russ., Greek-Orthodox.

p. 466. *das auch noch*: Germ., and that too.

p. 466. *pendant que je*, etc.: while I am skiing.

p. 473. *Vesti*: Russ., News.

p. 478. *Obst*: Germ., fruit.

p. 481. I love you with a brother's love, etc.: see *Eugene Onegin*, Four: XVI: 3–4.

p. 483. cootooriay, etc.: mispronunciation of *'couturier'*, dressmaker, *'vous avez entendu'*, you've heard (about him).

p. 483. *tu sais*, etc.: you know it will kill me.

p. 484. *Insiste*, etc.: quotation from St Augustine.

p. 485. Henry: Henry James' style is suggested by the italicized *'had'*.

p. 487. *en laid et en lard*: in an ugly and fleshy version.

p. 487. *emptovato*: Anglo-Russian, rather empty.

p. 489. *slip*: Fr., panties.

p. 492. *pudeur*: modesty, delicacy.

p. 492. *prosit*: Germ., your health.

p. 493. *Dimanche*, etc.: Sunday. Lunch on the grass. Everybody stinks. My mother-in-law swallows her dentures. Her little bitch, etc. After which, etc. (see p. 478, a painter's diary Lucette has been reading).

p. 494. Nox: Lat., at night.

p. 499. *Cher ami*, etc.: Dear friend, my husband and I were deeply upset by the frightful news. It was to me—and this I'll always remember—that practically on the eve of her death the poor girl addressed herself to arrange things on the Tobakoff, which is always crowded and which from now on I'll never take again, slightly out of superstition and very much out of sympathy for gentle, tender Lucette. I had been so happy to do all I could, as somebody had told me that you would be there too. Actually, she said so herself; she seemed so joyful to spend a few days on the upper deck with her dear cousin! The psychology of suicide is a mystery that no scientist can explain. I have never shed so many tears, it almost makes me drop my pen. We return to Malbrook around mid-August. Yours ever.

p. 502. And o'er the summits of the Tacit, etc.: parody of four lines in Lermontov's *The Demon* (see also pp. 142–144).

p. 503. *le beau ténébreux*: wrapt in Byronic gloom.

p. 508. *que sais-je*: what do I know.

p. 508. *Merci*, etc.: My infinite thanks.

p. 510. *cameriere*: Ital., hotel manservant who carries the luggage upstairs, vacuum-cleans the rooms, etc.

p. 511. *libretto*: that of the opera *Eugene Onegin*, a travesty of Pushkin's poem.

p. 513. *korrektniy*: Russ., correct.

p. 513. *hobereau*: country squire.

p. 513. cart de van: Amer., mispronunciation of *carte des vins*.

p. 514. *zhidovskaya*: Russ. (vulg.), Jewish.

p. 514. *je veux*, etc.: I want to get hold of you, my dear.

p. 514. *enfin*: in short.

p. 514. Luzon: Amer., mispronunciation of 'Lausanne'.

p. 515. *lieu*: place.

p. 517. (a pause): This and the whole conversation parody Chekhov's mannerisms.

p. 518. *muirninochka*: Hiberno-Russian caressive term.

p. 519. *potins de famille*: family gossip.

p. 519. *terriblement*, etc.: terribly grand and all that, she likes to tease him by saying that a simple farmer like him should not have married the daughter of an actress and an art dealer.

p. 519. *je dois*, etc.: I must watch my weight.

p. 520. *Olorinus*: from Lat. *olor*, swan (Leda's lover).

p. 520. *lenclose*: distorted 'clothes' (influenced by 'Ninon de Lenclos'), the courtesan in Vere de Vere's novel mentioned above.

p. 521. Aleksey, etc.: Vronski and his mistress.

p. 522. *phrase*, etc.: stock phrase.

p. 522. She Yawns: Chillon's.

p. 523. D'Onsky: see p. 13.

p. 523. *comme*, etc.: shedding floods of tears.

p. 523. *N'a pas le verbe*, etc.: lacks the gift of the gab.

p. 524. *chiens*, etc.: dogs not allowed.

p. 525. *rieuses*: black-headed gulls.

p. 526. *Golos*, etc.: Russ., *The Phoenix Voice*, Russian language newspaper in Arizona.

p. 527. *la voix*, etc.: the brassy voice telephoned . . . the trumpet did not sound pleased this morning.

p. 527. *contretemps*: mishap.

p. 530. *phalène*: moth (see also p. 138).

p. 530. *tu sais*, etc.: you know it will kill me.

p. 530. *Bozhe moy*: Russ., oh, my God.

p. 536. *et trêve*, etc.: and enough of that painted-ceiling style of mine.

p. 538. ardis: arrow.

p. 539. ponder: pun on Fr. *pondre*, to lay an egg (an allusion to the problem what came first, egg or hen).

p. 541. *anime*, etc.: Lat., soul.

p. 541. assassin pun: a pun on *pointe assassine* (from a poem by Verlaine).

p. 541. Lacrimaval: Italo-Swiss. Pseudo-place-name, 'vale of tears'.

p. 543. *coup de volant*: one twist of the steering wheel.

p. 546. dream-delta: allusion to the disintegration of an imaginary element.

p. 550. unfortunate thinker: Samuel Alexander, English philosopher.

p. 552. Villa Jolana: named in honor of a butterfly, belonging to the subgenus *Jolana*, which breeds in the Pfynwald (see also p. 128).

p. 553. Vinn Landère: French distortion of 'Vinelander'.

p. 553. *à la sonde*: in soundings (for the same ship see p. 521).

p. 555. *Comment*, etc.: what's that? no, no not 88, but 86.

p. 558. *droits*, etc.: custom-house dues.

p. 558. *après tout*: after all.

p. 558. *on peut*, etc.: see p. 247.

p. 559. lucubratiuncula: bit of writing in the lamplight.

p. 559. *duvet*: fluff.

p. 561. simpler: simpler to take off from the balcony.

p. 562. mermaid: allusion to Lucette.

p. 567. Stepan Nootkin: Van's valet.

p. 575. *blyadushki*: little whores (echo of p. 411).

p. 575. *Blitzpartien*: Germ., quickies (quick chess games).

p. 578. *Compitalia*: Lat., crossroads.

p. 578. E, p, i: referring to 'epistemic' (see above).

p. 584. *j'ai tâté*, etc.: I have known two Lesbians in my life, that's enough.

p. 584. *terme*, etc.: term one avoids using.

p. 587. *le bouquin . . . guéri*, etc.: the book . . . cured of all its snags.

p. 587. *quel livre*, etc.: what a book, good God.

p. 588. *gamine*: lassie.

Notes to
Vivian Darkbloom's Notes to *Ada*

J. E. RIVERS AND WILLIAM WALKER

Who is Vivian Darkbloom? Since "Vivian Darkbloom" is an anagram of "Vladimir Nabokov," one might be tempted to say that Darkbloom is Nabokov himself in the thinnest of disguises. However, there is a character in *Lolita* named Vivian Darkbloom, a writer who collaborates with Quilty on the play *The Lady Who Loved Lightning* and who survives the deaths of the major characters to write a biography, *My Cue*, presumably about Quilty. We are also told in *Lolita* that "Vivian Darkbloom" is a pseudonym, and Humbert catches one glimpse of this "hawklike, black-haired, strikingly tall woman," where, in spite of Darkbloom's femininity, Nabokov's features seem to burn through the mask (*The Annotated Lolita*, pp. 6, 33, 223).

In the "Notes to *Ada*," as in *Lolita*, Nabokov is and is not Vivian Darkbloom. Nabokov is Darkbloom in the sense that he wrote the commentary signed with Darkbloom's name, which is his own name rearranged. He is not Darkbloom in the sense that he adopts for the "Notes to *Ada*" a pseudonym, which tends, in turn, to create, or re-create, a fictional persona. This disguise, thin though it is, allows Nabokov to remain at a certain remove from his text and obviates any requirement that he speak here as the ultimate authority on *Ada*. The text of *Ada* is a metaphor for Nabokovian "reality," and "reality," as Nabokov tells us in *Strong Opinions* (p. 11), cannot be known: it can only be approached. The partial explication contained in the "Notes to *Ada* by Vivian Darkbloom" thus allows the "reality" of *Ada* to continue to recede even as it seems to be explained by this *ad hoc* identity invented and controlled by Nabokov.

If the pseudonym helps to preserve the ambiguity of *Ada*'s "reality," it also helps to make possible the playfulness, allusiveness, and ambiguity sometimes found in the "Notes" themselves. Inadequate or inaccurate commentary signed by Vladimir Nabokov would be, at the most, shocking, at the least, irritating. Inadequate or inaccurate commentary signed by "Vivian Darkbloom" automatically becomes a puzzle and a game. The Darkbloom persona bedevils readers even as it seems to enlighten them. Take the matter of translation, for instance. Sometimes Darkbloom gives only a literal translation from a foreign language when an idiomatic translation is also needed, or, conversely, only a figurative translation when a literal translation is required as well. Even more fiendishly, Darkbloom introduces foreign-language passages into the notes and leaves them untranslated, though one apparent purpose of the notes is to translate passages in foreign languages. Several of the puns on which Darkbloom comments are incompletely or obliquely explained. Darkbloom's identification of literary allusions is highly elliptical and often itself allusive. Sometimes Darkbloom even deliberately misleads us. In addition to these complexities, Darkbloom's notes have their own recurring themes and motifs and their own interconnections and cross-references. There is, in short, a whiff of Kinbote about Mr. (or Ms.?) Darkbloom.

Darkbloom's occasional unreliability as an annotator challenges us to exercise our own minds in order to approach one step closer to the "reality" of *Ada*. One way of doing this is to treat Darkbloom's notes as a text which itself invites and requires a commentary. In the annotations that follow, we have, for ease of reference, reprinted the problematic note by Darkbloom verbatim before adding our own commentary. Where Darkbloom is implicit, we have tried to be explicit. Where Darkbloom is vague, we have tried to be precise. And where Darkbloom is playfully and deliberately misleading, we have tried to be reliable guides. When Darkbloom alludes to little-known or previously overlooked literary texts, we quote extensively from these texts in order to place them conveniently at the disposal of other scholars. But we also offer our own interpretations of the function of these texts in *Ada* and in Darkbloom's annotations. Translations, unless otherwise noted, are by the authors.

This commentary supplements and expands Carl R. Proffer's "*Ada* as Wonderland: A Glossary of Allusions to Russian Literature," in *A Book of Things about Vladimir Nabokov* (ed. Proffer, pp. 249–79). For discussions of allusions to Russian literature not treated below, the reader is directed to Proffer's annotations.

p. 3. All happy families, etc.: mistranslations of Russian classics are ridiculed here. The opening sentence of Tolstoy's novel is turned inside out and Anna Arkadievna's patronymic given an absurd masculine ending, while an incorrect feminine one is added to her surname. 'Mount Tabor' and 'Pontius' allude to the transfigurations (Mr G. Steiner's term, I believe) and betrayals to which great texts are subjected by pretentious and ignorant versionists. *Commentary*: Mount Tabor in Palestine is the traditional site of Jesus' transfiguration. "Pontius" refers to Pontius Pilate, who figures prominently in the story of Jesus' betrayal. Hence the "transfigurations" and "betrayals." "G. Steiner" is George Steiner, author of numerous works on language and on the theory and practice of translation. Steiner's article on Nabokovian linguistics ("Extraterritorial," in *Nabokov*, ed. Appel and Newman, pp. 119–27) drew a blistering response from Nabokov (*Strong Opinions*, p. 288).

p. 3. Sevemïya Territorii: Northern Territories. Here and elsewhere transliteration is based on the old Russian orthography. *Commentary*: *Ada*'s "Severn Tories" is translated in the text as "Sevemïya Territorii," which in turn is translated in the notes as "Northern Territories." "Sevemïya Territorii," however, has nothing to do etymologically with "Severn Tories," which is the name of the Severn, Britain's longest river, coupled with the designation for one of the most important British political groupings. "Sevemïya Territorii" does mean "Northern Territories" in Russian. The implication of the text is that "Severn Tories" is an Antiterran translingual pun on "Sevemïya Territorii." Darkbloom's literal translation of the Russian, juxtaposed with the punning but inaccurate translation in the text, adds an additional level of complexity to the satire of translation and mistranslation that begins on the first page of *Ada* and continues throughout the novel. The declaration that "here and elsewhere transliteration is based on the old Russian orthography" makes Darkbloom's annotation seem serious and scholarly, when it is actually the second trapdoor in a linguistic fun house.

p. 3. granoblastically: in a tesselar (mosaic) jumble. *Commentary*: According to *Webster's Third New International Dictionary* the adjective "granoblastic" is part of the "International Scientific Vocabulary." Webster's definition is more detailed than Darkbloom's: "*of a rock*: having a texture in which the fragments are irregular and angular and appear like a mosaic under the microscope." Like many words in *Ada* and in Nabokov generally, "granoblastically" will not be found in every dictionary—not even in some of the best-known "unabridged" works.

p. 4. Tofana: allusion to 'aqua tofana' (see any good dictionary). *Commentary*: Darkbloom's injunction to "see any good dictionary" is a red herring—unless we define a good dictionary as one that contains a definition of "aqua Tofana." The phrase is not in *The Oxford English Dictionary*, nor in *Webster's Third New International Dictionary*. It is, however, in the *Funk & Wagnalls New Standard Dictionary*, and it also merits an entry in Sir Paul Harvey's *Oxford*

Companion to English Literature (4th ed., rev. Dorothy Eagle). Aqua Tofana, or Toffana—"Tofana water"—was a poison invented and sold by an Italian woman, Toffana, who lived in Palermo and Naples in the seventeenth century. She labeled it "Manna di S. Nicola di Bari" ("Manna of St. Nicolas of Bari"). Its main ingredient was probably arsenic.

p. 5. Lake Kitezh: allusion to the legendary town of Kitezh which shines at the bottom of a lake in a Russian fairytale. *Commentary*: According to this tale, the Virgin Mary, in answer to prayers from the inhabitants of Kitezh, made the city invisible to save it from being sacked by the Tartars. The reflection of the invisible city, however, could still be seen in a nearby lake. When the Tartars beheld the reflection, they fled before this evidence of the Christian God's power. The tale of Kitezh combined with the tale of St. Fevronia is the basis for an opera by Rimsky-Korsakov with libretto by Vladimir Belsky, *The Tale of the Invisible City of Kitezh and the Maiden Fevronia* (composed 1904, first performed 1907). An interesting feature of Rimsky's opera is the singing of the sirin, a mythical bird that lives in paradise, to herald the final transfiguration and apotheosis of Kitezh. Another sirin associated in the Russian tradition with fairy tales and magical transformation is, of course, Vladimir Sirin, né Nabokov, who puts his personal and artistic signature on the passage in this allusion to Kitezh. For a depiction of the sirin and of its companion bird the alkonost, see Yuri Ovsyannikov, *The Lubok: Seventeenth and Eighteenth Century Russian Broadsides* (Moscow: Sovetsky Khudozhnik, 1968), pp. 80–82.

p. 5. Mr Eliot: we shall meet him again, on pages 459 and 505, in company of the author of 'The Waistline' and 'Agonic Lines'. *Commentary*: T. S. Eliot (1888–1965), author of *The Waste Land* (1922) and *Sweeney Agonistes* (1932). Nabokov's distaste for Eliot's poetry is well known.

p. 5. Counter-Fogg: Phileas Fogg, Jules Verne's globetrotter, travelled from West to East. *Commentary*: Phileas Fogg is the protagonist of *Le Tour du monde en quatre-vingts jours* (*Around the World in Eighty Days*), a novel by Jules Verne (1828–1905). This novel appears as a leitmotif throughout Nabokov's career. It is, as he records in *Speak, Memory*, one of the books his French governess read aloud to him when he was a child (p. 105). And in *The Defense* it is mentioned, in lines that could apply equally well to Nabokov himself, as one of the books with which the boy Luzhin "had fallen in love for his whole life, holding [it] in his memory as if under a magnifying glass" (p. 33). The allusion to Phileas Fogg helps to establish the importance of travel and exile in *Ada*. We are told that Dan Veen traveled around the world three times "in a counter-Fogg direction" and thus hear of a triple *tour du monde* before the novel is five pages old. Nabokov himself, of course, traveled "counter-Fogg" when he went from East to West in his permanent exile from Russia.

p. 8. Stabian flower girl: allusion to the celebrated mural painting (the so-called 'Spring') from Stabiae in the National Museum of Naples: a maiden scattering blossoms. *Commentary*: Stabiae, an ancient town on the Italian coast at the eastern extremity of the Gulf of Naples, was destroyed along with Pompeii and Herculaneum by the eruption of Vesuvius in A.D. 79. The mural painting of the "flower girl," recovered from the ruins of Stabiae, is apparently a fragment of a larger work, or sequence of works. A reproduction may be found in Alfonso de Franciscis, *Il Museo Nazionale di Napoli* (Naples: Di Mauro, 1963), plate LXXI ("La 'Primavera' da Stabiae"). The Stabian flower girl is depicted as barefooted, as Ada indicates in her pun on "Bear-Foot" and "bare foot." This is one of many allusions to painting in *Ada*.

p. 14. Aardvark: apparently, a university town in New England. *Commentary*: *Ada*'s "Aardvark, Massa" corresponds to Cambridge, Massachusetts. Calling Harvard "Aardvark" is a very old joke.

p. 14. Gamaliel: a much more fortunate statesman than our W. G. Harding. *Commentary*: The full name of W. G. Harding, twenty-ninth president of the United States, is Warren Gamaliel Harding (1865–1923). Harding's administration is considered one of the most corrupt in American history. The "idealistic President" Gamaliel in *Ada* has more in common with the Biblical Gamaliel, "a teacher of the law, held in honor by all the people," who in Acts 5: 34–39 gives wise advice to the Sanhedrin on how to deal with the apostles.

p. 16. Lolita, Texas: this town exists, or, rather, existed, for it has been renamed, I believe, after the appearance of the notorious novel. *Commentary*: The town has not been renamed. Lolita (pop. 400, in Jackson County, Texas, southeast of Houston and north of Port Lavaca) is still listed in *The National Atlas of the United States of America* (Washington, D.C.: U.S. Department of the Interior, 1970). In a telephone conversation with William Walker on 2 April 1978, Mr. Grover Klaus, the town historian, said he had been living in Lolita for fifty-four years and that it always had been and still was Lolita. He added that there may have been some talk of changing the name, but nothing ever came of it. Incidentally, the inhabitants of Lolita pronounce the name of their town "luh-lée-dah."

p. 17. Faragod: apparently, the god of electricity. *Commentary*: The god of electricity takes his name from Michael Faraday (1791–

1867), the English physicist celebrated for his research on electricity and magnetism. The "-god" in Faragod is perhaps a translingual pun on "-day" via the similar-sounding Latin word *dei*. (*Dei* is the genitive singular and nominative plural cases of *deus*, "god.")

p. 17. braques: allusion to a bric-à-brac painter. *Commentary*: French painter Georges Braque (1882–1963). Braque and Picasso are regarded as the joint creators of Cubism. The pun in *Ada* and in Darkbloom's note is pilfered from the poem "Pale Fire," where John Shade says, "I loathe such things as jazz [and] abstractist bric-a-brac" (vv. 924–26). In an interview Nabokov says that Shade's opinion of "abstractist bric-a-brac" represents his own opinion. Nabokov has, however, expressed admiration for the work of Picasso before *Guernica* (1937) (*Strong Opinions*, pp. 18, 167).

p. 23. lammer: amber (Fr. *l'ambre*), allusion to electricity. *Commentary*: A real word, not an invented one. Under "lammer" *Webster's Third New International Dictionary* gives "chiefly Scot: AMBER." Darkbloom's note echoes the accepted etymology of "lammer," which derives the word from the French for amber (the *l* apparently reflects the definite article in French *l'ambre*). Lammer is an "allusion to electricity," because amber, when rubbed, can be made to produce static electricity. The word "electricity" comes from the Greek word for amber (*ēlektron*).

In *An Etymological Dictionary of the Scottish Language*, ed. John Jamieson (Paisley: Gardner, 1880) we learn that the ancients regarded lammer as having magical power and used it as a charm against illness, poison, and sorcery. We also learn that in Scottish folklore an imaginary liquor, lammer-wine, "was esteemed a sort of elixir of immortality." These occult and magical associations accord well with Nabokov's half-comical, half-serious treatment of electricity as a mysterious, quasi-magical force. For a time in *Ada* electricity is banned and is a taboo subject on Antiterra. When it comes back into use and re-enters polite conversation, it does so under the auspices of its own deity, Faragod, the god of electricity (see our first note to p. 17 above). This perspective on electricity is not limited to *Ada*. In *Pale Fire* John Shade writes a poem called "The Nature of Electricity," about which Charles Kinbote says, "Science tells us . . . that the Earth would not merely fall apart, but vanish like a ghost, if Electricity were suddenly removed from the world" (pp. 192–93). And in Andrew Field's *Nabokov: His Life in Part*, Nabokov is quoted as saying, "Electricity. Time. Space. We know *nothing* about these things" (p. 87).

p. 23. my lad, my pretty, etc.: paraphrase of a verse in Housman. *Commentary*: A paraphrase of the penultimate line of the fifth section of *A Shropshire Lad* by A. E. Housman (1859–1936): "Be kind, have pity, my own, my pretty,—." Nabokov's distortion of the line ("my lad, my pretty, my love, take pity") emphasizes the homosexual implications of the poem. Nabokov is fond not only of alluding to Housman's homosexuality but also of using him as a means of alluding to the homosexuality of others. In *Pale Fire* Charles Kinbote is satirized for his vegetarianism and homosexuality in a skit performed by drama students: "I was pictured as a pompous woman hater . . . constantly quoting Housman and nibbling raw carrots" (p. 25).

p. 23. ballatetta: fragmentation and distortion of a passage in a 'little ballad' by the Italian poet Guido Cavalcanti (1255–1300). The relevant lines are: 'you frightened and weak little voice that comes weeping from my woeful heart, go with my soul and that ditty, telling of a destroyed mind'. *Commentary*: Darkbloom translates the first four lines of the final (fifth) stanza of Cavalcanti's poem. The original of the translated lines reads:

> Tu, voce sbigottita e deboletta
> ch'esci piangendo de lo cor dolente,
> coll'anima e con questa ballatetta
> va' ragionando della strutta mente.

The complete text may be found in Guido Cavalcanti, *Le Rime*, ed. Guido Favati, Documenti di Filologia, No. 1 (Milan and Naples: Ricciardi, 1957), pp. 268–69. Dante Gabriel Rossetti's *The Early Italian Poets* (1861) includes a translation of the poem. For a modern reprint of this translation, see D. G. Rossetti, *Poems and Translations, 1850–1870* (London: Oxford University Press, 1959), pp. 414–15.

Like Nabokov himself and like several other writers alluded to in *Ada*, Guido Cavalcanti endured the experience of exile. Banished from Florence for political reasons in 1300, he returned there to die in the same year. The "Ballatetta" opens with a reference to his enforced absence from his beloved Tuscany: "Perch' i' no spero di tornar giammai, / ballatetta, in Toscana" (in Rossetti's version: "Because I think not ever to return, / Ballad, to Tuscany").

p. 27. horsepittle: 'hospital', borrowed from a passage in Dickens' *Bleak House*. Poor Jo's pun, not a poor Joycean one. *Commentary*: The word "horsepittle" occurs in chapter 46 of the novel *Bleak House* by Charles Dickens (1812–1870). It is arguably no pun at all, or if it is, it is ascribable to Dickens, not Jo. Nothing in the context suggests that Jo means anything but "hospital." His pronunciation of other words is similarly distorted, and he seems far too dim for sallies of verbal wit. Dickens says of him in chapter 16: "It must be a strange state to be like Jo! . . . To see people read, and to see people write, and to see the postman deliver letters, and not to have the least idea of all that language—to be, to every scrap of it, stone blind and dumb!" Thus the allusion in *Ada* to "the Mondefroid bleakhouse horsepittle" (p. 27) holds a double dose of Nabokovian contempt, since it combines a reference to illiteracy with a reference to Freudian psychology and allows the negative connotations of the one to rub off on the other (cf. the "Dr. Froid" and the "Dr. Froit of Signy-Mondieu-Mondieu" mentioned on the same page). The allusion also may be intended to remind the reader that *Bleak House* has as two of its central characters the cousins Richard Carstone and Ada Clare, who live with an elderly relative in the mansion Bleak House and love and marry in secret.

p. 29. *Princesse Lointaine*: Distant Princess, title of a French play. *Commentary*: The poetic drama *La Princesse lointaine* (1895) by Edmond Rostand (1868–1918), based on a legend about the Provençal poet Jaufré Rudel. Jaufré Rudel supposedly fell in love with the countess of Tripoli, whom he had never seen but whom he nevertheless celebrated in a famous poem about his *amor de lonh* ("distant love"). The legend says he set sail to see the woman, fell ill during the voyage, and died in her arms upon his arrival.

p. 37. Lady Amherst: confused in the child's mind with the learned lady after whom a popular pheasant is named. *Commentary*: Lady Amherst's Pheasant (*Chrysolophus amherstiae*) is named after Sarah, first wife of William Pitt Amherst (1773–1857), second Baron Amherst. William Pitt Amherst served as governor-general and viceroy of India, and the bird was introduced into England in 1828 from the mountainous regions of southwest Burma.

p. 46. lovely Spanish poem: really *two* poems—Jorge Guillén's *Descanso en jardín* and his *El otoño: isla*. *Commentary*: Of the two Spanish words Van knows, *nubarrones* ("thunderclouds") comes from Guillén's "Descanso en jardín" ("Calm of Gardens"), where it stands as the second line and the last line, and *canastilla* ("little basket") from "El otoño: isla" ("Autumn: Island"), where it is the third word of the ninth line. The "schoolbook" containing an *en regard* translation could be a fictive reflection of Jorge Guillén, *Cántico: A Selection*, ed. Norman Thomas di Giovanni (Boston: Little, 1965), which contains both "Descanso en jardín" and "El otoño: isla" in Spanish with *en regard* English translations. There are, however, several other books containing Spanish poems by Guillén with facing English renderings. Another well-known poem by Guillén, "Ardor," echoes part of the title of the novel now under discussion.

When the Spanish Republic fell in 1938, Jorge Guillén (1893–)

went into exile and settled in the United States. He taught at Wellesley College from 1940 to 1957 and was a colleague there of fellow exile Vladimir Nabokov. Like Nabokov, Guillén created his major *oeuvre* outside his native land. Also like Nabokov, who said that his art was his passport, Guillén found that exile sharpened the universality of his vision. He said that "exile has not been for me a totally alienating experience, because I find anywhere on earth the essential things: air, water, sun, man, human companionship. . . . I have never been able to consider myself completely exiled. I am always in this home country called the planet earth" (quoted and translated in Ivar Ivsak and Juan Marichal, eds., *Luminous Reality: The Poetry of Jorge Guillén* [Norman: University of Oklahoma Press, 1969], pp. vii–viii). Jorge Guillén has been called the greatest living Spanish poet, just as Nabokov during his lifetime was regarded by many as the greatest living English-language novelist. These references to Guillén in *Ada* are, then, a tribute to a man with whom Nabokov had a great deal in common.

p. 52. *infusion de tilleul*: lime tea. *Commentary*: The translation "lime tea" reveals only one of the meanings present in the passage. The *tilleul* in French is the lime or linden tree. The light filtering through the branches of the linden under which the children are playing thus becomes, punningly and metaphorically, a "lime infusion." And "lime infusion" in the sense of "lime tea" is perhaps an allusion to the *Combray* section of *A la recherche du temps perdu* (1913–1927) by Marcel Proust (1871–1922), where the involuntary memory set in motion by the tea and madeleine reminds the narrator of his own childhood and of the "infusion de thé ou de tilleul" ("tea or lime infusion") he drank in his aunt's room in Combray. Like Proust's narrator, Van and Ada eventually recapture their childhood through memory and through art. For a detailed discussion of Proust's role in *Ada*, see J. E. Rivers, "Proust, Nabokov, and *Ada*," *French-American Review* 1 (1977), 173–97.

p. 53. *Les Amours du Dr Mertvago*: play on 'Zhivago' ('*zhiv*' means in Russian 'alive' and '*mertv*' dead). *Commentary*: The French title means literally *The Loves of Dr. Mertvago* and is an allusion to the novel *Doctor Zhivago* (1957; Eng. tr. 1958) by Boris Pasternak (1890–1960). The substitution of *mertv* for *zhiv* communicates Nabokov's low opinion of the work, which vied with *Lolita* on the American best-seller lists in 1958. In an interview Nabokov says: "I regard [*Dr. Zhivago*] as a sorry thing, clumsy, trivial, and melodramatic, with stock situations, voluptuous lawyers, unbelievable girls, and trite coincidences. . . . I applauded [Pasternak's] getting the Nobel Prize on the strength of his verse. In *Dr. Zhivago*, however, the prose does not live up to his poetry" (*Strong Opinions*, p. 206).

p. 53. *grand chêne*: big oak. *Commentary*: An allusion to a poem by François René de Chateaubriand (1768–1848), explained in Darkbloom's first note to p. 138. See also the note below to p. 106.

p. 55. *Les Malheurs de Swann*: cross between *Les Malheurs de Sophie* by Mme de Ségur (née Countess Rostopchine) and Proust's *Un Amour de Swann*. *Commentary*: This title, though invented by playfully combining Proust and Mme de Ségur, is nonetheless an apt description of Swann's experiences in *Un Amour de Swann*, where Swann's love for Odette is equated with suffering and misfortune. Sophie Rostopchine, comtesse de Ségur (1799–1874), wrote a famous series of children's books, which figured prominently in Nabokov's early reading and which, as he relates in *Speak, Memory*, had the power of evoking later in life involuntary, Proustian memories of his childhood in Russia (pp. 76–77). The cross between the two titles, then, not only comments on Proust's work, but also reflects a blending of Proustian and Ségurian experience in Nabokov's own life. Mme de Ségur's *Les Malheurs de Sophie* was published in 1864. For other allusions to Mme de Ségur, see pp. 114 and 384 of *Ada* and Darkbloom's notes to those pages.

p. 61. *monologue intérieur*: the so-called 'stream-of-consciousness' device, used by Leo Tolstoy (in describing, for instance, Anna's last impressions whilst her carriage rolls through the streets of Moscow). *Commentary*: A reference to part 7, chapter 30, of Tolstoy's *Anna Karenina* (1875–1877).

p. 64. Mr Fowlie: see Wallace Fowlie, *Rimbaud* (1946). *Commentary*: In Wallace Fowlie's *Rimbaud* (New York: New Directions, 1946) there is an analysis of the posthumously published poem "Mémoire" (1895) by Arthur Rimbaud (1854–1891). The discussion begins with a quotation of the French text followed by "a literal translation of it" (p. 74). In the seventh line of the poem "ayant le ciel bleu pour ciel de lit" ("having the blue sky for a bed canopy") is mistranslated as "having the blue sky for the sky's bed" (p. 76). And in the fourteenth line "le souci d'eau" ("the marsh marigold") is mistranslated as "the care of the water" (p. 77). Fowlie's translation of "Mémoire" does not appear in the British edition of his book, *Rimbaud: The Myth of Childhood* (London: Dobson, 1946).

Several years before *Ada* appeared, Fowlie corrected the errors in his early translation of the poem. In a revised and expanded study, *Rimbaud* (Chicago: University of Chicago Press, 1965), he comments specifically on "le souci d'eau" and points out that it should be translated as "marsh marigold" (p. 17). And in his edition and translation *Rimbaud: Complete Works, Selected Letters* (Chicago: University of Chicago Press, 1966), "ayant le ciel bleu pour ciel de lit" is correctly translated as "having the blue sky as a canopy" and "souci d'eau" as "marsh marigold" (p. 123). Darkbloom either is unaware of or purposely ignores Fowlie's later rectification of these mistakes.

When J. E. Rivers wrote to Wallace Fowlie (now a professor emeritus at Duke University) and asked for advice about this passage, he received the following reply: "Those two bad errors in my translation of *Mémoire* appear (alas) in the American edition of *Rimbaud*. . . . A few students these last years have mentioned the reference in *Ada* and I have never had the courage to read the book or the passage. Now you have given it to me, and I feel better knowing that you and Mr. Walker may point out my own corrections." For additional comments, which appeared after this note had been written, see Bryan Boyd, "A Marsh Marigold Is a Marsh Marigold Is a Marsh Marigold," *Vladimir Nabokov Research Newsletter* 1 (Fall 1978), 13–16.

p. 64. *les robes vertes*, etc.: the green and washed-out frocks of the little girls. *Commentary*: The eleventh line of Rimbaud's "Mémoire."

p. 65. *en vain*, etc.: In vain, one gains in play
The Oka river and Palm Bay . . .
Commentary: In the text Ada translates into French the first two lines of "The Garden" by Andrew Marvell (1621–1678) as follows: "En vain on s'amuse à gagner / L'Oka, la Baie du Palmier" (p. 65). The lines from Marvell are: "How vainly men themselves amaze / To win the Palm, the Oke, or Bayes." Ada's French, which is a pun on Marvell's lines rather than a translation of them, is given a literal translation back into English in Darkbloom's note. The result is a wild distortion of Marvell's meaning and further satire of the translation process (e.g., "themselves amaze / To win" becomes "s'amuse à gagner," which then becomes "gains in play"). Cf. our second note to p. 3 above ("Severnïya Territorii"). For another allusion to Marvell's poem, see the note to p. 159 below.

p. 69. *groote*: Dutch, 'great'. *Commentary*: The word can also mean "large" or "big." In his "Dutch Footnotes to Nabokov's *Ada*" (in *A Book of Things about Vladimir Nabokov*, ed. Proffer) Francis Bulhof says that *groote* is "the pre-1934 spelling" (p. 291). This is incorrect. There was a partial Dutch spelling reform in 1934 and another attempt in 1938, the latter mainly to consolidate the orthography used in Holland and Belgium. But the war intervened, and it was not until 1947 that conclusive reforms were made. Thus *groote* is the pre-1947, not the pre-1934, spelling. In post-1947 Dutch the un-inflected form of the adjective is spelled *groot*, the inflected form *grote*, and the spelling *groote* is considered incorrect. In *Ada* the word occurs in a "Dutch-language illustrated paper," and the authors have verified that the spelling *groote* continued to be used in Dutch newspapers after 1934.

Even such a minor detail as this may be intended to underscore the chronological confusion of life on Antiterra. Exactly where are we in Terran time? In the nineteenth century, where Mlle Larivière is writing Maupassant's stories? In the latter half of the twentieth century, where people wear bikinis and say "I goofed"? Or in a vague "pre-1947," where Dutch newspapers still use the spelling *groote*?

p. 71. pensive reeds: Pascal's metaphor of man, *un roseau pensant.* Commentary: The French philosopher Blaise Pascal (1623–1662) wrote *Pensées* (*Thoughts*), first published in 1670. In the third chapter of this work, "Marques de la grandeur de l'homme" ("Signs of the Greatness of Man"), Pascal says: "L'homme n'est qu'un roseau, le plus faible de la nature; mais c'est un roseau pensant" ("Man is but a reed, the frailest in nature; but he is a thinking reed").

p. 77. Osberg: another good-natured anagram, scrambling the name of a writer with whom the author of *Lolita* has been rather comically compared. Incidentally, that title's pronunciation has nothing to do with English or Russian (*pace* an anonymous owl in a recent issue of *TLS*). Commentary: The anagram refers to Jorge Luis Borges (1899–), Argentinian writer. Perhaps it also glances at "Oseberg," the name of a farm in Norway where a famous Viking ship (the Oseberg Ship) was found in 1904. (We are grateful to Dr. Philip Anderson for this suggestion.) Since the Oseberg Ship was a burial ship containing skeletons, the anagram may not be as "good-natured" as Darkbloom claims but may instead communicate Nabokov's opinion of the vitality of Borges' work and its likelihood of survival. Cf. our note to p. 53 above (*Les Amours du Dr Mertvago*). When an interviewer asked Nabokov about critics who link his work with that of Borges, he responded, "They would do better to link . . . Borges with Anatole France" (*Strong Opinions*, p. 155). And Nabokov was quoted in *Time* (23 May 1969) as saying of Borges, "At first Véra and I were delighted by reading him. We felt we were on a portico, but we have learned that there was no house" (p. 83).

The "anonymous owl" reviewed Carl R. Proffer's critical book *Keys to "Lolita,"* his edition of the *Letters of Nikolai Gogol*, and his translation of Gogol's *Dead Souls.* The owl also reviewed Nabokov's

Russian translation of *Lolita* and the English translation by Dmitri
and Vladimir Nabokov of *King, Queen, Knave* ("Profferings," *TLS*,
10 October 1969, 1153–54). The offending passage reads in part:

> Nabokov's rough and recalcitrant English coruscates with
> brilliant impurities absent from his exquisitely modulated—
> but docile—Russian.
>
> The essential un-Englishness of Nabokov's English is em-
> phasized in the lyrical passage at the beginning of *Lolita*,
> where he gives instructions about the pronunciation of his her-
> oine's name ("the tip of the tongue taking a trip of three steps
> down the palate to tap, at three, on the teeth"). Unfortunately,
> however, the English "t" does not tap on the teeth at all,
> being—phonetically speaking—alveolar. Dental "ts" begin,
> one might note, at Calais. Or—to put the same point rather
> differently and in transatlantic terms—the genius of Nabo-
> kov's prose must surely derive in part from the presence of an
> invigorating homoeopathic infusion of Hyman Kaplanism.

The ignorance of the reviewer is apparent when we recall that Nabokov has been very specific about the pronunciation of "Lolita" and
about the various languages that can be imagined as contributing to
it. The following comments in *Strong Opinions* (pp. 25, 53, 138) are
from interviews published, respectively, in 1964, 1965, and 1969.
The first two therefore predate the comments by the anonymous
owl; the third comes eight months later.

> ["Lolita"] should not be pronounced as you and most
> Americans pronounce it: Low-lee-ta, with a heavy, clammy "L"
> and a long "o." No, the first syllable should be as in "lollipop,"
> the "L" liquid and delicate, the "lee" not too sharp. Spaniards
> and Italians pronounce it, of course, with exactly the necessary
> note of archness and caress.

> Note that for the necessary effect of dreamy tenderness
> both "l"s and the "t" and indeed the whole word should be
> iberized and not pronounced the American way with crushed
> "l's," a coarse "t," and a long "o": . . . Now comes the Russian.
> Here the first syllable of her name sounds more like an "ah"
> sound than an "o" sound, but the rest is like Spanish.

> Let me take this neat opportunity to correct a curious mis-
> conception proffered [*sic*] by an anonymous owl in a London
> weekly a couple of months ago. "Lolita" should not be pro-

nounced in the English or Russian fashion (as he thinks it should), but with a trill of Latin "l's" and a delicate toothy "t."

Furthermore, since Humbert is neither English nor Russian but like his father "a salad of racial genes," there is no reason his pronunciation of "Lolita" should accord with conventional notions of how Continental or English or transatlantic speech ought to sound.

p. 83. *La Rivière de diamants*: Maupassant and his *'La Parure'* (p. 87) did not exist on Antiterra. *Commentary*: *La Rivière de diamants* means *The Diamond Necklace*. In *Ada* this is the title of a short story by Mlle Larivière that is the antiterrestrial version of "La Parure" ("The Finery"; 1884) by Guy de Maupassant (1850–1893). In Maupassant's tale Mathilde Loisel, the attractive wife of a poor clerk, borrows a diamond necklace from her rich friend Jeanne Forestier to wear to a ball. At the ball she is a great success and is favorably noticed by her husband's superior, who is their host. But on the way home Mathilde loses the necklace. She and her husband borrow money, buy a new necklace for 36,000 francs, and return it to Jeanne as if nothing had happened. They then work for ten years to pay off the debt. Mathilde's beauty fades as she does menial chores to earn money, but finally the debt is paid. Soon afterwards she encounters Jeanne, who is still youthful-looking. Proud of her accomplishment, Mathilde tells Jeanne about the substitution and about her years of toil to pay the debt. The twist in the tale arrives when Jeanne exclaims in the story's final words: "Oh! ma pauvre Mathilde! Mais la mienne était fausse. Elle valait au plus cinq cents francs!" ("Oh! My poor Mathilde! But mine [i.e., my necklace] was false. It was worth five hundred francs at the most!").

In the summary of Mlle Larivière's story given in *Ada* some of Maupassant's details are parodically exaggerated (the couple work "for thirty or forty horrible years," the new necklace costs half a million francs). But the French words quoted in the summary are lifted directly from Maupassant: "he, half-paralyzed by a half-century of *copie* [copy-work] in their *mansarde* [garret], she, unrecognizably coarsened by the washing of floors *à grande eau* [by the 'swilling' of floors]" (p. 83). Mlle Larivière's title, in addition to echoing the name Larivière, is the phrase Maupassant uses to denote the necklace in his story. In English the story is known as "The Necklace." Larivière is also the name of the eminent physician in Flaubert's *Madame Bovary* (1857) who visits Emma after she has poisoned herself. Emma dies anyway, of course, just as the art of fiction, in Nabokov's view, dies under the ministrations of Maupassant-Larivière. For another possible allusion contained in the name Larivière, see our second note to p. 142 below.

Although Nabokov makes fun of "La Parure" and of its *pointe assassine* (see our second note to p. 541 below), the story nonetheless mirrors one of his key artistic concerns: the interplay between chance and determinism. One central passage from the story could almost stand as an epigraph to novels such as *The Defense, Pale Fire,* and *Ada:* "Que serait-il arrivé si elle n'avait point perdu cette parure? Qui sait? qui sait? Comme la vie est singulière, changeante! Comme il faut peu de chose pour vous perdre ou vous sauver!" ("What would have happened if she had not lost that finery? Who knows? who knows? How strange life is, how changeable! How little it takes for you to be lost or saved!").

p. 83. *vibgyor:* violet-indigo-blue-green-yellow-orange-red. *Commentary:* In other words, a rainbow. "Vibgyor" is a word invented by reversing the Terran acronym for the colors of the visible spectrum, "roygbiv," often written as the name Roy G. Biv and used as a mnemonic device. Such a reversal of the spectrum can be seen in the secondary rainbow that is sometimes visible above the primary rainbow. "Vibgyor" seems to allude specifically to this mirror-image of the rainbow and, more generally, to the many mirrorings and distortions of primary "reality" in *Ada.*

p. 87. *pointe assassine:* the point (of a story or poem) that murders artistic merit. *Commentary:* See our second note to p. 541 below ("assassin pun").

p. 92. *ce beau jardin,* etc.: This beautiful garden blooms in May, but in Winter never, never, never, never, never is green, etc. *Commentary:* Another literal English translation of a French pun on an English original (see our note to p. 65 above). The original is the following passage from Shakespeare's *King Lear:* "Why should a dog, a horse, a rat, have life, / And thou no breath at all? Thou'lt come no more, / Never, never, never, never, never!" (5.3.306–8). Lear's monologue refers to Cordelia's death. Ada's "revised monologue"

Ce beau jardin fleurit en mai,
    Mais en hiver
Jamais, jamais, jamais, jamais, jamais
N'est vert, n'est vert, n'est vert, n'est vert,
    n'est vert.

puns on "n'est vert" ("is not green") and the similar-sounding "never." It helps the pun to imagine the trochee of "never" being pronounced as an iamb and changed into "n'est vert" by a speaker with a French accent.

This pun on Lear's five-fold "never" recurs in a passage of *Ada* that parodies the interior monologue in part 7, chapter 30, of *Anna Karenina* (see our note to p. 61 above): "Tolstoy's novel. First exponent of the inner monologue. . . . *N'est vert, n'est vert, n'est vert.* . . . Never, never shall I hear again her 'botanical' voice . . ." (p. 300). There is also an allusion to the five-fold "never" in a speculation on the afterlife in *Despair*: "never, never, never, never, never will your soul in that other world be quite sure that the sweet gentle spirits crowding about it are not fiends in disguise" (p. 112). In a letter to Nabokov dated 20 April 1942, Edmund Wilson writes: "Beside the verse of Shakespeare's later plays, Pushkin seems pedantically regular. He almost never varies the iamb, whereas with Shakespeare any substitution is possible. I don't remember in Pushkin even any such verse as 'Never, never, never, never, never!' in *King Lear*. It may be that neither you nor Mirsky, trained on classic Russian verse, quite realizes what English verse is like" (*The Nabokov–Wilson Letters*, pp. 59–60). Perhaps this comment by Wilson helped to fix Nabokov's resolve to show in his English fiction and poetry that he indeed realized "what English verse is like."

p. 106. *Ada who liked crossing orchids: she crosses here two French authors, Baudelaire and Chateaubriand. Commentary:* Specifically, Ada's lines

Mon enfant, ma soeur
Songe à l'épaisseur
Du grand chêne à Tagne;
Songe à la montagne,
Songe à la douceur—

cross the first two lines of "L'Invitation au voyage" ("Invitation to the Voyage") from *Les Fleurs du mal* (1857) by Charles Baudelaire (1821–1867) with the twenty-sixth line of the *romance* sung by Lautrec in *Les Aventures du dernier Abencérage* (*The Adventures of the Last Abencérage*; 1826) by François René de Chateaubriand (1768–1848). The lines from Baudelaire are "Mon enfant, ma soeur, / Songe à la douceur" ("My child, my sister, / Dream of the sweetness"). The line from Chateaubriand is "Et ma montagne, et le grand chêne" ("And my mountain, and the big oak"). The other words of the pastiche are supplied by Ada. The line from Chateaubriand and the line that precedes it in the original poem are, as Darkbloom points out in his note to p. 138, "one of the leitmotivs of the present novel."

Chateaubriand composed his *romance* not later than 1804. It appeared in the *Mercure* on 31 May 1806 and was published separately two more times before finally being incorporated into *Les Aventures du dernier Abencérage*. As Chateaubriand points out in a footnote to the novella, he wrote the *romance* to be sung to a traditional mountain tune of Auvergne. The music is reproduced in *Atala, René, Le Dernier Abencérage*, ed. Aug. Dupont (Paris: Larousse, n.d., p. 139).

There is in *Ada* a mosaic of allusions to travel and exile, drawn from the lives and works of several writers. (Chateaubriand himself lived in exile in England from 1793 to 1800.) These allusions serve in part as a fictive refraction of Nabokov's own exile from Russia and his subsequent cosmopolitan life. They also help to create *Ada*'s pervasive atmosphere of nostalgia and underscore its concern with recovering and preserving lost time in art. Here the intertwining of Chateaubriand's *romance* and Baudelaire's "L'Invitation au voyage" reflects several facets of these themes. The *romance* is performed in *Le Dernier Abencérage* by a Frenchman longing for his homeland and for the happiness he knew there as a child. The opening lines are:

> Combien j'ai douce souvenance
> Du joli lieu de ma naissance!
> Ma soeur, qu'ils étaient beaux les jours
>   De France!

> How sweetly I remember
> The pretty place of my birth!
> My sister, how beautiful they were, those days
>   In France!

"L'Invitation au voyage" expresses a longing for escape to a realm of enchantment and artifice. It begins:

> Mon enfant, ma soeur,
>   Songe à la douceur
> D'aller là-bas vivre ensemble!
>   Aimer à loisir,
>   Aimer et mourir

> Au pays qui te ressemble!
> . . . .

> Là, tout n'est qu'ordre et beauté,
> Luxe, calme et volupté.

> My child, my sister,
>   Dream of the sweetness
> Of going over there to live together!

Loving at leisure,
Loving and dying
In the country that resembles you!

.   .   .   .

There, all is but order and beauty,
Luxury, calm and sensual pleasure.

Both poems open with an apostrophe to a "sister," who is invited to
share the poet's thought and emotion. They thus echo the sibling
relationship and the creative collaboration of Van and Ada. Furthermore, the movements of the two poems—in Chateaubriand a movement into the past to recover lost time, in Baudelaire a movement
out of "reality" to a region of aesthetic delight—become in *Ada* interlocking aspects of the same creative impulse.

Not only is Chateaubriand's *romance* about exile and loss: so is
the novella that contains it. *Le Dernier Abencérage* is the story of
Aben-Hamet, the last member of the Moorish tribe of Abencérage,
who returns to his homeland in Spain, falls in love with a beautiful
maiden, and finally ends his days in exile in Africa. The novella
begins:

> Lorsque Boabdil, dernier roi de Grenade, fut obligé d'aban-
> donner le royaume de ses pères, il s'arrêta au sommet du mont
> Padul. . . . A la vue de ce beau pays . . . Boabdil se prit à verser
> des larmes. La sultane Aïxa, sa mère . . . l'accompagnait dans
> son exil. . . . Ils descendirent de la montagne, et Grenade dis-
> parut à leurs yeux pour toujours.
>
> Les Maures d'Espagne . . . se dispersèrent en Afrique. . . .
> les Abencérages se fixèrent dans les environs de Tunis. . . .
>
> Ces familles portèrent dans leur patrie nouvelle le sou-
> venir de leur ancienne patrie. Le *Paradis de Grenade* vivait
> toujours dans leur mémoire. . . .

> When Baobdil, the last king of Granada, was obliged to
> abandon the kingdom of his fathers, he paused at the summit
> of Mount Padul. . . . At the sight of this beautiful country . . .
> Boabdil began to shed tears. His mother, the sultana Aïxa . . .
> accompanied him into his exile. . . . They came down from the
> mountain, and Granada disappeared from their eyes forever.
>
> The Moors of Spain . . . were scattered throughout Af-
> rica. . . . the Abencérage tribe settled around Tunis. . . .
>
> These families took with them into their new homeland
> the memory of their former homeland. The "Paradise of Gra-
> nada" lived always in their memory. . . .

The Ardors and Arbors of Ardis, the Russian childhood of *Speak, Memory*, Charles Kinbote's Zembla, Humbert Humbert's princedom by the sea—the tone and mood of many works by Nabokov is implied in these opening lines from *Le Dernier Abencérage*. Chateaubriand's *romance* reflects in miniature the novella that contains it. Nabokov's allusions to the *romance*, the novella, and the Baudelaire poem reflect, in turn, the aims and purposes of *Ada*. And *Ada* itself reflects and allegorizes the exile, the losses, and the aesthetic compensations of Nabokov's own life.

Similar ideas are articulated in *Speak, Memory* in another passage that alludes to Chateaubriand's poem: "Tamara, Russia, the wildwood grading into old gardens, my northern birches and firs, . . . *et la montagne et le grand chêne*—these are things that fate one day bundled up pell-mell and tossed into the sea, completely severing me from my boyhood. I wonder, however, whether there is really much to be said for more anesthetic destinies. . . . The break in my own destiny affords me in retrospect a syncopal kick that I would not have missed for worlds" (pp. 249–50). Here "anesthetic" is used in two senses: (1) lacking in pain and suffering, and (2) lacking in artistic feeling and aesthetic perception ("an-aesthetic"). *Speak, Memory* is an explicit and *Ada* an implicit commentary on how exile ensures that the anaesthetic destiny will never be Nabokov's.

For other direct and indirect references to travel and exile in *Ada*, see the discussions in our notes of Jules Verne and Phileas Fogg (p. 5, third note), Guido Cavalcanti (p. 23, third note), Edmond Rostand and Jaufré Rudel (p. 29), Jorge Guillén (p. 46), John Hanning Speke (p. 120), Thomas Mayne Reid and Alexander Pushkin (p. 171), François Coppée (p. 246), Jules Verne and Captain Grant (p. 334), Cyrano de Bergerac (p. 339, first note), Seneca (p. 355), and John Steinbeck (p. 403, first note).

p. 114. Mlle Stopchin: a representative of Mme de Ségur, née Rostopchine, author of *Les Malheurs de Sophie* (nomenclatorially occupied on Antiterra by *Les Malheurs de Swann*). *Commentary*: See the note to p. 55 above.

p. 114. Ashette: 'Cendrillon' in the French original. *Commentary*: "Cendrillon" is the French for "Cinderella." "Ashette," like "Cendrillon" and "Cinderella," means "little cinder" or "little ash." For other allusions to Cinderella, see pp. 228 and 397 of *Ada* and Darkbloom's notes to these pages.

p. 120. The Nile is settled: a famous telegram sent by an African explorer. *Commentary*: According to Alan Morehead, *The White Nile* (New York: Harper, 1971), p. 78, these words were not telegraphed. They were spoken by John Hanning Speke on 22 June 1863 before the Royal Geographical Society in London. Speke meant that the mystery of the Nile's source had been settled.

p. 127. *leur chute*, etc.: their fall is slow . . . one can follow them with one's eyes, recognizing— *Commentary*: The French lines here translated by Darkbloom are from the sonnet "Matin d'octobre" by François Coppée (1842–1908). The poem appeared in the collection *Le Cahier rouge* (*The Red Notebook*) in 1874:

C'est l'heure exquise et matinale
Que rougit un soleil soudain.
A travers la brume automnale
Tombent les feuilles du jardin.

Leur chute est lente. On peut les suivre
Du regard en reconnaissant
Le chêne à sa feuille de cuivre,
L'érable à sa feuille de sang.

Les dernières, les plus rouillées,
Tombent des branches dépouillées;
Mais ce n'est pas l'hiver encore.

Une blonde lumière arrose
La nature, et, dans l'air tout rose,
On croirait qu'il neige de l'or.

This is the exquisite morning hour
That a sudden sun reddens.
Through the autumn mist
The garden's leaves are falling.

Their fall is slow. One can follow them
With the gaze, recognizing
The oak with its leaf of copper,
The maple with its leaf of blood.

The last ones, the most rust-colored,
Fall from the denuded branches;
But it is not yet winter.

A yellow light besprinkles
Nature, and, in the air, all pink,
One would think it was snowing gold.

It is appropriate that this sentimental sonnet be associated here with

Mlle Larivière, since she is frequently an expounder of trite art in *Ada.*

p. 127. Lowden: a portmanteau name combining two contemporary bards. *Commentary*: Robert Lowell (1917–1977) and W. H. Auden (1907–1973). The two bards are linked because of Nabokov's low opinion of their accomplishments as translators. He says in *Strong Opinions*: "I do not parody Mr. Auden anywhere in *Ada*. I'm not sufficiently familiar with his poetry for that. I do know, however, a few of his translations—and deplore the blunders he so lightheartedly permits himself. Robert Lowell, of course, is the greater offender" (p. 151).

p. 132. *Chiron*: doctor among centaurs: an allusion to Updike's best novel. *Commentary*: In Greek mythology Chiron is a wise and just centaur, and a "doctor among centaurs" because he teaches the art of healing to Asclepius. John Updike (1934–) published *The Centaur* in 1963.

p. 136. Heinrich Müller: author of *Poxus*, etc. *Commentary*: German version of novelist Henry Miller (1891–). Just as Nabokov later invokes "the Burning Swine" (Swinburne) and calls down "A pest on his anapests" (p. 367), Darkbloom here puts a pox on Henry Miller's trilogy *The Rosy Crucifixion*, consisting of *Sexus* (1949), *Plexus* (1953), and *Nexus* (1960).

p. 138. *Ma soeur te souvient-il encore*: first line of the third sextet of Chateaubriand's *Romance à Hélène* ('Combien j'ai douce souvenance') composed to an Auvergne tune that he heard during a trip to Mont Dore in 1805 and later inserted in his novella *Le Dernier Abencérage*. The final (fifth) sextet begins with '*Oh! qui me rendra mon Hélène. Et ma montagne, et le grand chêne*'—one of the leitmotivs of the present novel. *Commentary*: Darkbloom forgets to translate the two lines that form the leitmotif: "Oh! who will give me back my Helen / And my mountain and the big oak?" See also our note to p. 106 above.

p. 142. Rockette: corresponds to Maupassant's *La Petite Rocque*. *Commentary*: The title of the story by Guy de Maupassant is "La Petite Roque" ("Little Roque"; 1885), not "La Petite Rocque," as in the Darkbloom note. The distortion is slight but perhaps intentional. "Roque" is the family name of the girl in the Maupassant story; *rocque* is the French word for the rook in chess, thus giving Maupassant's title a Nabokovian twist. The name given the girl in Mlle Larivière's version of the story, "Rockette," means "little rock" and may be intended whimsically to recall the capital of Arkansas or, perhaps, the famous dancing troupe at Radio City Music Hall, the Rockettes. See also our notes to p. 154 and p. 155 below.

p. 142. *chaleur du lit*: bed warmth. *Commentary*: Mlle Larivière's preference for writing in bed may allude to a famous French author who also found inspiration in *la chaleur du lit*: Marcel Proust. Much of Proust's *A la recherche du temps perdu* was written in bed. There is, moreover, a family in Proust's novel named Larivière. Or perhaps it alludes to Vladimir Nabokov, who says in *Strong Opinions*: "Thirty years ago I used to write in bed, dipping my pen into a bedside inkwell" (p. 139).

p. 145. *mironton*, etc.: burden of a popular song. *Commentary*: Not the burden of a particular song but one that frequently occurs in popular songs in France.

p. 154. *au cou rouge*, etc.: with the ruddy and stout neck of a widower still full of sap. *Commentary*: A distortion and embellishment of the description of M. Renardet, the rapist and murderer in Maupassant's "La Petite Roque." Maupassant speaks only of "son cou puissant et rouge" ("his powerful and red neck"). The rest of the phrase does not appear in the story.

p. 155. *gloutonnerie*: gourmandise. *Commentary*: The phrase "gloutonnerie impardonnable" ("unforgivable gluttony") is presented in the text of *Ada* as if it might be a quotation from Maupassant's "La Petite Roque." In fact the phrase does not appear in the story. Darkbloom's translation of *gloutonnerie* ("gluttony") as "gourmandise" is a whimsical understatement in light of the gruesome events of Maupassant's tale.

p. 159. Stumbling on melons . . . arrogant fennels: allusions to passages in Marvell's 'Garden' and Rimbaud's 'Mémoire'. *Commentary*: Andrew Marvell's poem "The Garden" contains the lines "Stumbling on Melons, as I pass, / Insnar'd with Flow'rs, I fall on grass" (stanza 5, vv. 39–40). Lines 17–19 of Arthur Rimbaud's poem "Mémoire" read: "Madame se tient trop debout dans la prairie / prochaine où neigent les fils du travail; l'ombrelle / aux doigts; foulant l'ombelle; trop fière pour elle" ("Madame holds herself too erect in the prairie / adjoining, where the sons [threads] of toil are snowing; umbrella / in her fingers; treading upon the umbellate flower; too proud for her"). *Fils* can be translated either as "threads" or "sons," and critical opinion varies as to what Rimbaud meant. The word *ombelle* is a generic term for plants with umbellate flowers (umbellifers), of which the fennel (French *fenouil*) is one. See also our notes to p. 64 and p. 65 above.

p. 168. *amour propre, sale amour*: pun borrowed from Tolstoy's 'Resurrection'. *Commentary*: The pun consists in the possible double meaning of *amour propre* ("self-love" and "clean love") and the paradoxical clash of the latter with *sale amour* ("dirty love"). It occurs in the following passage from book 1, chapter 27, of *Resurrection* (1899; quoted in the Traill translation with the French translated by the authors of these notes):

> "What does all this mean? *Comme cela m'intrigue* [How it intrigues me]," said Katerína Alexéyevna. "I must find out. Probably some *affaire d'amour propre, il est très susceptible, notre cher Mitya* [affaire of *amour propre*, he is very susceptible, our dear Mitya]."
> "*Plutôt une affaire d'amour sale* [Rather an affair of *amour sale*]," Missy was about to say, but she stopped and looked in front of her with a face from which all the light had gone, quite different from when she looked at Nekhlúdov. She could not utter the vulgar little pun even to Katerína Alexéyevna. . . .

p. 169. *quelque petite*, etc.: some little laundress. *Commentary*: An allusion to the laundress of Touraine, with whom the narrator suspects Albertine of having an affair in Proust's *A la recherche du temps perdu*.

p. 171. *The Headless Horseman*: Mayne Reid's title is ascribed here to Pushkin, author of *The Bronze Horseman*. *Commentary*: Thomas Mayne Reid (1818–1883) was born in Ireland and came to the United States in 1840, where he worked at a variety of jobs including actor, Indian fighter, journalist, and storekeeper. He returned to Europe in 1849, then visited the United States again from 1867 to 1870. He drew upon his broad travels in some seventy novelistic romances, many of which dealt with the American West. His books were enormously popular with boys all over the world. In *Speak, Memory* Nabokov includes a half-loving, half-ironic discussion of *The Headless Horseman* and of its reverberations throughout his life (pp. 70, 197, 200–203). Alexander Pushkin (1799–1837) wrote the narrative poem *The Bronze Horseman* in 1833. The combination of Pushkin with Mayne Reid is appropriate not only because both authors wrote about horsemen but also because both careers were marked by travel and exile. In May 1820 Pushkin was banished from St. Petersburg for his political poems and exiled to southern Russia. Transferred to Kishinev (1820–1823) and then to Odessa (1823–1824), he once again offended the authorities and was exiled, this time to his mother's estate of Mikhaylovskoe. Nicholas I allowed him to return to Moscow in 1826.

p. 176. Shivering aurora, laborious old Chose: a touch of Baudelaire. *Commentary*: A touch of Baudelaire's "Le Crépuscule du matin" ("Morning Twilight"). The poem, an evocation of Paris at dawn, ends with the following lines:

L'aurore grelottante en robe rose et verte
S'avançait lentement sur la Seine déserte,
Et le sombre Paris, en se frottant les yeux,
Empoignait ses outils, vieillard laborieux.

Dawn shivering in a pink and green dress
Was slowly advancing over the deserted Seine
And somber Paris, rubbing its eyes,
Picked up its tools, a laborious old man.

Nabokov also quotes a line from this poem in *Bend Sinister* (1973), p. 115, and some words from it in *Lolita* (*The Annotated Lolita*, p. 164). "Chose" is the Antiterran version of Cambridge, England, where Nabokov studied at the University from 1919 to 1922.

p. 187. Yellow-blue Vass: the phrase is consonant with *ya lyublyu vas* ('I love you' in Russian). *Commentary*: When Nabokov was teaching Russian at Wellesley College, he used a technique of "interlingual association," whereby students were taught to remember Russian phrases by associating them with similar-sounding English phrases. One of the associations was *ya lyublyu vas* and "yellow-blue vase." See Field, *Nabokov: His Life in Part*, p. 248.

p. 190. *mais, ma pauvre amie*, etc.: but, my poor friend, it was imitation jewelry. *Commentary*: A slightly distorted version of the concluding words of Maupassant's "La Parure." See our first note to p. 83 above.

p. 191. *elle le mangeait*, etc.: she devoured him with her eyes. *Commentary*: In *Speak, Memory* Nabokov says his Uncle Ruka used to sing a French song that contained the line "Ils se regardent tous deux, en se mangeant des yeux" ("They both look at each other, devouring each other with their eyes"; p. 70). But the echo may be accidental: *manger des yeux* is a common expression in French.

p. 192. *petits vers*, etc.: fugitive poetry and silk worms. *Commentary*: Ada's comment: "I've given up all that stuff—*petit vers, vers de soie*" puns on French *vers*, which means both "verses" and "worms." *Vers de soie* (more properly, *vers à soie*) are "silkworms."

p. 203. Ero: thus the h-dropping policeman in Wells' *Invisible Man* defined the latter's treacherous friend. *Commentary*: Neither the policeman nor anyone else in *The Invisible Man* (1897) by H. G. Wells (1866–1946) drops his aitches. In most editions of the work the passage in question reads, " 'Dr. Kemp's a hero,' he said." Two editions have a variant: " 'Dr. Kemp's in here,' he said." But this variant makes no sense in light of the context. Griffin, a scientific genius who has made himself invisible, blunders into Dr. Kemp's house. Kemp at first tries to help him but subsequently becomes frightened and attempts to turn him over to the police. Griffin, however, escapes. In chapter 27, "The Siege of Kemp's House," Griffin returns to take revenge. He forces his way into Kemp's house despite resistance from two policemen. During the ensuing melee Kemp flees in terror from a back window. The policeman's remark, "Dr. Kemp's a hero," is a sarcastic comment on Kemp's lack of courage.

In order to remain completely invisible Griffin wears no clothes and no shoes. When in the following chapter Kemp tries to elude Griffin, he does so by running over broken glass, flints, gravel paths, and so forth. Thus in *Ada*, Van, followed by barefooted Ada and Lucette, "changed his course from gravel path to velvet lawn (reversing the action of Dr. Ero, pursued by the Invisible Albino in one of the greatest novels in English literature)" (p. 203). For another allusion to *The Invisible Man*, see p. 133 of *Ada*.

p. 231. Beer Tower: pun on 'Tourbière'. *Commentary*: Blanche's family lives in a village that Blanche calls "La Tourbière." The name means "the peat bog" in French (see p. 228 of *Ada*). If the syllables were divided and the second syllable construed as an adjective, the result would be "Beer Tower" (*tour* is "tower" and *bière* is "beer").

p. 232. *cousinage*: cousinhood is dangerous neighborhood. *Commentary*: This adage is lifted from Tolstoy's *War and Peace* (book 1, part 1, chapter 9).

p. 237. *kontretan*: Russian mispronunciation of *contretemps*. *Commentary*: *Contretemps* means "mishap" or "untoward event" in French.

p. 243. *filius aquae*: 'son of water', bad pun on *filum aquae*, the middle way, 'the thread of the stream'. *Commentary*: If we read the phrase as "son of Aqua," then the pun is not as bad as Darkbloom would have us believe, and Demon's words become a wicked, if unintentional, reference to Van's parentage.

p. 245. *seins durs*: mispronunciation of *sans dire* 'without saying'. *Commentary*: *Seins durs* means "hard breasts" in French.

p. 246. *Lorsque*, etc.: When her fiancé had gone to war, the unfortunate and noble maiden closed her piano, sold her elephant. *Commentary*: The lines here translated are a comical distortion of the opening lines of the sentimental narrative poem "La Veillée" ("The Vigil") by François Coppée. The poem appeared in the collection *Les Récits et les élégies* (*Narratives and Elegies*; 1878) and is one of Coppée's so-called *récits épiques* ("epic narratives"). In the poem Roger, the fiancé of Irène de Grandfief, goes to war. While Irène waits anxiously for news of him, there is a skirmish near her castle. Irène takes in one of the enemy wounded and promises the doctor she will watch over him all night. Alas! She discovers that this very man has killed her fiancé. Should she take revenge by stabbing the man in his sleep? Should she withhold the medicine the doctor has left and allow the man to die? She turns her eyes to an image of Christ hanging over the bed and there finds the strength to put her wicked thoughts behind her and minister to her fiancé's killer. When the doctor arrives in the morning, he finds Irène still caring for the wounded man and sees that during the trials of the night her hair has turned white. The poem's opening lines are:

> Dès que son fiancé fut parti pour la guerre,
> Sans larmes dans les yeux ni désespoir vulgaire,
> Irène de Grandfief, la noble et pure enfant,
> Revêtit les habits qu'elle avait au couvent,
> La robe noire avec l'étroite pèlerine
> Et la petite croix d'argent sur la poitrine.
> Elle ôta ses bijoux, ferma son piano,
> Et, gardant seulement à son doigt cet anneau,
> Seul souvenir du soir de printemps où, ravie,
> Au vicomte Roger elle engagea sa vie,
> Aveugle à ce qu'on fait et sourde à ce qu'on dit,
> Près du foyer, stoïque et pâle, elle attendit.

> The moment her fiancé had left for the war,
> Without tears in her eyes or vulgar despair,
> Irène de Grandfief, the pure and noble child,
> Put on again the clothes she wore in the convent,
> The black dress with the narrow cloak
> And the little silver cross upon her breast.
> She took off her jewels, closed her piano,
> And keeping only that ring on her finger,
> Sole reminder of the spring evening when, enraptured,
> She pledged her life to the Vicomte Roger,
> Blind to what people do and deaf to what they say,
> Near the hearth, stoical and pale, she waited.

Demon's "gobble *enfant*" (p. 246) is a mocking distortion of the phrase "noble enfant," the sound of which it approximates. But "gobble *enfant*" is not, in fact, "genuine," as Demon claims, for Coppée's phrase "la noble et pure enfant" has been changed in the text to "la pauvre et noble enfant," thus making Demon's pun possible.

Ada shares Irène's pale skin and preference for black dresses. But there is ironic humor in the equation of Ada ("Ada de Grandfief" [p. 246]) with the chaste and patient Irène, since Ada, unlike Irène, is neither chaste nor particularly patient in matters of love.

The allusions to Coppée in *Ada* (see also our first note to p. 127 above and our note to p. 558 below) obliquely reflect the motif of exile. One of Coppée's collections of poems was called *L'Exilée* (*The Exiled Maiden*).

p. 300. *marais noir*: black tide. *Commentary*: *Marais noir* means "black swamp," not "black tide." But in the text of *Ada* a different phrase appears—*marée noire*, which literally means "black tide" and is used colloquially to mean "oil slick." In the text we read, "Poor Stream of Consciousness, *marée noire* by now." But the note invites us to read, "Poor Stream of Consciousness, *marais noir* by now." *Marais* and *marée* are homophones in French. But since the genders of the nouns differ and since the adjectives agree with the nouns in both places, this almost seems a deliberate alteration or revision of the text by the notes. Could it be that Darkbloom decided to perpetrate a Kinbotean distortion and mistranslation of the text in order to suggest that the stream of consciousness technique, which had changed from a stream to an oil slick by the time *Ada* was written, had changed from an oil slick to a black swamp by the time Darkbloom wrote the notes?

p. 304. Tapper: 'Wild Violet', as well as 'Birdfoot' (p. 306), reflects the 'pansy' character of Van's adversary and of the two seconds. *Commentary*: This passage is a cat's cradle of allusions to homosexuality and is much more complex than Darkbloom's note suggests. "Birdfoot" alludes to the Bird's-Foot Violet, whose scientific name is *Viola pedata*. This scientific name yields a double allusion to homosexuality: (1) in *Viola*, since violet or lavender is a color traditionally associated with homosexuality and since the *Viola pedata* has large purple or blue flowers; (2) in *pedata* (Latin, "footed"), since this word suggests the French term *pédéraste* ("homosexual") and its colloquial derivatives *pédé*, *pédale*, and *pédéro*. The name "Tapper" alludes to another French term for a homosexual man: *tapette*. Both "Wild Violet" and "Birdfoot" allude to "pansy" and thence to homosexuality, since "pansy," in addition to being a slang term for a homosexual man, is a flower belonging to the violet family. "Wild Violet" may contain a further allusion to one of homosexuality's most famous exponents: Oscar Wilde.

p. 321. *encore un*, etc.: one more 'baby ghost' (pun). *Commentary*: The crucial word here, *enfantôme*, is a telescoping of French *enfant* ("child") and *fantôme* ("ghost").

p. 325. the last paragraph of Part One imitates, in significant brevity of intonation (as if spoken by an outside voice), a famous Tolstoyan ending, with Van in the role of Kitty Lyovin. *Commentary*: The passage imitated is the ending of part 5, chapter 20, of *Anna Karenina*: "The doctor confirmed his former suppositions in regard to Kitty. Her indisposition consisted of pregnancy" (the Garnett translation, revised by Guerney).

p. 331. *bateau ivre*: 'sottish ship', title of Rimbaud's poem here used instead of 'ship of fools'. *Commentary*: A literal translation of the title of Rimbaud's poem "Le Bateau ivre" (1871) is "The Drunken Boat." Darkbloom's translation—"sottish ship"—indicates that the reader should extract from this title an allusion to the painting *The Ship of Fools* (c. 1500) by Hieronymus Bosch (c. 1450–1516). An older meaning of "sottish" is "foolish."

p. 334. Grant, etc.: Jules Verne in *Captain Grant's Children* has *'agonie'* (in a discovered message) turn out to be part of 'Patagonie'. *Commentary*: Jules Verne's novel of adventure, exile, and exploration *Les Enfants du capitaine Grant* (*Captain Grant's Children*) was published in 1867. The message to which Darkbloom refers is the leitmotif of Verne's narrative. The explorer Captain Grant, castaway on an island in the South Pacific, commits the message to the waves in a sealed bottle. It is recovered near his native Scotland and sets off the search leading to his rescue. In part 1, chapter 2, the water-damaged fragments of the three versions of Grant's message—in English, French, and German—are superimposed by its finders, and the message is reconstructed. But it is reconstructed with mistakes, which lead the rescue party to the Chilean coast of Patagonia. Successive misreadings of the fragments account for the subsequent divagations and adventures, over vast areas of South America, Australia, and New Zealand, until Grant is found and restored to his children. Darkbloom's *agonie*, however appropriate to the passage from *Ada* on which Darkbloom here comments, does not occur in Verne's description of the fragments. But *-gonie* does occur in the French fragment, and it is this which is correctly interpreted by the finders as part of *Patagonie*. (Later on it is reinterpreted—incorrectly—as part of *agonie*.)

Darkbloom's "Grant, etc." invites a good deal more explicitness than Darkbloom provides. The climactic portion of the letter by Ada containing the reference to Captain Grant begins with the assertion that she is *"sur la verge* . . . of a revolting amorous adventure."* The phrase *sur la verge* is a translingual pun suggesting English "on the verge." The meaning in French is "on the penis," or, to follow Nabokov's ribald lead, "on the horn." The passage continues with references to "the burning tip of Patagonia" and "Captain Grant's Horn." The first, taken literally and geographically, is Tierra del Fuego, the "Land of Fire," and the second, of course, is Cape Horn. Both localities, as well as Patagonia, figure in *Les Enfants du capitaine Grant*, and all acquire explicitly phallic and erectile associations here—somewhat outrageously, one may feel, given the thoroughly unamorous character of Verne's narrative. There is considerable temptation to carry on the process begun by Ada in her letter with the aid of a good atlas, which reveals a "Cockburn Channel" and other suggestive place names near the Horn.

The allusion to Captain Grant's message calls attention to Verne's word games by playing word games with those word games and thus redoubling the linguistic playfulness of *Ada*. Grant's message—polyglot, elliptical, and inviting of multiple and continually expanding interpretations—is like the very passage in *Ada* that alludes to it and like many another passage in Nabokov's fiction. And, of course, the references to the far-flung travels described in *Les Enfants du capitaine Grant* provide yet another stone in the vast mosaic of allusions to travel and exile in *Ada* (see our note to p. 106 above).

For another allusion to Captain Grant, which also brings Verne's hero into association with amorous adventures, see p. 220 of *Ada* and Darkbloom's first note to that page.

p. 339. *Cyraniana*: allusion to Cyrano de Bergerac's *Histoire comique des Etats de la Lune. Commentary*: In two posthumous works by Cyrano de Bergerac (1619–1655)—*Histoire comique des états et empires de la lune* (*Comical History of the States and Empires of the Moon;* 1656) and *Histoire comique des états et empires du soleil* (*Comical History of the States and Empires of the Sun;* 1661)—the author visits the moon and the sun and describes their inhabitants and social institutions. Both works use their fantastic settings as vehicles for refracting and commenting upon life on earth, somewhat in the manner of *Ada* with its Antiterra.

p. 339. *Nekto*: Russ., quidam. *Commentary*: *Quidam* is Latin (and also, rarely, English) for "somebody" or "a certain person."

p. 340. *Sig Leymanski*: anagram of the name of a waggish British novelist keenly interested in physics fiction. *Commentary*: Kingsley Amis (1922–). His interest in science fiction is manifested in his study *New Maps of Hell: A Survey of Science Fiction* (1961) and in the anthologies *Spectrum* (1961) and *Spectrum II* (1961), which he edited with Robert Conquest.

p. 342. *Abencérage, Zegris*: Families of Granada Moors (their feud inspired Chateaubriand). *Commentary*: Another allusion to Chateaubriand's *Les Aventures du dernier Abencérage*. See our notes to pp. 106, 138, and 428.

p. 355. *subsidunt*, etc.: mountains subside and heights deteriorate. *Commentary*: The line is from a poem by Lucius Annaeus Seneca (c. 4 B.C.–65 A.D.), generally taken to have been written during Seneca's exile on Corsica:

> Omnia tempus edax depascitur, omnia carpit,
>   Omnia sede mouet, nil sinit esse diu.
> Flumina deficiunt, profugum mare litora siccant,
>   Subsidunt montes et iuga celsa ruunt.
> Quid tam parua loquor? moles pulcherrima caeli
>   Ardebit flammis tota repente suis.
> Omnia mors poscit. Lex est, non poena, perire:
>   Hic aliquo mundus tempore nullus erit.

> Greedy time consumes everything, plucks up everything,
>   It moves everything from its place and allows nothing to
>   endure for very long.
> The rivers ebb, the shores dry the fleeing sea,
>   Mountains subside and heights deteriorate.
> Why speak of such insignificant things? The beautiful expanse
>   of heaven
> Will suddenly and totally catch fire with its own flame.
> Death claims everything. To perish is a necessity, not a
>   punishment.
> A time will come when the universe will be annihilated.

In the text of *Ada* the line quoted from this poem seems at first to serve as little more than a joke about impotence. In reality, it represents one of the most suggestive allusions in the novel. Since the line comes from one of Seneca's poems of exile, it forms a part of the network of allusions to travel and exile in *Ada* (see our note to p. 106). When set within its full context, the line can be seen to reflect other major themes of *Ada*: the passage of time, the mutability of experience, and the threat of death and annihilation. For Nabokov these sources of pain and suffering are mitigated and redeemed by artistic creation. For Seneca, a Stoic, they can be withstood when viewed as parts of the inevitable cycle of creation and destruction envisioned by Stoicism, in which the universe is periodically born from fire and returns to fire ("The beautiful expanse of heaven / Will . . . catch fire with its own flame"). The cyclical view of experience, of course, is not foreign to Nabokov either. He often compares time to a spiral and suggests in the conclusion of *Ada* that the end is the beginning: "One can even surmise that if our time-racked, flat-lying couple ever intended to die they would die, as it were, *into* the finished book, into Eden or Hades, into the prose of the book or the poetry of its blurb" (p. 587).

The Latin text of Seneca's poem may be found in *Anthologia Latina*, ed. F. Buecheler and A. Riese (Leipzig: Teubner, 1893), pt. 1, fasc. 1, no. 232; or in *Poetae Latini Minores*, ed. A. Baehrens (Leipzig: Teubner, 1882), vol. 4, p. 55.

p. 365. *sturb*: pun on Germ. *sterben*, to die. *Commentary*: *Sturb* is both a neologism derived from and expressing the meaning of German *sterben* and an obsolete English synonym of "disturb." The pun consists in the combination of both meanings in Rattner's use of *sturb*.

p. 368. Larousse: pun: *rousse*, 'redhair' in French. *Commentary*: The pun is on French *rousse* ("redhead") and on *Petit Larousse* (*Little Larousse*), the well-known French dictionary and encyclopedia.

p. 375. *cogner*, etc.: pun ('to coin a phrase'). *Commentary*: *Pour cogner une fraise* is a translingual pun (French: "to thump a strawberry"; English: "to coin a phrase").

p. 375. *vanouissements*: 'Swooning in Van's arms'. *Commentary*: A distortion of French *évanouissements* ("swoons"), in order to pun on Van's name. "Swooning" in Darkbloom's translation should be "swoonings," since the word is plural.

p. 378. I have not art, etc.: Hamlet. *Commentary*: *Hamlet*, 2.2.121. The line occurs in Hamlet's love letter to Ophelia, read to Gertrude and Claudius by Polonius.

p. 400. *lit*, etc.: pun on 'eider-down bed'. *Commentary*: The pun depends upon the similarity in sound of *lit d'édredon* (French "eider-down bed") and *lidderons*, Ladore slang for "liriodendrons" ("tulip trees").

p. 403. Beckstein: transposed syllables. *Commentary*: John Steinbeck (1902–1968). "Old Beckstein's *Tabby*" is probably John Steinbeck's *Travels with Charley: In Search of America* (1962), an account of the author's tour of America in the company of his poodle.

p. 403. *Love under the Lindens*: O'Neill, Thomas Mann, and his translator tangle in this paragraph. *Commentary*: The imaginary author of *Love under the Lindens*, "Eelmann," is a combination of Thomas Mann (1875–1955) and Eugene O'Neill (1888–1953). The title evokes Mann and O'Neill by mixing O'Neill's play *Desire under the Elms* (1924) with the Schubert song "Der Lindenbaum" ("The Linden Tree"), which figures in Mann's *The Magic Mountain* (1924). The title *Love under the Lindens* may also echo the fact that Van's and Ada's love begins under the lindens (see pp. 51–52 of *Ada* and our note to p. 52 above). H. T. Lowe-Porter ("a firm of Packers & Porters") was widely regarded as the "official" translator of Mann's works into English and received the author's praise on many occasions. See Thomas Mann, *Gesammelte Werke*, 13 vols. (Frankfurt: Fischer, 1960–1974), vol. 11: pp. 148, 250, 281, 572, 680.

p. 406. *foute*: French swear word made to sound 'foot'. *Commentary*: The French swear word is the verb *foutre* ("to fuck").

p. 406. *ars*: Lat., art. *Commentary*: There is also a quibble on the English word "arse."

p. 406. *Carte du Tendre*: 'Map of Tender Love', sentimental allegory of the seventeenth century. *Commentary*: The *Carte de Tendre*, an allegorical map of the tender feelings and sentiments, was published in the ten-volume romance *Clélie* (1654–1660) by Madeleine de Scudéry (1607–1701). It is often erroneously called the Carte *du* Tendre, as it is in the text of *Ada* and in the Darkbloom note.

p. 408. *Knabenkräuter*: Germ., orchids (and testicles). *Commentary*: In German *Knabenkräuter* (literally "boy plants") means "orchids" but not "testicles." Van and Darkbloom, however, punningly mean both "orchids" and "testicles." Presumably they are alluding to the derivation of "orchid" from Greek *orchis* ("testicle"). (The roots of the orchid, as this derivation reminds us, resemble testicles.) They may also be pointing up the echo in *Knabenkräuter* of the other German terms for "orchid" that contain words meaning "testicle": *Orchidee* (the usual German term for nondomestic varieties of orchids), *Orchis* (the German botanical term for the family to which the orchid belongs), and *Hodenkräuter* (a German synonym for *Knabenkräuter* that means literally "testicle plants").

p. 416. *Vorschmacks*: Germ., hors-d'oeuvres. *Commentary*: *Vorschmack* does not mean "hors-d'oeuvre" but rather "foretaste." Perhaps in Van's use of the word *-schmack* is intended to suggest English "snack." *Vorschmack* is a variant of the usual term, *Vorgeschmack*, and is extremely rare in modern standard German. However, Grimm's *Deutsches Wörterbuch* provides many attestations for the nineteenth century and earlier. Grimm's opines that *Vorschmack* has a more figurative connotation than *Vorgeschmack* and is most often used in theological contexts, as, for example, in the notion of a foretaste of heaven—or hell. The plural in -s is an anglicization. The German plural is *Vorschmäcke* or, facetiously, *Vorschmäcker.*

p. 428. *oh qui me rendra,* etc.: Oh, who'll give me back
my hill and the big oak.
Commentary: A distortion of vv. 25–26 of the *romance* from Chateaubriand's *Le Dernier Abencérage.* The original reads: "Oh! qui me rendra mon Hélène, / Et ma montagne, et le grand chêne?" ("Oh! Who will give me back my Helen, / And my mountain, and the big oak?"). The distortion (*"Oh! qui me rendra ma colline / Et le grand chêne and my colleen!"*) rhymes French *colline* ("hill") with Anglo-Irish *colleen* ("girl"), a near homophone. See also our note to p. 106 above.

p. 430. *en robe,* etc.: in a pink and green dress. *Commentary*: A simultaneous reference to Natasha's pink dress and green sash in act 1 of *The Three Sisters* (1901) by Anton Chekhov (1860–1904) and to the concluding lines of Baudelaire's "Le Crépuscule du matin." See our note to p. 176 above.

p. 434. R 4: 'rook four', a chess indication of position (pun on the woman's name). *Commentary*: The woman's name is Mrs. Arfour (see p. 433 of *Ada*).

p. 443. ridge: money. *Commentary*: "Ridge" is an English cant term of obscure origin, apparently obsolete since the end of the nineteenth century, with the general meaning of "gold" or "gold coin" and the specific meaning of "a guinea." It appears to have been used mostly by criminals, or in reference to criminal activities, and is therefore an appropriate word for Demon to employ while upbraiding Van for Van's incestuous relationship with Ada.

p. 466. *das auch noch*: Germ., and that too. *Commentary*: "And that too" is a literal translation of the phrase, which expresses resignation and annoyance and could be more idiomatically rendered by "*That,* on top of everything else!" or "That's all I need!"

p. 466. *pendant que je,* etc.: while I am skiing. *Commentary*: Darkbloom's "etc." glosses over some scabrous word play. Lucette says, *"pendant que je shee in Aspenis."* "Shee" is "ski" as pronounced in German and the Scandinavian languages. "Shee" is also a homophone of French *chie,* the first person singular of *chier* ("to shit"). It could also be understood as a whimsical verb formation, "to she," that is, to engage in sexual activities with women (in this case, lesbian activities). "Aspenis" seems to be a gratuitously obscene combination of "ass" and "penis," with a quibble on Aspen, the famous ski (and "she") resort in Colorado.

p. 484. *Insiste*, etc.: quotation from St Augustine. *Commentary*: The quotation is from the *Confessions* of St. Augustine (354–430). It is the opening sentence of chapter 27 in book 11, in which Augustine, like Van in this section, wrestles with the concept of time. The Latin is translated in the text of *Ada*.

p. 494. Nox: Lat., at night. *Commentary*: In Latin *nox* does not mean "at night" but simply "night." "At night" could be expressed by the ablative *nocte* or by the adverb *noctu*.

p. 508. *que sais-je*: what do I know. *Commentary*: Darkbloom's translation "what do I know?" is literally correct, but *que sais-je* as used here could be more idiomatically rendered as "etc." or "Who knows what else?"

p. 513. cart de van: Amer., mispronunciation of *carte des vins*. *Commentary*: *Carte des vins* means "wine list" in French.

p. 518. *muirninochka*: Hiberno-Russian caressive term. *Commentary*: "Hiberno-" comes from "Hibernia," the Latin name for Ireland. In Irish *muirnín* is a term of endearment meaning "sweetheart" or "darling"; *-ochka* is a Russian feminine diminutive ending that here connotes affection. The Hiberno-Russian word thus means "little darling."

p. 520. *Olorinus*: from Lat. *olor*, swan (Leda's lover). *Commentary*: In Greek mythology Zeus takes the form of a swan in order to rape Leda. In the celebrated sonnet "Leda and the Swan" (1923) by William Butler Yeats (1865–1939) Leda's neck, like Ada's in this scene, is subjected to her lover's "tender fury" (vv. 3–4): "her nape caught in his bill, / He holds her helpless breast upon his breast."

p. 522. She Yawns: Chillon's. *Commentary*: An allusion to the castle of Chillon near Montreux on Lake Geneva and to the poem "The Prisoner of Chillon" (1816) by George Gordon, Lord Byron (1788–1824).

p. 538. ardis: arrow. *Commentary*: The Greek word *ardis* means "point." It can refer to the point of an arrow, but it is not limited to that meaning. Cf. p. 225, where we are told that "it was pitiful to see Lucette" play Antiterra's version of Scrabble and "cling to her last five letters (with none left in the box) forming the beautiful ARDIS which her governess had told her meant 'the point of an arrow'—but only in Greek, alas."

p. 541. *anime*, etc.: Lat., soul. *Commentary*: *Anime meus* is "my soul" or "my mind." See p. 484 of *Ada* and our note to it above.

p. 541. assassin pun: a pun on *pointe assassine* (from a poem by Verlaine). *Commentary*: The poem is "Art poétique" ("The Art of Poetry") by Paul Verlaine (1844–1896). The relevant lines are:

Fuis du plus loin la Pointe assassine,
L'Esprit cruel et le Rire impur,
Qui font pleurer les yeux de l'Azur,
Et tout cet ail de basse cuisine!

Flee as far as possible from the assassin Point,
From cruel Wit and impure Laughter,
Which make the eyes of Heaven weep,
And from all this garlic of low cuisine!

Nabokov comments on this allusion in an interview published in *Strong Opinions*: "In a poem about poetry as he understands it, Verlaine warns the poet against using *la pointe assassine*, that is introducing an epigrammatic or moral point at the end of a poem, and thereby murdering the poem. What amused me was to pun on 'point,' thus making a pun in the very act of prohibiting it" (p. 129).

p. 550. unfortunate thinker: Samuel Alexander, English philosopher. *Commentary*: Samuel Alexander (1859–1938) taught philosophy at Oxford and at the University of Manchester. His major work, *Space, Time, and Deity* (1920; rpt. London: Macmillan, 1966), was first presented as the Gifford Lectures at Glasgow from 1916 to 1918. *Ada* attributes to Alexander the quotation "looking forward to a promotion or fearing a social blunder" (p. 550). But this is really a blending of two sentences from book 1 ("Space-Time"), chapter 4 ("Mental Space-Time"), of *Space, Time, and Deity*. The first is: "Think of the expectation of some promotion or the fear of some disaster" (p. 118). The second is: "I remember the feeling of shame felt at a social blunder" (p. 129). Van changes "expectation," the term preferred by Alexander, to "anticipation" (p. 550 of *Ada*).

Van's treatise *The Texture of Time*, like Alexander's *Space, Time, and Deity*, grows out of a series of lectures. Furthermore, it is filled with the sorts of homely analogies and metaphors favored by Alexander. Alexander holds that Space-Time is that from which all things are engendered. In his own philosophizing Van tries to discard the notion of Space-Time. He speaks of "'Space-Time'—that hideous hybrid whose very hyphen looks phoney" (p. 543) and says that "one can be a hater of Space, and a lover of Time" (p. 543). Part 4 of *Ada* can therefore be read as a parody of Samuel Alexander's style combined with an attempt to forge beyond his thought.

p. 558. *on peut*, etc.: see p. 247. *Commentary*: "One can follow them and recognize. . . ." An echo of the lines by Coppée quoted on pp. 127 and 247 of *Ada*. See our first note to p. 127 above.

p. 584. *j'ai tâté*, etc.: I have known two Lesbians in my life, that's enough. *Commentary*: In Darkbloom's translation "known" should be understood in the Biblical sense. In French *tâter de* means "to feel," "to taste," "to prod," "to try."

p. 584. *terme*, etc.: term one avoids using. *Commentary*: This comment is appended to the definition of *tribade* ("tribade," "lesbian") in Emile Littré's *Dictionnaire de la langue française* (*Dictionary of the French Language*). Emile Littré is the "Dear Emile" to whom the remark is attributed in *Ada*.

The Problem of Text: Nabokov's Last Two Novels

PAUL S. BRUSS

Nabokov's last two novels may not measure up to the achievement of *Lolita*, *Pale Fire*, and *Ada*, but both show the deft touch of an artist who knows the intricacy of his craft. The two novels are, to be sure, very different, for while the narrative strategy of *Look at the Harlequins!* has much in common with the retrospective texture of *Ada*, *Transparent Things* lacks that sophisticated, mazelike quality which readers have come to associate with Nabokov's fiction. In his *Encounter* review of *Transparent Things*, Jonathan Raban disparaged it as the work of "a novelist who has grown tired and irascible at his own cleverness" and who has thus merely created "a paper chase of transparent metaphors which lead back to the groaning novelist, weighed down by a world he has himself created."[1] Because the artist always faces the dilemma of having to re-create himself as well as his world with each succeeding text, however, Nabokov's last two novels deserve to be examined in their own terms. Both works continue the familiar Nabokovian concentration upon the problems of establishing a text, and thus it may be possible to regard the two novels as Nabokov's final statement concerning the essential nature of his art. In order to provide some focus to my discussion of these works, I intend first to explore their narrative strategies and then to comment upon the appropriateness of these strategies as a "final statement."

That the establishing of text remains a significant problem in Nabokov's last novels is evident in the characterization of Mr. R. in *Transparent Things.* As an accomplished writer, Mr. R. has possessed, throughout his life, that expansive and fluid perspective which is in touch with the essential arbitrariness of human experience. When it comes to writing his own fiction, however, Mr. R. has created a world of stature and significance that belies this fundamental arbitrariness. The narrator of *Transparent Things* provides a shrewd insight into the contradiction of Mr. R.'s position when he recounts how Mr. R.'s editor, Hugh Person, tries to cajole him into modifications of the characters and the title of his latest novel, *Tralatitions*. Mr. R. determinedly refuses on the ground that any alteration would radically disfigure the character of his conception for the work. Indeed, when reminded of the libel suits the book would be likely to encounter in its present form, Mr. R. merely suggests that he has "paid for [his art] once in solitude and remorse, and now was ready to pay in hard cash any fool whom his story might hurt."[2] Obviously confident and self-assured, Mr. R. has generated over the years a profound respect for his own handling of experience and thus, without hesitation, thinks nothing of committing himself completely to the development of his own peculiar text. With such an insistent claim to the realization of his own text, however, he seems to transgress the one law common to all of Nabokov's fiction —that there exists no text of authority whereby human experience can finally be measured and judged.

The irony that attaches to Mr. R.'s stance applies even more specifically to his editor. *Transparent Things* focuses upon Hugh Person, whom Mr. R. himself regards as "one of the nicest persons I knew" (p. 83), but who, by failing to explore the textures of his own imagination, finally becomes conscious of having squandered his life "in a sick dream" (p. 96). Hugh does possess some genius, but because he lacks originality, or because he does not act upon his genius by challenging and extending it, he ends up throwing his life away—first as a secretary to Atman (a fraudulent symbolist), then as an entrepreneur in stationery (who markets the Person fountain pen), and finally as an editor for a publishing firm (where he eventually takes charge of Mr. R.'s texts). At one point in the novel, shortly after meeting Armande, he even confides in his diary that "I am an all-round genius" (p. 28), but by then it is evident that something has gone wrong with his life. Lacking that confidence which is crucial to the success of the artist in any field and which certainly underlies Mr. R.'s distinguished career as a writer, Hugh at that point not only finds himself separated from a life of achievement but also at a serious disadvantage when dealing with other people. His relationship with Armande is a good case in point.

Hugh is fearful of approaching Armande, and from the beginning he allows her to define the character of their relationship, particularly in matters of sex. Such allowance is disastrous. Armande fancies herself a realist, one who reads "hard realistic stuff" (p. 26) and who thus expects Hugh to be likewise "serious, and plain, and believable" (p. 63). Moreover, by depending upon ideas derived from other people, she has moved completely out of touch with the imaginative character of being that is the source, throughout Nabokov's fiction, of emotional vitality. In her presence, therefore, Hugh himself never has the opportunity to develop that same primary source of energy. Not surprisingly, having deferred to her perspective, he eventually discovers in himself a profound core of hate: "I hate Witt. . . . I hate life. I hate myself" (p. 55). By marrying Armande, Hugh has fully separated himself from any lingering sense of responsibility for exploring his own world of perceptions, and finally, having given up the one marginally original game that has continued into his adult life (the tennis played while he lulls himself to sleep), he becomes the complete victim of his own folly. Throughout the marriage, instead of examining his own perceptions, Hugh engages only in what amounts to an editorial examination of Armande's unpredictable behavior. By regarding the strange aspects of her conduct "as absurd clues in a clever puzzle" (p. 63), he tries to establish the emotional equivalent of an authoritative text for her life. Despite his repeated analyses of her behavior, however, he never locates reasonable explanations, and all his effort turns out to have been for naught.

Hugh's editorial relationship to Armande's life is obviously inferior to Mr. R.'s authorial relationship to the texts he creates, but both characters, by committing themselves to the establishment of their respective texts, seem to violate that fundamental textlessness which is at the heart of Nabokov's fiction. In Nabokov's work all "reality" is a text in need of editing. If, however, the process of editing assumes that there is an ultimate "reality" that is discoverable by careful scrutiny of the available evidence, then that process must emerge as self-defeating and dangerous to its originator. One of the dictionary definitions of "text" is "an ultimate source of information or authority." This is the sort of text for which many of Nabokov's characters search—Armande in her admiration for "hard realistic stuff," Hugh in his editorial search for the "reality" of Armande's life. But there is another kind of text, the Nabokovian literary text, which imitates the shifting nature of reality and becomes an authoritative source by virtue of showing that there are no authoritative sources. In his last two novels and throughout his career Nabokov parodies the first kind of text in order to establish the second kind, the text that creates "reality" by dramatizing the many ways in which it eludes human perception.

At the very beginning of the novel the narrator provides a telling comment concerning the delicacy that must attend any relationship to a text. Recognizing that the past is particularly seductive because the future enjoys "no such reality . . . as the pictured past and the perceived present possess" (p. 1), the narrator suggests that most people, in the process of perceiving an object (person, place, or thing), "involuntarily [sink] into the history [the text] of that object." For the narrator, consequently, any sustaining of the imagination requires, above all, a facing up to this dangerous skewing of perception toward the past. As he suggests, "Novices must learn to skim over matter if they want matter to stay at the exact level of the moment" (p. 1). Jonathan Raban, in disparaging such skimming, has cited both Lolita and Armande as good examples of skimmers.[3] In actuality, however, Lolita and Armande represent the opposite tendency, for both of them have submerged themselves in the attitudes and conceptions that over the years have created the social fabric of their respective milieus. The narrator makes their position clear: "A thin veneer of immediate reality is spread over natural and artificial matter, and whoever wishes to remain in the now, with the now, on the now, should please not break its tension film" (p. 2). Lolita and Armande simply do not take such care. They are both so dominated by prevailing attitudes that they repeatedly break through the tension film at the surface. If, in Nabokov's world, genius and originality depend upon maintaining sufficient distance between oneself and the texts of the past so that imaginative responses to the present remain viable, then Lolita and Armande represent colossal failures.

The narrator's emphasis upon skimming over matter shows Nabokov's determination to clarify in this novel his uses of the past. While critics have sometimes applauded his characters' retreat into the past, Nabokov himself recognizes that all texts, even those of the past, are multi-faceted, very complex, and frequently contradictory. When his most original characters mine the resources of the past, therefore, they are not so much retreating into it as attempting to create a web that can contain it in all its complexity. Whether I cite Pnin or Shade or the elder Van Veen, it should be clear that none of these characters inhabits a stable past from which he can extract a single, authoritative text. Instead, each of them, with each succeeding moment of the present, finds himself in the predicament of having to create a new web for the past that takes into account all the adjustments in attitude and insight that have emerged in the present. Van Veen's extensive modulation of his past and present relationship with Ada is probably the best example of this process, but Pnin's juxtaposition of Russia and America also serves nicely. In Nabokov's fiction, static texts—those that presume to possess a final authority—are dangerous commodities because they no longer engage their originators in the modifications that are crucial to sustained vitality and creativity. In *Transparent Things*, which begins and ends with Hugh's return (at age 40) to the Ascot Hotel, where he expects to recover "a moment of contact with [Armande's] essential image in exactly remembered surroundings" (p. 95), the danger becomes fully apparent. For when Hugh commits himself to the recovery of an exact configuration of the past, he divorces himself from the necessity of making his present act of perception a condition of that past. The consequence is that he cuts himself off from the processes of perception and virtually commits aesthetic suicide. In these terms, of course, the difference between Hugh and Mr. R. finally emerges. Both men may commit themselves to their texts, but while Hugh's commitment reflects an editorial relationship in which the text dominates him, Mr. R.'s commitment reflects an authorial relationship in which the text, even when located in the past, remains a function of his acts of perception in the present. In the letter he writes as he is dying, Mr. R. declares (p. 84):

> I used to believe that dying persons saw the vanity of things, the futility of fame, passion, art, and so forth . . . but now I feel just the contrary: my most trivial sentiments and those of all men have acquired gigantic proportions. . . . The more I shrivel, the bigger I grow. . . . Total rejection of all religions ever dreamt up by man and total composure in the face of total death! If I could explain this triple totality in one big book, that book would become no doubt a new bible and its author the founder of a new creed. Fortunately for my self-esteem that book will not be written—not merely because a dying man cannot write books but because that particular one would never express in one flash what can only be understood *immediately.*

Mr. R. scrupulously establishes the texts of his various books, but he is not, finally, dominated by their versions of the truth. On the contrary, he dies with a sense of his insufficiency as an artist and of his previous failure to express the "totality" of things.

It is striking that the narrator of *Transparent Things* himself seems to fall into the textual trap he forswears. Repeatedly, as when he recounts the history of the pencil located in the desk in Hugh's room at the Ascot or the history of the room in which Hugh takes his first prostitute, the narrator seems to indulge in the kind of textual re-construction of the past with which he associates Hugh. Finally, though, Hugh is engaged in an editorial (or sentimental) pilgrimage, in the "enforced re-creation of irrecoverable trivia" (p. 94), whereas the narrator plays with the texts of the past in the fashion of Mr. R. He is not directly involved in the history of the pencil or of the room and thus does not seek to establish the exact configuration of the past. Knowing, in fact, that such an attempt is impossible, he moves well beyond Hugh's stance and allows himself the luxury and the imaginative stimulation of playing with the open textures inherent in all texts, even those of the past. Whereas Hugh has victimized himself by committing himself to the pursuit of exact texts, the narrator constantly expands his play with the multidimensional texts before him and takes genuine delight in ferreting out each new facet or "flavor" (p. 36). In a somewhat paradoxical sense, then, the source of this narrator's genius is that he suspends himself in as "textless" a reconsideration of his experience as possible. Such suspension, much like Pnin's, allows him to bring the texts of experience into genuine contact with his present mode of being. More than that, however, once in this new contact with each other, the play between the texts of the past and of the present can create those wonderful, sometimes completely unanticipated textures which readers have come to associate with Nabokov's fiction. At the same time, this narrator has avoided the pursuit of an avant-garde text, which in his mind "means little more than conforming to some daring philistine fashion" (p. 34). Having created for himself a spaciousness of mind that separates him from conformity to the sentiments of the past, he also has recognized the dangers of succumbing to the prevailing fashions of the present. He is—as much as any narrator can be in Nabokov's fiction—his own man.

The narrator of *Transparent Things* reinforces the creative character of his relationship to the text by developing the contrast between Mr. R. and Hugh Person and then indicating his own similarity to Mr. R. The doubling of his own situation in these two men is of crucial importance to his narrative, but when contrasted to the narrator's use of doubling in *Look at the Harlequins!*, its role in *Transparent Things* seems fledgling at best. There is a good reason for this. Once Nabokov has clarified his use of the past—the fact that it is predicated upon a creative rather than an editorial relationship to the texts of the past—he can free his narrator to seek out facets in the texts of the past that still lie unrealized. One of the best—and now very familiar—means of realizing such facets is the technique of doubling. By its very nature, doubling separates the narrator from the obligations of realism or, more properly, from the requirement of textual exactitude. Not surprisingly, therefore, in *Look at the Harlequins!*—which is a retrospective on a whole career— doubling serves as the structural principle for the novel. Not only does Vadim N.'s career play off that of Nabokov himself,[4] it also plays off the lives of other characters who represent what Vadim N. might have become had he not pursued a career as an author. The novel, consequently, enjoys a very ambiguous status. Whereas the reader might be tempted to regard Vadim N. as a loose disguise for Nabokov himself (and the considerations of Vadim N. as Nabokov's own), it eventually becomes apparent, if only because Vadim N. is such an adroit gamer, that he must be given his due as a character in his own right. By giving him his due, moreover, the reader will perceive Vadim N. as the full realization of that creative relationship to text which supports the narrator's genius in *Transparent Things.*

Vadim N. frequently employs the double as a means of measuring a particular aspect of his experience. Near the beginning of the novel, for example, while recounting the history of his "'numerical nimbus' syndrome,"[5] Vadim alludes to a "Mr. V.S." with whom the doctor treating his syndrome has associated him. A little later, he alludes to a Lieutenant Starov who has taken the job in the White Cross that Vadim himself has turned down. Then it turns out that it is this man—a "White Russian, Wladimir Blagidze, *alias* Starov" (pp. 69–70)—who guns Iris down. And finally, much later in the novel (and in this instance within a parenthetical remark), Vadim considers whether "Count Starov [presumably the lieutenant's father] . . . was my real father" (p. 227). By the time readers have accumulated all these references, they should have begun to suspect that the lieutenant—with the frustrations of a boring job that lead him, perhaps, to the act of murder—represents what Vadim believes he himself might have become, had he not concerned himself with the very difficult but enlivening creation of texts. While the lieutenant—in the manner of Hugh Person—has wedded himself to a well-defined, rather restrictive career, Vadim has plumbed the depths of the imagination and has created for himself a texture of experience far beyond the lieutenant's ability to conceive.

Professor Notebooke and his wife are also doubles for Vadim N. Notebooke, while described as "meek myopic old" (p. 131), is at least a skilled translator whose sister is rather suggestively named Phoneme (p. 159). He, too, much like Vadim, has interested himself in the deployment of texts. Unlike Vadim, however, who is chiefly concerned with exploring and fostering his own texture of experience, Notebooke seems interested only in the extension of other writers' texts. In this context, therefore, the distinction already cited between Mr. R. and Hugh Person again surfaces with some intensity. As a translator who attends to the subtle dimensions of language, Notebooke does not have as narrow a relationship to text as Hugh Person, but it is clear, especially given Vadim's rather summary presentation of Notebooke's abilities, that he does not enjoy the spacious fields of imaginative play that belong to Vadim himself. Notebooke simply represents that academic dryness of mind that would have been Vadim's had he not devoted himself to the evocation and the extension of his own being. The contrast between Vadim and Notebooke, while rather boldly hinted at in the latter's name, is probably most evident in the fact that it is Notebooke's wife who suggests that Vadim purchase a "Junior Manicure Set" (p. 163) for Bel and encourages him to hire "an experienced, preferably German, governess to look after [Bel] day and night" (p. 173). The wife represents the text of propriety—a text from which Vadim, by virtue of the rather idiosyncratic character of his life as an artist, has increasingly separated himself. Because the hiring of a governess would interfere with his relationship with Bel, Vadim ignores the views of the Notebookes.

A third—and perhaps the best—example of Vadim's use of doubling occurs late in the novel, when Vadim repeatedly alludes to the man who shadows him on his trip to Leningrad. Vadim believes that he has known the man in Paris in the early thirties, and he suspects throughout the trip that the man is Russian at least by birth. When the mystery man turns out to be Oleg Orlov, all his earlier suspicions prove to be well founded. Some forty years ago, Oleg "joined the small number of *littérateurs* who decided to sell the bleak liberty of expatriation for the rosy mess of Soviet pottage," but during this long association with the Soviets he has achieved little more than a "medley of publicity pieces, commercial translations, vicious denunciations" (p. 217). In the novel, therefore, he serves as a sharp contrast to Vadim himself. Once he has identified himself, Oleg may attack Vadim's "obscene novelette about little Lola or Lotte," as if he—Oleg—were morally superior to Vadim and his work, but in the end the reader recognizes that it is Vadim who is superior—especially when Vadim deals Oleg a blow "with the back of my left fist . . . of quite presentable power" (p. 218). Vadim's reference to Oleg in the narrative certainly indicates that Vadim himself has realized that his decision to surrender to the difficulties of life as an émigré rather than to settle for "the rosy mess of Soviet [or, for that matter, American] pottage" has become the basis for a life of genuine moral distinction.

All three of these doubles, while hardly exhaustive of the technique, clearly point to the lack of textual stability within Vadim's own tenuous grasp on existence. Because of the possible combinations of level and attitude available to him, during his lifetime an almost continuous modulation of text has emerged that is once more evident in this—his final—narrative. This continuous modulation of imaginative consciousness has in the past served to goad Vadim through a succession of marriages and relationships—from Iris to Annette to Louise, with some additional attention to Dolly and even to Bel—and now, in the very face of his desire to assess his life, to give it a final shape by establishing the character of his relationship with "You," he discovers that this process of modulation is as relentless as ever. In the past the complexity of Vadim's marital (and extramarital) experience has only served to corroborate his difficulty in accepting any one text as the final basis for his existence. The first two sentences, which focus on a doubling situation, say it as well as any other passage in the novel: "I met the first of my three or four successive wives in somewhat odd circumstances, the development of which resembled a clumsy conspiracy, with nonsensical details and a main plotter who not only knew nothing of its real object but insisted on making inept moves that seemed to preclude the slightest possibility of success. Yet out of those very mistakes he unwittingly wove a web, in which a set of reciprocal blunders on my part caused me to get involved and fulfill the destiny that was the only aim of the plot" (p. 3).

While somewhat enigmatic, and perhaps even deliberately ambiguous, this passage seems to extend the distinction between text and texture that underlies John Shade's artistry and probably serves as the principal key to Nabokov's fiction. First, in the terms of *Look at the Harlequins!*, it helps to explain why Vadim's relationship with "You" will remain tenuous even in this narrative of retrospective self-definition. For Vadim the web of this present relationship is simply not yet complete and, in the world of textual insufficiency, never will be complete. Second, and more generally, the passage alludes to a "main plotter," who, as opposed to Vadim himself, initiates certain actions that resemble "a clumsy conspiracy," of whose existence even the plotter himself is unaware. Despite all their complex posturing in full view of each other, apparently neither Vadim nor the "main plotter" possesses an authoritative text of experience to which he is committed. For both of them existence is problematic and elliptical. Third, because Vadim lacks a preconceived text that can organize his experience, he actually has no choice but to give over the ground of his being to that plotter who makes decisions at least in the sense that he initiates action. On the surface, such a transfer of authority may seem a desertion of moral responsibility, but finally it is this stance which ensures the continued vitality of Vadim's existence. Having avoided the rigorous observance of a specific text, Vadim is free—much like the narrator of

Transparent Things—to suspend himself in the imaginative possibilities that have emerged, over the course of several decades, in the strange dialogue between the plotter's "inept moves" and Vadim's own "blunders." On the surface, again, this suspension may not seem very promising, but to the extent that it separates Vadim from that sterile observance of a preconceived text which characterizes Hugh Person's existence, the suspension guarantees Vadim a life rich in realization and understanding. His life will never be predictable, but in light of his preference for imagination rather than stable text, there is little doubt that his life will be intense.

This relationship between Vadim and the main plotter possesses a double-edged character. Given the presence of the main plotter, Vadim must remain conscious—even to the very end of his life—that there is no means of achieving absolute control over the field of his experience. He may over the years have become an accomplished writer, with many texts written under his name, but despite the long accumulation of success he remains prey to the notion that his life is "the non-identical twin, a parody, an inferior variant of another man's life, somewhere on this or another earth" (p. 89). While this notion obviously alludes to the shadow of Nabokov himself stalking his narrator, the notion also recovers, it seems to me, that profound sense of self-doubt which must accompany the artist's suspension of self in the textures, rather than the texts, of human experience. Try as they may to establish the character of their own art, all true artists are in the end conscious only of the insufficiency of their achievement. Vadim himself is such an artist, and thus it is not surprising that he remarks late in the novel, "The hideous suspicion that even *Ardis*, my most private book, soaked in reality, saturated with sun flecks, might be an unconscious imitation of another's unearthly art, *that* suspicion might come later" (p. 234), but come it must. In this instance, too, what the urbane Vadim finally recognizes is that he will never possess a text that fully recovers the character of his deepest (his most private) imaginative experience and that must, therefore, be associated only with his name. The artist craves identity, specifically the identity that emerges in his best art, but in view of the ultimate insufficiency of all texts he is—as Vadim here realizes—forever disappointed. Late in the novel, following a stroke, Vadim actually loses all sense of his own identity. At that point Nabokov's shadow almost completely overwhelms him: "Poor Vivian, poor Vadim Vadimovich, was but a figment of somebody's—not even my own—imagination" (p. 249). When he suggests on the same page that "in rapid Russian speech . . . 'Vladimir Vladimirovich' becomes colloquially similar to 'Vadim Vadimych,'" there may exist no further reason for maintaining the distinction between this narrator and Nabokov himself. Even then, nevertheless, the reader must realize that Vadim's difficulty is not so much with Nabokov (although that is a significant problem) as it is with the limited character of texts in general. Vadim, like any determined artist, wants the authority of text that is finally available to no one. When he loses his bearings, his sense of identity, it is because the struggle for what is impossible has finally overwhelmed him.

The Vadim who has heeded the advice of his grand-aunt to "look at the harlequins!" (p. 8) and who has chosen for himself the "essential, hysterical, genuine [muse]" rather than "her apprentice, her palette girl and stand-in, a little logician" (p. 44) is an artist who has reached for the heights. Aware, in fact, of a fundamental inability to "cope with the abstraction of direction in space," he has turned the peculiarities of his own perceptions into the foundation for a very idiosyncratic art: "My battle with factual, respectable life . . . consisted of sudden delusions, sudden reshufflings—kaleidoscopic, stained-glass reshufflings!—of fragmented space" (p. 85). Reshuffling is, of course, the key term. Just as Joan Clements in *Pnin* characterizes the texts of a particular novelist as the attempt "to express the fantastic recurrence of certain situations,"[6] so Vadim has allied himself with that openness of text which allows for continuous modulation of one's experience, past or present. Indeed, lacking the concrete text that organizes, say, Hugh Person's life, he actually has found that he must rely upon the process of reshuffling in order to retain his sanity. As he himself acknowledges, "only the writing of fiction, the endless re-creation of my fluid self could keep me more or less sane" (p. 97). An even better self-assessment, however, probably appears a few pages later when he remarks that his "average age has been thirteen" all his life (p. 103). Vadim has become the artist adroit at turning his dreamlike reshufflings into the texture of art and thereby has discovered Nabokov's fountain of youth.

Nabokov's last two novels, then, while very different, serve as a summation for his art. Together, the novels establish the precise character of that relationship to text (whether of the past or the present) whereby Nabokov's best artists gain and sustain their brilliance and intensity. Nabokov's fiction is always complicated, always a contest between author and reader, but if its complexity is regarded as a function of the textual difficulties that confront all people, not merely the old writer who has become sensitive to the slightest textual nuance, then that fiction can also serve as a basis for sustaining the reader's own vitality. Nabokov would have it no other way.

NOTES

1. Jonathan Raban, "Transparent Likenesses," *Encounter* 41 (September 1973), 75.
2. Vladimir Nabokov, *Transparent Things*, p. 74. Hereafter cited in text.
3. Raban, "Transparent Likenesses," p. 74.
4. Richard Patteson, in "Nabokov's *Look at the Harlequins!*: Endless Re-creation of the Self," *RLT* 14 (1976), 84–98, has begun to establish some of the more significant parallels between the two careers.
5. Vladimir Nabokov, *Look at the Harlequins!*, p. 15. Hereafter cited in text.
6. Vladimir Nabokov, *Pnin*, p. 159.

Notes on Contributors

LARRY R. ANDREWS, Associate Professor of English and comparative literature at Kent State University, has published articles on Russian literature and translations of Russian poetry. He recently spent a year as exchange professor at the University of Warsaw.

ALFRED APPEL, JR., was Nabokov's student at Cornell and subsequently became the dean of world Nabokov scholars. He is the author of *Nabokov's Dark Cinema* and of several articles about and interviews with Nabokov. His standard edition of Nabokov's masterpiece, *The Annotated Lolita*, is quoted throughout this book and discussed in the essay by James M. Rambeau.

BEVERLY GRAY BIENSTOCK has taught English and journalism at UCLA, the University of Southern California, and Hebrew Union College. In addition to her work in contemporary American fiction, she writes on theater and film for such publications as *Performing Arts*, *Theatre Crafts*, *New West*, and the *Los Angeles Times*.

MARGARET BYRD BOEGEMAN is Professor of English at Cypress College in California.

PAUL S. BRUSS is Professor of English at Eastern Michigan University. His book on Joseph Conrad was published by Bucknell University Press in 1979 and *Victims*, his study of Nabokov, Barthelme, and Kosinski, in 1981. During 1975–1976 he held an NEH Fellowship in Residence in the Art Department at Brown University, and during 1980–1981 he served as Visiting Professor at Johannes Gutenberg Universität in Mainz, West Germany.

WILLIAM C. CARROLL is Associate Professor of English at Boston University. His well-known article on *Pnin* and "Signs and Symbols" is discussed in this volume by Larry R. Andrews. His book *The Great Feast of Language in "Love's Labour's Lost"* was published by Princeton University Press in 1976.

BEVERLY LYON CLARK teaches English at Wheaton College in Massachusetts. Her essay "Contradictions and Affirmations in *Ada*" appeared in a recent issue of *College Literature.*

GLADYS M. CLIFTON teaches in the English Department of the University of Pittsburgh at Johnstown.

JULIAN W. CONNOLLY teaches in the Department of Slavic Languages and Literatures at the University of Virginia. He has published a number of scholarly articles on Russian literature and his book *Ivan Bunin* is soon to be published by Twayne.

MARILYN EDELSTEIN is a Ph.D. student in the Department of English at the State University of New York at Buffalo.

WALTER EVANS teaches English at Augusta College in Georgia. He has published several scholarly articles and short stories.

THOMAS R. FROSCH is Associate Professor of English at Queens College of the City University of New York. His study of William Blake, *The Awakening of Albion* (Cornell), appeared in 1974. He has also published a book of poetry, *Plum Gut* (New Rivers Press, 1979).

DMITRI NABOKOV frequently collaborated with his father in translating his father's work. His essay "Father's Room" appeared in Peter Quennell's *Vladimir Nabokov: A Tribute.*

VLADIMIR NABOKOV is one of the twentieth century's finest writers.

CHARLES NICOL, Professor of English at Indiana State University, has written frequently on Nabokov and is past President of the Vladimir Nabokov Society. His criticism has appeared in *Harper's*, *Atlantic*, *Saturday Review*, the *New York Times Book Review*, and elsewhere.

JAMES M. RAMBEAU teaches English and American Studies at The Pennsylvania State University. He has published essays on several American writers, assisted on the third edition of the Henry James bibliography, and is currently the Assistant Bibliographer of *American Literature.*

J. E. RIVERS is Professor of English at the University of Colorado, Boulder. He directed the first MLA seminar devoted to Nabokov and has published several articles on his work. His book *Proust and the Art of Love* was published by Columbia University Press in 1980.

PHYLLIS A. ROTH is Associate Professor of English at Skidmore College. A past Vice-President of the Vladimir Nabokov Society, she has published frequently on Nabokov. Her book *Bram Stoker* is published by G. K. Hall. Currently she is editing *Critical Essays on Vladimir Nabokov*, also for G. K. Hall.

EARL D. SAMPSON teaches Russian in the Department of Oriental and Slavic Languages and Literatures at the University of Colorado, Boulder. He has published a book and several articles and reviews dealing with the poet Nikolay Gumilev. He has also previously published a translation of Pushkin's *History of Pugachev* and a translation of a story by Yury Nagibin.

CAROL SHLOSS teaches English at Wesleyan University in Connecticut.

WILLIAM WALKER teaches English at the Ruhr-Universität Bochum in Bochum, West Germany. He has previously published commentary on *Ada* in collaboration with J. E. Rivers.

Bibliography

PRIMARY SOURCES

Ada or Ardor: A Family Chronicle (novel). New York: McGraw-Hill, 1969.

The Annotated Lolita (novel). Edited by Alfred Appel, Jr. New York: Mc-Graw-Hill, 1970.

Anya v stranye chudes (Nabokov's translation into Russian of *Alice's Adventures in Wonderland*). 1923. Reprinted, New York: Dover, 1976.

Bend Sinister (novel). 1947. Reprinted, New York: McGraw-Hill, 1973.

Camera Obscura (novel: English translation of *Kamera obskura*). London: Long, 1936.

Conclusive Evidence (autobiography). New York: Harper, 1951.

Dar (novel). Paris: *Sovremennye Zapiski* (émigré journal), 1937–1938. Printed without chapter four. Book version, New York: Chekhov, 1952.

The Defense (novel: English translation by Nabokov and Michael Scammell of *Zashchita Luzhina*). New York: Putnam's, 1964.

Despair (novel: English translation by Nabokov of *Otchayanie*). New York: Putnam's, 1966.

Details of a Sunset and Other Stories. New York: McGraw-Hill, 1976.

Drugie berega (autobiography: expansion and Russian translation of *Conclusive Evidence*). New York: Chekhov, 1954.

Eugene Onegin (English translation of and commentary on the poem by Aleksandr Pushkin). Revised edition. 4 vols. Princeton: Princeton University Press, 1975.

The Gift (novel: English translation by Nabokov and Michael Scammell of *Dar*). New York: Putnam's, 1963.

Glory (novel: English translation by Nabokov and Dmitri Nabokov of *Podvig*). New York: McGraw-Hill, 1971.

"Hodassevich: A Note and Translation." In *New Directions in Prose and Poetry, 1941.* Edited by James Laughlin. Norfolk, Conn.: New Directions, 1941.

Invitation to a Beheading (novel: English translation by Nabokov and Dmitri Nabokov of *Priglashenie na kazn'*). New York: Putnam's, 1959.

Kamera obskura (novel). Paris: *Sovremennye Zapiski* (émigré journal), 1932.

King, Queen, Knave (novel: English translation by Nabokov and Dmitri Nabokov of *Korol', dama, valet*). New York: McGraw-Hill, 1968.

Korol', dama, valet (novel). Berlin: Slovo, 1928.

Laughter in the Dark (novel: English translation by Nabokov of *Kamera obskura*). New York: Bobbs-Merrill, 1938.

Lectures on Literature. Edited by Fredson Bowers. New York: Harcourt/Bruccoli Clark, 1980.

Lolita (novel). 2 vols. Paris: Olympia, 1955.

Lolita (novel). New York: Putnam's, 1958.

Lolita (novel: translation into Russian by Nabokov). New York: Phaedra, 1967.

Lolita: A Screenplay. New York: McGraw-Hill, 1974.

Look at the Harlequins! (novel). New York: McGraw-Hill, 1974.

Mary (novel: English translation by Nabokov and Michael Glenny of *Mashenka*). New York: McGraw-Hill, 1970.

Mashenka (novel). Berlin: Slovo, 1926.

Nabokov's Dozen (short stories). Garden City, N.Y.: Doubleday, 1958.

The Nabokov–Wilson Letters: Correspondence between Vladimir Nabokov and Edmund Wilson, 1940–1971. Edited by Simon Karlinsky. New York: Harper, 1979.

Nikolai Gogol (criticism). 1944. Reprinted, New York: New Directions, 1961.

Nine Stories. Norfolk: New Directions, 1947.

Notes on Prosody and Abram Gannibal (excerpts from the commentary to *Eugene Onegin*). Princeton: Princeton University Press, 1964.

Otchayanie (novel). Paris: *Sovremennye Zapiski* (émigré journal), 1934. Book version, Berlin: Petropolis, 1936.

Pale Fire (novel). New York: Putnam's, 1962.

Pnin (novel). New York: Doubleday, 1957.

Podvig (novel). Paris: *Sovremennye Zapiski* (émigré journal), 1932.

Poems and Problems (English poems, English translations of Russian poems, and chess problems). New York: McGraw-Hill, 1971.

The Portable Nabokov (selections). Edited by Page Stegner. New York: Viking, 1971.

Priglashenie na kazn' (novel). Paris: Knigi, 1938.

The Real Life of Sebastian Knight (novel). Norfolk: New Directions, 1941.

A Russian Beauty and Other Stories. New York: McGraw-Hill, 1973.

Speak, Memory: An Autobiography Revisited (autobiography: expansion in English of *Conclusive Evidence* and *Drugie berega*). New York: Putnam's, 1966.

Strong Opinions (occasional prose). New York: McGraw-Hill, 1973.

Three Russian Poets: Translations of Pushkin, Lermontov, and Tiutchev. Norfolk, Conn.: New Directions, 1944.

Transparent Things (novel). New York: McGraw-Hill, 1972.

Tyrants Destroyed and Other Stories. New York: McGraw-Hill, 1975.

Vozvrashchenie Chorba (stories). Berlin: Slovo, 1930.

Zashchita Luzhina (novel). Berlin: Slovo, 1930.

SECONDARY SOURCES

Alter, Robert. *Partial Magic: The Novel as a Self-Conscious Genre.* Berkeley: University of California Press, 1975.

Alvarez, A. "'A Tale of a Tub' for Our Time." Review of *The Annotated Lolita,* by Vladimir Nabokov, edited by Alfred Appel, Jr. *Saturday Review of Literature* 53, no. 24 (13 June 1970), 27–28, 45.

Appel, Alfred, Jr. *Nabokov's Dark Cinema.* New York: Oxford University Press, 1974.

———. "Nabokov's Puppet Show." *New Republic* 156 (14 January 1967), 27–30; (21 January 1967), 25–32.

——— and Charles Newman, eds. *Nabokov: Criticism, Reminiscences, Translations, Tributes.* Evanston: Northwestern University Press, 1970.

Bader, Julia. *Crystal Land: Artifice in Nabokov's English Novels.* Berkeley: University of California Press, 1972.

Boegeman, Margaret Byrd. "Paradox Gained: Kafka's Reception in English from 1930 to 1949, and His Influence on the Early Fiction of Borges, Beckett, and Nabokov." Ph.D. dissertation. University of California, Los Angeles, 1977.

Charyn, Jerome, ed. *The Single Voice.* New York and London: Collier, 1969.

Dembo, L. S., ed. *Nabokov: The Man and His Work.* Madison: University of Wisconsin Press, 1967.

Dupee, F. W. *The King of the Cats and Other Remarks on Writers and Writing.* New York: Farrar, 1965.

Field, Andrew. *Nabokov: A Bibliography.* New York: McGraw-Hill, 1973.

———. *Nabokov: His Life in Art.* Boston: Little, 1967.

———. *Nabokov: His Life in Part.* New York: Viking, 1977.

Fowler, Douglas. *Reading Nabokov.* Ithaca: Cornell University Press, 1974.

Frosch, Thomas R. "Parody and the Contemporary Imagination." *Soundings* 56 (1973), 371–92.

Grayson, Jane. *Nabokov Translated: A Comparison of Nabokov's Russian and English Prose.* New York: Oxford University Press, 1977.

Hyde, G. M. *Vladimir Nabokov: America's Russian Novelist.* London: Boyars, 1977.

Josipovici, G. D. "*Lolita*: Parody and the Pursuit of Beauty." *Critical Quarterly* 6 (1964), 35–48. Reprinted in his *The World and the Book: A Study of Modern Fiction.* London: Macmillan, 1971, pp. 201–20.

Kostelanetz, Richard, ed. *On Contemporary Literature.* New York: Avon, 1964.

Lee, L. L. "Duplexity in Vladimir Nabokov's Short Stories." *Studies in Short Fiction* 2 (1965), 307–15.

———. "Vladimir Nabokov's Great Spiral of Being." *Western Humanities Review* 18 (1964), 225–36.

Levy, Alan. "Understanding Vladimir Nabokov: A Red Autumn Leaf Is a Red Autumn Leaf, Not a Deflowered Nymphet." *New York Times Magazine* (31 October 1971), pp. 20–23, 28–30, 36–39.

Mason, Bobbie Ann. *Nabokov's Garden: A Guide to "Ada."* Ann Arbor: Ardis, 1974.

Moynahan, Julian. *Vladimir Nabokov.* Minneapolis: University of Minnesota Press, 1971.

Murray, Isobel. "'Plagiatisme': Nabokov's 'The Vane Sisters' and *The Picture of Dorian Gray.*" *Durham University Journal* 39 (1977), 69–72.

Naumann, Marina Turkevich. *Blue Evenings in Berlin: Nabokov's Short Stories of the 1920s.* New York: New York University Press, 1978.

Nemerov, Howard. "The Morality of Art." *Kenyon Review* 19 (1957), 313–14, 316–21. Reprinted in his *Poetry and Fiction: Essays.* New Brunswick: Rutgers University Press, pp. 260–66.

Nicol, Charles. "Don Juan Out of Hell" (review of *Ada*, by Vladimir Nabokov). *Atlantic* (June 1969), pp. 105–6.

———. "Pnin's History." *Novel* 4 (1971), 197–208.

Patteson, Richard. "Nabokov's *Look at the Harlequins!*: Endless Re-creation of the Self." *Russian Literature TriQuarterly* 14 (1976), 84–98.

Poirier, Richard. *The Performing Self: Compositions and Decompositions in the Languages of Contemporary Life.* New York: Oxford University Press, 1971.

Proffer, Carl R. "From *Otchaianie* to *Despair.*" *Slavic Review* 28 (1968), 258–67.

———. *Keys to "Lolita."* Bloomington: Indiana University Press, 1968.

———, ed. *A Book of Things about Vladimir Nabokov.* Ann Arbor: Ardis, 1974.

Quennell, Peter, ed. *Vladimir Nabokov: A Tribute.* New York: Morrow, 1980.

Raban, Jonathan. "Transparent Likenesses." *Encounter* 41 (September 1973), 75.

Rivers, J. E. "Proust, Nabokov, and *Ada.*" *French-American Review* 1 (1977), 173–97.

Roth, Phyllis A. "The Psychology of the Double in Nabokov's *Pale Fire.*" *Essays in Literature* 2 (1975), 209–29.

Rowe, William Woodin. *Nabokov's Deceptive World.* New York: New York University Press, 1971.

Schaeffer, Susan Fromberg. "*Bend Sinister* and the Novelist as Anthropomorphic Deity." *Centennial Review* 17 (1973), 115–51.

Stark, John O. *The Literature of Exhaustion: Borges, Nabokov, Barth.* Durham: Duke University Press, 1974.

Stegner, Page. *Escape into Aesthetics: The Art of Vladimir Nabokov.* New York: Dial, 1966.

Stuart, Dabney. "The Novelist's Composure: *Speak, Memory* as Fiction." *Modern Language Quarterly* 36 (1975), 177–92. Reprinted as "*Speak, Memory*: Autobiography as Fiction," in his *Nabokov: The Dimensions of Parody.* Baton Rouge: Louisiana State University Press, 1978, pp. 163–191.

Swanson, Roy Arthur. "Nabokov's *Ada* as Science-Fiction." *Science-Fiction Studies* 2 (1975), 76–88.

Trilling, Lionel. "The Last Lover: Vladimir Nabokov's *Lolita*." *Encounter* 11 (1958), 9–19.

Williams, Carol T. "'Web of Sense': *Pale Fire* in the Nabokov Canon." *Critique* 6 (1963–1964), 29–45.